THE MATHERS

*Three Generations
of Puritan Intellectuals,
1596-1728*

Robert Middlekauff

UNIVERSITY OF CALIFORNIA PRESS
Berkeley   Los Angeles   London

University of California Press
Berkeley and Los Angeles, California

University of California Press, Ltd.
London, England

First University of California Press paperback, 1999

Preface to new edition © 1999 by Robert Middlekauff

Library of Congress Cataloging-in-Publication Data

Middlekauff, Robert.
  The Mathers : three generations of Puritan intellectuals,
1596–1728 / Robert Middlekauff.
      p.   cm.
  Originally published: New York : Oxford University Press, 1971.
  Includes index.
  ISBN 978-0-520-21930-4 (pbk. : alk. paper)
    1. Mather, Richard, 1596–1669.   2. Mather, Increase, 1639–1723.
3. Mather, Cotton, 1663–1728.   4. Puritans—Massachusetts—
Biography.   5. Massachusetts—Intellectual life—17th century.
6. Massachusetts—Intellectual life—18th century.   I. Title.
F67.M47M53   1999
285′.8′0922744—dc21   98-50840
  [B]   .   CIP

For Edmund S. Morgan

Preface to the Paperback Edition

When I wrote *The Mathers* (1971), the study of Puritanism was well established; indeed, it constituted a subfield in both the history of religion and intellectual history. Some historians considered it virtually a field in and of itself, set off by the depth and sophistication of its scholarship. Several of the great American historians of this century had given it a wonderful foundation and enormous energy.

An obvious beginning point in what became a flood of scholarship on Puritan experience in seventeenth-century New England does not exist, but the splendid studies of Kenneth Murdock and Samuel Eliot Morison can surely serve as exemplary texts. In 1926, Harvard University Press published Murdock's *Increase Mather*, a biography that is still worth reading. Morison provided books and articles—among them studies of Harvard, Puritan ideas, and the founders of New England—that suggested how fertile a field the study of Puritanism in America might become. Both Murdock and Morison attracted students eager to study at their feet and both—Morison in particular—wrote with such clarity and grace as to draw educated laymen to their writings.[1]

Morison and Murdock had broad interests and their work was

not confined to any single line of study. To a certain extent this is also true of Perry Miller, who arrived at Harvard as a young man from Chicago determined to make the study of Puritanism his own. He succeeded in extraordinary ways and today the study of Puritanism still bears the impress he first began to make on it in 1933 with his brilliant book on church polity, *Orthodoxy in Massachusetts, 1630–1650.*[2] Whatever one might say about Miller's range of interests, he was primarily an intellectual historian and the books, articles, and editions of Puritan writings he produced in the twenty years following the publication of *Orthodoxy in Massachusetts* fall largely into the field of American intellectual history. The greatest of Miller's works appeared on either side of World War II under the general title *The New England Mind.*[3]

In defining the field, Miller gave Puritan theology, and what happened to it in the hundred years between 1630 and 1730, a central place. In fact, he insisted that these subjects deserved attention above all others because they shaped more than anything else what would now be called Puritan culture. He was not, as his critics have claimed, indifferent to social history, but his method of extracting it from such sources as sermons and tracts left something to be desired. His method of discovering what was happening in the society of New England was to rely on indirection, on hints in sources not ordinarily the grist for the mills of social historians, and then, invariably, to point out how far actual social development deviated from the intentions of those under study. Obliqueness and irony have their uses in historical works, but they cannot provide a full or satisfactory account of society. Yet Miller's conclusions, especially as presented in *The New England Mind*, were not only original and exciting, they were indispensable to an understanding of the early history of New England.

Since Miller's death in 1963, Puritan studies have ranged widely over the literature and society of Puritan New England. Virtually all of this scholarship owes something to his inspiration. Even the studies of towns and families that began to pour out in the 1970s are in Miller's debt—some, to be sure, in a peculiar way—insofar as they repudiate his method and his focus on the mind.

A worthy field in its own way, social history has thrown up a serious challenge to traditional conceptions of the study of New England Puritanism. The most important of these works have concentrated for the most part on small-scale studies of towns, counties, families, women, and the law. E. S. Morgan's *The Puritan Family*, first published in 1942, is in part responsible for some of this interest, though family studies have taken different directions from his book and wandered into the social sciences in ways his book did not. For example, John Demos' *A Little Commonwealth* considers the family in old Plymouth Colony with Erik Erickson's psychology of identity clearly affecting its argument. On another track, Philip Greven's books on Andover and on the Protestant temperament provide superb studies with a blend of traditional and social science methods.[4]

But the most remarkable of all the recent social histories of New England, David Hall's *Worlds of Wonder, Days of Judgment*, turns the study of religion in New England in a new direction.[5] Puritanism as historians have understood it is not missing from his book, but it is not at its heart. Instead Hall gives us popular religion, a folk religion, a religion that existed alongside and sometimes within the formal worship of the Puritan churches. Hall's achievement is to make plausible a religious scene in which ministers and laymen alike shared belief in a world of wonders— of tales, providences, and magic. His book shows that the occult was accommodated to the Puritan version of Christianity; it did not replace it.

The books by Demos, Greven, and Hall are examples of fresh and different approaches. Along with a multitude of others on aspects of New England society, they have relevance for more traditional understandings of Puritanism even though such a relevance was not usually a part of their authors' intentions. But the fact is that they provide a richer context for study of colonial New England in all its aspects.

That study has proceeded apace and with a continuing emphasis on Puritanism. There has been valuable research into Puritan churches, for example. Perhaps the most provocative example is E. S. Morgan's *Visible Saints* (1963), on the importance of the requirement Puritan churches imposed on candidates for membership that they give evidence of their conversions.[6] Morgan argues that compromise in admissions of members soon followed stringency. Robert Pope has told the story of the Half-Way Covenant in all its fascinating detail; especially valuable is his finding that laymen initially opposed the extension of baptism to the children of the unregenerate and that ministers led the way to reform.[7] Ministers and church polity, as the studies of Miller and E. S. Morgan forecast, proved to be major subjects for study and over the years a spate of such works has appeared—studies of John Cotton, the Winthrops, Thomas Hooker, and Samuel Willard, for example.[8] There have also been several valuable books on worship, religious experience, and "radical" religion. Among such studies, several stand out: Charles Cohen's *God's Caress*, E. Brooks Holifield's *The Covenant Sealed*, and Philip F. Gura's *A Glimpse of Zion's Glory*.[9]

In addition, many have attempted to provide a larger look, a kind of post-Miller synthesis, albeit on a smaller scale and in a less dramatic style: Sacvan Bercovitch, Harry Stout, Stephen Foster, and Theodore Dwight Bozeman.[10] Their studies are impressive and all deserve close readings. Several are innovative in research and argument. Harry Stout, for example, has studied an impressive number of sermons in manuscript and reminds us that sermons in manuscript may reveal more of the Puritan spirit than the carefully wrought preaching that made its way into print. Bozeman challenges much in current scholarship on Puritan millennialism by insisting that the Puritans looked back to the New Testament for the model of their churches. Stephen Foster suggests, by implication at least, that many studies of Puritanism have begun in the wrong place—that New England Puritan culture has to be seen as an extension of Puritanism in old England. And Sacvan Bercovitch argues in several books that much of American identity and in nineteenth-century culture can be traced to the seventeenth-century movement.

Most of the ideas and the subjects found in the books I have discussed here can also be found in biographies. For example, in the case of popular religion my own book on three generations of the Mather family points to the ways in which both Increase and Cotton Mather used the "Wonders in the Works of Creation"— Increase's words in *An Essay for the Recording of Illustrious Providences*—to reinforce the sense of mystery in life which was at the center of popular religion.[11] More importantly, all of the biographies of the three Mathers that were published after my own treat the major problems first opened up in the studies of Miller, Morison, Murdock, and Morgan.

There have been two excellent biographies of Increase Mather published in recent years: Mason Lowance's short but thoughtful *Increase Mather* (1974), and Michael Hall's *The Last American Puritan* (1988).[12] Hall does not explain why he considers Increase the last American Puritan, but this omission is of minor importance. Hall has written a superb study that makes full use of Mather's work in manuscript as well as in print, and his account of Increase's mission to England for a new charter is especially fresh. David Levin, in *Cotton Mather: The Young Life of the Lord's Remembrancer, 1663–1702*, has provided a balanced and sympathetic account of Cotton Mather's life up through 1702. The ending year saw the publication of Mather's great *Magnalia Christi Americana*; his assessment of that work is, in a sense, the most sophisticated of a variety of subtle insights in the book.[13] Unfortunately, Levin died before he could write a second volume. The only modern full biography of Cotton Mather was published by Kenneth Silverman in 1984.[14] It is a rich and complex book, full of careful and shrewd assessments, but perhaps on occasion it is unfair to its subject. Still, it is an extraordinarily valuable book and, together with Levin's, it is indispensable to our comprehension of Cotton Mather's life.

The Mathers appears in this edition in its original form. For the most part, its main conclusions have held up. I refer to its interpretations of Puritan mission, the "invention" of New England by Increase Mather's generation, its emphasis on the importance of Cotton Mather's millennialism, his devotion to the spirit over reason, his transformation of covenant theology, and his pietism. On this last point, Richard F. Lovelace's *The American Pietism of Cotton Mather* has added much to our knowledge.[15]

The Mathers and their Puritan colleagues are rich subjects for further study. We also need modern editions of many of their works. I trust that scholars coming into the field of Puritan studies will find much to do.

Robert Middlekauff
October 1998

Notes

1. Kenneth Murdock, *Increase Mather: The Foremost American Puritan* (Cambridge Mass.: Harvard University Press, 1926); Samuel Eliot Morison, *The Founding of Harvard College* (Cambridge, Mass.: Harvard University Press, 1935), *Harvard College in the Seventeenth Century*, 2 vols. (Cambridge, Mass.: Harvard University Press, 1936), *Builders of the Bay Colony* (Boston: Houghton Mifflin, 1930).

2. Perry Miller, *Orthodoxy in Massachusetts, 1630–1650* (Cambridge, Mass.: Harvard University Press, 1933).

3. Perry Miller, *The New England Mind: The Seventeenth Century* (Cambridge, Mass.: Harvard University Press, 1939) and *The New England Mind: From Colony to Province* (Cambridge, Mass.: Harvard University Press, 1953).

4. Edmund S. Morgan, *The Puritan Family: Religion and Domestic Relations in Seventeenth-Century New England* (Boston: Boston Public Library, 1944, book form, in *More Books*, 1942); John Demos, *A Little Commonwealth: Family Life in Plymouth Colony* (New York: Oxford University Press, 1970); Philip J. Greven, Jr., *Four Generations: Population, Land, and Family in Colonial Andover, Massachusetts* (Ithaca: Cornell University Press, 1970), and *The Protestant Temperament* (New York: Knopf, 1977).

5. David D. Hall, *Worlds of Wonder, Days of Judgment: Popular Religious Belief in Early New England* (New York: Knopf, 1989).

6. Edmund S. Morgan, *Visible Saints: The History of a Puritan Idea* (New York: New York University Press, 1963).

7. Robert G. Pope, *The Half-Way Covenant: Church Membership in Puritan New England* (Princeton: Princeton University Press, 1969).

8. Larzer Ziff, *The Career of John Cotton: Puritanism and the American Experience* (Princeton: Princeton University Press, 1962); Edmund S. Morgan, *The Puritan Dilemma: The Story of John Winthrop* (Boston: Little Brown and Company, 1958); Sargent Bush, Jr., *The Writings of Thomas Hooker: Spiritual Adven-*

ture in Two Worlds (Madison: University of Wisconsin Press, 1980); Ernest Benson Lowrie, *The Shape of the Puritan Mind: The Thought of Samuel Willard* (New Haven: Yale University Press, 1974).

9. Charles Lloyd Cohen, *God's Caress: The Psychology of Puritan Religious Experience* (New York: Oxford University Press, 1986); E. Brooks Holifield, *The Covenant Sealed: The Development of Puritan Sacramental Theology in Old and New England, 1570–1720* (New Haven: Yale University Press, 1974); Philip F. Gura, *A Glimpse of Sion's Glory: Puritan Radicalism in New England, 1620–1660* (Middletown, Conn.: Wesleyan University Press, 1984).

10. Sacvan Bercovitch, *The Puritan Origins of the American Self* (New Haven: Yale University Press, 1975); Harry S. Stout, *The New England Soul: Preaching and Religious Culture in Colonial New England* (New York: Oxford University Press, 1986); Stephen Foster, *The Long Argument: English Puritanism and the Shaping of New England Culture, 1570–1700* (Chapel Hill: University of North Carolina Press, 1991); Theodore Dwight Bozeman, *To Live Ancient Lives: The Primitivist Dimension in Puritanism* (Chapel Hill: University of North Carolina Press, 1988).

11. (Boston, 1684), p. 99.

12. Mason Lowance, *Increase Mather* (New York: Twayne, 1974); Michael Hall, *The Last American Puritan: The Life of Increase Mather, 1639–1723* (Middletown, Conn.: Wesleyan University Press, 1988).

13. (Cambridge, Mass.: Harvard University Press, 1978).

14. *The Life and Times of Cotton Mather* (New York: Harper and Row, 1984).

15. *The American Pietism of Cotton Mather: Origins of American Evangelicalism* (Grand Rapids, Mich.: Christian University Press, 1979).

Preface

———————

ᏱᎥᎥ

This study of the three leading Mathers of colonial New England should not be confused with a rounded biography, a full-scale family study, or a sociological analysis of a group of Puritan intellectuals. To some extent I have been concerned with these subjects, but only as they bear on my rather different interest— the intellectual history of Puritanism. I began my research into the Mathers with this interest, and though my understanding of it has profoundly changed, it has continued to absorb me.

As subjects for study, the Mathers first attracted me because of their obvious importance in the seventeenth and eighteenth centuries in New England, and because as intellectuals and personalities they seemed fascinating. When I began to read their work, I also had some vague sense that they were probably representative of their kind—ministers who were also intellectuals—and that they might be made the means for a fresh telling of the history of Puritanism in America. This hunch has paid off in ways which have surprised me. Like most historians of Puritanism in New England I had thought of Puritan development as a slow accommodation to the requirements of a new "secular" world. The terms historians have used to describe this change suggest the lines of this story: it is one of the degeneration of Puritan mission, of "piety" becoming "moralism," of the "covenant legalism" yielding "Arminianism," of the gathered Church merging with society, of faith transformed by reason, science, and business, and finally becoming a mild benevolence. In the standard studies of the New England mind, these changes do not just affect laymen rushing into modernity; they also capture a clergy especially sensitive to cultural shifts by a recognition that their leadership—and their political influence—will depend upon their ability to assimilate the new secularism to the old religion.

A summary account cannot convey the sophistication of many of these histories. And I have no wish to separate completely my own work from that of other scholars. There is much of value in their studies, but I have found that the history of Puritanism in New England departs from these accounts in important matters. I have seen things differently in part because my method, or more accurately, my research, has been different. The concentration on the three great Mathers—reading their private as well as their public writings, their manuscripts as well as their published work, has given me a perspective not only on the larger contours of Puritanism but on inner experience as well. Of course, I have also read the work of the Mathers' contemporaries—and many of their English forebears and colleagues—too. I have also found what the Mathers said to common men, those they faced every week and those they tried to convert and comfort, as revealing as anything they published in formal treatises and books.

This research has excited and moved me in several ways. It has proved exciting because it has convinced me that Puritanism in New England changed in rather different ways than I had believed—that Puritan mission was defined more by the second generation in America than the first, that religious psychology and covenant preaching were more "affective" than has been suspected and that they helped Puritan intellectuals use "reason" and the new science in the development of a theory of religious experience and eschatology which were anything but accommodations to or rationalizations of the existing order of things early in the eighteenth century. There was, in fact, in the Mathers' thought and feeling much that was creative. They were not original in the sense that Augustine and Calvin were, but because they were men of powerful minds and, especially, because they were men of intense piety—everything they did, they attempted to do in the service of God—they succeeded at times in transcending the limits of the emerging lay culture of their time. Thus they did more than "respond"; they did more than "accommodate" their creed to the American environment. Cotton Mather went farther along this road than his father and grandfather, and in the process gave away much in the synthesis of piety and intellect that they—and he—expressed. Indeed, Cotton Mather's piety threatened to destroy his reason—he died before it did. He is, nonetheless, I think, the most admirable of the three because he was the most daring (and the most driven). Before he died he had refashioned, with the aid of his father, much in Puritanism—ecclesiastical theory, the psychology of religious experience, covenant preaching, and conceptions of Christian history and prophecy. He had failed to reconcile science and faith, but he had begun to grasp some of the difficulties of their reconciliation. He had also failed to persuade his society to reform itself, surely the easiest of his failures to understand. In success and failure he had lived up the best standards of his family.

I have been moved by this story because though all three Mathers had unattractive sides, they also had intellectual—and moral—courage. Their lives—and the lives of Puritan intellectuals generally—are not the stories of those sad men who find ways of giving in while they persuade themselves that they are holding fast to their principles. But perhaps my own feeling should not be discussed; it is probably clear in my work, though I hope it is not obtrusive.

I have no wish, however, to repress my feelings of gratitude to those who helped me in my work. Among them, I wish to thank the University of California Library, Berkeley, where I did most of my research; the American Antiquarian Society, for providing microfilm of manuscripts in its possession; the Massachusetts Historical Society, for the same service and for guidance in using its holdings; the Yale University Library, for aiding my work there and for providing film. (The Henry Martyn Dexter collection of Puritan tracts at Yale proved especially valuable to me.) The Henry E. Huntington Library also furnished film of several rare tracts in its collections.

The Mathers, I am certain, would regard uneasily the amount of financial aid that I have received in the course of my work.

They managed to turn out solid edification without the grants and fellowships that I have enjoyed. The University that has been my academic home for the last eight years never behaves puritanically —at the risk of striking an unappreciative note, I might say that it might be better if it occasionally did so—and has been anything but ascetic in its support of scholarship. I am grateful to the University's Regents and the Committee on Research for funds for travel, film, typing, and for a Faculty Humanities Fellowship. The American Council of Learned Societies generously provided a fellowship for the academic year 1965–66, a year I spent in research and writing.

My friends and colleagues have, as always, been extraordinarily generous and encouraging. At the University of California Gunther Barth and Richard Johnson provided several important bibliographical leads; Roger Hahn, Winthrop Jordan, and Kenneth Stampp read major portions of my study and gave me suggestions and encouragement; I am particularly indebted to two old friends, Lawrence Levine and Irwin Scheiner, for reading my work and urging me on—despite their scorn for Puritanism of any form in any century.

David Levin of Stanford University lent me notes and has given me wise counsel; Leo Marx of Amherst suggested a way of thinking about conversion (I have used some of his language in three paragraphs in Chapter One); Max Savelle, now of the University of Illinois, Chicago Circle, has given me good advice in my studies over the years.

By dedicating this book to Edmund S. Morgan I hope to express something of my regard for him and my indebtedness to his inspiration and his scholarship. He has not only read my manuscript closely, he has helped me to see what was crucial in the history of Puritanism in New England.

R. M.
Oakland, California
November 1970

Contents

BOOK ONE

の

RICHARD MATHER
(1596–1669)

HISTORY

I

The Founder

━━━━━━━
oᴚ

The question "who am I?" is often in the mouths of men in the twentieth century. Uncertain of their values, men today feel rootless and lament their inability to locate themselves by fixed points in the world. A part of their plight, they recognize, lies within themselves: they distrust themselves, their ideas, their motives, and their impulses. But the world is suspect too: it offers no stability, only change, unthinking and, what is worse, unfeeling change. Ransack it for meaning as they will, they discover that the world will not answer the question of their identity. And so they continue to search and to suffer. At their most desperate, they resemble Saul Bellow's Gene Henderson, who listened to an unsuppressible voice in his heart saying only "I want, I want, I want!"

Puritans did not ask the question of the moderns, "who am I?" but they seem to have endured a similar anxiety. Like men today, they were fascinated by their own mental states; and this absorption with themselves yielded great uneasiness. But the resemblance is superficial. Modern men yearn to find themselves, they search for values, and they want to discover how to live. Puritans shared none of these concerns. They knew who they

3

were; man, after all, was elaborately described in Scripture, and the scholastic psychology and Reformed theology also told them much about themselves. Nor were values unclear—the word in the modern connotation would have bewildered them—God's will shone in the Scriptures. In fact they had at hand in the body of belief we call Puritanism an explicit philosophy covering all aspects of human existence. This philosophy defined man's place in the world with absolute clarity: it told him who he was and what he might become; and it told him what God expected of him. But if man's fate was clear, the fate of individuals was not. In its doctrines of predestination and election, Puritanism offered a man the assurance that his future had been decided. But it gave him no infallible indication of the nature of the decision. All he could know with absolute certainty was that God in His justice had predestined some men for salvation and others for damnation.

Predestination summed up a set of ideas conventionally identified with the Christian inheritance. In the form of Calvinism that permeated New England's culture, predestination took its meaning in the context of the relationship of God and man. God was sovereign and omnipotent: man was dependent and helpless, sunk in original sin. The Puritan knew that it had not always been so: God created Adam in His image, endowed him with free will, and charged him to live within the covenant of works. With Adam's fall, free will was lost and man was left without power, his fate locked in an iron determinism: whether he would live eternally or burn forever was decided not by himself, by his own merit, or anything he did or could do, but rather by the pleasure of God—almost, Richard Mather once observed— "as if by lot." [1]

And how was he, a totally helpless creature, expected to respond to this universe that took its decisions about his eternal state as easily as a man casts dice? With the most strenuous efforts to secure from God the grace that could save his soul. The paradox is obvious: the creed the community lived by, the ministers that preached to it, the books and tracts that came from its presses, all told the Puritan "you are helplessly and hopelessly sunk in sin, your will is corrupt, your understanding impaired, your emotions base, but though only God can save you, you must strive after the grace that will bring eternal peace, you must exert yourself to all your capacity." We have difficulty comprehending a creed that tells a man he is without power and then exhorts him to use all his power to save himself. We can refuse to consider such a situation as a description of reality; men in seventeenth-century New England could not. But some of them too found the doctrine paradoxical and responded by saying that they could do nothing for themselves. Their repetition of the doctrine of human depravity had a hopeless and desperate ring to it—yes, we admit our guilt, but we are helpless, they said, we cannot rescue ourselves; only God can give us saving grace.

The rejoinder to such plaints reveals remarkable—though limited—psychological insight: to be sure, Puritan ministers replied, you are helpless. But sinners always ignore the dreadful truths about themselves. "Sinners," Increase Mather once noted in a great sermon, are not only "wicked," they are "unreasonable. Ask them why they don't reform their Lives, why don't you Turn over a new leaf, and amend your ways and your doings, they will answer, God does not give me Grace. I can't Convert my self and God does not Convert me. Thus do they insinuate as if God were in fault, and the blame of their Unconversion to be imputed unto him." Increase Mather, as clearly as any Puritan preacher, saw the weakness in these protestations. Of course, he agreed, it is true that "Sinners cannot Convert themselves, [but] their *Cannot* is a wilful *Cannot*. *They will not come*. It is not said they could not (though they could not of themselves come to Christ) but that they *would* not come." This explanation which emphasizes the willfulness of the refusal is reminiscent of the Freudian theory of neurosis. The Freudian analogue holds that what makes it difficult to cure the neurotic of his sickness is his attachment to it, his willful (to use the seventeenth-century term) clinging to his neurosis and all its unhealthy gratifications. And why do men will not to convert? "If it were in the power of a Sinner to Convert himself, he would not do it: For he hates Conversion. It is an abomination to fools to depart from evil. . . . Their hearts are in Love, and in League with their Lusts, yea they hate to be *turned* from them." [2]

Forcing the sinner to recognize his complicity in his inability to act had the effect of subduing the will, robbing it of its arrogance and power. You cannot act, the minister says, because you will not; your inability, your sin is deliberately chosen. The intention of this preaching was achieved when humility was induced; the sinner was in despair; he looked at himself honestly and saw only depravity. In this state of diminished will, he was at last ripe for conversion. He, or his heart, that is, his psyche or will, was now an empty vessel; its corruption had been drained away; and once emptied, the vessel of the heart might be filled with the saving grace of the Lord. He had endured, in modern terms, a crisis of identity. When his ego loss had reached the point where he was reduced to desperation, he experienced the new birth and became a new man as his personality attained a fresh integration, the components of the new birth being implied, of course, by the Calvinist version of Christianity.

This experience, and the explanations of it offered by theology, reinforced a bent towards self-awareness in men eager to determine whether or not they were of the elect. Puritanism achieved the same result in yet another way—by explicitly demanding a self-consciousness that made a man aware of his emotions and sensitive to his attitudes towards his own behavior. It accomplished this by describing in elaborate detail the disposition of a godly mind. Sin, it taught, might be incurred as surely by attitudes as by actions. In the process of performing his religious duties a man might sin if his feelings were not properly engaged. Prayer, for example, was commanded of every Christian; but prayer without inward strain, even agony, is mere "lip-labour," a formality that offends God.[3] Prayer for spiritual blessings without faith that those blessings will be granted implies a doubt of God's power and is equivalent to unbelief. Ordinary life, too, must be lived in a Christian habit of mind. A man getting his living in a lawful calling, though staying within the limits imposed by the State, might nevertheless violate divine imperatives by overvaluing the creatures, as Puritans termed excessive esteem for the things of this world. The "manner of performances," Increase Mather once said, was the crucial thing in fulfilling the duties imposed by God.[4]

Puritanism thus bred a deep concern about a state of mind. The norms of good thought and feeling were clear, and every Puritan felt the need for effort to bring his consciousness into harmony with these norms. Doing what he must was another matter and much of his anxiety arose in the attempt to live according to God's stringent requirements. The most familiar figure among Puritans is the tormented soul, constantly examining his every thought and action, now convinced that hell awaits him, now lunging after the straw of hope that he is saved, and then once more falling into despair. He wants to believe, he tries, he fails, he succeeds, he fails—always on the cycle of alternating moods.

The sources of Puritan anxiety then were vastly different from those of modern anxiety. Puritan anxiety in a peculiar sense was a conscious uneasiness, deliberately imposed or at least clearly seen and accepted by its sufferers. It rose from the objective world; it was, paradoxically, reasoned anxiety, and there lay its difference from modern anxiety which is neurotic and which has its sources in the irrational and the abnormal.

What surprises one is that this anxiety did not often produce morbidity among the Puritans. Children who had been taught, almost as soon as they left their mothers' breasts, that they reeked of sin, continued in this belief and tormented themselves over their inner condition but still grew into adults who worked productively, married, reared childen and lived useful lives by any standard. As a young man, Michael Wigglesworth, who earned fame through the apocalyptical poem *The Day of Doom,* not only worried constantly over his own but over his neighbors' souls. As a tutor at Harvard, the innocent play of students reminded him of the torments of Hell, and he resolved to suppress their Sabbath evening activities, which he saw as "mad mirth." Wigglesworth did not shed these concerns with his youth, as far as one can tell. Rather he obtained a forum for expressing his opinions of them when he became a minister. But no one minded; his prying into his neighbors' lives was not resented; and his preoccupation with sin seemed—and was—perfectly normal in the seventeenth century. His life contained spheres other than the pastoral: he married—not once—but three times. The last time at age seventy-four he took his servant-girl to be his wife; she gave him his last child.[5]

The records of these lives suggest that morbidity did not occur more often because of what seemed the restrictive side of Puritanism generated tremendous energy and compelled its release. Beyond any question man was depraved. By nature he loved only himself; he should try to love his fellows and to love God. He lusted after the things of this world, but he should love the world with weaned affections and concentrate on God. His model for living existed in his sinful makeup, but he should seek to conform to Christ. The imperative which Puritans most insisted upon was that as helpless as man was, he should act, and act according to divine prescriptions. The total self had to be enlisted in God's cause. Every life must be lived with this requirement in mind; inwardly and outwardly men were to conform to Christ in "our soules, our bodies, our understanding, will, memorie, affections, and all we have to the service of God, in the generall calling of a Christian, and in the particular callings in which hee hath placed us." [6]

Probably no Puritan understood these injunctions in exactly the way any other Puritan did. From these differences in understanding came differences in styles of life. The more literally the command "live with the self fixed on God" was taken, the greater religious intensity life had.

The three distinguished Mathers of the seventeenth century—Richard, his son Increase, and his, Cotton—all took this injunction to heart as a standard of life. And none confined intensity to inner experience. Their general callings as Christians affected everything they did and thought and felt, but their particular callings as ministers were hardly less important. In fact the two cannot be separated, for the voice of God was clearly heard in both.

These three men lived passionate lives, but their determination to get the best out of themselves for the glory of God did not rest on untutored enthusiasm. All three respected ideas and knowledge; all three proved themselves as scholars as well as ministers. Perhaps in the long history of their service to New England, their ideas about the conduct of life influenced their society more than anything they did. Yet, most of their contemporaries seem to have been as impressed by the sustained example of their religious devotion. And a few sensed what was significant in all three Mathers—their desire to fuse piety and intellect, to pursue ideas with the heart as well as with the mind, and to bring their thinking constantly to bear on their love of God.

Inevitably they did not all love God in the same way and inevitably they chose, or were forced to choose, different ways of expressing their love of God's glory. Inevitably they differed in their abilities to sustain the union of mind and spirit. And inevitably because their faith was deep and because they strove so mightily in God's service, their differences reflected in most ways the intellectual development of three generations of clerical intellectuals in New England.

This development, which includes much of the intellectual history of Puritanism, is usually taken to parallel the transformation of Puritan into Yankee, a process that sees piety replaced by secular values. Surely the process of secularization of society began in the seventeenth century as business and the market, farms and fields, and styles of life separated from the meeting-house, assumed an increasing importance. The State gave ground, too, as internal diversity and external imperatives forced the abandonment of an official policy of intolerance. And while these changes occurred, children were born and reared who experienced distress, incomprehension, and indifference at their inability to recapitulate in their lives the religious psychology of their fathers.

But just as surely as it began, this process was not completed. Standing apart from it, though not unaffected by it, were Puritan laymen and divines, who continued to maintain that life must be shaped by the necessity of advancing God's glory and who persisted in measuring every alteration in society against what they could conceive of as its effects on the true religion. These men did not—as much of the written history of Puritanism has it—accommodate or rationalize the gradual decline of religious faith. Those who hold that they did describe them as unself-conscious Arminians, subtle exponents of the free will of man, who encouraged the drift from the Calvinist creed by preaching a covenant legalism. Such preaching did occur within the Congregational churches of New England, though it is significant that the group commonly taken to be the most worldly in New England, the merchants trading overseas, found their way into the Church of England, an institution far more committed than the Congregational churches to the power of human abilities. A more prevalent preaching upheld the old creed, however. This preaching represented a largely clerical culture increasingly at variance with the chief dispositions of society in New England.

The Mathers—particularly Increase and Cotton—felt the gradual divergence of religious and secular life with great acuteness. Their responses came out of their hearts and minds. As they watched their society move from what they considered the true road to God's glory, they suffered and resisted and sought the means to bring it back. They were not reactionaries or even conservatives—the words have no value in this context—for they attempted to contain within their thought what they considered the best in the new science and social organization. They proved remarkably resourceful in discovering "unessentials" in religion and Church polity which, they said, ought to be sacrificed to rally men to the Lord's cause. And in the end they both compromised and still held fast.

All this cost Increase and Cotton much. Yet their piety, which was only slightly more intense than most of their ministerial colleagues', had probably increased over that of the founders. Certainly it had assumed more extravagant forms and had carried them into rapturous dreams of the next world. These changes reached their highest expression in the mind and heart of Cotton Mather. Within him the old balance had collapsed in favor of the spirit. The society in which he died, the society of the Franklins, the *Courant,* the Hell-Fire Club, and much more that he despised, may have been as "reasonable" as it claimed and as he for a brief time acknowledged. But that sort of reasonableness he learned could not be incorporated into the spirit to which he finally gave himself. At the end of his life then, he had given over the synthesis of piety and intellect which had so distinguished his grandfather's era. And in the process he had transformed the life of passionate commitment, and contributed to the alteration of Puritanism itself.

The founder of the family in America, Richard Mather, established this pattern of passionate commitment. Increase and Cotton Mather felt his moral authority and commented on it throughout their lives. Had they wished to escape it they could not have done so, for what gave Richard's example its compulsive power was, of course, the fact that it measured up to the highest Puritan ideals. Richard embodied as fully as any man among the fathers of New England the reasoned intensity all Puritans held before themselves as a model for living.

Richard Mather was born in a substantial, timbered house in 1596 in the village of Lowton, not far from Liverpool in Winwick Parish in Lancashire. Richard's father, Thomas, seems to have been a yeoman whose family had lived in Lowton for several generations. His mother, Margarite, must have come from yeoman stock, and she too traced her family back over several generations of Lowton stock. Thomas and Margarite were probably not Puritans for they once considered apprenticing Richard to Catholic merchants. Neither were they wealthy but they resolved to give their son an education and sent him off to grammar school in nearby Winwick.[7]

Lowton boys usually did not get much schooling. Their parents were poor and the longer a boy stayed at his books, the longer his father had to feed and clothe him without any return. Richard studied with a Mr. Horrocke who, if he observed the conventions of most schoolmasters, expected his charges to read and write English almost immediately after beginning school, if indeed they had not come with such skills, and who spent most of his time exercising them in Latin and Greek. Latin came first and remained the center of the curriculum. Lily's *Grammar,* a book first authorized under Henry VIII and continued by Elizabeth, furnished the text. Boys memorized the rules of grammar, translated Latin into English and then turned their versions back into Latin, wrote themes in Latin and acted out Latin plays and spoke dialogues. As their facility in Latin increased, the scholars turned a part of their attention to Greek grammar. There the favorite text was the New Testament.[8]

This regimen did not permit much variety, and masters did not encourage their students to develop their capacities for originality, especially since the prevailing view held that in boys as in all men these capacities were depraved. Masters who grew tired of their lives and their charges sometimes became more exacting, and they sometimes accompanied their increasing demands with increasing punishments.[9]

Mr. Horrocke may have been such a master. In any case his scholars discovered that as he laid on the grammar he also laid on the rod. Resenting harsh treatment and hoping to escape it, Richard appealed to his father to take him out of the school. But Thomas Mather, indulgent as he was in other ways, refused and contented himself with a talk with the master in which he evidently appealed for less severity.[10]

Thomas Mather handled the interview tactfully and Richard continued in school with his standing unimpaired. Perhaps the episode forced Horrocke to look more carefully at him, for a little later, when Thomas Mather was about to apprentice his son to Catholic merchants from Wales, it was Horrocke who interceded on the boy's behalf. The merchants were looking for "pregnant wits," and they had heard that young Richard Mather was a very bright youth.[11] Keeping his son in school was costly, and Thomas Mather thought that he could reduce his expenses by signing his son over to these merchants. At this point William Horrocke stepped in and reminded the parents that their son had considerable talent and should be kept in school. Besides, he pointed out, apprenticing Richard to these merchants assured that he would be "undone by Popish Education."[12] Horrocke's appeal turned the elder Mathers from their resolve, and their son continued in Mr. Horrocke's school until 1611, the year of his fifteenth birthday, when he left the school as the result of another friendly act of Master Horrocke. The schoolmaster, asked by citizens of nearby Toxteth Park to recommend someone who might conduct a grammar school for their children, named Richard Mather. Horrock's opinion carried weight; Richard Mather was given the job.[13]

Serving as a schoolmaster marked another decisive point in Richard Mather's life. From the scholar's dependency he moved, though still a boy, to the independence and responsibility of a master. He now had to exercise others in grammatical studies; he had to maintain discipline; and he had to give an accounting to the community. As far as we know, he did these things ably; yet there must have been considerable strain and exertion. He did not break down, but in 1614, three years after beginning, he experienced the agonizing and exhilarating crisis of conversion.[14]

It began simply enough. Mather was living with Edward Aspinwall and his family. He took his meals at the Aspinwall table and saw much of the household. Edward Aspinwall did not rule the household rigidly nor did he make unusual demands upon his boarder. Still, he and his family, in their quiet piety, exerted a subtle influence upon Richard. What impressed the boy most, he later recalled, was the difference between the spiritual condition of the Aspinwalls and his own. They evidently felt God's grace working in themselves; he did not, though he hoped to feel it. The Aspinwalls were not the only ones affecting his spiritual condition. In these years Richard was listening to the minister of nearby Hyton, a Mr. Harrison, who was preaching the Pauline doctrine of the new birth. Richard was especially moved by Harrison's explication of the statement of Jesus that "Except a man be born again, he cannot see the Kingdom of God." [15] What he meant was simply that men had to experience regeneration. They could not be satisfied with knowing that their lives were moral or that intellectually they believed in Christ. They must feel the spirit in themselves; they must believe on Christ—as it was customarily phrased. They must accept Christ's sacrifice as payment for their sins and feel themselves joined to Him.

Feeling of this sort bewilder and perhaps frighten most men who experience them. For Richard they were most intense in his eighteenth year. He later described them in the language of birth —he felt, he said, "terrible pangs." [16] His misery arose in part from his feeling that he would not be saved; in his worst moments he avoided everyone, staying away from meals and nursing his sorrow and grief. Encouraging this process and perhaps ultimately helping him escape his despair was a book by William Perkins.

Born in 1558 Perkins had lived only until 1602, but in his brief life he became one of the two or three most important divines in the English Church. Perkins, like many preachers of his day, attempted to comprehend the mysterious working of grace in men. As he saw it, ordinary men were baffled by the problem of separating natural feeling from divine. Only God could save men, of course, and He drew only those He elected. But common sense told a man that he had some power over his own feelings and that these feelings were affected by impressions supplied by his senses. How could a man determine the origins of what exactly he was feeling—especially when God worked through his senses too, sending His grace as a passenger on the vehicle of a minister's words or shooting into a man's heart with the message of the Gospel. And a man might bring himself to believe—in a certain manner—that Christ died to save men, that Christ was the son of God, and that men required Christ's intercession for their salvation. Even reprobates might go this far—and farther: they might succeed in leading moral lives in the eyes of the world, though not in the eyes of God.[17]

Perkins schooled ordinary Engilshmen in these facts and explained to them how God's workings might be identified. He made comprehensible what Richard Mather was experiencing and thereby aided in the completion of the process of conversion. Richard Mather later remembered that he had been extraordinarily affected by Perkins' caution about "how farre a Reprobate may go." The danger facing the sinner was that he would confuse his own efforts with God's and become complacent. If he fell into this trap, his chances for grace were slim.[18]

In several books which young Richard Mather may have read, Perkins reviewed these problems and analyzed experience in terms which troubled men were able to apply to themselves. Perkins told men that conversion did not change their substance, the stuff out of which they were made, nor did it give them new powers, or faculties of the soul, as the old language he employed put it. All conversion did was to renew what they already had; it restored a measure of the purity that Adam had possessed before his fall. Perkins likened the process to rebuilding an old house but with one difference: a house is restored piecemeal, a room at a time, a window first, and then a wall; but a man who receives grace has his whole being—his reason, his will, his affections, all his faculties—reconstructed at once, and simultaneously. And yet this restoration occurred over a time, and could be broken down into identifiable periods.[19]

Initially, a man might become sensible of his sin, feeling fear and terror in response to the accusations of his conscience. Such feelings are "no graces of God" but fruits of the law. But they do help "tame" a man's nature.[20] Anyone could achieve this much on his own, though God usually got things going. At this point a man may be likened to the breaking of dawn, Perkins said; the darkness remains, but there is light in the air. If the process is genuinely from God, the Holy Spirit next begins to work restraining the worst of the natural impulses and leading the person to moral behavior. A reprobate might proceed this far but no farther. The final step occurred when renewing grace was infused into the soul: the man was now Christ's, he had been born again.[21]

By itself Perkins' description, though enlightening, was scarcely comforting. The reader of one of Perkins' tracts would find little encouragement for feelings of ecstasy. Perkins told him that in the beginning he should be afraid and should feel guilt, but at the end he should not expect that raptures would follow. But in a sense Perkins did provide tests for determining the validity of the process. Grace was "counterfeit" unless it grew, he said. The sinner should expect his faith to increase, and he should strive to see that it did. His very striving was evidence that his grace was genuine. Thus he should pray, listen to sermons, read the gospel, and examine himself—his impulses, his feelings of every sort, and his thoughts. He could expect to fail his God, and his own best intentions, at various times. How he responded to his failures gave further indication of the state of his soul. If he felt grief at his failure to grieve over his sins he should be reassured. If he sorrowed because his desires to close with God were weak, he should be encouraged. Complacency, or as Puritans customarily put it "security," was a great danger and suggested that the grace he claimed was fraudulent.[22]

During his conversion in 1614, Richard Mather required no help to avoid security. His heart was broken, and he craved the comfort that reaching the end of the conversion process conferred. Finally, after a prolonged period of misery, he began to feel that he was God's. He was never to feel secure, though he did enjoy the feeling of assurance, the feeling that he had been converted. Still, there were pangs of uncertainty; the last lengthy period of anxiety came after his arrival in New England and his acceptance of the Dorchester pulpit. Then for several years, he was troubled by doubts. He was characteristically quiet about his uneasiness, talking only to John Norton, the pastor of Ipswich, who gave him as much reassurance as he could.[23]

Mather continued to teach throughout the period of his conversion and remained in Toxteth Park as master until 1618, when on May 18 he matriculated in Brasenose College, Oxford. His stay was short, probably a little more than a year. It is impossible to say what lasting effect, if any, Oxford had on him. If he was placed with the freshman class, he received the beginnings of the liberal arts course with instruction in the *trivium* and *quadrivium*. Certain it is that he liked Oxford: several of his former students were there, and he enjoyed seeing them (though if they were juniors and seniors he must have had mixed feelings in greeting them); he admired the learned instructors and delighted in his studies. The only disturbing feature of Oxford life was the profaneness he encountered there. So perhaps, given his Puritan cast of mind, he was disposed to leave when he received the call from Toxteth Park to return as minister of the church. In any case, he departed his college and in 1619 took holy orders.[24]

At his ordination an incident took place that reveals how highly his spiritual gifts were valued. The Church official in charge was Doctor Morton, the Bishop of Chester. When the ceremony ended the Bishop took Richard Mather aside, saying to him: "I have an earnest Request unto you, and you must not deny me, It is that you would pray for me: for I know the Prayers of men that fear God will avail much, and you I believe are such a one." [25]

The Bishop might not have been so eager for Mather's prayers had he known that Mather took the holy orders of the Church of England with considerable reservations. For Mather was a Puritan and already tending to embrace openly Congregational notions of Church organization. Still he accepted the vows of the Church and continued to preach, though not to conform outwardly to all its rites and ceremonies.[26]

Mather's congregation shared his scruples and made no trouble for him. But his views caused problems of a personal sort: it took time to persuade Edmund Holt of Bury to give permission for the marriage of his daughter, Katharine, to Mather. Holt did not care for nonconforming churchmen. But the marriage took place nonetheless in September 1624, and six sons followed over the next fifteen years.[27]

The next few years were good ones for Richard Mather and his family. He enjoyed good health all his life, never missing an opportunity to preach the Sabbath sermon in fifty years; and his wife and children, if not so robust, at least escaped the early death that dogged people in the seventeenth century. Richard Mather's sermons for these years do not survive, but we know that he preached heavily from Samuel, Isaiah, and the Epistles of Paul. These books provided texts for many Puritan ministers in the seventeenth century. From them the preacher could remind his people of the obligations of Israel, another people highly favored by God. Many ministers seized the opportunity to liken England to Israel, urging that the English too were a chosen people with extraordinary obligations to keep the faith with the Lord. Israel had failed and Israel had suffered; the gentiles in England should profit from this example. The words of Paul suggested other kinds of lessons. The need for conversion was obvious; and Paul had insisted that men were saved by faith. But no minister could be content with simply announcing this doctrine. The converted had to be exhorted to live up to their conversions, to demonstrate their grace by leading holy lives. Faith implied a good conversation, as ministers styled the godly life. And the ordinary day-to-day constituents of gracious behavior could be extracted from Paul.[28]

Richard Mather preached these doctrines plainly but with great vigor. Like most Puritan preachers of his day, he favored the plain style. His sentence structure was clear and simple; he avoided Latin words and phrases; where a homely word or phrase would most affect his simple village auditory he used it. In this way he hoped to appeal to as wide an audience as possible. Without vanity himself, he sought not to impress his flock but to instruct those already in the faith and to bring those who were without it into the fold.[29]

While he was going methodically through these Scriptures, he was not altogether easy inwardly. He did not conform to the Church in most ways and in 1630, when Archbishop Laud became the leading ecclesiastical official of Charles I, he knew he was in for trouble. Trouble came in the person of a visitor from the bishop, who after suitable investigation recommended suspension, which followed in August 1633. Happily, Richard Mather had influential friends who succeeded in getting him restored in November. Still, Mather refused to change his practice. Laud and his party insisted; Richard Mather like so many others in these years continued to refuse to conform and the next year he was suspended again. This time there was no possibility of a return to his pulpit without conformity.[30]

Richard knew this, and after a month of soul-searching he decided to seize the opportunity of preaching on the Lord's terms rather than on the Church of England's. That opportunity, of course, lay in New England. And in the Spring of 1635, Richard Mather, his wife, and their children set out on the Atlantic, bound for the colony of Massachusetts Bay.

The voyage provided a number of new experiences and problems. The Mathers sailed on the *James,* a vessel which carried many other Puritans to America. "Our Land stomachs grew weary of ship diet," Richard Mather noted in the journal he kept while on the *James.*[31] This entry, like many others made during the passage, betrays a concern with the conditions of life on the ocean. Such interest is understandable, for Mather knew some-

thing of the history of voyages. Most ended well, with ship intact and crew and passengers breathing, but even these usually
brought some kind of suffering. When stomachs grew weary of
salted fish and beef, the staples of ship diet, scurvy was usually
not long in coming.

A woman and her child did suffer with scurvy near the end of
the voyage, but Mather and most of his company came through
in good health. An unusual variety of diet proved to be possible
when they tired of salt fish for they had brought provisions with
them—"sometimes we used bacon and buttered pease, sometimes
buttered bag-pudding, made with currants and raisins; and sometimes drinked pottage of beer and oatmeal, and sometimes water
pottage, well buttered."

Most of the passage was like hundreds of others. Summer on
the Atlantic can be surprising with treacherous storms, but the
murderous gales of the winter are usually absent. The *James* ran
into some bad weather about ten days out, and her passengers
discovered that a tiresome diet would not be all that would keep
them from the dinner table. On several of these days, rain beating in through the sides of the ship to soak the beds joined the
wind in making life miserable. There were other rough days, but
there were calm ones too. Some days the sun burned down so
hotly than any breeze was welcomed; at still other times the heat
vanished and the cold reminded Mather of December at home.
When the sea ran smoothly enough, the company enjoyed watch-
ing the porpoises and dolphins that played around the ship. The
crew took a porpoise occasionally, one of which when opened
brought to mind a familiar country scene, the slaughter of hogs.
Mather was delighted by the spectacle, and the women and children found the dissection of the porpoise—"his entrails, as liver,
lights, heart, guts, etc., for all the world like a swine"—to be
"marvellous merry sport." The guts of a pig were a comfortable
sight for most, and out on the sea anything that evoked the smells
and the day-to-day quality of the countryside was reassuring.

The voyage ended in an experience which in its own peculiar
way was even more reassuring. On Saturday, August 15, while
anchored at the Isles of Shoals (off the coast of Maine), the
James was struck by an easterly wind which drove the rain before it. The ship's master first attempted to hold his vessel with
anchors but two gave way, taking their cables with them, and a

third cable had to be cut before the sea dragged the ship aground. With rocks looming through the spray, the captain next hoisted sail with the hope of escaping to the open sea. The wind destroyed the hope, tearing the sails from the masts and shredding them, "as if they had been but rotten rags."

As the sails flapped in tatters, the ship drove out of control toward a "mighty rock" standing out of the water. Ordinary men would have bid their lives farewell at this point, but the *James* was not carrying ordinary men. Mather and his fellow Puritans called on God for His mercy, and "he was pleased to have compassion and pity upon us." By God's "overruling providence" the ship cleared the rock, and the wind and sea quieted long enough for the crew to rig the ship with fresh sails. The Lord also "sent us a fresh gale of wind" which allowed the *James* to navigate out of danger towards Cape Ann. Two days later, on August 17, 1635, the ship put into Boston.

When the Puritans on the *James* learned that the storm would not take their lives, Richard Mather reports, "O how our hearts did then relent and melt within us!" Richard Mather was more than grateful for his escape—even at the worst moment he seems to have expected it. He had felt fear, of course, but when he remembered "the clearness of my calling from God this way," that is to New England, his fear abated somewhat. He knew that God would do with them what He wished. Christian resignation probably does not describe Mather's attitude; resignation implies a passivity, and Puritans were rarely passive. He welcomed God's actions, even if they entailed the loss of his life. But God did not claim his life; He simply demonstrated to the passengers of the *James* the ease with which He could make His claim successful and then in His mercy spare them for His other purposes. They had escaped the sea because God wished them to go to New England. This was comforting knowledge; and it strengthened Richard Mather's sense of purpose and his expectation that since Providence had steered him safely once, it would probably do so again.

2

The Antichrist

Richard Mather arrived in Boston singing the praises of the Lord. The Lord had helped him and his companions escape their persecution in England. The Lord had conducted them safely over the sea without the loss of a man and without the suffering that usually dogged ocean voyages. The Lord had delivered them from a fearsome storm that boiled the sea and snapped anchor cables as if they were string. And so Richard Mather sang, "Praise the Lord, O my soul; and all that is within me, praise his holy name!" [1]

Mather had not left England so full of confidence. The two years preceding his departure in 1635 had been marked by uncertainty about his ministry. Sometime between 1618, when he had accepted episcopal ordination at Toxteth Park, and 1633, when he was suspended, he had become convinced that Congregationalism was the true Church polity. His failure to conceal this persuasion had, in August 1633, brought visitors from the bishop who had suspended him, but in November he had been restored to his pulpit. He had returned to his church without promising to conform. The chances are that in 1633 Mather had simply requested action which would return him, and had not been required to make any declaration of his principles. In the tangle of ecclesiastical politics and the unevenness and inconsistency of Anglican determination to smash dissenting ministers, his case had been favorably decided. The next year Mather had not been so fortunate. The Archbishop of York had dispatched visitors who again suspended him. When Mather's friends had appealed for a lifting of the suspension they were asked how long Mather had been a minister. The answer was "fifteen years." And how often had he worn the surplice? The response was that Mather had never worn it. The visitor's cynical comment had left little room for hope that Mather could return to his church: "*'What* (said the Visitor, swearing as he spake it) *preach Fifteen years and never Wear a Surpless? It hath been better for him that he had gotten Seven Bastards.'*" [2]

Mather had been banished but he probably did not immediately consider leaving England. By his principles, though not his bishop's, he was still pastor of his church. His flock needed him and wanted him to continue at its head. The idea of removal to New England may have been planted by John Cotton and Thomas Hooker who wrote him about this time. In any case, he was soon considering leaving. With characteristic respect for balance, Mather began drawing up arguments for removal. These statements, which reveal his indecision, suggest what moved him most in the months before he decided. Most of his "arguments"— Mather arranged them in a kind of order—revolved around the necessity for godly worship to be conducted in purity and freedom. His first proposition, for example, contended that "'To remove from a corrupt Church to a purer, is necessary for them that are not otherwise tyed, but free. . . .'" The Scriptures after all enjoin men to choose "the best gifts." The best gifts included the true Church discipline. In England such discipline no longer existed, if it ever had: ministers were prevented from executing their sacramental functions and their preaching; and, of course, the full enjoyment of the ordinances was vital to a pure Church. England threatened persecution; the Scriptures required men to escape persecution in favor of peaceful enjoyment of worship. Even nature taught one to seek "ones own preservation." Richard Mather's mood in this part of the argument was hardly exalted. Hope was gone, and he was looking for a way out. [3]

Mather's feelings about the plight of the faithful received

scant comfort when he turned to the present state of religion in England. As he looked at England, Mather found many signs of "fearful Desolation." His recapitulation of them reads like an indictment presented in court. Degenerate England gloried in its sin and sinners; where sin did not exist, security or indifference prevailed. God had attempted to warn England's stiff-necked people but they persisted in their corrupt ways, impervious to the meaning of afflictions, contemptuous of the warnings delivered by the Lord's faithful ministers, and ungrieving, though the Lord was fast stripping the land of His faithful servants.[4]

But why should the Lord manifest such terrible concern for England? Like other commentators of his day, Richard Mather turned to the past for an answer. He began his study with the assumption that England was in covenant with God who valued her above other nations, an assumption which so pervaded Reformed thought in England as to be commonplace. God's extraordinary interest in England had first become clear to men at the time of the Reformation when He began leading the nation out of Antichrist's dreadful clasp. Since then His blessings had been great—He thwarted Mary's attempts to return the land to Rome's control and in Elizabeth He gave the people a sovereign who continued to pour the vials of God's wrath upon the Antichrist. The list of God's covenant kindnesses could be extended but what especially touched Richard Mather was the shocking return made for them by His nation.[5]

Mather was especially impressed by one chronicle of this dismal story, John Brinsley's *The True Watch and Rule of Life*.[6] In it he found an elaborate analysis of the declension of another body of God's chosen, the people of Judah. And as Brinsley hastened to point out to those slow to make the application for themselves, the sins that sent Judah into seventy years of captivity in Babylon abounded in England.[7]

Brinsley's tract purported to rest on the ninth chapter of Ezekiel, and in fact its mood of imminent destruction awaiting England is supplied by Ezekiel's vision of the slaughter of the unworthy in Jerusalem. But its substance draws widely on the Old Testament in its account of a people chosen by the Lord who paid the Lord in pride and sin for His protection. The Lord, Brinsley wrote, took the people of Judah to be "his peculiar people of all the earth, plucking them out of the iron furnace.

He gave them his Covenant, and the seales of it, his word and Sacraments, his lawes, ordinances and statutes. He planted them in Canaan the garden of the earth . . ."; and when they proved rebellious He took His vengeance on them.[8]

The application of this melancholy history to England should, said Brinsley, send shivers over every Englishman, "for feare of the same denunciation, and desolation to light upon us." For, he continued, "who knoweth not that the Lord did take us to him-selfe, as a vine out of Egypt: I mean that he fetched us out of that Romish bondage, by a most high hand and notable over-throw of our oppressors; getting us in our habitation and re-newing his covenant with us; as he did Israel from Egypt, plant-ing them in Canaan?"[9]

Brinsley's relentless insistence that England must repent and reform or face destruction relied, as all such literature of this type had to, on the figure of the Beast, the Antichrist of Daniel and Revelation. The Book of Daniel portrays four great beasts rising out of the sea, the first "like a lion," the second, "like to a bear," the third, "like a leopard," and the fourth, the ten-horned Beast, "diverse from all the rest." All were dreadful, and unre-pentant sinners were assured that at the Day of Judgment should they "scape the Beare, yet a Lion shall teare them in peeces."[10]

At the time Richard Mather was pondering his fate and Eng-land's, the interpretations of these scriptures had reached a com-plexity so tangled as to give them a mystery which rivaled the prophesies themselves. Virtually all Protestant interpreters agreed, however, that the Beast from the sea was the Antichrist and that the Antichrist was the Papacy with its episcopal para-phernalia. For these Protestants, history was a great cosmic drama of the struggle between good and evil, between God's faithful in His Church arrayed against Antichrist and his master, Satan. The ultimate outcome of this conflict was clear: the Book of Revelation forecast it. At the climactic moment the warrior-Christ and His angels would descend in a cloud of fire which would consume Antichrist and his followers. Satan would be bound and eventually consigned to the pit of fire and brimstone. At this point the story became less clear. Some Protestants, in-spired by the Book of Revelation, insisted that a millennium fol-lowed during which Christ and the faithful reigned on earth. This period would see a restoration of the Edenic paradise—

poverty and pain banished, sin and suffering dispelled and happiness and harmony ensuing. But other interpreters offered a view remarkably like Augustine's which held that the millennium has already occurred and that, with the Second Coming of Christ, history ended.[11]

Puritans of Richard Mather's generation often disagreed on the question of the periodization of history and the location in time of the millennium. And yet they almost unanimously agreed that the end was approaching. For most, the Protestant Reformation of the sixteenth century marked the beginning of the end. These reformers believed that by the split in the Roman Catholic Church, the papacy, or Antichrist, suffered the first of a series of blows which would end only when he slid downward into the pit. The popular expression of this apocalyptical history was written in the sixteenth century by John Foxe in the *Book of Martyrs*. This book helped to form Richard Mather's mentality in these years of imminent exile.

Foxe announced near the beginning of his book that he did not intend to show the Church in England as "any new church of our own," but rather as "the renewing of the old ancient church of Christ." [12] As part of the old order of Christ, the English Church experienced the long cycles of purity and decay that supplied the common pattern of history. According to Foxe's calculations, the first period of the Church extended from the year of Christ's death to the victory of Constantine over Maxentius, almost three hundred years later. The following one thousand years marked an era of spiritual prosperity, for the angel of John's vision had appeared with the key to the bottomless pit and had bound Satan. During this epoch the Church enjoyed the freedom of preaching the gospel as the brethren listened without the fear of persecution. But even before this bright day gave way to the inevitable darkness, signs of degeneration appeared. They had been especially clear in England in whose history Foxe found this universal rhythm of purity and corruption.[13]

According to Foxe, the spiritual conquest of England had begun during the time of the Apostles. The true faith, in other words, had not come from Rome, though later the Roman church had sent its emissaries. Joseph of Arimathea, sent by Philip the Apostle in the year of the Lord 83, had brought Christianity to pagan England. A little more than one hundred years later King

Lucius established the Church in Britain: Lucius banished heathenism so far as possible by converting pagan temples into Christian churches, and transforming the "flamins," or head-priests, into bishops and archbishops. Lucius accomplished all this without interference from Rome, which had not yet fallen away from the true religion. Unhappily, Lucius died without issue and soon after the realm began to experience what was to be a familiar pattern: Roman Catholic ambassadors, Saxons and Danes, the forces of darkness intruded themselves to be met by godly kings and faithful people. Christian kings—the model is Alfred—defend the truth, and ungodly ones betray it; obedient people worship in the faith and disobedient ones desert it. There was, Foxe reported, about a millennium of this history, the period of the binding of Satan during which true Christianity was sustained in England.[14]

Difficulties grew, however, in the fourteenth century as Satan gained his release and began persecuting the elect. For the next two centuries the corruption of the faith proceeded, doctrine degenerated, and the Roman overpowered the true Church of Christ. Though scripture and learning disappeared from men's lives in these centuries, replaced by Roman rites, scholastic philosophy, idolatory, and error, God did not choose to abandon England completely. In fact, He raised up Wyclif and though the Antichrist suppressed Wyclif, he did not do so until Wyclif begot Huss. Foxe was as certain of this as he was that Huss begot Luther, and Luther the Truth. With Luther and the Protestant Reformation the long struggle reached its climax, an historical moment which Foxe was convinced would encompass his own lifetime and extend to the final judgment.[15]

With this understanding of the course of history, the religious character of England and role assigned to it in the final drama assumed great importance in any calculation of whether one should stay or remove himself. Certain factors in the calculation seemed inescapable to Richard Mather. The reasons for God's wrath abounded in England. A covenanted people now harbored sin that exceeded that which had sent Judah into a seventy-year captivity. Remaining in England held the possibility that even the godly would become corrupt.

The godly had a responsibility to preserve the visible Church. As John Winthrop, the first great civil leader of the Bay Colony, pointed out, Christ's Church on earth is everlasting. The past threw up examples of God's preservation of a covenant people in His Church. As long as they remained faithful, the Antichrist was held at bay. But as soon as they yielded to sin, as Israel had, God permitted them to perish. History suggested, then, that preservation of the Church required removal to New England—or, as Richard wrote, "to some such like place." [16]

Separated from corruption but not from the world, nor from the Church of England, which despite its degeneracy still remained a part of Christ's visible Church, the saints would enjoy God's protection. John Winthrop gave Puritan aspirations their most exalted expression: in Massachusetts Bay Colony, he told his followers on the *Arbella,* they would be "as a city upon a hill." Winthrop meant by this phrase that the rest of the world would watch them to see if they held to their professed dedication to purity and Christian love. It seems doubtful that the hard-headed Winthrop, or any of the Puritans who arrived in the years after 1630, held any hope that the watchers would profit from New England's example. The past offered too many cases of men who, despite divine warnings and afflictions, persisted in their degeneracy.[17]

The general path of history seemed clear to Richard Mather though the details were obscure. As destitute as the times were of goodness, the Antichrist in his apparent triumphs was approaching his end. Richard came to believe, as he decided to leave England, that the Puritans in the wilderness might contribute to the effort of pushing him into the pit. Surely God would not abandon His people in the wilderness if they were true to Him. History contained melancholy examples of people rejected by the Lord but they were people who had repeatedly broken their covenant with Him. God had patiently endured Israel's violations of their pact, mercifully calling them back until the stiffness of their hearts made their defection permanent. So the Lord's children in New England could depend upon their opportunities to serve. The Lord might try them and certainly would afflict them when they earned His disapproval. But He would not desert them unless they renounced Him.[18]

A godly company had arrived in New England five years before Richard Mather landed in Boston. Their mood when they settled was filled with the expectation that the end of the "line of time" was approaching and with it cataclysm perhaps, but also judgment and eternal bliss for the righteous.

Mood was one thing. The Puritans craved the certainty and the substance that would convert it into knowledge about the final sequences which would bring the end. To gain this knowledge they consulted the Prophecies, but the metaphorical quality of these Scriptures invited disagreement as surely as they raised expectations. The gaining of knowledge required practical study. And so Puritan historians, who aspired to become prophets, began the process of searching the past for the fulfillment of scriptural prophecy. Their method was to compare theory and reality, the predictions of the Bible and the events of the "objective" world.

The Scriptures disclosed the signs of the last days in a bewildering variety. David sang of the "wondrous works" that signalled the end; the Puritans could not help but believe that they would be wondrous, but their apparently infinite number made them hard to sort out from Providence and other divine intrusions into the affairs of men. Daniel promised that knowledge would increase in the last days, and apparently it was increasing, especially as it concerned the number and extent of the prophecies. But Paul, while apparently agreeing that men would in the last days be "ever learning," also concluded that they would be "never able to come to the knowledge of the truth." Paul was not exactly happy at the prospects for moral behavior during the last days either. They would be "perilous times," and men "shall be lovers of their own selves, covetous, boasters, proud, blasphemers, disobedient to parents, unthankful, unholy." The list went on; happily, other passages promised better things in statecraft: revolution, for example, that would overturn the ungodly, and upheavals that would shake the wicked from power. Nature, too, would give tokens of the impending end. They were not calculated to sooth lovers of quiet—there would be earthquakes, said John; and the prophet Joel scanning the universe discerned the promise of the earth of "blood, and fire, and pillars of smoke," and in the heavens, of the sun "turned into darkness, and the moon into blood, before the great and terrible day of the Lord come." [19]

Reading the events of the past—and the present—in the light of the prophecies could be a stimulating but nevertheless an unsatisfactory business. From the beginning of history, there had been revolutions and earthquakes; periodically, too, there were revivals of learning; and Puritans could not find a time when men had not been covetous and filled with pride and self-love. Comets had appeared before the seventeenth century; the moon had taken on shades of red; and eclipses had darkened the sun. The signs, then, had appeared before and proved themselves misleading.

The conviction that history had entered its last phase persisted nonetheless. And with good reason. In the last century the events on the line of time had begun to take a different shape; there was nothing, for example, to approach the Reformation in earlier centuries. Not only did it alter the central institution of history, the Church, it affected politics, the conduct of life, the spread of people. The Reformation, like all other events, had to be understood in the context of history. In particular, its meaning had to be apprehended with two, more reliable, signs in mind. Most Puritan commentators, while conceding the difficulty in sorting out the portent of earthquakes and comets, insisted that Scriptures proposed two infallible points by which progress towards the end could be charted. Just before the end, the Jews, who had been scattered throughout the world since their release from the Babylonian captivity, would be converted to the faith of Christ; and the Antichrist—the Bishop of Rome—would be pulled from his throne and destroyed. These events had a particularity and a concreteness that would permit verification. Either the Jews were in the Christian Church or they were not; either the Pope held power or he did not.[20]

These events would occur over a period of time; presumably—according to most authorities—the Pope would be brought low first, and the conversion of Israel would follow when the Church had regained much of its old purity and authority. When these occurrences were accomplished, their meaning would be clear; the difficulty arose in detecting the evidence of their beginning, for the early stages were not so clear as Puritans would have liked.

There were variations in this general interpretation of the signs. Puritan commentators relished the account in Revelation of the pouring of the vials of wrath, which they took to be the story of the destruction of the Antichrist. The question they paused over—and threatened to debate endlessly—involved discovering the correspondences in history to this figurative description. Had the angel poured the first vial upon the earth? Had all seven been emptied? Almost all scholars agreed at the time Richard Mather pondered these questions that at least several vials of wrath had been emptied and that several more remained full, ready to spill over on the ungodly. Richard Mather's friend, John Cotton, the closest student of the subject in New England, believed that history had progressed through the pouring of four vials of wrath. The first, on the earth, referred to the afflictions visited upon laymen of the Roman Catholic Church, "the lowest and basest Element in the Antichristian world." Catholics since Henry VIII's time, he explained, had learned that their old religion was nothing but the worship of God "after the devices of men." God's agents in history who tilted over this vial counted among their number ordinary men, who as good Catholics had formerly worshipped according to the laws of the Church. In Revelation, the wrath of the second vial spreads over the sea like the blood of a dead man; its referents in reality were the ordinances, the doctrine, the worship of the Church, all foul and corrupt. The men who poured this vial were Reformed ministers, who exposed the falseness and evil of the ordinances. Cotton named these men and included two especially familiar to Puritans in New England, William Perkins and William Ames. Cotton dated the emptying of the third vial "upon the rivers and fountains of waters" even more precisely. Rivers and fountains designated the priests of the Catholic Church who felt the wrath of the third vial in 1581, when Parliament under Elizabeth's tutelage passed a statute making the preaching of Catholicism high treason. Jesuit priests received the full force of the Lord's wrath in the extraordinary statutes of a few years later. The King of Sweden joined Elizabeth in pouring the fourth vial "upon the sun," the House of Austria, the most glorious light in the Antichristian world. Scripture described the "seat of the beast" receiving the wrath of the fifth vial; this reference, Cotton insisted, designated the system of papal government, specifically the Episcopacy. It did not refer to the Pope himself, or to Rome, as some held. This vial had not yet been emptied, though Cartwright, Paul Baynes, and other powerful critics of the bishops had "sprinkled a few drops" here and there. When its wrath was poured, it would spread from England to Catholic countries and eventually flow into the gates of Rome itself.[21]

Like others, Cotton's sureness in interpretation vanished when he faced the events of his own day. What was to be made of the persecution of Puritans in England? And of their immigration to America? The meaning of the English Civil War was especially puzzling. But Puritan authorities in New England in the first generation agreed on most essentials. The differences in their views were less important than their agreement on one important particular: how New England's role fitted into the general pattern of history. On this matter their agreement reflected a general consensus of their purposes in coming to the New World.

In the year 1635, while he was trying to decide whether to leave England or to remain, Richard Mather pondered the prophecies and reflected on history. He lacked John Cotton's gift for handling metaphor and he seemed reluctant to draw exact correspondences between the figures in Revelation and the facts of his own day. But if he resisted the temptation to fix in time the pouring of each vial of wrath, he could not escape what seemed to be the obvious meaning of the general course of events: the struggle with the Antichrist was coming to a climax. In 1635 the prospects for the success of that struggle in England did not appear bright. The English Civil War, with its conflict with Episcopacy, was still more than five years away—and the possibilities of a Presbyterian triumph and the beheading of a King were still inconceivable. (Most of John Cotton's prophetical works are the products of the next wartime decade.) Not surprisingly, then, Richard's historical thought lingered upon Israel of the captivity and defeat rather than victory. But he also noted earlier deliverances of God's chosen out of situations fraught with disaster. He was much impressed by the Lord's charge to Lot to flee Sodom before it was destroyed; the preservation of Noah out of a world drowned because of its corruption was in his mind too. The lesson of these events was clear: God preserved the faithful; God never permitted His Church to be extinguished whatever the evil around it. The obligation of the faithful seemed to be to protect themselves, in order that the Church might survive. If they could not worship in purity in their old homes, they must remove themselves. This obligation became an absolute necessity when the Lord threatened to destroy the land of their birth. Richard noted carefully in the arguments he wrote at this time that even nature agreed that a man must preserve himself and his own in the face of danger. Richard thus came to New England as an avowed exile; he had been banished because of his attachment to purity in the Church of Christ. His purpose in coming was to protect himself and help maintain the ordinances of Christ in His Church. His mood and his understanding of what he was doing was widely shared among the immigrants of the 1630's.[22]

The sense of exile lasted until the early years of the English Civil War, an event which convinced Mather that New England was no longer isolated in the conflict with the Antichrist. With the war he discovered that God had raised up in England a number of faithful supporters in His cause. To be sure, while the fighting continued they suffered, but they had the consolation—Richard Mather pointed out—of suffering in God's cause. Their sufferings in fact were similar to the afflictions he had endured while still preaching in England. Grievous though afflictions were, they revealed God's interest in the afflicted, and His intention of punishing them until they were purged of their corruption.[23]

This was one meaning Mather discovered in the war. It had still another dimension: it marked the death throes of the Beast. The servants of Antichrist had forced the issue; they had attacked true Christians just as they formerly had presecuted them. Now Christians were defending themselves in a sacred cause, and in the process of destroying the prelacy they were ushering in a period of purity in doctrine and worship. The struggle was worth it, Richard insisted, for the New Jerusalem would follow Christ's triumph.[24]

If, in the 1640's, the war promised the end of the Antichrist, events seemed less favorable to the prospect of the conversion of the Jews. And yet Richard Mather had hopes for this prophecy too. If the Lord had intervened to forestall the bloody conquest of England by the Beast, He had chosen America to give a prevision of the salvation of Israel. He had planted Indians in America, another nation of heathen, and now as the conflict with the Beast in England rendered its climax, He had begun to snatch the Indians from Satan. What impressed Richard was the fact that the Indians had resisted all attempts to convert them before. The English had preached without avail for almost thirty years; and not until 1650 did their message begin to take hold. And if the Indians could be brought out of the wasteland of America after all this time, he asked, was not there hope for the Jews? Perhaps the Lord had selected this means to give impetus to further attempts to salvage them.[25]

Whatever their hopes for the future, Richard Mather and his colleagues who led the migration to New England did not ever expect that the Congregational Church polity would serve as a model for others; nor did they expect that, as Perry Miller contends, "ultimately all Europe would imitate New England." [26] The first generation had no such conception of history; and they did not even begin to think of what they were doing as an errand. (In fact, they did not ever use the word "errand" to describe their purposes; its first use came in the next generation.)

An interpretation of their mission in such terms simplifies their conception of the historical process. It fails to concede their psychological subtlety—they did not believe that men followed rational models—and it strips from the historical process the power they attributed to conflict as a determinant in human affairs. It also discovers in them a pride they did not possess. Richard Mather, John Cotton, Thomas Hooker, and most of the great figures of the first generation continued to follow English events after their removal to America. Their interest, however, was not marked by a feeling of superiority, or a belief that the truth resided in New England and nowhere else. Ten years after Richard Mather arrived in Boston, he joined William Thompson, an old friend from England and then minister to the Braintree Church, in writing a long letter of advice to their old congregations in England. The two presumed to offer advice, yet their mood as they wrote was humble: they were out of touch with events in England, they admitted, and they hesitated to give suggestions to their friends. The result was that what they wrote was more in the nature of consolation than advice to people distressed by war. They loved their old countrymen, they explained, and wanted only the best for them. Most of all, they did not want to be understood as posing as the representatives of a morally superior culture: "We doe not think our selves to be the only Prophets, nor that we only are able to give a word of counsel or comfort to our countrymen: . . . such arrogant apprehensions are far from us." [27]

These Puritans began by thinking of themselves in exile. Richard Mather was only one of many who had been deprived of pulpits. Unable to practice the true religion, surrounded by Antichristian practices, and banished from their homes, they held out little hope for the country of their birth. Though there were good men there, and a few true churches, it belonged to the Kingdom of Darkness. Hence they fled to the only Kingdom they valued, the Kingdom of Light. It would be more accurate to say they took the Kingdom of Light with them to New England. It was this Kingdom that concerned them, not New England. While still in England Richard Mather thought of escaping to New England—or, as he said in a revealing phrase, "some like place." And once safe in the New World, these Puritans continued to think in terms of the old abstractions: the conflict between the forces of light and darkness and the grand development of history towards the ultimate end.

Place did not preoccupy them in these years of beginning; and it lost even what initial importance it had when the great conflict between Parliament and the King broke out. Though at first cautious in attributing meaning to this struggle, many Puritans soon invested the war with cosmic significance: if the war did not bring down the Beast, it would inaugurate a greater effort which eventually would destroy him. Their part in New England in these grand events was clear: they had preserved a saving remnant; they had worked out Christ's ideas of the true Church polity; now they had the opportunity to join the faithful called by God to the climactic war. What could they do: watch and wait, strive to perfect themselves, and pray for their brethren in England.[28]

They could help in the struggle in still another way: since the Lord had not revealed all His light even to them on matters of Church polity, they must continue to probe into the meaning of Christ's word. When the Antichrist was brought low, they would have something to contribute to the new order of things. In the New Jerusalem they would help fashion true institutions, according to the Word of Christ; in this effort they could join their victorious brothers in England.

Obviously such a view of history—and their own role in it—could not provide a definition of New England, nor did it in fact prescribe a dramatic role for New England conceived separately from Europe. When these Puritans thought of place, in the 1630's and 1640's, they thought of the Kingdom of Light extending all over the Western World, linking the people of God—the saving remnant—wherever they might be. Richard Mather, and his kind, were not Americans and never would be; they did not think of history in terms of America. Their vision was greater, extending to the godly to the ends of the earth.

3

The Church

Richard Mather's expectation that the Lord would again soon strike the Antichrist evoked a jubilation that was touched with sadness and foreboding. England, shrouded in Antichristian darkness, seemed headed for afflictions—blows landed on the Antichrist, he feared, would leave her reeling. In the New World Mather's feeling for England was one of nostalgia, though not of sentimentality. Not only had he grown and matured there, he had left behind friends he would never forget. Fifteen years after his departure he was still gently instructing his old church in Lancashire.[1] Two of his sons, Nathanael and Samuel, returned to spend their adult lives in England and Ireland; and Increase took an M.A. at Trinity College, Dublin, after he was graduated from Harvard. His father watched him go, fully expecting never to see him again; Increase, he supposed, would make his career abroad.[2]

Mather felt his mind and heart pulled towards England by other considerations too. England figured in his understanding of Biblical prophecies about the Church and the end of the world. And, of course, the Church, even more than the Antichrist, dominated his thought.

At the time Richard went to New England there was a good deal to ponder about the Church. It, of course, had been the occasion for the first appearance of the Puritans. When Henry VIII broke with Rome he did not reform the Church wholesale —his was a reformation at the top supported at the bottom by men who helped themselves to the riches of the Church. The old doctrine and the traditional Church hierarchy satisfied Henry, who thought the bishops needed English direction, not Roman; and he knew none better than himself to supply it.

Reformers with visions of a new purity and simplicity and with a greater respect for Scripture, especially their own reading of it, did not like Henry's notions. They thought that they had a chance to alter things when he died, but Henry's young son, Edward VI, who came to the throne in 1547, lived only six more years. During those six years a satisfactory beginning was made—satisfactory to some at least—but the changes under Edward were repealed by Mary Tudor, who craved the opportunity to return the English Church to Rome. She did her best (her worst, the Puritans said), restoring bishops friendly to her plans, reinvigorating the old doctrine, and driving nonconforming ministers from their pulpits. At least eight hundred fled England, their departure warmed by pyres on which martyrs burned.[3]

The Puritans greeted Mary's successor, Elizabeth, with great hope. But however much the middle way of the Elizabethan Church satisfied—or left undisturbed—most men, it did not please Puritans. They were gratified at the elimination of the Mass and of the Pope's authority, but were appalled by the Popish remnants which were left untouched—bishops, corrupt ministers, to say nothing of pluralities and sinecures, and favors and fees. Moreover, the Queen's Church retained a system of ecclesiastical justice including the Commissary's Court which was probably the most corrupt, and therefore most detested, institution in the entire arrangement. All these vestiges of the old order offended men who valued godliness above everything else.

Although the Puritans, uneasy in this sloppy and comfortable structure, attacked it on all fronts, they could not make the Church over in the face of the Queen's desire for the middle way. Elizabeth stopped their attempt to discard vestments and ceremonies in the Convocations of 1563. To be sure, individual ministers modified the liturgy and refused to wear the surplice; but individual practice, fearless as it sometimes was, could not alter policy. And dissent took casualties as it always does. Thomas Sampson, Dean of Christ Church, Oxford, for example, lost his post when he refused to conform. The challenge to the surplice and the liturgy soon broadened as the Puritans took on the bishops who enforced practice in vestments and ceremonies. The Queen saw the ultimate threat in these attacks—her own authority as Supreme Governor of the Church was clearly called in question by the attack on her appointees, the bishops.[4]

The climax to this phase of the Puritan struggle came in the Admonition Controversy of the 1570's. This engagement, which took its name from two Puritan appeals, the Admonitions to Parliament, followed soon after the expulsion of Thomas Cartwright from Cambridge in 1570, by Dean Whitgift, Vice Chancellor of the University and the future Archbishop of Canterbury. But Commons provided the main arena for this contest and Parliament, encouraged by the Queen, rejected all the Puritan demands for reform of doctrine and ecclesiastical polity.[5]

The Commons contained Puritans and men sympathetic to their cause. One, William Strickland, in 1571, made the mistake of introducing a bill to reform the Prayer Book, and was temporarily barred from the House at the order of the Council for his temerity. The Queen also squelched other attempts to modify the established religion in the next year.[6]

The Puritans could not stop trying to make the Church godly but they could—and did—give up most of their attempts to work through Parliament. When they realized that they could not make Parliament serve reform, they began to work from within the Church, first by holding "prophesyings," weekly discussion meetings which brought clerics and laymen together to open the Scriptures. Elizabeth recognized that such devices threatened her control of the Church, and when in 1577 Archbishop Grindal refused to halt them she suspended him from his administrative duties. His successor, John Whitgift, despised Puritans and took on the task of stopping these meetings without any hesitation. Whitgift invigorated the Court of High Commission and set it after clergymen who refused to subscribe to key articles. In particular the Court demanded that they accept Royal Supremacy, the Thirty-nine Articles, the Prayer Book, and the Ordinal. He also presecuted the leaders of the "Classical Movement," so named after the Presbyterian "classis," or synod, which had as its objective the transformation of episcopal polity into Presbyterian organization. By the early 1590's Whitgift had succeeded: Puritanism had not been killed, but it was stifled as Presbyterian leaders, including Cartwright, were jailed and their oganization smashed. Spurred on by the disdainful laughter of Martin Marprelate, who directed his scorn at the bishops, Whitgift pushed his inquisition as far as he could. For the remainder of the reign, the Puritans were in flight.[7]

Their hopes for James I in 1603 were touchingly like those they held fifty years before at the accession of Elizabeth. James had been bred on Calvinism and might prove receptive to their appeals for modest reform—and for a toleration of their differences. James denied their appeals at the Hampton Court Conference and thereafter their way was rough. Most Puritan clergy conformed but hundreds did not. James's bishops drove them from their pulpits, suppressed their meetings, and rejected their suggestions that pluralities be abolished and the clergy be educated. But the worst was to come under Charles I, a pious but dull and vindictive man who left them no hope at all.

So matters stood in England before the Puritan migration. Events had settled very little as far as the critics of the established Church were concerned. In fact they disagreed with the orthodox on the meaning of the events themselves. They also disagreed among themselves. These disagreements were important, for how the Church's history was understood determined in part the attitude held toward the Church as it was presently constituted.

Anglican divines traced the founding of the Church to the time of the Apostles when, they said the Church of Christ was established in England. But though they argued for the Apostolic founding, they denied that the polity of the Church must be identical with that of the primitive Church. They dismissed such a view as one of the many delusions of the Puritans. Nor did they see any reason to discard any practice just because it had fallen into corruption under the Pope. The Puritans were much too rigid: God—John Whitgift asserted—did not impose any particular Church organization on men, but rather left it to be varied according to circumstances of time and place. Of course, the Church should have ministers, but how they garbed themselves was not a critical question. The surplice affected no one's eternal state; nor indeed did anything related to the Church's organization—its government, its discipline, or its rites. That, however, did not mean that the Church should permit Puritan ministers to appear without the surplice (as Richard Mather was to discover); nor did it mean that they and their flocks should feel free to abandon the liturgy or the Prayer Book. Rather the decisions of the Church about such matters ought to be accepted without controversy, as a bishop said, "for order and obedience sake." [8]

None knew better than Anglican divines how little regard some Puritans paid to order and obedience. Among the most disobedient and disorderly were the Separatists. The Separatists (they took the name because of their insistence that in forming churches good men must separate themselves from evil ones) rejected virtually every contention of the Anglicans. Although they did not agree among themselves on every point, they all echoed Robert Browne's confident assertion about the Church of England and its bishops—"It is the Beast and they are the Ryders." [9]

The first true churches, according to John Robinson, minister of the church that eventually founded Plymouth Colony, were established by the Apostles. Christ himself formed no churches; He lived and died "a minister of the circumcision." [10] The churches of the Apostles, and those established since then, appeared when believers voluntarily covenanted among themselves. Compulsion could not be used in the forming of these bodies since the substance of a church had to be gathered from men of faith, and faith could not be coerced. The means by which it was obtained was teaching and instruction by Christ's disciples. [11]

The Church of England, Robinson said, could not claim such an origin. It was the offshoot of the Church of Rome and the Roman Church had never been a true church freely gathered. To be true, saints had lived in Rome during Christ's time, and true churches had also maintained themselves. The Antichrist, or the Church of Rome, made his appearance long after the Apostles' time. The Antichrist existed "as an embryo in the womb," the Pope was his head, the hierarchy, his body. [12] The

Antichrist grew in size until he dispossessed Christ of His leadership of the Church in the world. Until the Protestant Reformation, the English Church served her parent, the Antichrist, without interruption and without serious challenge. The Church of England was never Christ's Church, it never—despite its claims—comprised the body of the people of England. What saints there were in England lived in defiance of the diabolical efforts of the Antichrist and enjoyed Christ's truth only precariously.[13]

If the saints were few in these days of the long apostasy from the primitive Church, their number, by the Separatists' computations, did not increase much with the Protestant Reformation of the sixteenth century. The Reformation in England began, according to Separatist accounts, with young Edward VI. His father, Henry VIII, made so few changes in matters close to their hearts that they dismissed him with hardly a word. In Edward's short reign the Antichrist in England received a few injuries, a part of the old doctrine was revoked and a few of his servants, the bishops and their minions, were dismissed. The saints took heart and gathered churches which they thought approached the purity of the primitive Church. The Antichrist had barely quailed before these meager assaults when his creature, Mary, acceded to the throne. Yet something was achieved even under the bitter persecutions of Mary's dreadful reign. For, as Henry Ainsworth, a Separatist divine, put it, the martyrs "by their faithful testimonyes and patient sufferings, [did] throw down a great part of Antichrists church." [14] But Christian suffering could achieve only so much and with the death of Mary, progress towards purity came to an end. The few churches of the saints were swept into the national Church and all its branches with the dissolved congregations joining "the unhallowed rout in the popish and profane parishes under their late mass." [15] Deluded and unsanctified men who expressed a desire to bring the Antichrist down chose the wrong means: they appealed to the State to reconstitute the Church and to remove Popish abuses. After failing they cravenly joined their oppressors once more.[16]

Their means were improper, in the judgments of Separatists, because although the State was charged with the responsibility of suppressing idolatry and rooting out error, it could not constitute the Church. Churches took their beginning in good men, who could be brought to faith only by instruction divinely countenanced; force could never yield faith. But it was force they faced, the Separatists insisted, and force had stopped all progress towards purer churches. The self-styled reformers who chose to stay within the Church had not only stopped reform, they had conspired to reincarnate the Antichrist. Weren't Popish practices common once more? the Separatists asked. And as further evidence of decay they cited the persecution of themselves.[17]

History had paused in England. It was clear to the Separatists that the development which had been arrested at the end of Mary's time had not resumed. And so after sixty or seventy years of discontinuity, they felt justified in taking new action, especially in leaving England for Holland, and later for America.

There is an unyielding quality in the history written by the Separatists. They did not shrink at dismissing others as the agents of the Devil. They did not draw back at the smell of the pit, nor was it difficult for them to imagine generations of Englishmen drowning in floods of smoking brimstone.

When Massachusetts was founded, the Separatist version of the history of the Church of England was at least thirty years old. The Puritans who came to Massachusetts Bay probably knew its details as well as they knew the Scriptures. They shared many of the Separatists' ideas about the English Church and its history: they agreed that the Church of England was corrupt; it retained a disgusting reverence for Roman ritual; its episcopacy was the legitimate heir of the Catholic hierarchy; its entire history exposed its early Antichristian origins. While holding these views, these Bay Colony Puritans always insisted that they had not separated from the Church. Despite its imperfections it remained a true Church. They were a part of it, though far removed from it physically.[18]

This refusal to take the path of the Separatists has been explained in Perry Miller's *Orthodoxy in Massachusetts*.[19] The non-Separatist Congregationalists, he writes, refused to follow these assumptions to the Separatist conclusion because they shared their age's commitment to uniformity in religion. Separation opened the door to "social demoralization" and to political chaos.[20] The State had responsibilities to enforce the true worship and they would support it, corrupt though it was. The Separatists—as Miller points out—would not have stripped the State of its coercive power, even while it struck at them in the name of uniformity. In fact the Separatists derided separation; they would not split Christ's Church; they would not countenance any departure from it. But the Church of England was not Christ's own; the Church of England belonged to Antichrist. They had not separated from Christ's Church, they had removed themselves from evil.[21]

At this point non-Separatist Congregationalists diverged from their Separatist brethren. But they did not do so primarily on the basis of the elaborate sophistry that Miller so brilliantly reconstructs. Miller concentrates on the defense they made of the Elizabethan Church: against Separatist protests that the churches had not been truly gathered of the faithful, because the State had constructed them by sweeping all but the openly scandalous within, the non-Separatist divines answered that there were many in the churches who voluntarily served Christ without the spur of the State. They had joined implicitly in covenant by their coming together. As for the force of the State which throbbed behind the whole structure, it did not affect most religious exercises which were conducted voluntarily. Nor did these non-Separatists boggle at the ministry, which in existing practice was appointed by a patron and installed by a bishop, even though their theory required that the people—the saints—choose their ministers. Within Anglican practice—these ingenious divines argued—the procedure demanded by Christ might be met. Nothing prevented the people from giving their silent assent to the appointment by a patron: this tacit approval conferred a genuine calling upon the minister. And he, by silently making certain reservations in the course of his appointment and installation, remained free from impurity. It was regrettable that the whole matter could not be conducted in the open, but in this maze of unspoken calls and silent answers, the saints were certain that Christ heard and saw true visible churches where others detected only the traditional establishment.[22]

This is the burden of the story Miller tells. Subterfuge, evasion, elaborate pretense, all were resorted to in the service of the ideal of religious uniformity. The non-Separatist shrank before the alternative of separation, Miller contends, "for events had proved in the way of Separation political madness lay." The Separatists had incurred the guilt of "rending the seamless garment of the church. . . ." [23]

In England of the late sixteenth century the contention of the non-Separatists that they had not separated from the Church of England was a farce, but in America in the first half of the seventeenth century, it was not. Perry Miller's reconstruction of these arguments rests largely on the writings of the sixteenth-century group which he then attributes to the founders of Massachusetts Bay. But this later group, while always professing admiration for their fathers, largely ignored the form of their argument, while accepting its conclusion that the Church of England was a true Church.

The problem of the non-separating reformers in England was to demonstrate that a strain of purity had survived and would continue to do so, despite corrupt ecclesiastical practices and ideas. To show that Christ's true Church lived amidst Antichristian degeneracy, they resorted to a history of Church polity which had the pure Church surviving unseen within the impure. Their American tutees did not have to contend with hostile bishops and Romish remnants, and they could construct their churches any way they liked. There was no point in cleaving to the stratagems of the English reformers. Still, they maintained that they were a part of the old Church of England. They did so out of a commitment to one of the oldest beliefs about Church history: the Church of Christ would survive to the end of the world. It would struggle and suffer; indeed, since its inception it had always engaged the forces of evil, led for most of history by the Antichrist. Though it had hidden itself, the true Church had found life for centuries in the midst of the English establishment. And now in the freedom of the New World, far away from the prying eyes of the bishops, it could declare the truth openly and follow the faith to the glory of Christ.[24]

The group around William Ames, perhaps the non-Separatist divine most admired in New England, had held similar views but had not emphasized them. Their immediate necessity was to establish how in fact the true Church polity existed within the practices of parish churches created by the State and led by a minister appointed and ordained from outside the congregation.

What kept them from going the whole way and joining the Separatists was their belief that a holy remnant had preserved in England the Church of Christ over the ages. So they admitted that the Church harbored some of the unfaithful, and that its procedures should be altered, but they insisted that it also contained God's elect. For rejecting the Church of England, as the Separatists did, meant consigning these people to the Antichrist.[25]

The desire to preserve Christ's Church free of corruption carried Richard Mather and thousands of others out of England in the Great Migration. By 1639, the last year of that human flood, Richard Mather had almost given up hope for the country of his birth. The England that had received the Church in the times of the Apostles only to lose it to Rome was in danger of seeing it vanish altogether. This dreadful possibility had followed the promising beginning made under King Edward VI and Queen Elizabeth, who had apparently begun the destruction of the Antichrist. Four years after his landing in Boston, Mather warned that the Lord was about to "unchurch" England.[26]

England's apostasy made the American task all the more urgent. The Church must be preserved; the polity that Christ had prescribed in the Gospels must be worked out. This much could be done in the expectation of Christ's imminent coming.

When Richard arrived in New England, the New England way in Church organization had been almost completed. Puritan divines in England had worked out the theory over a period of two generations. Their conclusions amply and brilliantly described by modern historians as non-separating Congregationalism held that Christ's Church in the world should be restricted to visible saints, as those who gave some evidence of holiness were called. The visible Church was to be composed of self-governing particular churches, separated from the State and other institutions though depending upon them for support. These particular churches of the faithful were to be gathered out of the world and formed on the basis of a covenant, a joint agreement of the saints with one another, and with God, to worship together according to the criteria laid down in the Gospel.[27]

Ministers called by the Church in an election would preach and govern; once selected, ordained, and installed in their godly offices they could require obedience, for their offices were divine though their call—mediately—came from the people. Ministers preached, administered the sacraments of baptism and the Lord's Supper, catechized children, and provided moral and religious leadership and supervision in the community. Their flocks, the laymen of the Church, held a kind of power from Christ to call their leaders, though once in office ministers were to be obeyed, and at "liberty" to give their consent to major decisions taken by the elders—the admission of new members and the discipline of strays among the faithful.

This system, if it may be called that, proved more susceptible to amendment and change in practice than in theory. A strong pastor could render the liberty of the lay brethren almost meaningless if he chose; and in a few cases, the church expanded their liberty from consent to an authority to rule. Ministerial associations, and synods, special meetings of pastors and lay representatives, also presented a challenge to the autonomy of the individual church. The relationship of these bodies and of the competing authority of clergy and laymen preoccupied churches and their leaders throughout the seventeenth century. In a variety of forms, the same questions were asked in New England's churches: What authority did ministers have? Should not lay members participate in the governing of the church? And where could the associations of churches and ministers enter the ecclesiastical arrangement, if indeed they could at all?

Richard Mather possessed the qualities which equipped him to make an important contribution toward the resolution of such questions. And his belief that the survival of Christ's Church was intimately tied to its fate in New England gave the task its importance. In his first years in America two kinds of questions were heard often in discussions of the Church. One, sounded in England and Scotland by Presbyterians, challenged the Congregational dedication to the autonomy of the particular church. News of New England's practices had reached nonconformist ears in England soon after the founding. To those still in the mother country, the news was disturbing and smacked of repression—and, at the same time, of anarchy as well. Two of the leading critics of the New England way were Charles Herle, a Presbyterian minister who preached before the Long Parliament, and Samuel Rutherford, a Scottish divine who had lost his pulpit for opposition to the extension of Episcopacy to Scotland and then became a Professor of Divinity at St. Andrews. Their attacks on New England were considered serious enough to draw answers from Thomas Hooker and John Cotton, as well as Richard Mather.[28]

Mather rooted his replies in the sources Puritans respected: his studies are especially rich in the citation of New Testament Scriptures. But his work does not display either the massive scholarship of the comparable studies by Thomas Hooker, *A Survey of the Summe of Church Discipline* (1648), or the originality of John Cotton, *The Keyes of the Kingdom of Heaven* (1644).

What distinguished Richard's work was its judicious quality and its devotion to finding the truth. Thus he rose above mere defense; he provided more than a rationale of a system; he sought as honestly as possible to discover what Christ intended for His Church in the world. One other characteristic marked his efforts—the concern that the true way—Christ's way—survive in order that His coming might be hastened by the certainty of a holy reception on earth.

In his heart of hearts, Richard Mather was absolutely convinced, of course, that Christ's Church would survive—it could depend upon Christ's promise for its being. What he, and others like him, faced in the Presbyterians was an indirect challenge to demonstrate that the New England way embodied the continuity of the Church from Israel's day to their own. The Presbyterians Herle and Rutherford indicated that they were skeptical about this contention. If New England was the Gentile version of Israel, they asked, why did it not hold true to the Jewish ecclesiastical pattern and establish a hierarchy of synods and classes which could review the practices of local churches and weed out the errors that inevitably sprang up in bodies with no checks on their autonomy? Israel had its judicatory in Jerusalem, Herle pointed out. The implication was plain: New England needed synods, located, perhaps, across the ocean. If the Church embodied the saving remnant, it must not depart from this Holy pattern—presumably the pattern set by Israel. Richard conceded that self-governing churches might make mistakes; the concession came easily to him for he was then enabled to point out that review bodies would fall prey to the same inherent propensities. The Presbyterian argument on the grounds of efficiency might be dismissed on those same grounds of efficiency. Could New England continue as the Lord's Israel without following exactly the Israelites' ecclesiastical practices? Richard believed emphatically that it could. The polity of Israel resided in the nation and hence was inapplicable; the Gospel had opened the Congregational way, a way unknown to the Church of the Old Testament. The judicatories in Israel included civil authorities and extended to civil administration; and besides, they met on a regular basis. Judicatories were not synods then; the Presbyterians ought to resist whatever inclinations they had to wrap themselves in Jewish banners. Nor should the particular congregations of the Jews be regarded as churches invested with the authority to administer the ordinances—none could administer the Passover which was reserved to the supreme body in Jerusalem. Yet, though New Testament Church polity differed greatly from Old, the covenant cherished by saints everywhere remained the same in substance as that of the Israelites. The covenant, Richard expained, would endure until the Second Coming of Christ even though it was embodied in a Congregational rather than national polity. More light on true Church organization had appeared with Christ, and more shone forth as the end of the world approached. It would be unforgivable not to revise the constitution of churches in accordance with this brighter knowledge of Christ's desires. Mather announced all these views in a series of tracts written over a twenty-five-year period and in the definitive statement of the Congregational way, *A Platform of Church Discipline Gathered Out of the Word of God*, which he composed under the direction of the Synod meeting at Cambridge in 1648.[29]

The Synod did not spend most of its time on matters dear to the hearts of Herle and Rutherford. Questions about the organization and the government of churches concerned it deeply, as they had Presbyterians, but it recognized that for most men in New England, these issues were largely theoretical. Not that disputes between ministers and their people did not occur in New England's churches. They did, and they caused concern; and men felt troubled when they attempted to define the jurisdictions of the synods that occasionally met to ease conflicts. But most such contests involved the wills and characters of the participants and victory in them depended upon power—not upon

scholarship and theology. For these reasons the brotherly exchanges in tracts which solemnly examined Old Testament
precedents for synodical authority probably did not obsess most
laymen in Massachusetts Bay—nor did the precise constitutional
lines drawn in the Cambridge Platform. The other issue taken
up by the synod—the question of Church membership—did,
however.[30]

Along with every member of the Synod, Richard Mather also
pondered the question: what made a man a member? How did a
man qualify? What separated him from the sinful world? Could
anything separate him in the reality accessible to mere mortals?
After all, every man in this life carried the original corruption
in his heart and this corruption sprouted each day as surely as
the seeds in springtime.

The official answers to these questions—so far as any answers
could be official in Massachusetts—had been pretty well given by
the time of Richard Mather's arrival in 1635. Accepting the
Augustinian distinction between the invisible and the visible
Church—the first composed of the truly pure of all times and
places, the second of those claiming to be saintly (though in fact
the claims were not equally true)—these Puritans in New England resolved to make the visible conform to the invisible as
closely as possible. Christian churches had always excluded the
obviously profane, but despaired for the most part of isolating
hypocrites from the genuine saints. Not so the non-separating
Congregationalists of the Bay who worked out tests of saving
faith which they hoped would lend themselves to the task of
making certain that visible saints would be drawn from the invisible.

The tests of saving faith, which were just being established in
practice when Richard Mather arrived in 1635, reflected the
suspicions of his ministerial colleagues that by themselves good
behavior and professions of belief told little about a man's
internal state. Good behavior might help in identifying the elect,
but it could originate in morality as well as graciousness; the
claim to believe accompanied by knowledge of the Scriptures,
testified to a good disposition, but it, too, could be faked. A few
miles from Boston the Puritans of Plymouth stopped with these
tests—good behavior and profession of faith—and built their
churches on them. It may seem curious that the Puritans of the

Bay carried the search for purity farther than the Pilgrims of Plymouth. The Massachusetts group seems less intense in most respects—they refused to separate from the Church of England and they did not bounce from Amsterdam to Leyden to the New World to avoid the world's taint. Yet they attempted to make the visible and the invisible Church congruent by means of a test of internal experience. By 1636 they had institutionalized a requirement that candidates for membership describe the inner experience that convinced them that saving grace had entered their souls. Only the context of the founding of Massachusetts Bay, the sense of exile in America of these men, and their powerful conviction that they must preserve the Church in the world can explain the framing of this requirement. For they believed that if escape from Antichristian England was worth the effort, the Church they sought to save must be made to conform to the elect as closely as human means could contrive. The men who could tell of Christ working in their souls were the Church; they were for substance the seed of Abraham. They continued the true Church—the Church God had located first in the Jews, and then in the Gentiles. God had chosen to deal with His Church through His covenant; He had promised Abraham that His covenant would be "everlasting," extending to "thy seed after thee." [31]

Giving a description of one's conversion experience provided the key test for saving faith and seemed at first to provide the solution to the problem of identifying the visible Church. A people who used this test and who insisted that it be accompanied by a knowledge of the Scriptures and by sanctified behavior surely had discovered the means for making the visible conform to the invisible. But whatever comfort the first-generation divines may have taken from this conviction did not last, for their "system" soon came to be questioned—from without, by their English brethren, and from within by their anxious flocks. [32]

The issues raised from both outside New England and within it began, and in a sense ended, with children. The nature of Church membership seemed clear, deceptively so, Puritan divines came to realize. All agreed that the Church should admit only visible saints, and to make certain that it did, churches and the State worked out the tests of inner experience, all designed to make the invisible visible to rational charity. But what should be done about the children? At first the answer was easily given

—baptize the babies born to members. The churches proceeded in this way until they discovered that many of these children, as they came of age, failed to give evidence of their inner worth. The painful necessity of denying them the Lord's Supper was then recognized in practice and institutionalized in the Cambridge Platform of 1648.[33]

No one proposed denying these unconverted, but baptized, persons marriage; and marry and procreate they did. Because of disagreements within itself, the Cambridge Synod remained silent about the children born of these marriages, but the question remained: should the children of unconverted, but baptized, members receive baptism? Their parents were usually good, although perhaps over-scrupulous of their own fitness for membership, and could not accept lightly the prospect that their children would burn in Hell, which was exactly the fate implied by the denial of the sacrament of baptism.[34]

Richard Mather read of these issues before he faced them in his own ministry. In his first great tract on Church government he begged off questions about the intentions of New England toward its children with the claim that the churches were too young to know.[35] He apparently never had any doubts about qualification for the Lord's Supper and throughout his career insisted that only the fit, those who demonstrated that grace resided in their souls, should eat of the body of Christ. All the founders agreed, and he wrote their judgment into the Cambridge Platform. In 1636, twelve years before the Platform was drafted, Mather had professed uncertainty about baptizing the children of baptized, but unconverted, adults. But sometime in the next seven or eight years he shed enough of his uncertainty to announce in his most ambitious study of Church polity, "A Plea for the Churches of Christ in New England," that he believed such children should receive baptism.[36]

Mather did not make this announcement full of confidence. The entire matter was "dark and doubtfull," he wrote in the "Plea." [37] His doubts did not extend to adults who offered themselves for membership, and who thereby requested the sacraments of baptism and the Lord's Supper. He never believed that they should be admitted.[38]

Mather had come to New England convinced that the Church of Christ must be preserved in all its purity. In the Spring of

1636, less than a year after the *James* entered the port of Boston, he agreed to serve the Dorchester group which was just gathering itself into a church. Ministers and magistrates from nearby communities appeared on the appointed day to examine the company that was seeking to establish itself. To the distress of everyone concerned, the faith of some of the candidates proved hard to discern, and the examiners withheld their permission. Thinking on this episode a few days later, Richard Mather, whose own grace had not been challenged, regretted that he had agreed to sponsor the Dorchester group. "They pressed me into it with much importunity," he explained to Thomas Shepard, who among the examiners had been least satisfied that the Dorchester candidates possessed the requisite qualifications. Richard was "ashamed" not to yield—if he did not "a tribe . . . should perish out of Israel." Not wishing that to happen and not wanting to be considered "stubborn and of a stiff spirit," he gave in to the people of Dorchester—with unhappy results.[39]

This episode marked the last and perhaps the only time that Mather allowed himself to apply less than rigorous standards in assessing the fitness of an adult company. Later in 1636 he and the Dorchester faithful succeeded in gathering a regenerate group out of the world and into a church. A few months before they did so, a chastened Richard Mather was writing friends in England that hypocrites must be kept out of the Church and that the fitness of all who applied must be searched. Mather must have succeeded in impressing his own sense of rigor on his church; for years afterwards they resisted his belief that the children of unconverted members should be baptized. Perhaps they knew of his own doubts in the 1640's, doubts that weakened his plea that the Church extend baptism to such children.[40]

The resolve to keep out "counterfeit Christians," in Mather's pungent phrase, did not weaken.[41] He meant the term to refer to adults only, of course; there was no way of telling about an infant, or a small child, until reason and knowledge were attained with maturity. But those adults in the community who presented themselves for membership were another matter. While the least spark of faith ought to bring their acceptance by the Church, they must be examined carefully beforehand. Mather made the conventional bow to the need for conducting this scrutiny with "rational charity," a phrase that echoed through three generations of Puritan writing on Church polity. The question that the modern must ask is what he, and other divines of the seventeenth century, meant by the term. How rational was it, and more to the point, how far did this charity extend into a corrupt world? Richard Mather impressed his own generation as a kind and sympathetic man, a view that justifiably persists in our own century. He was not one of the eager tormenters of Anne Hutchinson; he did not sniff heresy behind every bush—and he looked at children with far more hope than many of his age. Yet probably because he had been burned in the first attempt to draw the Dorchester men into a church, and certainly because he despised impurity in God's house, he proved himself more dedicated than most to keeping the counterfeit out. Although he often went to William Ames, John Ball, Paul Baynes, and even Cartwright for guidance in his thought about the Church, on this matter of examination none of the scholars gave him his lead. Rather it was Calvin he found most persuasive—Calvin who counted it "foolish credulity" to accept "meer verball acknowledgments" as satisfying the requirements of faith.[42] Nothing ought to be taken at face value—or so Richard Mather read Calvin. The Church must "search and examine" into men's hearts, otherwise sinful men, hypocrites, liars, designing men would find their way into the Lord's house.[43]

Calvin carried great authority but Scripture even more, and Mather went to the Old and New Testament for proof of the need for preventing charity from developing into foolishness. The second book of Kings told the melancholy story of Gedaliah who lost his life for being "over charitable" to the treacherous Ishmael—even after a warning against such weakness was delivered to him.[44] Other holy passages reported the results of examinations, however, of Philip searching the heart of the eunuch, of John The Baptist who "sifted the very thought of them that came to his Baptisme," and most gloriously of the Angel of Ephesus who earned Christ's praise for trying those claiming to be Apostles and discovering them to be liars. As Mather read Revelations, Christ "commended" the Angel for "suspiciousness," and provided a standard that His Church must honor.[45] Rational charity for Mather clearly implied a willingness to accept weak Christians but to receive none without suspicion that they might be fraudulent. He might well have substituted "suspicious" for rational. In any event, he summed up his views by urging that charity not be suspicious without cause yet it must "not trust all faire pretences too farre." [46]

Mather's colleagues in the pulpits of New England, and his son Increase, and his grandson Cotton, all were to agree that rational charity should be exercised so as not to exclude any Christian. Better to admit ten hypocrites, John Cotton once wrote, than keep out a single Christian.[47] Richard Mather heard this argument often and rejected it specifically—better keep out many Christians, he urged, than admit a single hypocrite. The "hurt" in denying membership to one with saving faith, he explained, was "negative"; the Church would miss the good that the saint had in him, but it would not receive the evil that a hypocrite carried in his soul.[48] In the history of the Church what impressed Richard was how much wickedness a single corrupt person might do, as Satan's desire to sow the tares among the wheat demonstrated. And Ecclesiastes reported that "one sinner destroyeth much good." [49]

If Scriptural history and his own experience made Mather wary of unexamined avowals of graciousness, they did not dampen his confidence that the Church could judge accurately the experience of applicants. We can see today that among the effects of much preaching about predestination and the process of conversion was the appearance of a large number of laymen uncertain of their inner states. Perhaps some were over-scrupulous, at any rate they hesitated to claim that their private experience revealed the working of grace. Others simply said that they had not undergone conversion, but the pattern of their lives seemed to suggest that they might entertain hopes. In the 1640's Richard Mather was still full of confidence, and he urged them all to trust the churches by telling the elders how things stood within their minds and souls at the moment. Those knowledgeable in such matters would decide whether their experience was gracious. The Church would make mistakes, but Mather did not consider those errors sinful, even when they resulted in the admission of hypocrites. An unregenerate man sinned when he entered the Church, but the Church, in acting honestly on the evidence, did not.[50]

What all this implied for the character of the Church is clear: it would contain hypocrites. Mather recognized this, admitted it freely though he deplored it and wished to preserve the Church from taint whenever possible. Unlike several colleagues, he never claimed that hypocrites had their uses, that indeed their presence in some way strengthened the Church. Such assertions were made by divines who were even more concerned about an orderly society that he. They emphasized the advantage of having unworthy men directly under the watch of the Church—as all of the baptized, of any age, were. The Church could exhort them to live up to the promises of their baptismal covenant, and to observe the law and live decent and moral lives. Mather rarely delivered such exhortations and never rejoiced that unregenerate men within the Church were subject to its supervision.[51]

Despite his demand that the Church regard prospective members with suspicion, Mather urged as early as 1644 that the children of unconverted members receive baptism. To many of his peers, such practice guaranteed that the impure would pollute Christ's Church. Despite his harsh, unforgiving attitude towards hypocrites, Richard possessed a gentle side. Certainly he found the grief of parents who dreaded the possibility that their children were unregenerate hard to bear. He spoke several times of the need to give them some comfort. But by itself this desire would not have carried him to his position on baptism. What he had was a profound organic sense, a tendency to see wholes—not just discrete parts—and to conceive of the interconnectedness of things. This sense shaped his historical understanding, especially his conception of the covenant and the persistence of the Church. The New Testament, of course, held that Christ's Church would endure until the end of the world. But if all Protestant reformers agreed on the persistence of the Church they did not agree on the unity of the covenant, at best a shadowy device in the New Testament, nor did they agree on the relationship of the Church of the Jews to the Church of the Gentiles. Richard Mather's ideas on these subjects had a starkness and a clarity that gave them great power. The covenant, he was convinced, was one. Beginning with Adam, transferred to Abraham, and to the children of Israel, and extending through the New Testament history to the seventeenth century, the same covenant had endured. He conceded that it varied according to circumstances and accidents, but for substance—for the faithful of all ages within it—it was unvarying. It had always contained sinners and hypocrites; no one could deny that Ishmael and others of Abraham's household who had been sealed into it by circumcision were of the damned. They had been in the covenant externally, he explained: they, like many after them were in it, but unable to keep it, unable to receive grace. Eventually Israel itself arrived at this dreadful condition and the Lord cast Israel off, breaking the everlasting covenant with these unfaithful. When the everlasting covenant was shattered through the apostasy of Israel, the Lord chose a new people for His own, and the reformed saints everywhere in the seventeenth century survived as the chosen.[52]

It was the children's being in covenant that qualified them for baptism, Richard always believed, not their parents' fitness for the Lord's Supper. In the 1640's when he first argued for the baptism of children of unregenerate members, he may have expected many of them, and perhaps their parents also, to convert. He preached on the growth of grace in these years, insisting even as he begged men to come to Christ, that grace would show itself in those who had received it. It would grow, revealing itself in the attitude and the behavior of the saint.[53]

As the problem of membership—and baptism—came to a head late in the next decade, Mather reluctantly admitted that perhaps he had been mistaken about the visibility of grace. His admission came almost fifteen years after the Cambridge Synod had decided to ignore the entire issue. But in 1657 and 1662, when successive synods took up the question, the time for a reassessment and for candor had arrived. In *Defense of the Answer of the Synod of 1662*, Mather declared that grace might not work itself into men's actions.[54] Still its "being and truth" might be present even though its "exercise" was not.[55] And hence it was simply impossible to decide one way or another about those adults who had been baptized as children, but who had then failed to convert as they reached maturity. Perhaps they had grace, perhaps they did not, but in either event the Church could not attain certainty. All it could know was that they remained in the covenant and in the Church unless they were cast out for some notorious sin. Once these adults declared their belief in Christ and owned their covenant, their children too should receive baptism. Presumably the children of these children too would qualify as they were born.[56]

In the 1630's when the founders gave their ecclesiastical theory practical form, they had not realized the implications of having two methods of qualifying for Church membership. They had assumed that membership itself had its own integrity—it was one no matter whether a person qualified through birth to regenerate parents or through a relation of his own conversion experience. This assumption was challenged, first quietly in one church and another as the baptized grew up unconverted but still presented their own infants for baptism. By the time of the Synod of 1662, its opponents were openly arguing that there were not just two methods for qualifying for Church membership, but that there were two kinds of membership. Those who experienced grace and told about it publicly were one kind—personal, immediate members in John Davenport's phrase; and those who came in by virtue of their parents' sanctity were another—mediate members, Davenport called them.[57]

Mediate members faced a great responsibility—the obligation to experience the Holy Spirit working within themselves, and a dreadful penalty if they did not—the disannulment of their "mediate" covenant. In effect, as Davenport described their plight, they cut themselves off from the Church which did not have to take any formal action against them. And, of course, in cutting themselves off, they did the same for their children who must then go through life unbaptized and without hope, unless they felt and described God's grace working within themselves.[58]

Davenport and his leading supporter, the young Increase Mather, son of Richard, possessed a hard streak of perfectionism that experience had softened in most of the founders. Every Puritan divine of the first generation wished to close the gulf between the invisible and visible Church, but most had learned with Richard that tests of saving faith did not provide the means of closing the breach. Davenport's confidence in the churches' ability to identify the faithful never slackened. The Israelites had required that circumcised children covenant for themselves after they came of age, and so should we, he argued. Richard Mather, denying that such action constituted a new covenant, insisted that it involved only a renewal of the one covenant God had ever extended to men. Davenport hoped that the Church would attain the purity of the New Jerusalem before Christ's Second Coming. Richard shared those hopes but denied that they would be realized. The Church, he said, must be holy at the end of the world, but even then there will be hypocrites. The parable of the foolish virgins suggested as much—those without will, without faith, will be excluded from the glorious marriage chamber, that is, from Heaven, at the end.[59]

Yet he remained certain that the Church would endure if it could be protected from the over-zealous within. The covenant that gave it form continued as always, though ways of qualifying for membership varied. A child born into a family was not less a member than his parent, Richard once pointed out, even though he had done nothing himself to earn his place. The same principle applied to elect societies, states, and churches, all of which had been chosen without regard to their merit. The Church must remain as pure as possible, but it must also recognize that while some of its members would be able to demonstrate their graciousness, others would not. Some would possess qualifications for the Lord's Supper; others would not. Some would be truly holy, though men would never be able to identify them with absolute certainty; others, whatever evidence they gave or withheld, would be unregenerate. But as long as holiness existed, as long as the churches held fast to their covenant, they could serve the Lord. And glory was promised by God to His Church at the end of the world.

4

The Word

∽

The struggle between the forces of light and darkness, between the Church and the Antichrist, gave meaning to history. But this conflict not only explained the past, it also cast its lines into the future. Of course not even the prophets could make out the pattern of the future distinctly, but they could predict that its end would arrive in the triumph of Christ. Although there were other certain reference points in human history—the beginning in Eden, the fall into the hands of the Devil, the birth of Christ— none offered more reassurance than the knowledge that at the end of the world the glorious Christ awaited His own.

Richard Mather received comfort from this grand schema, though he no more than anyone else could rest complacently in it. He knew that much was required of men in this divine drama. Did not Christ command that men should make their calling sure? Like every man, Richard had to consider the state of his soul; unlike most, he had, as a minister, to concern himself with the souls of others. The salvation of the soul reproduced on a small scale the cosmic struggle of good and evil. For within history, as within the soul, the fundamental forces of the universe were arrayed.

A minister who was convinced, as Richard Mather was, that the earth had entered its last days, might be expected to connect the fate of the soul to cosmic history. Mather made the connection—not just in formal treatises on the Church in history —but in the ordinary course of his preaching to the people of Dorchester, who heard from his lips of the "miserys" of the Protestant Church all over Europe, and of the "warre and bloodshed in England."[1] Richard found a moral in these grim events for New England—close adherence to the true religion was necessary if New England were not to feel similar torments. Like most Puritan ministers, Richard could never resist the suggestion that pain and affliction would bring good results if only the warning of sin they carried were heeded. In examining the upheaval all over Europe, and the distresses of the Church, Richard discerned the "day-light of the Gospel" breaking.[2] Good men should use the light to examine themselves and practice the virtues in preparation for the glorious end. No reform was too small to be made, as he pointed out in 1647. "It is also a Tyme that is the latter age of the world and for the coming of the Lord draweth neere, and for this cause we should be temperate and sober."[3]

Although Richard Mather rarely missed an opportunity to link the fate of souls to the destiny of the cosmos, he usually dealt with his church in less dramatic ways. The conventional tasks of the minister were to convert sinners and to strengthen and support those who had been saved. A minister in a culture that defined man's relation to God in terms of the determinism of Calvin faced, as Richard Mather and his colleagues discovered, an extraordinary set of problems. One revolved around the apparent inflexibility of the Lord's choice. On considering the rigidity of God, the question we might ask is, "If a man was predestined to salvation or damnation without regard to his merit, why would he exert himself to come to God and to lead a life according to the moral law?" Some men must have put the question this way, perhaps more often to themselves than to their ministers. But one suspects that such a question occurred to men more often in the eighteenth century than in the sixteenth or seventeenth. It is a question born of an indifference and a logic that do not comport well with the anxiety of the seventeenth century. Puritan laymen undoubtedly felt despair more often than indifference; the questions they asked themselves and their ministers reveal a kind of paralysis of will, rather than a logical indifference. The problem that obsessed them was why should God choose the likes of me for eternal bliss? Following it came the accusations of self: I am too evil even for a merciful God to accept; no one soaked in sin as I am can hope to experience conversion. Apparently there was a darkness greater even than such black desperation, for a second kind of response reveals that some complained of an inability to feel anything. I want to believe, such men said, but I do not, in fact I cannot believe. God has not given me grace and I can do nothing for myself. I am dead and all that I can experience is deadness.[4]

Richard Mather, like every other Puritan divine, failed to recognize these plaints for what they were—the expression of psychological rather than moral scruples. In Richard's mind the causes were obvious: the despairing ones who bewailed their sins really loved them and did not give them up because they did not want to forego their filthy pleasures; and those who professed their inability to believe refused to admit that their "cannot" was a willful "cannot." Christ was available to all; the Lord's promise of everlasting life to those who believed in Christ was "general, excluding none but such as by unbelief do exclude themselves." The conclusion was clear to Mather: since God's grace was free, requiring no "money," no "price," "no man may say, I know not whether I be elected"; only his own willful unbelief deprived him of the Lord's gift of grace and assurance. Nor would he concede the legitimacy of the denial of ability to believe. Fallen man—he contended—had not sought out God; rather the Lord provided mercy out of His own free grace: "Which may answer the objection the soul is wont to make against believing, from its own unworthiness."[5]

When he told his flock about God's mercy, Mather sometimes spoke of the covenant of grace. The term described for him, as for most in New England, an agreement, or a contract, in which God gave His elect saving grace in return for belief in Christ. All ministers agreed that God provided the strength with which man believed and thereby fulfilled the terms for salvation.

Modern historians have in examining this language argued that in time it came to constitute a separate theology. Puritans, these historians hold, enamored of the covenant conception, with its implications of bargaining, terms, conditions, promises, and responsibilities, tended to attribute to it a solid reality in which God voluntarily bound Himself to save men in return for their faith in Christ. According to these historians, the whole paraphernalia enhanced the powers of men; and in time Puritans used it to describe a situation in which man could compel the Lord to save him. A bargain after all had been struck and a man, if he chose to be a party to it, could force the Lord to give him grace in return for his promise to honor the covenant's terms. Over a period of generations, the theory with its subtle Arminianism undermined the determinism of the doctrine of predestination and election.[6]

Like almost every minister of the founders' generation, Richard Mather referred to the covenant, he spoke of promises (though he did not always consider them as contractual), and he emphasized the responsibilities of the parties to the transaction. But the covenant did not govern or shape his thought about the relationship of God and the saints. For Mather, as for most Puritan ministers throughout the seventeenth century, the covenant was one of many figures describing a complex arrangement. It provided a language that men, pressed to comprehend an inherently mysterious—because supernatural—transaction, found useful because it somehow reduced the awfulness of what was involved to a comprehensible process. This language had its limitations, however. Its flatness and its concreteness, the power it had of diminishing mystery, also deprived it of an aesthetic and emotional power. Hence, it remained only one of several languages used to move sinners to exert themselves.

In his preaching Mather sometimes told the Dorchester Church that the covenant of grace had replaced the covenant of works; and he extolled the promises of eternal life it held out to believers. But he never suggested that it opened the possibility of bargaining with God—I suspect that the thought never really occurred to him—nor did he describe the covenant in the language of commerce. It was a contract but also a gift, and men should be grateful for the opportunities it opened to them. To explain how men might seize these opportunities was the task of the minister.[7]

Richard Mather responded to his charge in a way that showed the power of experience in America. At times in his sermons he explicitly acknowledged that some things were different in Amer-

ica. In 1646 he warned the people of Dorchester that they lived
in a wilderness where life must be simpler than what they had
grown accustomed to in England. John the Baptist after all had
lived in a wilderness on nothing more than wild locusts and
honey which, Mather suggested, ought to make the people living
in the American wilderness "content with playn and wholesome
dyett though we have but a few daintyies." [8] He explained his
meaning many times in these years: a people deprived of the
delicacies of English life ought to prize all the more the wholesome diet in the worship of Christ. If in this sermon he was concerned to teach his listeners something about the special quality
of life in New England, a few years later, in 1650, he seemed
troubled by their growing attachment to physical place. On this
occasion he reminded his church that men must not confuse holiness with geography. Holiness, he said, did not reside in the landscape—"neither Jerusalem *nor any other place*" was holy. [9] This
theme had undergone an important change when Richard rose to
give what he imagined to be his farewell sermon in 1657. By this
time he had come to recognize that it was not holiness in the
land his people valued but the land itself, and in a warning that
was repeated many times later in the seventeenth century he remarked on how "easy" it was in the midst of worldly business
to lose the "power of Religion." [10]

American experience shaped Richard Mather's preaching in
yet another—more pervasive—manner. It helped reinforce his
emphasis on an affective psychology. Like every Puritan expression of the faculty psychology, Mather's aimed to lay bare the
workings of the inner man and thereby help the soul to receive
the Holy Spirit. But unlike most, Mather's psychology concentrated on all the faculties, laying particular stress on the affections, as the passions, or emotions, were sometimes called.

Since Mather was a mature man who had preached for almost
twenty years when he arrived in New England, he probably did
not change the essentials of his theory there. Still, almost immediately after he agreed to lead the Dorchester Church, he had
to reckon with the Antinomian crisis in New England. His sermons, like those of his friends, indicate that Antinomianism had
spread outside of Boston, where the worst of the affair took
place. They also suggest that though the General Court of Massachusetts banished Anne Hutchinson, it did not rid the colony

of her beliefs. Much of what Richard Mather preached about religious experience was directed against Antinomianism. We can see, perhaps even more than he realized, that his sermons were composed as such a response.[11]

The issues in the Antinomian affair turned on the questions of what part a man took in his own conversion and how his soul was changed by the process. The Antinomians, invoking the authority of an uneasy John Cotton, proclaimed that men were psychologically helpless. God seized the souls of His elect by surprise. Just as nothing they could do could affect His choice, so nothing could induce Him to work at a particular time or in a particular manner. The other camp, the ministers the Antinomians branded as "legalists" and who have since been called "preparationists," did not at first sight seem to disagree with this description. They held that God prepared His elect before He converted them—He humbled them, He broke their sinful dispositions, and finally after purging them of their corruption He drew them to Christ. Conversion in this conception occupied a period of time, taking clearly discernible steps. If in these sermons the preparationists often began with a description of God working to prepare His elect, they sometimes ended by urging men to prepare themselves. They reminded their churches that every man could take advantage of the means of grace; specifically every man could listen to sermons and pray for salvation. After these simple steps, recommending that men repent of their sins and humble themselves did not seem like a giant leap. But as far as divinity was concerned such a suggestion was, because no man could savingly repent without God's aid. Preparationists ordinarily avoided this problem by arguing that "common grace," the working of the Holy Spirit *on* a man's soul—not *within* it— might carry him deep into a sense of humility and repentance, even though it could not save him. And every man, even the worst of sinners, could try to repent, even though he was doomed to fail. In all these arguments the preparationists sought to break down the claims of men that they were unable to believe and to rouse those who said that they were too depressed by their helplessness to do anything for themselves.[12]

The preparationists also believed that regenerate men were different from sinful men in their natures: born again, they harbored within themselves a disposition to love God and to live according to His law. The renewed soul did not contain any new light or new knowledge nor did it attain perfection—conversion was always in some ways incomplete—but it did possess faculties inclined toward a holy life.[13]

Although the Antinomians apparently suffered an irretrievable defeat with the banishment of Anne Hutchinson and the recantation (ambiguous though it was) of John Cotton, their following among ordinary men survived. Richard Mather, secure and stable as he was, complained for years of the familists and the Antinomians who, he said, persisted in New England and continued to believe that all a man had to do was to lie around waiting for a divine seizure. What was worse, they believed that once Christ was joined to the saint, He directed the saint's actions and was responsible for them. No need for anyone to worry about good works or individual obligations in this happy state of anarchy.[14]

Granted that Mather did not put the Antinomian case with the nice precision he used when he described safer theories, his misconceptions suggest the value he placed on order in the inner and outer lives of men. Yet he cannot be dismissed as a legalist though he emphasized the role of the law; nor can he be described as fearful of emotional religion. What he, and many of his peers, detested in Anne Hutchinson was not that she relied on the emotions excessively, but rather that she denied to the emotions any power at all. They remained in converted men what they had been in sinful men, vile, corrupt, and incapable of good feeling. If Mather understood the Antinomians correctly, they held that Christ was all and did all while man's mind and heart did nothing but stand idly by while the spirit acted within, autonomously. The conflict between preparationists and Antinomians, as Richard Mather saw it, did not pose reason against emotion, but an active against a static disposition.[15]

Mather's inclination in working out his psychology of religious experience, expressed most clearly in lucid sermons to Dorchester, where he had to explain things from the ground up, was to emphasize the affective side of religion all the while insisting that the affective did not conflict with the intellectual. Religious experience—in particular, conversion—involved a process which engaged all the faculties of the soul, but which was most deeply rooted in the affections. And the experience, whether in conversion or in the worship that followed, was one in which the believer acted, and was not just acted upon, in virtually every phase. At no point did he sit in slothfulness.[16]

In the early stages of the process of conversion the Holy Spirit drew the chosen to Christ, given that the man affected had been elected to receive what Mather called the grace of faith (a phrase with Thomistic implications). Mather agreed with most Puritan divines that a man who had been consigned to Hell might experience the same feelings that gripped a saint in the first steps of conversion. This type of man feels what Thomas Hooker designated "legal preparation" since it never departs from the realm of nature and law in contrast to evangelical preparation, which is ultimately saving. The law in this phase is used by God to inform the sinner of his vileness and corruption: the law, as Richard Mather said, "throw[s] down the soule in sense and feeling" of its sin and misery.[17] This period in a man's experience is the darkest of all as the full conviction of his sin grows within him. The conviction, if it is genuine, produces contrition and sorrow and eventually a state of humble dependence. At this point the sinner becomes aware of his helplessness; and emptied of his pride he is ready for knowledge of Christ, a knowledge that the law cannot convey. Comprehending this knowledge is the responsibility of the reason, or understanding, but not exclusively so if the whole soul is to be renewed. Mather pointed out that even Balaam, Judas, and the very Devil know intellectually of the efficacy of Christ's sacrifice. Hence the need for the heart —in this case Mather seems to mean both the will and the affections—to comprehend the meaning of the righteousness imputed to men by Christ. The knowledge must "affect" them in such a way that they approve and love it. At this point with all the faculties deeply informed, and moved, the grace of faith is infused by the Lord into the soul. The saint is justified by the righteousness of Christ, and sanctified by the Holy Spirit which renews the other graces of his soul—virtue, godliness, charity, knowledge, temperance, patience, and brotherly kindness—all of which have some origin, weak though it may be, in a man's nature. In time, as these graces of sanctification grow, they give him evidence of his salvation, and he enjoys the assurance that he is one of God's elect.[18]

In this description, Mather's theory of the conversion process appears completely conventional in all respects except in its supposition that good qualities inhere in unregenerate man and in its insistence that the affections are involved in every phase, even those phases, commonly deemed intellectual, when the knowledge of Christ's sacrifice is grasped. Not even Thomas Hooker, perhaps the most evangelical of the first generation, conceived of the process as one in which an emotional apprehension saturated every step. Hooker's preaching may have been more affective than his theory, which isolated the will as the faculty requiring the "greatest work" and giving the "greatest difficulty" in converting the soul.[19] The will in Hooker's theory assumes a cast remarkably like the reason in other analyses—it functions as if it had intelligence and knowledge which enabled it to understand the Word of the Gospels. Its affective responses do not take on much importance except when in its sin it resists the force of Christ's sacrifice.[20]

The other great preparationist among the founders, Thomas Shepard, did not attribute a rational power to the will. Yet his conception of the process of conversion resembles Hooker's more closely than it does Mather's; for, like Hooker, Shepard did not attribute a prominent role to the affections. Shepard and Hooker's antagonist, John Cotton, was far too interested in the operations of the Spirit to concede power to the affections—even after the Antinomian crisis passed. And Cotton's successor, John Norton, who delivered an incisive criticism of the doctrine of preparation, remained essentially within Cotton's position.[21]

What gave Mather's theory of religious experience psychological subtlety and moral sensitivity were his insistence that the mind had to be thought of as a whole and his analysis of motive. Like most divines he was forced in his dissection of the psyche to speak as if the faculties functioned separately, but he made it clear that no faculty could escape the influence of others. The will might incline towards a particular decision, or choose it, but its inclination was disposed in some measure by the comprehension provided by the reason. Virtually all Puritan divines agreed that the reason and the will cooperated in this way, though they varied in the strengths they assigned to each faculty. In conversion, of course, this cooperation would always prove impotent, unless the faculties were renewed by supernatural grace. Richard Mather accepted this theory but modified it in one important way: conversion began in the affections, he told his flock, and true belief in Christ was as much an emotional disposition as it was intellectual. The regenerate man transcended the carnal through his love; this glorious passion saturated every faculty, set right the bias of his psyche, transformed the responses of his reason and will. A regenerate man would not achieve perfection in this world, of course: too much sin remained in his soul for that. But he had no chance at all of attaining goodness unless his affections were engaged in such a fashion that they moved his reason in its apprehending.[22]

Both Cotton and Hooker would have had difficulty in maintaining such a position—had they shared it—because their psychology was oriented around the will. The "greatest work of Reformation, Repentance, and the comfort of a mans spiritual condition, it lies mainly in the Will," Hooker once declared. And Cotton, concerned lest men too easily confuse the pangs of conscience for true grace, reminded them that the will "is the principall faculty of the soule, it rules all, it sets hand and tongue, all within, and all without a work." [23]

How Richard Mather conceived of the affective disposition of the faculties largely determined his answer to the question men asked in the agony of their uncertainty: How can I know that I am saved? Most listeners to Puritan sermons in Mather's day wanted to be saved, one suspects. From childhood on, they had been saturated with the Christian version of the good life; and even those who mysteriously imbibed a spirit of opposition evidently felt uneasy in their recalcitrance. They did not count many of their number among the founding generation; the majority evidently yearned for the central experience of their culture— the union with God that converted men enjoyed. Naturally enough, ordinary men were often confused by what they heard from their ministers. They asked: how can I know that I am saved? and the minister answered with uncompromising disquisitions about inward and outward calls, the distinctions between common and supernatural grace, true signs and false, and the gulf between genuine and counterfeit assurance. They wished to have true assurance, and he gave them divinity.[24]

Anyone listening to the sermons in the meetinghouse and the discussions in private meetings that followed church services could learn something of the process by which God claimed His own. Every minister urged self-examination, a technique that involved applying general principles to one's own condition. With the conversion process laid out like a map, one followed the pilgrimage of the self along a route stretched between the familiar reference points of humiliation and joy—humiliation in conviction of sin and joy in the assurance of the Holy Spirit.[25]

For many, the principles appeared clearer than their own progress, and they begged for some reassurance. To all, Richard preached the importance of the right "bent" of the soul. Of the fearful who complained about their lack of broken-heartedness, their inability to attain a humble spirit, he observed that perhaps they were the most humble of all though they were hesitant to see their own lack of pride, while those "that are proud and puffed up because of their humility" were "the farthest off from true humility." [26] Nor was lack of comfort and joy to be taken as an indication of an unredeemed state if one had gone through the earlier phases of conversion. Comfort and joy were the gifts of God as much as His grace was; and uncertainty and tension because one did not enjoy them might well suggest that one had in fact received God's grace.[27]

Mather recognized that tension and uncertainty were difficult to bear. What he was saying in urging his flock not to give in to despair when they experienced such feelings was that anxiety was better than security and deadness which were dangerous though tempting for the ease of heart they afforded. A good man should avoid ease and the static state, recognizing that in such a condition he could never rid himself of sin. As long as he bent his mind and will to the salvation of his soul he could take hope that his heart harbored the grace of God.[28]

There were, however, other more reliable indications which could testify more eloquently than a mere hope. The conduct of a man's life revealed much—in particular his attitude toward his own sinful adventures and his "bent" in the performance of good works.[29]

In the technical language of divinity, Mather was contending that sanctification was evidence of justification. By this he did not mean that good works gave irrefutable proof of the existence of grace in the soul but rather that a right habit of mind, a right disposition, in the performance of lawful acts did. Sinners frequently observed the law, and they sometimes did good works. At least their action appeared good; but inwardly their minds and hearts resisted the good and were inclined towards evil. Their motive in their good behavior was to protect themselves from punishment just as a dog leaves his master's meat untouched, Richard said, "for feare of a cudgell." A genuinely good man regarded sin with horror; the revulsion he felt from it permeated his faculties and grew out of a sense of its "filthiness." [30]

Moral choices, then, came out of the natural stuff of the self. A man renewed by grace did good naturally; nothing outside himself inclined his soul; with the Holy Spirit united to the soul, he takes a "natural delight in good dutyes" just "as the oxe followes hay, grasse, not through feare of punishment, or hope of reward, but because it is naturall to him to delight in his fodder." [31]

For those tormented by anxiety over their inner condition, the meaning of this argument was unavoidable. They must examine the frame of mind they carried into their actions. If a life of faith was burdensome, they lacked grace; if they pursued the right course with delight, grace inhered within them. But they should not always expect the bent of the redeemed soul to be free of baser impulses. When a man was converted, his faculties did not become altogether pure, though he received in grace the strength to avoid excesses of sin and the worst of self-seeking. He would desire to make his external life conform to the law, but he would not succeed perfectly. [32]

Mather did not intend that his flock should regard a lack of perfection complacently because they knew it would always escape men. The Lord required that a man constantly strive and that he examine himself while striving in order to make his calling sure. With this injunction in mind, all Puritan divines urged self-scrutiny. Private assurance was possible even though it might not be possible to give a demonstration of it publicly. Mather had good reason to pause at the difficulty of attempting to persuade others of one's inner worth: his church had failed in its first try at gathering itself because it could not convince the outside examiners that grace resided in its applicants. But he more than any of his great colleagues insisted that assurance could be attained by the individual Christian. His friends counseled caution in claiming certainty: the will was devious, they said, capable of disguising its motives and prone to do so. Mather agreed, but because he insisted that a man's entire nature was altered by

grace, he trusted more readily than they the evidence of vigorous self-examination. Only the grace of faith came completely
from the Lord, Richard Mather believed. The other graces, the
disposition to charity, to patience, to godliness, to virtue, all had
some natural base. In a natural man they remained as unripened
fruit, in a carnal man they withered and died, but in a man watered by grace, they grew and increased. Such was the transforming power of the Holy Spirit.[33]

Almost all of Richard Mather's sermons to the Dorchester
Church contain exhortations—to convert, to grow in grace, to
mend wicked behavior. Yet his preaching cannot simply be called
hortatory; it offers too much analysis of the psychology of good
and evil for that. In fact, like most Puritan ministers of his
generation, Mather used psychological analysis as a method of
inducing a saving religious experience. Telling men what was
right and wrong and what they must do to attain the right
was only one part of his technique. He also told them what they
must feel, how to achieve the proper feeling, and what happened
to their faculties as they succeeded or failed. To a stranger to
Puritan homiletics, one of Mather's sermons on the Second Epistle of Peter might well appear to be a short monograph on the
faculty psychology.[34]

Mather contended throughout his ministry that the inner man
and the outer were inextricably connected. In other words, what
a man was in his soul would affect the face he presented to the
world. Of course hypocrites existed and of course some would
succeed in deceiving themselves and the world as to their true
conditions. But a self-conscious man, one who examined himself,
would not find it easy to escape the discovery of his real being.
And because the conduct of life could be made to give assurance
of one's election, if all its aspects were examined—thoughts, feelings, actions, and the connections among inner dispositions and
behavior—it was all the more necessary for a minister to instruct
men in the right manner of living.[35]

In all the varieties of men that a minister faced—the complacent who stood on their own merits, the fearful who protested
that they were unworthy of grace, the numb who wished to believe but could not, the anarchic who claimed they learned from
an inner light, and even the saints who had received God's grace
—Richard detected the power of nature. Nature disposed every

man to think not only that he could save himself but also that he could govern himself without any aid from the Lord. So inclined, Mather pointed out, unregenerate men interpreted the law mechanically as involving obligations and rights. They saw the law much as they did a business contract, and claimed everything due them under its terms. They insisted on using the creatures as they chose; meat, drink, and sex, which God provided for man's survival and perpetuation, were often misused. And if through fear of God or from social pressure ordinary men did not transgress the law in the use of any of the creatures, they secretly wanted to. So they compromised and, avoiding fornication and gluttony and drunkenness, they contented themselves by abusing the law while technically staying within its terms. For within the law they acted without restraint in amassing as much wealth as they could; they indulged themselves in fine apparel and fine foods; and they used the marriage bed immoderately. Good men, in Mather's view, would do none of these things but stop short well within the limits of the law. They know, he reminded his church, that one should not always go to the utmost bounds of liberty. Sinning, after all, occurred most commonly in the abuse of lawful things.[36]

The conviction that men must act against their sins, that they conceive of their daily lives as an opportunity to grow in grace filled Mather's sermons to his flock. For most of his ministry he preached as if he were absolutely convinced that grace would always show itself in discernible ways. A church as a corporate group might experience difficulty in identifying the godly, but each member could know himself by the record of his thought and action in this world. "There is," Mather said in 1648, "an inseparable connection of the gifts and graces of Christ, so that if he give conversion and justification, he will sanctification also."[37] Christ, he explained in a figure often used by Puritan ministers, would not open a man's eyes to see "the things of heaven" without giving him the graces of sanctification. A man, Richard pointed out, should see the meaning of his life: if he proves incapable of living a sanctified life it is "a signe the man is in blindness still."[38]

Mather often likened grace to "fire" and to "springs of water," a comparison he contended that Scripture made. The "nature" of fire and springs of water, he reminded his church, "is to be active and to show forth themselves." [39] His sermons suggest that he was more concerned about the activity of grace than its visibility, a concern perhaps that arose from his conviction that the good activities of men would inevitably make themselves known to others. Translated into the language familiar to both divinity and ordinary discourse, what he was talking about were good works. He denied that one who urged good works was a "legal" preacher—he was not, he said, because he did not claim that works were efficacious by themselves. But they were evidence of what went on in a man's heart, and hence men who pursued them in a right frame of mind could gain assurance that they were saved.[40]

Moreover, good works were commanded by God—a fact Mather never tired of proving from Scripture. For example, he was especially concerned in his sermons on Second Peter to show that the King James version robbed the eighth verse of the first chapter of its force. James's translators had rendered its declaration about the graces to read:

> For if these things be in you, and abound, they make you that ye shall neither be barren nor unfruitful in the knowledge of our Lord Jesus Christ.

Richard objected to the word "barren," which he argued was tautological because it preceded "unfruitful." The word should be "idle" rather than "barren," he believed. He was on solid scholarly ground, for the Geneva Bible and, as he noted, Beza, Calvin, Estius, and Piscator all used "idle." The point of this seemingly trivial issue was that the graces all had work to do, or as Mather put it, all have "their actings and operations." To be idle was to admit that one lacked the grace of faith. The most compelling reason, after all, for striving was to "proove" at least to the self that one had received God's spirit. Mather proposed to show that men who have supernatural gifts, such as the servant in the parable who was given five talents, would use them. The spirit worked, it struggled, it fought, it wrestled—it struck at evil. This bent towards action inhered within grace itself; just as fire burned, so would grace consume wickedness. Christ furnished the model for every Christian, of course; and as Mather pointed out, the graces in a Christian are the "image" of the graces that were in Christ. His were active; and it followed that theirs must be also.[41]

These themes which are so directed to making good visible and influential in the conduct of life betray in almost every phrase Mather's persistent fear of Antinomianism. Nowhere does he describe conversion as a rape of the soul; nowhere does he suggest that it is anything but the result of experience over a period of time. A man does not become gracious in a moment, rather he finds his way to God through striving and effort. God draws him of course, but slowly, even painfully, and the process takes time. In these contentions Mather does not seek to confine the spirit in any conventional sense; he does not attempt to persuade his flock that the spirit is dangerous. Rather, he enlarges ordinary claims for grace by arguing that if it has entered into a man it affects his attitude toward the law of God. If it does not give him raptures and visions—Mather knows that such psychic events have their origin elsewhere—it assists him in living according to the law. Mather despised the common prejudice that placed grace in opposition to the law; in fact grace enabled one to observe God's commands. Not gracious excesses but satanic delusions carried men into Antinomian ecstasies.[42]

There were men in Dorchester who listened to Richard Mather speak of the transforming power of supernatural grace and then asked, "If grace infused be so active and efficacious, then what needs a Christian to depend on Christ and his assistance?"[43] These men were not Antinomians and they deserved a reply. Mather took the opportunity to say that Christ and grace were not "opposites but concurring." And in any case "A man may have money in his purse, bread in his house or other supplies, and yet this needs not, ought not to hinder his dependence upon the providence and blessing of God, even for his daily bread."[44] This answer put the matter in concrete terms that bore on the immediate lives of men.

Mather sometimes linked such questions to the ultimate fate of the elect. Their hope finally lay in the Second Coming of Christ, and that coming was near. We live in the daylight of the gospel, he told the Dorchester Church; the end of the world is near. But before it comes, Christ's chosen must be converted; in other words, they must accept the sacrifice of Jesus for their justification.[45]

Men who were even capable of hinting that they might not need Christ did not quail before a minister's authority. A few in Dorchester evidently expressed resentment at paying a minister's salary; and others suggested that perhaps they did not need pastors after all. Richard felt their "contempt" and their "reproaches."[46] They desperately needed ministers, he told the church. God had chosen to reveal some things to ministers, and to ministers only. Of course, there were some men in every community with talents rivaling those of the pastor, but these men were not the transmitters of the Word. And what could only the ministers pass on? The news about Christ, Richard replied: the full explication of the meaning of His birth and death, His sacrifice and miracles, and finally the news of the imminence of His glorious return.[47]

Firmly convinced of this magnificent calling of the minister, Richard frequently demanded that his flock "submit" and give obedience to the commands he spoke in the name of the Lord.[48] In his swan song, preached when he imagined himself approaching death, he reminded New England of the greatness of a minister's calling. His description of the relationship of the minister and the church was wholly conventional: the church should strive to get "a faithful and able Minister, to be set over you in the Lord"; ministers should be received as "Overseers and Rulers" who are to be obeyed. They deserve obedience; they are not ordinary men—indeed, Richard announces, a minister, is a "rare man," especially fitted for his role by his "learning" and "understanding." These qualifications are at the center of Richard Mather's recommendation to his flock, for, as he pointed out, it takes brains and learning to explain the truth and to "convince gainsayers." The repetition of this call for submissiveness suggests that convincing gainsayers was no small task even in Dorchester.[49]

Although there is no evidence that Richard ever flagged in this role, late in his career he conceded that grace did not inevitably show itself. He made this sad concession to reality in the defense he made of the Half-Way Covenant. But his preaching to his flock does not seem ever to have accommodated this reality. Richard indeed, like his generation of Puritan divines, continued to urge men to strive after God while he insisted that only God could draw them. And he continued to urge them to beg for the return of Christ even while he assured them that the Lord could not be coerced or even persuaded. The Lord would as always act according to His own Being, not in response to the imperatives of men.[50]

Whatever anxiety Richard Mather felt, striving in the moral order of God's sovereignty, his piety continued to burn brightly. In his last few days of life, blind in one eye, suffering painfully from the stone, he insisted on spending as much time in his study as his strength allowed, pushing his mind and spirit in the Lord's service. Among his last words to Increase was a plea that the children of New England should be baptized and brought into the Church.[51]

Increase's generation proved no less determined to serve the Church, but their resolve was inevitably affected by the fact that their origins were in New England. They could not summon the detachment that kept the founders' eyes fixed on the Church above all things. Exile made the founders suspicious of place and reminded them that the elect might survive anywhere. The sons inevitably saw men and the Church not only as parts of a reformed tradition but as part of New England's history as well. As it turned out, this narrowed vision brought its own anxieties, but it also helped to sustain the piety so profoundly felt by the founders.

BOOK TWO

INCREASE MATHER
(1639–1723)

TYPOLOGY

5

An Unripened Puritan

A prophet, Benjamin Colman carefully explained in a sermon mourning the death of Increase Mather in 1723, was one of those great figures in the Scriptures who performed such miracles as revelation of "things secret and future." The word still appeared useful to Colman, who suggested that in a "lax and improper Sense" it might be applied to the preaching ministry. Colman teetered on the edge of saying that it was in this "improper" sense that he would call Increase Mather a prophet, but finally drew back before the plunge. There was no need to extend the definition explicitly to Increase anyway; simply making the distinction between ancient and modern prophets left the mourners in no doubt of what he meant.[1]

On the face of it, Colman did not diminish Mather's immense reputation; Increase Mather could not claim prophetical powers for himself nor could anyone else. But Mather was someone "dear to God" as the Puritans sometimes said; and he had long insisted upon a particular version of New England's history and an extraordinary vision of its future. Colman's labored distinctions about prophets served notice to the community that he, for one, dissociated himself from Mather's views of New England.[2]

The remainder of Colman's message rehearsed old themes in a conventional way. At the time of Increase Mather's death, funeral sermons had taken a form which everyone understood and approved. The minister giving the sermon improved his opportunity to give moral instruction, directed either at individuals or the land and on some occasions, at both. Death, he might tell his listeners, should remind them of their mortality; and when they considered their own impending deaths they should seize the chance to repent and reform and to believe on Christ. If the public concern was uppermost in his mind, he might use the occasion to suggest that God sometimes took some of the living from the people as a kind of chastisement; their recourse in such times was a general reformation.[3]

Benjamin Colman followed this line in his sermon. Little that Colman said could have surprised his listeners. Increase deserved praise as a Christian, a scholar, a minister; he had served his God and his people with wisdom and strength for over fifty years. They knew that Mather was a great man, and it seemed natural to look upon their loss as an affliction from God—even though the dead man had reached his eighty-third year.

This part of Colman's eulogy contained nothing that was not safely within the conventions of the funeral sermon. Increase had preached many similar sermons warning the people of the dread meaning of the loss of leaders. He had also regularly predicted his own death for thirty years. And although he accepted his death as inevitable, he clearly considered it as evidence of God's displeasure with New England.[4]

Colman's agreement would have pleased him, but Colman's subtle rejection of his view of the meaning of New England would not. But he would not have been surprised by it; Colman, with others, had said as much before in terms unrestrained by the occasion of a funeral sermon. Increase had grown accustomed to such rejection, but it always frustrated him.

The first half of Increase Mather's life, though hardly free of tension and struggle, was largely free of such frustrations. When he was born in Dorchester, Massachusetts, on June 21, 1639, his father was already recognized as a good man who could be depended upon to serve the colony. Richard not only filled an important pulpit, he also possessed a mind fruitful of Congregational theory. Encouraged by his fellow ministers, he was engaged in explaining the New England way to its critics in England. Busy as he was, Richard took the time to help in his son's education: first by teaching him to write and then by giving him instruction in Latin and Greek.[5]

Increase's mother, Katharine Mather, began her son's education, teaching him to read when he was a small boy. There is not much known of her—Puritan men usually did not mention women except as models of piety in the way of Ruth or as agents of the Devil in the way of Jezebel. Richard praised his wife's devotion to God, her loving care of her family; and Increase described her as a "very Holy praying woman." There is evidence that she harbored a strength that these conventional descriptions fail to suggest. Early in her life when Richard began to court her she was not discouraged by her father's opposition. Her father, Edward Holt, may not have liked Puritans and especially disliked the notion of his daughter's marrying one, but when Katharine declared her love for Richard and persisted in her attachment to him, Holt gave way.[6]

In Richard, Katharine married a very strong man, and if before her marriage she was not wholly disposed to share his religion, after it, she was. She became a Puritan wife lavishing care on her six sons, helping them to learn to read and worship, and seeking after God in the way of her husband. These things were expected of a wife; anything less from one married to a minister would have been unthinkable. But Katharine Mather did more, at least in the case of Increase, her youngest child, and probably in the cases of the others too. She told Increase that all she prayed for him when he grew up was that God should give him grace and learning. Although there is no way of calculating the effects of Katharine Mather's hopes, Increase, we know, remembered them all his life.[7]

Writing as an adult, Increase admitted that he could not understand why as a boy in school he had proved the best in class. We can discount his characterization of himself as a boy of "dull wit" but there is no reason to discount his claim that he cared nothing for his studies until he was fourteen years old. Yet as he said, "I was much forwarder in learning than any Boy in the school my age." A bright boy he surely was, but bright boys did not do well in Latin and Greek grammar without steady application. Something must have pushed Increase Mather very hard;

his family's expectations as his mother expressed them doubtless provided the force.[8]

Increase matriculated at Harvard in 1651, when he was twelve years old, but he left Cambridge after about six months in his freshman year. His parents had decided that because of his "weak natural constitution of Body," he should be entrusted to the Reverend John Norton of Ipswich who would tutor him in the regular college curriculum. In April 1653 Increase followed Norton to Boston and lived and studied with him until the year 1656, when he rejoined his class, then seniors.[9]

The year before he was graduated, Increase went through conversion. Long afterwards he said that the process began with a serious illness in 1654. As far as the observable experience was concerned he was right in dating its beginnings. But in another sense, he was mistaken: his conversion began much earlier, at the time his mother told him that she desired only that God should give him grace. In the language customarily used to describe the conversion, the period between the moment that he became aware of his mother's hope and the first quickening of grace in his soul was preparation. His mother's desires were presented as hopes for him, but they were also expectations as he must have realized even as a child who supposedly cared nothing for his studies. He cared very much (for he had made his mother's wish his own), but in conversion he had to recognize his own inclinations.[10]

Katharine Mather's death in March 1655 followed hard on the heels of his return to health. On her deathbed his mother thrust upon him another great burden, a wish expressed in great emotion, that if it were God's will, Increase should become a minister. Filled with doubt that he was even one of God's own, Increase shook before his mother's parting words; as he later recalled, "the Lord broke in upon my conscience with very terrible convictions and awakenings." For almost three months he suffered dreadfully from his sense of sin and his worry that he was not one of God's chosen. His behavior reflected his unease—on several days he shut himself up in a room and listed his sins while appealing to God for mercy. His occasional isolation probably would have gone unnoticed by his friends, except that it was accompanied by "preciseness" and a "tender conscience." Increase's altered behavior made his companions uneasy; and they made him feel their scorn for his new scrupulosity. The changes in actions doubtless amounted to little in behavior—he was always a good boy—but a greater seriousness in attitude and a conscientiousness in observing the simple pieties of Puritan life would have been enough to alarm his friends.[11]

Their derision did not deter Increase from his new purpose and his quest for God continued. Increase respected, even revered, his tutor John Norton, but something prevented him from seeking comfort from Norton. He loved his father and it was to him that he turned, asking for his prayers. The end to this agony came on election day in May 1655. Norton and his family left the house for the day and Increase, after hours in prayer, finally attained peace and the assurance that he had received God's grace. Assurance came after he achieved a complete sense of psychological dependence upon God: "At the close of the day, as I was praying, I gave my selfe up to Jesus Christ, declaring that I was now resolved to be his Servant, and his only and his forever, and humbly professed to him that if I did perish, I would perish at his feet. Upon this I had ease and inward peace in my perplexed soul immediately; and from that day I walked comfortably for a considerable time, and was carefull that all my words and wayes should be such as would not offend God." [12]

As in the case of most of the converted, pangs of doubt returned after this initial exaltation. The words of Christ, "Him that cometh unto me I will in no wise cast out," had helped give him assurance, but now the words of one of Christ's ambassadors frightened him.[13] Norton said that one might repent of his sins and still not be converted; Norton here was making a distinction between legal and gracious repentance as Increase knew. But how to detect the difference in one's own soul between the two? Happily, at this time Richard Mather preached a sermon answering the question to Increase's satisfaction. His father showed that new and genuine obedience to God, and an actual change in the heart, or the will, which might be detected if love of God replaced love of sin, indicated that true conversion had occurred. Increase studied himself, applying these subjective tests, which seemed objective to him and other Puritans, and decided that he had experienced real conversion.[14]

A little more than a year after these momentous happenings, Increase was graduated from Harvard. Commencement offered an opportunity to candidates for the bachelor's degree to distinguish themselves in arguing a thesis. Increase, of course, presented one, but the Ramean logic he selected to demonstrate his views displeased the President, Charles Chauncy, who favored the Aristotelian logic. The President was on the verge of cutting Increase short when Jonathan Mitchell, afterward tutor and Cambridge minister, and one of the leading divines among the founders, pleaded *"Pergat, Quaeso, Nam-doctissime disputat"* (Let him go on, I beg, for he is arguing like a great scholar).[15]

The question of a career for Increase does not seem to have come up when he was graduated. For a long time, perhaps from the time of his mother's death, he was pledged to the pulpit. In June 1657, after a year of further study, he was ready to preach. He delivered his first sermon in a small village belonging to Dorchester, and the next week he filled his father's pulpit in the town. Increase's maiden effort very nearly became his swan song in New England, for two weeks later he was on board a ship sailing for England. At this time he seems to have planned to make his way in the service of the Lord in the mother country.[16]

His destination was Trinity College, Dublin, where Samuel, his older brother, a nonconformist minister, had arranged for his entrance to pursue studies leading to an M.A. degree. Increase reached Dublin after stops in Portsmouth, London, and Lancashire, where he visited the former parishioners of his father. Trinity College received Increase but it did not accept him with open arms. The proctor, several fellows, and most of the students disliked his Puritanism. His scholarship and his obviously sincere application won them over to at least a grudging acceptance, however, by the time he received the M.A. in 1658. To cap his success he was offered a fellowship.[17]

Increase turned the fellowship down for the pulpit: as the son of a minister and with three brothers preaching, he wanted to serve within a church. Serve he did, in Torrington in Devonshire, and as the chaplain of the garrison on Guernsey from April 1659 to March 1661, with a short interruption early in 1660 when he served a Gloucester church. None of these places was very secure, and Guernsey proved dangerous. The time was wrong for a Congregationalist anywhere in England because Episcopacy promised to return with Charles II. And Charles had been awaiting his chance on the throne for years. With his restoration, his ministers and his bishops began demanding conformity to the established Church and its ways.[18]

Increase held out as long as he could, but the commander of the Guernsey garrison was neither a Puritan nor a patient man. For a time there was doubt that Increase would escape arrest, and then that he would be paid. Discouraged, he finally gave up in March 1661. Return to New England was all that was left—short of a repudiation of what he regarded as the true Church polity. He sailed for Boston on June 29, 1661 and was greeted with joy by his father.[19]

It seems likely that his step-sister, Maria Cotton, also greeted him with warmth. She was the daughter of the great John Cotton whose widow had married Richard Mather in August 1656. Increase may have carried the aura of a hero to Maria; in any case she came to love him and they were married in March 1662. Cotton Mather, the first of six children, was born to them in the following February. Maria was a happy choice, an ideal Puritan wife, kind, devout, fruitful of children—a loyal and devoted spouse who supported her husband in all his works.[20]

The works came hard and fast in the next few years. Increase was called to the Second Church (the old North Church) in Boston in 1664, a post he occupied until his death. He soon established himself as a voice of authority throughout New England. His sermons were well attended and many were published at the instigation of admiring parishioners. Most of these publications of the 1660's and 1670's have genuine intellectual distinction, if not originality. They included works of scholarship as well as of piety; they speak to individuals but most often to all New England. They betray the intensity of Increase's sense of personal mission during these years—in 1675 he declared that "untill my work be done, I am immortall," a sense that he conveyed to men of power in Church and State.[21] Men who counted in both realms respected him, though they did not always like him, and they came increasingly to call upon him for public service. The first opportunity appeared in the Synod of 1662, convened to ponder the problem of baptism. Increase's part was on behalf of a lost cause, the adherence to the traditional policy of baptising children of members in full communion, while the majority of the Synod chose the way of extension of baptism to the children of half-way members, so designated because they had been baptised but not received at the Lord's Supper. Increase joined John Davenport in opposing the Synod but in time changed his mind and became an eager defender of the Half-Way Covenant, as the Synod's solution was labeled.[22]

Although he doubtless switched sides in this controversy out of altered convictions, the change ensured his availability for further services. For most of the ten years after his acceptance of the new baptismal arrangement, he found little opportunity to serve outside the pulpit. He preached regularly in Boston, and occasionally filled in for colleagues of neighboring churches. Richard Mather invited him to Dorchester several times a month and clearly enjoyed Increase's sermons as fully as anyone in the colony.[23]

The death of Richard in 1669 left Increase desolate. He was physically ill at this time, but the melancholy he experienced after his father died does not seem to have arisen from physical sources. He felt sadness, of course; Richard, a warmly understanding man, had been precious to him. The sadness deepened three months later when Increase's younger brother Eleazar, who occupied the pulpit in Northampton, died.[24]

The loss of Richard seems also to have left Increase with a vague feeling of guilt. He had not failed his father in any direct sense, but he yearned to prove himself useful, perhaps in some service resembling Richard's during the days of controversy with the English Presbyterians. While Increase tried to handle these desires, his melancholy grew worse as he discovered himself doubting the very genuineness of his faith.

The physical illness continued to be serious from the fall of 1669 until the spring of 1670. His depression lasted even longer, troubling him seriously for at least two more years. During this time, he performed the conventional acts in search of a cure, praying, fasting (which probably weakened him further), and going to the healing waters of Lynn, Massachusetts. The crisis passed gradually, leaving its mark in the shape of an intense desire to get the best out of himself before his life ended. He expressed his hope in his Diary in January 1670. "I *wish!* I *wish!* I *wish!*," he wrote, "that I might do some special Service for my dear God in Jesus Christ. . . . I would feign do good after I am dead." And, "After I have finished my doing work, I would feign suffer and do for the sake of my dear God, and for Jesus

Christ." The desires to do good and to suffer never left him. To survive he required both; and somehow he obtained the assurance during these years that they would be granted to him.[25]

Although Increase's recovery followed, he continued to suffer as he gave his Lord public service. His service was great and made him the most powerful minister in New England for the next thirty years. He took a leading part in the Synod of 1679, writing the preface to its "Result," and presided over its second session in 1680. A few years later he encouraged the Boston meeting and the General Court to resist attempts to deprive the colony of its original charter. When resistance failed, and the charter was abrogated in *Quo Warranto* proceedings in 1683, he continued to defend New England's autonomy. This fight carried him to England in 1688, where he remained until 1692, when he returned with a new charter which provided greater self-government for Massachusetts Bay than any royal colony in America enjoyed. And during sixteen of these years, from 1685 to 1701, he held the honored position as head of Harvard College.[26]

The suffering that blotted these services and their distinction bewildered Increase at times. He could not lay it all at the Devil's door. The source of his discomfort at the Synod of 1679 was Solomon Stoddard, who did not share his views on qualifications for the Lord's Supper. Stoddard was a decent and good man—everyone recognized that, even Increase, who did not conceal his belief that Stoddard, for all his sanctity, was misled. The dissatisfaction with the charter of 1691, of which he was justly proud, came from other good men who did not appreciate the difficulties of his achievement. He, an American provincial, had spent four years at two English courts and had emerged with almost everything a loyal son of the founders could desire. Yet his success was flung back into his face as failure and weakness by men who argued that nothing less than the restoration of the original charter could be accepted. Service at Harvard also brought pain. To secure its charter and to protect it from Anglican infiltrators seemed essential to Increase. But what seemed to concern the Corporation, and the General Court that supervised the College, was that he reside in Cambridge, and give up commuting from Boston—where his church still needed him. This tangle eventually forced his retirement from Harvard, amidst petty bickering and backbiting.[27]

Despite the fact that Increase sometimes encountered what he took to be the same meanness of spirit, the gossip, and the squabbling in his church, he took profound satisfaction in his ministry. Increase took up his duties as teacher of the North Church in Boston on May 27, 1664, and preached until just before the end of his life in 1723. The church was a large one and grew under Increase's tutelage. On most Sabbaths his auditory numbered around 1500 souls. Except for his first few years as pastor, Increase enjoyed good relations with his church. His first years, however, were made worrisome by a low salary and his growing family. His church and its deacons may have believed that poverty would inspirit him; in any case they did nothing as his debts and anxieties mounted. Mather, as was his custom, drew a perverse pleasure from his penury, comforting himself with such reflections as "when I am gone, my poor people will believe that the grief which I sustained by their neglect of me and mine, was unprofitable for them." [28] He gained security soon after this entry when several wealthy members of his church came to his rescue, helping him pay his debts and raising his salary.[29]

In his ministry, Increase performed the usual tasks of a Puritan clergyman, but with one difference. He slighted the pastoral functions, visiting the sick and catechizing the young, in favor of studying and preaching. During most weeks he preached on the Sabbath and on Thursday. For at least two years in the 1670's he attempted to follow a regular schedule of instructing his own children, preaching, studying, and meeting his flock. He even laid out a routine for each day. On the Sabbath he preached and gave instruction in his own family. The next day he gave to the study of Scripture, reading several commentators and theologians. Tuesday was much like Monday except that he seems to have instructed candidates for the ministry part of the afternoon, at least in the summer. He spent all of Wednesday in his study; and on Thursday he revealed some of the fruits of this labor in his sermon. But in the early part of the morning before he preached, he studied. Late in the afternoon after his lecture, he met with other ministers "to promote what shall be of publick advantage." [30] The last two days of the week were given to his books and to preparation for the Sabbath. On days preceding the celebration of the Eucharist, Increase ordinarily fasted.[31]

There was not much time reserved for pastoral visits in this schedule, and there were murmurings about this lack. When Cotton Mather joined his father as pastor, he took the responsibility for this side of ministerial life, and the criticism may have been silenced. Increase Mather obviously believed that his greatest contribution to his God came in his sermons to his flock; and hence the long, hard hours spent in his study. His sermons reflect this effort in their tight construction and solid substance.[32]

Although Increase did not hold to this schedule all his life—there were too many interruptions which carried him out of his routine—it reveals his respect for the need of scholarship. When he gave up the systematic division of his day he did not give up his studies. Politics and government called him; the social life of Boston consumed an increasing part of his time as he grew older; and he traveled in New England and out of it, but he managed to find time for study and for writing.

Near the end of his life Increase Mather likened the heart of man to a mint "in which evil thoughts are coined continually." [33] This phrase represented one pole of his thought about men, their infinite capacity for evil, and lust for sin. Throughout his life Increase also preached, as his father had before him, on the need of men to grow in grace. He meant that men could change, they could improve. To be sure, no real alteration of their character was possible without God's help through grace; and, of course, no man could secure grace of his own efforts. To grow in grace implied that once the soul had been infused with God's gift, it should continue to improve. Puritans as different as William Perkins and Thomas Hooker agreed that in this process of improvement a gracious man could take a hand. Perkins said the best evidence that a man had grace was its growth. Once he had grace his helplessness ended. He could act effectively and God expected him to act.[34]

Over a lifetime a man should strive to strengthen his faith by worship, study, good works. If he tried he could expect God's aid. By living in faith he would lose a part of his love of himself —he would love God more and make every act of his life an expression of his love of God. Ordinary acts, Increase included even eating and sleeping, should be accomplished with one's attention on God; and work and good works should be a testimony to the greatness of God.[35]

As a man grew in grace he grew dead to the world; and as the creatures lost their savor to him so also did the self. His whole being was turned to God—his will, his understanding, his affections. His love of the Lord, his rejection of the world did not leave him somber or joyless, but vanities no longer could please him. As he grew in grace, his very manner changed: he had gravity without heaviness and patience without weakness.[36]

Richard Mather's character was cut closer to these specifications than Increase's, though they shared many similar experiences and, by any standard, held the same values. The central event of their psychic lives, conversion, wracked them both and left each of them filled with doubts about its genuineness. Although Richard's recovery did not carry him into complacency, his assurance was sooner achieved and more certain than Increase's. Each proved an extraordinary minister by the lights of the world, but Increase endured secret dissatisfaction in the midst of success. Richard departed the world in peace, full of years and wisdom; Increase, full of years, but haunted by fear that he was damned.[37]

Although Increase proved more imaginative than Richard, he was also more literal. Age and experience softened Richard's personality while they failed to alter Increase's. Life mellowed Richard but it left Increase unripened—unyielding in matters of the law, self-righteous in his rectitude, and incapable of exercising what was called Christian charity.

The tendency of Increase's character was to push thought and feeling to their extremity. Thus even his literalness assumed a peculiar intensity and in dealings with men, a harshness. This unbending quality inevitably found expression in his language and in his style. Most of his expression, of course, did not depart from the conventions of his generation, and resembled the usage of his father. But Richard's mind had rarely strayed far from the idioms of the Scripture and Puritan theology, and though for many of Increase's purposes these were appropriate, the urge to express his intensity had to be met too. Here he bade his father's practice farewell.

Richard Mather had been a devoted practicer of the plain style all his life. His sermons followed the classic Puritan structure—Text, Doctrine, Propositions, Uses—and yet managed to convey his strong feeling and his subtle sense of what motivates human beings. A similar simplicity of structure and style appeared in

Mather's tracts and polemical works. He was a direct man and he went directly to the point as, for example, in *Church-Government and Church Covenant,* he used the questions asked by English Presbyterians about New England's ecclesiastical polity to give his defense of Bay Colony practice a systematic expression. His longest treatise on this subject, a "Plea for the Churches of New England," responded directly to English criticisms and then provided a reasoned statement, embellished with scholarly citations, in Mather's own terms.[38]

Increase Mather admired the plain style, praised the simplicity it gave his father's sermons, and used it himself. He was a self-conscious writer who read other men for their styles as well as their substances. He did not confess to feeling any anxiety about the forms his son Cotton employed in his writing, but he may have had Cotton in mind in several of the complaints he sounded late in his life about the new elegance that was creeping into the pulpit.[39]

Increase never allowed any of these new fashions to find a place in his sermons. But he did strive for unusual effects using the conventional style. He was no more concrete than his father; indeed, in his typological references he was much less so. He sought, however, to achieve the graphic, to paint in the minds of his listeners and readers pictures of themselves and their fates. Hence, though both Richard and Increase preached about the end of the world, Richard usually limited himself to discussions of the historical process that carried nations and peoples along the line of time to the inevitable conclusion of all things. Increase shared Richard's historical sense, but he could not find contentment by focusing his sermons on anything so abstract. Rather, he provided a fare that deliberately sought to evoke the terror the unworthy should feel as they contemplated their inevitable sufferings in Hell. Throughout the seventeenth century, ordinary preaching in New England did much with this device and with a vocabulary of fire, burning, and the odor of brimstone. Richard recognized the power of such techniques but he could not have said to his listeners, as Increase did, "Thy soul is hanging over the mouth of hell by the rotten thread of a frail life: if that breaks, the devouring Gulf will swallow thee up for ever." [40]

Richard and Increase both composed muscular sermons which

abound in references to striving, wrestling, and laboring with sin, and searching and running after Christ. These figures evoke images of straining bodies, mortified flesh, as well as of psyches taut in the worship of God. Frequently they are accompanied by references to moral lapses which are often drawn with oblique sexual references. A Puritan layman recognized the special horror of an offense described as "unclean" or "filthy." Richard Mather, like every minister, used these words to describe such sins as fornication and adultery. Increase Mather pushed this terminology farther, using these words to describe offenses having no connection with sex. These rhetorical, or stylistic, choices suggest a character less confident of itself, less certain of its goodness perhaps, and striving for reassurance that it measures up to the best in the past.[41]

The differences in the characters of Richard and Increase may also be seen in certain instances of their applications of Puritan ideas to life. Near the end of his life and feeling his death was near, Richard attempted to recall New England to the divine mission. New England had strayed; the founders' expectations had been subjected to a good deal of battering. Had Richard been a man to insist upon the letter of the law, he would have found good company. But without weakness, he continued to make distinctions between errors that damned and those that did not. Some errors he told his church *"subvert the soul"* excluding it from Heaven, while others are not so fundamental, "but are as *hay* and rubble upon the *foundation.* . . ." Increase did not make such distinctions—an error such as a lie was criminal, even a lie told to spare your neighbor grief and which did no ostensible harm dishonored God and was a damning sin.[42]

For Increase, Christian charity was a limited concept. The ungodly did not excite his sympathy; rather, he felt only revulsion from them, a feeling he expressed in his insistence that good men should avoid them. Necessity, say the demands of one's particular calling, might lead to some contacts but they should be kept to a minimum. The company a godly man kept constituted a test of his regeneration: a truly godly man, Increase said, delighted only in the company of other godly men; he resented wasting his time with sinners; he did not want them to throw his mental frame out of joint. The thrust of this attitude is towards a kind of moral separation, a fear of contamination.[43]

Increase's tendency to exceed the requirements of the moral law—and of piety—may also be seen in his message to children. Every child was told that a failure to experience grace implied eternal damnation. Increase assured those in his congregation that should they fail they would hear him accuse them on the Day of Judgment. His father had contented himself with reproaching the parents for their inability to bring their children to God. Increase, of course, did not neglect the parents; unless they had grace, he said, they were unfit even to pray for their children. In castigating the parents in this fashion, Increase strained the bounds of the creed, which made it a duty for all men—saints and sinners alike—to seek the mercies of the Lord in prayer.[44]

As extraordinary as Increase Mather's character appears, it was in most respects typical of his generation. Increases's generation were the sons of the founders—great men whose achievements had to be reckoned with. In Increase's case, the burden was heavier—his father was the last great survivor of a group of distinguished divines. With the exception of four years spent in England, Increase had to face his father almost every day for the first thirty years of his life. Although there were other reasons for his decision, Increase at one point in his life left the scene of his father's fame resolved to make his way in England. Rebellion, or a simple desire to disengage himself from Richard's influence, may not have been a part of this decision. Yet the fact is that on his return, which was forced by conditions completely out of his control, he resisted a cause his father advocated, the extension of baptism to children of half-way members. Increase took a hard line—saying in effect that he would uphold his father's principles, if his father was incapable of maintaining them.[45]

In some manner Increase had to deal with the fact that he was the son of a great man who was acting in a cosmic drama. The piety of both parents added to his problem—he would have to equal, if not surpass it. In a peculiar way his private success added to his public problems. As a boy he succeeded in making his mark as a scholar; he honored his mother's dying wish that he convert; in his father's footsteps he became a minister. In all these ways he satisfied his family's—and his own—expectations. But serving God was the highest goal, and all these other achieve-

ments were subordinate to it. They were largely meaningless unless he furthered God's plan in New England. To be sure, Increase became the most esteemed minister of his day, the re-
cipient of public trusts and honors, and a recognized force in the
government of Massachusetts. But these attainments meant less
than they might have in the face of departures from the true
polity, in the shock felt at the loss of the colony's charter, and
in the unhappy decline of godliness.[46]

His inability to control these events seemed to mark his private
experience—his encounters with the Lord. Understandably, he
sometimes confused this relationship and, forgetting to abide in
divine decisions, he appealed for help in his own devices.

His eagerness to succeed, to uphold the authority of his family,
to get his way with New England and—implicitly—with the
Lord led him to an extraordinary concern with himself. This
concern was an unavoidable development—his place in the family
and the community, conspired with Puritan impulses to introspection, all contributed to it. Psychologically, Puritan imperatives to self-examination could never be reconciled with the
ideals of humility and resignation of the self. The more Increase, or any Puritan, sought humility, the more he studied
himself to discern its attainment. The result was a self-consciousness at best painful, at its most excruciating worst, unbearable,
and which—in any case—implied the value of the self.[47]

Increase's self-evaluation led him, in prayers for his son
Samuel, who, he believed, was near death in 1672, to approach the
Lord with pleas that were as much for himself as for the boy.
In several of the prayers Increase was joined by his wife and
his son Cotton. Appealing to the Lord for Samuel, Increase
thought of the possibility that his prayers would not be granted,
and wondered what the effects of failure would be on his family.
Only obliquely did he reveal his knowledge that his reputation
as a man who got his prayers answered was at stake; but his
pitying reference to himself in his account of what he prayed—
doubtless privately—betrayed him: "Now I thought it might be
some discouragement to Cotton in case he should see that his
poor sinfull Fathers prayers, were not heard; [so] I humbly
pleaded that with the Lord." [48]

If Increase Mather worried over his family, over how it regarded him as well as how it fared, he also received unmixed

happiness from it. Though it is difficult to gain a sense of his wife's character from the conventional language used by all who described her, she seems to have given as fully of her love as of her obedience. Increase noted of her that he could always rely on her to keep the family well when he was called away, but she was clearly one who shared more with him than a concern for their children. Maria Mather understood her husband's hopes and fears for New England. When he went to England to retrieve the charter in 1688, she took his place in his study, praying and fasting for his success. Her prayers, recorded in her papers, reveal that she grasped something of the analogy of New England to Israel, and of the desperate plight of the people of God in America.[49]

Increase undoubtedly shared much of his private feelings with Maria Mather, but to the world he showed a highly controlled gravity. His thin face with its long nose was not harsh, but it did not invite light and frolicsome behavior. When Increase laughed, men did not believe their ears; everything about him suggested the gravity that Puritans cultivated inwardly as well as outwardly. Increase's presence, his awesome presence, testified to his belief in life's seriousness—and tenuousness on earth.[50]

Only in his church, and especially at the Lord's Table, did he unbend. There, even more than in the pulpit, he could release publicly the passion he felt for his God. The quality of his feeling cannot now be recaptured, of course, but we can gain a glimpse of his soul in these rapturous moments. Whatever else he experienced, he received an impression of the immensity of God's power and beside it the triviality of his own. His soul melted, he said, when immediately afterwards he tried to recapture the experience at the Supper. He wished God to treat him as a child; he felt like a child standing before the majesty of the Divine. Tears gushed from my eyes, he reported; and indeed, he usually wept at the Supper, wept in happiness, not in terror. He wept too, one suspects, for himself, as well as for the beauty and generosity of God in sacrificing His Son. He wept out of his sense of his imperfection, his impurity, which he could not escape—and could not hide from—in the celebration of what he considered the most perfect act in history.[51]

6

The Invention of New England

Richard Mather's generation settled the new land. They organized the Massachusetts Bay Company in England, raised money for ships and supplies, recruited the men and women for the venture, and transported the lot, including the Company's Charter, across the Atlantic. They suffered from heat and cold and disease and hunger while they peopled the landscape and built towns and laid out farms. As when they gathered their churches and listened to the word, they did all these things in the service of the Lord. They told themselves all their lives and they told anyone else who would listen that they had come to New England to preserve the true Church polity. In a sense, it was chance (or, as they said, Providence), that they came to New England for they would have gone anywhere to do what they did; they would have remained in England had it served the Lord's purposes.[1]

The fact is that the founders had no conception of New England apart from Old England. New England was the extension of the country they had left. And the new was sent out in the hope of reclaiming the old. The founders identified themselves with England—they had grown up there, and they were too old to cast off inherited conceptions of themselves. They revealed the bent of their minds in a number of ways: they referred to England as home, and when they spoke of their nation it was England they meant, not the outpost in North America. Their churches, of course, were a part of the Church of England and their struggle with Antichrist was a continuation of struggle that the English had taken up in earnest under Edward and, more forcibly, under Elizabeth.

The founders demonstrated repeatedly that they had a well-developed historical sense. They pored over the historical books of the Bible and the glosses that churchmen had been turning out for centuries. As rewarding as Biblical history was, it never sated their appetites, and they devoured the pagan historians along with the Pentateuch and the prophets. And finally there was Church history which they relished because in it they saw reflected much of their own experience; for their own experiences fitted neatly into others and were cast easily into epics describing their struggles with Antichrist as a part of the oldest experience of man, the conflict between good and evil. Their historical consciousness, then, was universalistic not particularistic—not especially time-orientated, and certainly not rooted in place.

The second generation shared their fathers' apocalyptic conception of history, but they held it with a different temper. Fresh from Europe, the fathers had a sense of the Reformation which they could not pass along to their children. The struggles of Luther and Calvin and their successors retained an immediacy for the first generation that the second could not quite recapture. The fathers' expectations of the end of the world had a concreteness that they could see and feel in the events and actions of their time. Henry VIII and his children, Edward VI, Mary, and Elizabeth, the Gunpowder Plot, the convulsions of the English Civil War gave reality to the theory of final things. The fathers were disappointed, of course, when the end did not come, and their children shared their disappointment but did not abandon their version of history. The timing was off, the second generation said, and the prophecies were cloudy, but their fathers' intuition remained sound: the end was coming. But they could not think about the end in their father's terms. Disappointment bred caution in drawing the line of time; it was presumptuous, they admitted, for mere men to claim to be able to chart precisely God's plans for men. But disappointment also bred frustration and out of it came a temperament prone to hope extravagantly for the future and to despair about the present. The second generation was divided within itself; in its hopes and fears it came to new conceptions of what history in the new land would be. Unfortunately for its ease of mind, these conceptions could never be wholly reconciled with the facts of its experience.

More than a sense of history contributed to the divergence of the second generation from the first. The second had to face changes in its society that the first generation had failed to anticipate. The founders conceived of their mission as one of preserving the Church of Christ in the form they found prescribed in the New Testament, and they bent their energies to defining the Church organization they called the Congregational way. They were not naive; history—they knew—afforded countless examples of unrealized expectations. Plans failed, good intentions miscarried, purity turned into corruption. Perhaps they expected disappointments in New England, though there is evidence that they expected the world to end before their hopes would be disappointed in the normal course of things. Time did not cease, and the normal course of things followed much sooner than they anticipated. Happily for their peace of mind, most did not live to see the full extent of the disaster that overtook their plans, but their children did and had to do something about it. The problem, as the second generation saw it, was to explain the decline of New England and to prevent the decline from becoming a fall. Somehow the inability of the third generation to undergo conversion had to be accounted for and so did the divisions in the community and what was understood to be the surprising moral decay.[2]

In rehearsing these desperate problems, the children of the first generation referred to the founders with veneration for not only establishing New England but for defining its ends as well. This respect was merited; the achievements of the first generation were remarkable. And yet, in a sense, the second generation credited their fathers too much and themselves too little: the fathers may have founded the colonies, but the sons invented New England.

The process of invention was not deliberate, nor even conscious. It arose in the agony of the knowledge that the Lord was not being served in New England and that they, the sons, were letting down the fathers. The great radical apostasy of New England lay, as Increase Mather said, in the fact that "the Interest of *New England* is now changed, from a Religious to a Wordly Interest." [3] New England had changed, it had shifted its concern from religion to trade, from God's business to Man's. In their evocation of their fathers' greatness, these intellectuals of the second generation formulated the idea of the mission of New England, the notion in Jonathan Mitchell's impressive phrasing that "it is our Errand Into the Wilderness to study and practice true Scripture-Reformation." [4] The founders had spoken in similar terms, but with a different understanding of history. They had come to New England because they had been banished from the old land. Their purpose in coming was to preserve the Church for the final climactic moments of history. Despite Winthrop's incantation "we must be as a city set upon a hill," they harbored no illusions that their practice would strike answering chords in Europe.[5] They were the Church in exile and destined to remain outside the English pale until the end of things. Their obligation was to preserve the Church—not to convert the world, which in any case would resist conversion until the proper point was reached on the line of time.[6]

In its essence, the founders' thought remained always anchored to the Church. The Church in history, its form and membership and government, almost totally preoccupied them. They conceded that it existed in other places as well as in Old and New England. Their particular churches were a part of a larger institution and their purpose was to keep them—and it—pure.

The sons no less than the fathers thought of the Church but in their hopes and fears for it, and for themselves, born of a generation of bitter experience, the Church in their minds became inextricably identified with New England as a people. While the first generation explained its coming to America as an effort to preserve the true Church, the second extended this purpose to include the preservation, at least temporarily, of an entire people. Strictly speaking—as they understood their fathers' stories of the migration—the Lord had not just dispatched the

Church to the wilderness, He had sent a people. And He expected not only the Church to honor Him, but the people as well, sinners as well as saints.

How this conception took form constitutes an important chapter in the history of American provincialism. The irony in the seventeenth-century development is that, while these sons of the founders proclaimed the universal importance of New England in Christian history, "a part of God's Israel," Jonathan Mitchell intoned, they simultaneously contributed to its isolation from the history of the Western World.[7] To be sure, the sons *felt* isolated in a way their fathers, accustomed to European practices in politics and scholarship, did not. The sons were different from their parents and insensibly confessed their difference, all the while declaring that they were continuing their fathers' divine errand. Richard Mather had never described himself as a "true New England man"; that designation would have had no meaning in the first generation.[8] But in the second generation, when it and similar expressions became common currency, a quarter-century of experience in the American setting had accumulated. Such appellations emphasized New England's difference as a people (incantations to the geography of the New World were still in the future). They implied that a Puritan in this tribe was more than a saint, more than the chosen of God. A true New England man had special obligations, because he was a part of a holy expedition. Having been established by the fathers, the ends of this expedition were fixed and could not be redefined.[9]

The sons did not dare to say that a saint in America was dearer to God than one in England, but that was what they believed. They were a peculiar people, and they had an extraordinary history. But they were failing to live up to the greatness of that history. They were unaware that by defining mission in terms of a people's obligations as well as of the Church's, they were imposing a far greater burden upon themselves than their fathers had felt compelled to carry. And hence they began to brand themselves apostates and to fashion a conception of New England as a failure. New England, as a construction of thought and feeling, took its rise in a profound sense of unease.

Increase Mather contributed more than he knew, or intended, to the invention of New England. At the time he came to manhood, worried explanations and accompanying warnings about the fate of New England were beginning to issue from its pulpits. The sermons usually began with a reference to the fathers, the the chosen of the Lord, an extraordinary group of the wise, the selfless, the faithful. They had been selected by God to carry His Church to safety out of degenerate England. God had offered them a covenant which promised, in return for service to His cause, blessings, in this world and in the next.

To the second generation, the founders assumed the proportions of the patriarchs of the Old Testament. Increase sometimes conceded that his own day had more knowledge of holy things than the fathers had, but he hastened to point out, only because God had chosen to reveal Himself progressively. Therefore the light that shone on the sons should not produce pride; Increase always insisted that knowledge grew brighter despite anything they did. In any case, the second generation divines agreed among themselves that they were inferior to their fathers in qualities that mattered—in the love of God, zeal for His work, and in piety in all its forms. The fathers' age was a "golden" one; theirs, an "Iron Age." [10]

Increase summed up these attitudes in *A Discourse Concerning the Danger of Apostasy,* one of the great sermons of this type.[11] The leaders among the founders, he said in this sermon, were "Abrahams." When God called Abraham out of Ur, he followed the Lord's instructions and "built an altar to the Everlasting God." And so did our fathers, Increase said; they moved "out of their own Land, when God called them, and came hither, to build an Altar here to the Everlasting God," and "upon its right Basis too." Increase meant that the fathers had placed the Church in a political state that excluded the errors and heresies that disfigured the English scene. Indeed, he explained, "Our Fathers have been *Davids,* that is to say, eminent *Reformers.*" Increase, in a sentence that appeared in slightly altered form in dozens of sermons by his colleagues, made no effort to suppress the admiration he felt for these men: "Let me speak freely (without offence to any) there never was a Generation that did so perfectly shake off the dust of Babylon, both as to Ecclesiastical and civil Constitution, as the first Generation of Christians, that came into this Land for the Gospels sake, where was there ever a place so like unto new Jerusalem as New England hath been?" [12]

Increase always found this theme congenial, and as an example of how God favored this band of His faithful, Increase cited the life of his own father. To Increase, it seemed clear in the circumstances of Richard's childhood that the Lord had selected him for an important role in New England. First of all, Richard, the son of poor parents, could not ordinarily have expected much schooling, but the Lord stirred up his parents to send him to school. Increase detected Providence in this occurrence, a Providence that again came to Richard's aid when his aptitude for books proved almost his undoing through the Catholic merchants from Wales who persuaded his father to apprentice the boy to them. This time the Lord interposed His Providence through the boy's schoolmaster who urged that he be kept at his studies. Finally, in Increase's understanding of his father's life, the Lord's special providence acted later to preserve Richard for the great work in New England, saving him when all seemed lost on the voyage to Boston in 1635.[13]

Richard served New England for thirty-four years; despite near blindness in one eye, he remained in his study and in his pulpit turning out solid edification for the Lord's people. In Increase's mind his father and his father's generation deserved veneration for much more than their stay in power: they had brought the true Church organization to New England. They set the pattern for sermons and worship; they discovered a way of examining for membership; they devised tests for the sacraments. In all these ways they made New England, in John Higginson's phrase, a plantation of religion, not of trade; they defined its meaning and established that the public interest should always take precedence over the private.[14]

To Increase and his great contemporaries—Willard, Higginson, Hubbard, Stoughton Oakes, Danforth—the land of their day presented a far different aspect. They painted their pictures in various dark hues for thirty years, and then were joined in their lamentations by their sons and heirs. They complained of their people's growing fascination with the creatures and their neglect of the things of the spirit. The people, they said, either avoided the sacraments or took them indiscriminately without qualifications. Families suffered as much from pollution as the churches: discipline was slack, servants unservile, children disobedient, and order was lacking everywhere. The land wallowed in filth, and as a return felt the barbs of the Lord. But if afflictions punishing the people came in abundance, they produced nothing more than temporary correction. The course of New England led downward; in the depth of his despair in 1697, Increase Mather suggested that his land served the Lord as a type of Hell, an emblem for the edification of other nations still capable of profiting by its dismal example.[15]

Out of this extended study covering almost forty years, one conclusion emerged. The land housed a people in decline, but the Lord still claimed the land to be His own, though He must soon blast it should New England fail to reform. In these years before the new century opened, Increase plotted New England's course as anxiously as a navigator trying to steer his ship out of the shoals. When the controversy over the Half-Way Covenant first broke into print, he denied that anything was seriously amiss. The Apostolic Church had survived disagreements, he pointed out, and so presumably would New England's. His reassurance masked uneasiness at being in the position of opposing the new baptismal covenant and seemingly incurring responsibility for the outcry. When a few years later he joined the majority and began insisting that the extension of baptism comported well with the first principles of New England, he admitted that the land suffered in its sins. From that time on he concealed neither his despair nor his hope. The situation looked darkest in King Philip's war, but with victory Increase decided that a partial reformation had been achieved—how else could the defeat of the Indians be explained but as a reward for repentance? New England at this moment, he said, was in the position of Israel under Samuel, a partial reformation had occurred but the land awaited a David to pull it back to its original goodness. David did not appear, and in a few years Increase was ready to admit that affairs were at a pass as bad as ever. Both the regenerate and the unregenerate were failing to live up to their obligations: the first group growing in worldliness to the point where their behavior almost proved indistinguishable from the second; and the second steadily showing its determination to go its own sinful way.[16]

There is, in Increase's assessments and those of his colleagues, an inability to regard change in any but moral terms. To his eyes, deviations from the norm appeared as decay, not as behavior based on a perception of reality different from his own. What made change so frightening was that its basis was concealed from ordinary observation; apostasy—he knew—always began in the heart which the outsider could not study. Heart idolatry preceded the better known variety that carried men into a worship of false gods. How could a minister tell when his flock began to yearn after such things as money, business, fashion, rather than the worship of Christ? We "slide back by degrees insensible," the younger Thomas Shepard said in 1672, an observation that echoed through the sermons of second-generation divines.[17] These men knew that they could rally their churches outwardly—they could warn backsliders and excommuncate them if warnings failed; they could exhort them to renew the Church covenant; they could force them to observe days of fasting and thanksgiving. But what of the hearts of ordinary men? [18]

The fear in these lamentations fed on still another development —the restoration of Charles II and the subsequent persecution of nonconformists in England. These New Englanders watched English events with despair and an increasing sense that they were isolated in the world. They heard periodically from friends in England about the silencing of dissenters under the Act of Uniformity; they heard too of the "drunken beastes" who replaced their friends in English pulpits. The stories of persecution and immorality discouraged them from whatever lingering hopes they may have had about returning to England. Increase of course could confirm these reports from his own experience; he had been driven back home in 1661.[19]

There were other sorts of stories too that arrived from across the sea—reports of ridicule of Puritan ideas and practice. William Hooke wrote to John Davenport of a scene in a play by Ben Jonson, enjoying a revival in Restoration England, which represented "the Puritan put in the stockes for stealing a pigg, and the stockes found by him unlockt, which he admires at as a wonderfull providence and fruite of prayer, upon which he consults about his call, whether he should come forth or not, and at last perceived it was his way, and forth he comes, lifting up his eyes to heaven, and falls to praye and thanksgiving." [20] After this sort of thing, they could not have been surprised by news in 1670 that the Archbishop's chaplain now insisted that grace must not be distinguished from virtue. Were that contention forced on them, they knew that they would have to discard their entire basis of Church membership. And that would render their land, already in decline, as vicious as old England. With news of all these English disasters arriving with depressing frequency, little wonder that they turned inward to study themselves.[21] The results of this study of their own experience, the perceived declension from the way of the fathers, probably contributed more than anything else to their definition of New England.

But the history of another chosen people also affected the second generation's understanding of themselves and a method of interpreting Scripture also played its part. The history was the story of Old Testament Israel and the method was the ancient one of typology.

Frequently the history of the first chosen people, the children of Israel, was told with the obvious parallel drawn to New England. The Lord had not broken His covenant with Israel, the Puritan ministers insisted; Israel had rejected the Lord despite afflictions and warnings which forecast its eventual disgrace. Surely New England would not permit itself to follow Israel's example; it need not; the time for reform still existed. And all that the Lord required of His people was reformation and repentance. New England–Israel could still save itself.

Perhaps more than anyone else in New England, Increase studied the history of Israel. His sermons brim with references to it, and he wrote one book and long passages in other works about it. Israel fascinated him all his life because of its past and because of what he took to be its future. Israel's history as the people of God had relevance for the Puritans of New England, he was certain. Israel's future promised to be important in the end of the world: Christ's Second Coming and the destruction of Antichrist would be signalized by the salvation of the exiled Jews who would be gathered from the four corners of the world. Obviously New England would be affected by these last climactic events, and in the meantime she could profit much by Israel's example.[22]

The problem for all such interpreters was in deciding what was meant by Israel in the Scriptures. Puritans, devoted to literal interpretation except where another sort served their purposes better, began with the assumption that most Biblical passages described historical Israel, but they conceded that in many cases something more than the literal sense was intended. Should Moses striking the rock for water be taken simply at face value or did the episode indicate something more? What of manna from Heaven and Jonah in the whale? Such passages had intrigued Christians for centuries, and long before the Reformation a means for understanding them had been developed.[23]

Perhaps it was natural to consider such episodes as allegorical. At any rate, men with imagination so construed them, and early in the Christian era they developed typology, a branch of allegory devoted to treating the mysteries of the Scripture. Typology as a method of Scriptural interpretation held that many passages in the Old Testament, whether they dealt broadly with Israel's history, or with specific incidents and characters, should be read as anticipations of Christian history recounted in the New Testament. The history of Israel, then, was not what it appeared to be but should be read figuratively. Thus typologists commonly took Moses as a "type" of Christ who, in theological jargon, became the antitype. Christ, as an antitype, had many types in the Old Testament: over a period of years Christian scholars decided that most of the prophets had been types of Christ. Given the initial assumptions it did not take much effort to decide that Adam, Noah, Joseph, Jacob, the most frequently cited, had forecast Christ. Things too were considered as figures of Christ —gold, jewels, especially a pearl, were to be considered allegorically. Augustine made the drunkeness of Noah comprehensible by demonstrating that it was "a figure of the death and passion of Christ." The English reformers of the sixteenth century, despite the warning of Luther and Calvin who distrusted the method, proved even more inventive. The water from the rock, they took to be a figure of the blood of Christ; the manna, of His body; the serpent of brass raised on the pole, of the crucifixion; Joshua's overthrowing of material Jericho, of the overthrowing of spiritual Jericho; the dark powers, of evil destroyed by God. Similarly, the pit into which Joseph's brothers cast him was a figure of Hell, or sometimes of the descent of Christ, and the swallowing of Jonah by the whale was a type of the burial of Christ.[24]

Although the founders of New England sometimes drew the parallel between Israel's experience and their own, they clung to the literal method of scriptural interpretation more often than not. They were a sober, practical lot and they had before them a dreadful example of what literary imagination might do in the person of Roger Williams. An enthusiastic typologist in every way, Williams used the method to challenge the most cherished prejudices of his solemn brethren in the Bay. Hence in comparing themselves to Israel, the founders kept their imagination under watch and relegated the bewildering passages the typologists were so eager to take under study to the useful category of the mysteries of the Lord.[25]

Increase Mather, like most of the leading intellectuals of his generation, simply ignored his father's fears. Matters that had appeared so clear, so self-evident to the founding generation, had proved extraordinarily murky. Protestants had always looked to the Scriptures, and he could not afford to confine himself to received interpretations. So, very early in his career he began to employ typology. Like scores of divines before him, he discovered that Moses, Solomon, and Samson were all types of Christ; the tabernacle of Israel was a "Type of Christ's humane nature"; the temple, a type of His body. He also understood the redemption of Israel out of Egypt as a type of the salvation of sinners by Christ, and he found in the "ceremonial Holiness of the Jewish Church" a type of the "real Holiness which ought to be in Gospel Churches." And throughout his life he insisted that Israel typified the elect in all times and places.[26]

In Increase's hand, typology became more than a technique for penetrating the puzzle of Scripture: it became a method for understanding the history of his own time. But though his use of typology was uninhibited, he never succeeded in reconciling the intellectual strains the method imposed.

Intended to solve so much, typology created an ambiguity that always resisted Mather's best efforts at resolution. The problem arose in the comparison of New England to Israel. Good typologist that he was, Increase insisted that two Israels were referred to in Scriptures, and by an extension of thought easy to make, he was led almost unknowingly to think of two New Englands. By two Israels, Mather meant first historical Israel, or as he sometimes called it, "carnal" or "natural" Israel. This was the Israel of Jacob, national Israel, the covenanted people whose literal history was told in the Old Testament. But there was another Israel as well. This was spiritual Israel. Like most

Puritan divines, Increase believed that the term sometimes served as a kind of shorthand for those chosen for salvation by God. The Scriptures worked back and forth between these two meanings and so, naturally, did he. In the same manner, he sometimes thought of New England as the entire people in covenant with God, and as that small body of saints who had been chosen for salvation.[27]

Early in his life carnal Israel drew his attention. Its history, as he read it in the Old Testament, presented a melancholy example of a nation in decline. Punctuating Israel's progressive decay were periodic revivals explicable largely in terms of generational changes. A saintly generation, he pointed out, invariably fathered a backsliding generation. Did not Abraham beget Ishmael and Isaac beget Esau? And was not Joshua's great example wasted on the children who came after him? The Scriptures suggested that it had always been so; the rebellion of the children provided a universal theme in all human history. Consider the beginning of history. The first Church of God resided in Adam's family in godliness, but Cain "foresook the Lord" and had to be excommunicated. Out of the Church, Cain became the father of an evil and corrupt generation. Purified by the expulsion of Cain, the Church "continued in some measure pure" until the time of Seth when once again the children reverted to form. In these years the reforming fathers accomplished their tasks with relative ease. Concentrated in one family, the Church could detect apostates within itself and cast them out. But as the world increased in number so did the multitude of sinners who enjoyed a kind of immunity from punishment because they were so many. At this point the Church separated from the profane in an attempt to secure purity. But corruption haunted almost every generation, and before long, the pure and the profane mingled within the Church. This second great apostasy provoked the Lord who sent the flood to wash evil from the earth. Religion revived in Noah's family, but Cham's apostasy followed about forty years later. Once again the Lord encouraged reform in the Church and once again the builders of Babel, the grandchildren of Noah, rebelled. Within a few generations the world was almost completely overrun by idolatry. By the time of Job, who—Increase calculated—lived three hundred and fifty years after the flood, religion had almost left the world. Abraham established a pure Church, but his children demonstrated their identity with all previous generations of ungrateful children. A thread of faith survived, however, which Jacob spun into a national Church.[28]

When the Church achieved national status after being joined so long to a family, the problems intensified. The expansion of the Church permitted men to sin with impunity, Mather explained, and the old dreary cycle of reform and decline persisted. So, of course, did the slow and steady downward progress of the life of religion. The godly of each passing generation never quite managed to equal their fathers' grace. "Solomon," Increase Mather once observed, "was a good man and his Soul is now in Heaven, yet he was not like David his Father as to measure of grace and faithfulness."[29] The absolute low point in this tale of decline came twenty years after the death of Josiah who had wrought "a great Reformation" but who had fathered offspring so graceless that "the Jewish State both Civil and Ecclesiastical" was quite overthrown.[30] Sent into the captivity, Israel learned nothing from its suffering and when it was released, fell again into its self-serving habits. Despite the warnings of the prophets, apostasy proceeded. The generation that went into captivity had been guilty of idolatry; the one emerging from it was guilty of covetousness, a kind of spiritual idolatry. To bring them to their senses, the Lord afflicted them as He had afflicted previous generations. As before, these judgments of the Lord had failed to yield a permanent change, and when Christ appeared, the Jews were once more in a degenerate state.[31]

This was one interpretation of Israel and its carnal History. In measuring New England's unfolding history against the record of natural Israel, the Lord's first chosen people, Increase Mather never found reassurance. If Israel was a type of New England, as Increase assumed, should Puritans expect that their history would parallel Israel's exactly? Since there were no clear rules for controlling the typological method when it was applied to history, as there were when it was applied to Scriptures, divergences between type and antitype could be expected. But such departures from the model remained possibilities, and over the years what impressed Increase Mather was the dreadful faithfulness in which New England followed Israel's road to destruction.[32]

The beginnings of the two covenanted people appeared strikingly alike. Just as the Lord led the children of Israel out of tyrannical Egypt into the wilderness, so he also carried the Puritans out of persecuting England into the wild New World. Like the children of Israel, New England's people remained true to the Lord's purposes in the first generation when they possessed gifted leaders. Apostasy did not begin until the great men of the founders passed from the scene, and then the godly leaders in the second generation took up the burden of directing a degenerating people back up the hill of purity. When Increase came of age he did not at first grasp how steep this hill would be nor how difficult it would be to persuade New England to scale its top. He may not even have understood that reform was needed. His first comments on the problems of the unbaptized children of his generation were uncomprehending. With John Davenport he insisted that the old rules furnished clear guides to action, or in this case as his opponents pointed out, to inaction. As he came to see the disaster that impended should the children fail to convert, he changed his mind about the Half-Way Covenant and became one of its leading advocates. But children, the rising generation, remained one of his concerns throughout his life.[33]

King Philip's War, which began in 1675, provided the next great shock following the Half-Way Covenant, and prompted a response in the familiar historical terms. By sending the war, God notified His people of His disappointment and anger with their growing defection from the covenant. So great was His wrath that He refused to be propitiated by the Day of Humiliation which the General Court called on June 29, 1675, sending on that day more dreadful scourges. Conventional ritualistic replies to His anger would not be enough, Increase noted: the Lord expected reformation. When the war ended with a victory, good men could take heart. A partial reform had been achieved under the lash of the Lord's afflictions, and New England appeared to have recovered a measure of holiness, but a full reformation awaited the future, if it was to occur at all.[34]

Strictly speaking, there was nothing in historical Israel's past comparable to the series of shocks that buffeted New England in the years following the war with the Indians. The Crown stripped the Bay Colony of its charter in 1684 and sent out in the person of Sir Edmund Andros a governor who was bent on following his instructions to centralize the government of New England.

Political struggles of a new magnitude occurred until revolution erupted in 1689. At this time Increase Mather and those around him dreamed of the old way which would be capped by the restoration of the charter of their fathers. But though they got rid of the detested Andros, they also got a new charter and with it a state in which political privilege rested no longer on Church membership but instead on property. They also received another innovation of doubtful benefit, a royal governor and a new method of selecting his council, the upper house of the legislature. A reconstituted state appeared even more shocking when it became known that it was committed to religious toleration.[35]

Israel's state had also endured transformations; it had suffered under foreign rulers; it had connived in the propensity of its subjects to worship false gods (and what else did toleration, the equivalent in New England, involve?). The parallels could be drawn for all their unevenness; but if Increase did not feel obligated to etch the differences precisely, neither did he seize the opportunity to insist that the experiences of the New England people conformed exactly to Israel's.[36]

The prophets had branded the children of Israel a stiff-necked people and in so doing expressed the Lord's displeasure at the pride of His chosen. Much of the anger of the Lord and the despair of the prophets arose in fact from the psychological perverseness of the chosen people. Brought out of Egypt by the Lord and spared the anger of Pharaoh and his people, they persisted in their complaints and grumbling. Receiving the manna rained down from Heaven to ease their hunger, they ignored the injunction to take their supply a day at a time. Warned not to worship false gods and images, they constrained Aaron to cast the molten calf of gold. These sad beginnings became a pattern, the sordid outlines sketched by the backbiting, stealing, divisions among themselves, and the uncleanness of the children of Israel. And so it went again and again even in defiance of repeated warnings and in violation of their covenant with God. Assured of the Lord's blessing and protection, were they to hold fast to His law, the children of Israel swelled themselves up and broke His Covenant.[37]

Increase detected the same cast of mind in New England and pronounced it more disturbing than any of the external shocks the society received. Israel's history suggested that a decline was almost inevitable; that a backsliding generation followed a good one seemed in the nature of things. But perhaps history could be reversed in New England; perhaps New England could escape the awful destruction that had befallen the first chosen people. Increase retained his hopes in the 1690's though the State seemed to be slipping out of orthodox hands. Happily the Church of the pure, though hard-pressed to keep its graciousness, still survived. If it could be kept undefiled it could save the land.[38]

7

The Church of the Pure

━━━━━━━━

What preserved hope for Increase Mather and his colleagues in
the pulpit in these years, what kept them assiduously preaching
to saints and sinners alike, was a confidence that the normal in-
stitutional order could be depended upon to work the Lord's will
on the land. More particularly Increase relied upon the State;
his bitterest jeremiads are efforts to compel the State to act or
expressions of despair at its lethargy.

The first jeremiads were election sermons, preached at the invitation of the General Court, and addressed to the people's rulers. But though, in a formal sense, the ministers delivering these
sermons addressed the magistrates, they used the occasion to
speak to the entire people. Only a small proportion of the people
of New England attended, of course, but the ministers knew that
the magistrates and representatives would transmit their messages and if they should neglect this obligation, the many other
ministers in attendance could be depended upon. The final resort
of the ministers lay in the printing presses of Boston and Cambridge, which produced hundreds of copies of the sermons year
after year. And so ministers seized their advantage, a magnificent
pulpit from which an entire society might be exhorted, and me-

thodically reminded New England of what God expected of it. The early efforts of the ministers summoned the whole community to reform, impartially denouncing all the people for their departures from the true way. God's controversy was with New England in Wigglesworth's epic poem and in these early jeremiads. John Higginson warned "Merchants and such as are increasing *Cent per Cent*" to remember that the Lord had planted the land for religion, not trade, but he reserved his gravest threats for "any man who made Religion as Twelve, and the world as Thirteen." William Stoughton preferred analogies from the family to those of trade and likened New England's people to the disobedient children of a mighty father. Jonathan Mitchell's majestic *Nehemiah on the Wall,* preached in 1667, attempted to evoke a "publick Spirit" among all. All erred, he insisted, all incurred the Lord's wrath for unbelief and idolatry. Samuel Danforth, who borrowed Jonathan Mitchell's metaphor of the errand into the wilderness in his election sermon of 1670, also persisted in calling on the body of the people as a whole. And Increase Mather himself in his first ventures into this melancholy form followed the example of his senior colleagues in, for example, *The Day of Trouble Is Near* (1674).[1]

By the end of the decade of the 1670's, the jeremiad began to change: as in the old form, ministers continued to summon the people as a body to reformation, but now specific groups and interests were singled out for exhortation, ministers, merchants, schoolmasters, fathers, children, servants, and, in particular, magistrates. The change of address marked a recognition of the fragmentation of the community. The people could still be appealed to as a body, and a minister ought to continue to remind them of the public interest. But private concerns demanded recognition too and perhaps if appeals to the group failed, approaches to men in their private capacities would not.[2]

Increase pioneered in the new form of the jeremiad. Its beginnings are clear in his great *Discourse Concerning the Danger of Apostasy.*[3] In this sermon as in others he directed the most feverish of his appeals to the magistrates. It was very well to remind a people of their duty, but fifteen or twenty years of that had proved of little value. The facts were, as he saw them, that the people had no inclination to reform, that sin would abound unless the State acted more vigorously. The magistrates were the "cornerstone" of New England Society—he told them in 1679. If they failed to act, New England's people would fail the Lord. The magistrates could do much, and he provided a list of recommendations. They should encourage the keeping of the record the founders had achieved in New England. A book of chronicles of New England was what he had in mind, comparable to the chronicles of the Old Testament. The State should also authorize the collection of the history of God's special providences towards New England. The record in marble in Geneva ought to inspire emulation, he said. And the magistrates should attempt to do what magistrates had always done in a Christian society—enforce the law. They would not convert men by insisting upon obedience to statutes, but at least they might effect an external reformation which would secure outward blessings and prevent judgments on the external affairs of men. You cannot stop "pride in the heart" Increase told them, but you can stop "pride in apparel." You cannot stop drunkenness in the sight of the Lord, but you can punish drunkenness in the sight of men.[4]

Increase's central recommendation, which he would regret making years later, concerned the organization of churches. At the time Increase preached the *Discourse,* he faced the prospect of further defections from the Congregational way in the West. There in the Connecticut Valley of Solomon Stoddard the old basis for admission to the churches had been discarded. To Increase, Stoddard appeared in the guise of the destroyer of the Church as an institution of the pure. Stoddard baptized indiscriminately, it seemed, and he was about to open Communion to the profane. His practice caught on and spread from Northampton throughout the West. Only the State could stop him—and it would not. But it might insert itself into the process of the selection of ministers, or so Increase urged. He paid his respects to the old idea of congregational autonomy in a sentence that betrayed his uneasiness at the disaster it threatened to bring to New England: "Though the just liberties of Churches should not be infringed, yet that every Plantation in the Country should have allowance to chuse, whom they please to labour in the publick dispensation of the word, may be in time a great inlet to ignorance, error, and profaneness." Increase proposed that the General Court find some "expedient" to ensure that only the qualified served in the churches of New England.[5]

Thirty-five years later Increase would oppose giving synods such powers, and he would stand as the defender of the autonomy of the particular church. But in 1679, when he still retained faith in the State, having given up on mere exhortations, he proved willing to invest it with authority far beyond anything his father would have approved. New England's case seemed desperate to him; and the magistrates, for the moment, seemed the only hope for it. The danger was that they would tolerate new practices. They could do nothing about Stoddard, except to attempt to restrain his influence, but they could stamp out error. They could resist toleration. Their fathers' example should remind them of their duty, and he invoked the great earthly trinity once more, Winthrop, Dudley, and Endecott. Increase must have suspected that even this appeal would fail, that the younger Winthrops and Dudleys and Endecotts were not the men their fathers were. And so, once more, in his hopelessness he threatened—if they failed—"God will *change* either *you*, or your Government *ere* long." [6]

The failure of the State to suppress competing faiths, which was clear to everyone by 1700, deprived Increase of much of his hope for New England as a people in covenant with God. His confidence in the external covenant which the Lord had made with the tares as well as with the choice seed had been diminishing for years. The loss of piety, the changes in sacramental practice, the lowering of standards for Church membership, all had shaken him. Afflictions would be understood—the blasting of crops, the incursions of the Indians, even the loss of the charter were occurrences which made sense within the rationale of the outward covenant of God. But when the State finally proved unreliable, no basis for recovery of the entire people appeared possible. [7]

Increase's hope that the State might prove capable of producing a reformation had survived almost until the beginning of the eighteenth century. When hope died, he believed that one resource remained to New England, the expectation that the saints, the people of God, might through their faithfulness rescue the entire land. The conception of New England as a people had grown slowly in Increase's mind. While the idea was taking form, his attachment to his father's notion of the true Church in New England as a saving remnant, holding itself in readiness for the final drama, remained strong. But he could not help but feel differently about the people and the land. He was a child of America, the son of an immigrant, born and reared in Dorchester and Cambridge. And for the first thirty years of his ministry, he had found himself placing his hopes in all the people, sinners as well as saints, though he knew in his heart he could do nothing for the sinners.[8]

But he seemed to assume that the sinners could do something for New England; they might help maintain its churches despite their own black sin and thereby ward off the blows from the Lord. How could they do these things? By external conformity, by obeying the law, by avoiding visible sins, they could give outward testimony to the value of its mission.

Yet he conceded that by themselves the unregenerate could save neither the land nor the churches. The protection of the land lay in the hands of the Lord's own chosen ones. For this premise Increase drew upon the theory of John Cotton, first expounded in *The Way of Life,* which Cotton had not written with New England in mind and had in fact phrased rather abstractly.[9] Cotton argued in this work that sinners would always follow their hearts' lead: they would sin and they would prove incapable of true repentance. By all standards of human justice they deserved destruction, but so wonderful was the mercy of the Lord that they might escape temporal judgment through the intervention of the saints. The saints might "mourn" for "the whole land," in Cotton's fine phrase; God loved them and He would spare the sinners on earth as long as His own people stood "in the gap." [10] To be effective the saints must not participate in the sins of the land; only by holding themselves aloof from the prevailing crimes of the unregenerate could they stay the Lord's hand. If they should join the multitude in its evil, they too could expect afflictions and even temporal destruction, though in the end they would share in God's eternal mercy. Cotton meant that saints could redeem New England's people on earth but not in Heaven. And the mass of people themselves could advance their own prosperity on earth. They could also damage themselves and, in the process, the saints as well. Though sinners were incapable of attaining the virtue of the regenerate, they owed saints an elementary kind of respect. If they could not bring themselves to follow the examples of the godly, at least they could restrain their impulses to persecute them. Not only must the saints not be persecuted by the State, they must direct it and see that it at least externally recognize the true religion. Should the sinners indulge the worst in themselves, and neglect the directions provided by the regenerate, or worse, persecute them, they would feel God's wrath. Unfortunately, the saints too would suffer as the Lord blasted the whole land.[11]

These assumptions guided Increase Mather's anxious reflections on New England until the turn of the new century. He began his ministry thinking in his father's terms about the Church, a pure institution transferred to the new world awaiting its destiny at the end of the world. But while he shared his father's vision, Increase and his generation insensibly tended to identify the Church with New England. Somehow in the period before 1700, the fate of the Church proved hard to separate from the fate of the people, saints and sinners alike. The warnings he issued, the trouble he predicted, the decline he charted in these years were directed to the society as much as to the people of God, the company of the faithful gathered out of the world.[12]

Increase Mather's ideas about the Church changed little throughout his life. The Church was an institution of the chosen of God; it had always been so; it would remain so until the end of the world. Hypocrites had always polluted it, and probably always would at least until the millennium dawned. But the gracious should deny hypocrites entrance whenever they were recognized and drive them out when they were unmasked. The Church belonged to the pure.

The theory of Congregational polity held by his father satisfied Increase in every respect after he changed his mind on the Half-Way Covenant. The covenant gave the Church its form; the minister ruled it with the aid and consent of laymen. Each particular church governed itself, though loving communion with others often provided necessary guidance on doctrine and worship. Like Richard, Increase felt no desire to take the Church out of the world; perfection was denied to men even in Christ's institution, and renunciation of the world would not secure sanctity or purity. But men should use all lawful means to make the Church holy. The best means, according to the experience of the fathers of New England, lay in restricting the sacraments to those in the covenant and in applying tests of saving faith to discover the regenerate. Some men would offer themselves for membership without saving qualifications; the Church had to find them out in order to protect itself.[13]

How to exclude the sinners and discover the saints, how to keep the Church pure were concerns that filled Increase's mind all his life. The Church of Christ, the true Church, had always been holy, and Increase's sense of its continuity increased as he grew older. This Church stretched from Israel to the primitive days in the time of Christ to the evangelical age of the New Testament. The one development which impressed him was the growing perfection of the Church. There had been great men in Israel's day and they had served the Lord well; they had preserved His Church; and God loved them and blessed them with His holy Church. But God loved His Son, Jesus Christ, infinitely more, and He gave His Son's followers a greater light on His ordinances. And now with the end of history approaching, the light shone even brighter and the Reformed churches of the evangelical age took on greater perfection.[14]

But though the evangelical Church conformed more closely to Christ's desires, it remained in essence the original Church, the Church of the patriarchs. The one unvarying qualification for the Church, if it were to follow divine prescription, was that it receive only the faithful, those who possessed the grace of God. In Increase's understanding of ecclesiastical history, the greatest reforms in the Church were in its substance, the selection of a holy membership. The contribution of New England had come when tests had been discovered which permitted a more effective separation of sheep from goats, the saved from the damned. This impetus to ecclesiastical progress exceeded even the discovery of the autonomy of particular churches. Congregationalism had made the covenant explicit and had located governance within the particular churches, but as important as these developments were, they would have no meaning should the world succeed in inserting itself into Christ's sanctuary. Hence Increase Mather's concern for purity and his insistence that it was the one unvarying mark of the true Church from Israel's time to his own.[15]

This concern led him into opposition to the Half-Way Covenant, an opposition he abandoned only when he became convinced that purity could be maintained under Half-Way terms. His initial view, announced in "An Apologetical Preface," a

long introduction to John Davenport's *Another Essay for the
Investigation of the Truth,* implied that the covenant with
Abraham, which had been extended to his seed, was so fragile
a contrivance that it collapsed in cases in which men failed to
demonstrate their inner quality to the Church.[16] For God's
promise of salvation to the seed of Abraham was interpreted by
Puritans in New England to mean that the children of full members were in the covenant. The children claimed membership by
their birthright, though presumably they possessed the inherent
qualifications which they would demonstrate publicly after their
conversion. This was the way Increase Mather first understood
New England's system of membership and sacraments.[17]

The theory appeared clearer than it actually was. One portion
of the New England way dominated all others: the requirement
that a candidate for membership in a church describe his conversion experience. The emphasis laid on this test warped the
remainder of the system and the sacramental theory had to be
adjusted so as to preserve this overruling stipulation. Many Reformed groups had long considered baptism a seal of the covenant signifying the regeneration of the baptized. The problem
was always in identifying the gracious; in New England with
the requirement that candidates prove their regeneracy to the
satisfaction of the church by describing their inner lives, the
problem was more complicated than elsewhere. Unbaptized adults
who satisfied the church that they had grace were to be baptized
because they had proved themselves to be Abraham's seed. Presumably their children, too, were in the covenant, and they were
baptized. But when these children succeeded in having children
of their own, but failed to experience grace, the entire sacramental theory seem endangered.[18]

The Synod of 1662 took advantage of the confusion of the
covenant language—it was possible according to the elaborate
covenant terminology to be in an external covenant and yet not
enjoy saving grace—to propose that these children of baptized
but unconverted parents also be baptized once their parents had
declared that they believed in Christ as far as their natural abilities enable them to believe. These parents still maintained some
relationship with God, unregenerate though they might be, and
their children should receive this first sacrament in the hope that
they might be among the faithful who in time would enjoy a

recognizable conversion. To refuse baptism to these infants, the Synod pointed out, would be to empty the churches of New England in a generation or two. The founders had not come to New England for such a purpose.[19]

The youthful Increase—he was twenty-three in 1662—listened to these proposals with scorn. The Church, he said in his introduction to Davenport's tract on the Half-Way Covenant, took its being in the purity of its members. The Church was the institution of Abraham's seed. And how did men prove themselves of the seed in the seventeenth century? By making clear their faith. The literalness of Increase's understanding conveyed his sense of the simplicity of the whole problem: requirements for membership had been established in the 1630's; the technique for working out membership had existed for a generation; the fathers had declared their satisfaction then. Why, he asked, if the system was true in the 1630's wasn't it true in the 1660's? In fact the situation was as old as the Old Testament; all New England had to do was to follow the wisdom of the patriarchs, which was expressed in typology for the instruction of Christian churches.[20]

At this point Increase parted company with John Davenport, who denied that Old Testament sacramental practice represented types for the New Testament churches. Circumcision, long considered to be the Jewish analogue of baptism, could be purchased, Davenport sneered. If faith adhered to the moneyed, then so presumably should sacramental practice, a conclusion, Davenport recognized, no one could accept. Increase read Old Testament practice differently: Israel required that parents demonstrate their fitness for Passover before offering their children for circumcision. Passover, which forecast the Lord's Supper according to typological theory, was reserved for the faithful. The Old Testament precedents for New Testament practice seemed abundant to Increase. Men who did not respond to the obligations of their circumcision lost their membership in the Church and with it the privilege of having their children admitted and circumcized. Esau cut himself off, "dis-Membered himself," Increase reported in a revealing phrase, by his failure to believe.[21] And so did the children of Abraham by Keturah; the Ishmaelites and Edomites, the descendants of Abraham, "were discovenanted by not promising nor performing those duties of Faith and Obedience, which God required on the peoples part." [22] These men cut themselves off; so also did those adults in New England, baptized as children on their parents' membership, who failed to give evidence of their conversion. The type forecast the practice. If the Church in New England, blessed by a superior eternal polity, were truly to prove its superiority to the Old Testament Church, it would have to be at least as pure. The children of half-way members should not receive the sacrament of baptism.[23]

By 1671, and perhaps as early as 1668, Increase Mather repudiated his opposition to the Half-Way Covenant. But his repudiation did not include giving up either his typological reasoning or his interpretation of the significance of Old Testament sacramental practice. He did not change his mind easily; nor did he rest comfortably in his new position as defender of the Half-Way Covenant.[24]

In his youthful literalness of 1662, Increase had been unmoved by Jonathan Mitchell's prediction that refusing baptism would produce vacant churches. As he grew older, youthful indifference could not be maintained, and by 1671 Increase himself was echoing Mitchell's warning with the question, "doth it at last come to this, that [the children] have no more Advantage as to any Church care about them, then [than] the Indians and Infidels amongst whome we live?" [25] As dreadful as this possibility was, Increase probably would not have switched sides had he not come to see that purity might be protected under the new baptismal practice as surely as under the old. The churches could assume that the baptized adults and their children stood in an external relation to the Lord, even if there were little direct evidence that the external corresponded to the internal condition. But what prevented the baptized from claiming full membership? What inhibited them from professing that their outward condition reflected their inner? Increase noted several possible answers as he returned to these questions over the years. Perhaps the baptized were not yet converted. And there was no escaping it, perhaps they never would be. On the other hand, perhaps they were over-scrupulous. Conversion was the most valuable experience available to man and many may have hesitated to claim it for themselves. They were modest, very much aware of their imperfections, and reluctant to suggest that they felt the movements of grace in their souls. This reluctance, he almost added, was the fruit of their sense of sin.[26]

Hypocrites might slip into the Church under the new baptismal dispensation, Increase conceded, but the Church had not been free of them before this agonizing problem arose. The fact was that the Church still retained means to maintain purity. By continuing to test for an experience of grace, it could keep the unworthy from the Lord's Supper, the sacrament intended to seal one's growth in grace. Increase gained reassurance from the practice of requiring an applicant for the Supper to give evidence of the working of grace in his soul.[27]

It may seem to us that the Half-Way Covenant implied that baptism was inherently of less value in the eyes of God than the Lord's Supper. After all, churches required more of a candidate for the Supper than they did of those offered for baptism. And if this was not implied, did not the new system threaten to debase baptism by making it available to those who lacked the promise of grace (a charge which could not be avoided in the seventeenth century)? Increase took great pains to refute this argument because he felt uneasy with the change and probably secretly suspected that the doors were open to the unregenerate.[28]

Part of Increase's perplexity in this entire problem grew from the fact that he, no more than anyone else, had clearly recognized that while baptism sealed the initiation of adults into Christ, it sealed only the promise of such an initiation for children and infants. According to traditional theory, election had been completed before men were born, but the infusion of grace in conversion must occur in time and space. God, Puritans knew, by working through such means as the preaching of the Scriptures, had pretty well limited Himself to bring men to Christ only after they reached the years of reason and knowledge.[29]

The new system perpetuated the old practice regarding unbaptized adults. Increase was at such pains to establish this continuity that one suspects he wanted to avert questions about the change in infant baptism. Adults, he emphasized, must prove their worth. Here the type from the practice of Israel was clear. The Jews required saving faith even of Abraham before he was circumcized. The Jews insisted so rigidly upon the sincerity of the adult candidate that few were circumcized in the time of David and Solomon "lest haply the Time-serving Ethnicks of those days might out of carnal fear or worldly Advantage take upon them the Profession of the then only true Religion. Now the same thing is true concerning Baptisme." A "meer Historical" faith was not enough for baptism; a "Justifying Faith" was required of adults. Even the Jews of Israel had understood this much about the sacraments though many of the "mysteries" eluded them. Hence the conclusion which confirmed the case for the continuity of purity in the Lord's Church: the Old Testament sacraments sealed "for the substance" the same "spiritual mysteries which are sealed in the Sacraments of the New Testament. . . ."[30]

Increase chose well in attempting to defend the practice of baptizing adults. No departure from the old way of treating adults was implied in the Half-Way Covenant. But the momentous change instituted in infant baptism could not be disguised. Increase revealed his uneasiness at the new practice in his febrile defense of the requirements for adults and in his oblique admission that "unmeet Subjects" might receive the rite under the Half-Way Covenant. This incautious slip of phrasing occurred in a cautious discussion of the symbolic meaning of the sacrament. The water used in the sacrament, he explained, represented the spirit of Christ, not His blood. Therefore Christ's blood was not profaned by unworthy subjects who participated in the rite.[31]

At the time that Increase Mather decided to support the Half-Way Covenant, the standard most dear to his heart was the pure Church which honored the typological model of the Old Testament. As long as the churches of New England insisted that only those who could describe the workings of the Lord's grace in their hearts should receive the Lord's Supper, Mather was convinced, purity would be maintained and consistency with the ancient models preserved. But fifteen years after the Half-Way Synod devised its compromise, purity in the ordinances was cast aside in favor of the corruption of open Communion first instituted by Solomon Stoddard of Northampton.[32]

Stoddard was an imposing man in every way. Physically powerful, and long-lived, he dominated the Connecticut Valley's churches until his death in 1729 at the age of eighty-six. In those years he never missed a Sabbath in his pulpit except on the infrequent occasions of his visits to Boston. The Valley produced a number of big men in these years, among them merchants whose power and ruthlessness later brought their designation as "River Gods." They were strong-minded men who wanted to run things their own way. Stoddard did not intimidate them, but neither did they bend him to their purposes. There were struggles within his church and he, within his own domain, emerged the master.[33]

Stoddard did not share Increase Mather's cherished concerns. A typologist like Mather, Stoddard was nevertheless capable of declaring in 1700 that "All typical laws are out of date."[34] He meant that Israel's ecclesiastical polity should not serve as a model for New England which, in keeping with the glorious dispensations of the New Testament, possessed brighter light on the nature of the Church. But if Stoddard denied that Old Testament ordinances were types for New Testament, and evangelical, emulation, he persisted in interpreting much Old Testament history in a typological mode. He did so not to demonstrate the straight and true line of purity in Christ's Church, but to persuade men that the Lord had always wished them to trust the power of Christ's righteousness as sufficient to save them. The sacrifices, for example, which were instituted immediately after the fall of Adam, and renewed on Mount Sinai, took shape as models of atonement to procure the remission of sins. The Israelites confessed their sins at these rites, and then slayed the sacrifice instead of the sinner. No one, Stoddard argued, should imagine with the Israelites that these gave a "real" satisfaction for their sins; the sacrifices gave a "legal" and a "typical" satisfaction, but "they were not a proportionable price to ransom men's souls by." Rather their purpose was to "shadow forth the satisfaction that Jesus Christ was to make for our sins." The Lord intended that they serve as types of the payment Christ would by His crucifixion render for our sins.[35]

Stoddard announced his hope of persuading men to put down their delusions of saving themselves in his great *Safety of Appearing in the Righteousness of Christ,* which he published in 1687. Ten years earlier he had opened Communion to all Half-Way members of age; he refused to give the Supper to children on the grounds that they lacked the knowledge to examine themselves before coming. He had already introduced the baptismal practice advocated by the Synod of 1662; the Church of North-ampton had urged his predecessor to do so and Stoddard agreed with his church. But Stoddard did not baptize all the children of the town then, or in later years for that matter, as modern his-torians have argued. Rather, he simply insisted that what quali-fied a person for baptism served to qualify him for the Supper. And Stoddard took pains to argue the importance of the quali-fications.[36]

And what were the qualifications? Visible sainthood—he said —in a position he never deviated from. What distinguished this view from Mather's was his definition of a visible saint, which held that historical faith, not saving faith, was all that was re-quired to qualify for visible sainthood. Any adult person who declared his faith in Christ and who was "Morally sincere" in his profession should be baptized.[37] Children of such a parent also qualified for baptism because they were presumed to be within the covenant of their parents. Stoddard also claimed a covenant interest for children of parents excommunicated from the Church, and for the children of any heathen, unconverted servants, for example, who were members of Christian families. None of these qualifications implied the existence of saving faith. And the essential qualification earned a person the full privileges of the Church, including the Supper, once he came of age. Mem-bership possessed an indivisible integrity for Stoddard; as he once observed in a phrase Increase Mather did not admire, "we never read of communicants and non-communicants in Scrip-ture." [38]

As these views came into the open, Stoddard stood revealed as a major critic not only of Increase Mather's use of typological interpretation but also of his advocacy of the Church of the pure. Stoddard did not admire the impure, but he despaired of the Church's ever attaining the discernment to identify them ac-curately. Some men would always possess the skill to act the part of saints, though they lacked the gracious qualifications; others would confuse the pangs of conscience, which might torment even carnal men, with the true movements of the Holy Spirit; and still others would be unable to recognize the faith within themselves even when it was genuine.[39]

The Church's problem of selecting its own was complicated by the yearnings of most men to save themselves unaided by any divine power. Because a man is a rational creature, Stoddard said, he flatters himself that his reason can find the way to God. It guides him in most actions of his life and so, he asks, why not in matters of religion? What a man's reason does not inform him of is the deceitfulness of the heart, and its propensity to serve the self at the expense of everything else. In pride and in self-righteousness, men trust their reason and refuse to accept the proposition founded in Scripture that men can be saved only by Christ's righteousness. Carnal reason, after all, is full of objections against the doctrine of our acceptance by Christ's righteousness. The one thing reason cannot tell men is how to deny itself; and men "do not carry a sense upon their hearts of the imperfections and deceits of their own reason: they know not what dim-sighted things they are. . . ." Hence they regret the testimony of the Lord and "make their understanding the rule and measure of Principles in Religion." Unfortunately for such men, the Lord, in choosing His elect, did not consult men's reasons, or their merits, but simply chose whom He would according to His own pleasure. And He gave His Son as payment to satisfy the exactions of His law for violations by men.[40]

Because men found this order of salvation so hard to accept and because men who were enabled to accept it were difficult to identify, Stoddard insisted that the Church should be made comprehensive enough to encompass all those not openly scandalous who professed belief in Christ. They were visible saints and visibility defined the Church so long as it existed on earth. Stoddard did not believe that men should trouble themselves about the invisible Church beyond accepting its existence. The bent of his mind favored not only the observed but the ordered. A church, he once commented, resembled an army—it had "orderly" lines of authority with some men serving the Lord as rulers and the others as the ruled, whose duty required obedience to their superiors.[41]

The sacraments in these orderly regiments did not differ from any other sort of worship except in form. The Lord commanded all men to pray, regenerate and unregenerate alike. He required them to listen to His Word, and He demanded that they take the sacrament of Holy Communion. Placing the sacrament in this context in effect reduced its symbolism and emotional significance. To be sure, throughout the course of his ministry Stoddard made the appropriate obeisance to the commemorative import of the Supper and he noted that it should provide comfort to those who received it. But these gestures, while carrying conviction, did not carry intensity of feeling. As long as Stoddard's army mustered in the proper ranks, and marched to the beat of duty and law, he was content. He approved when the soldiers found joy in their discipline, but he did not concern himself overly about their morale at the Communion Table, or away from it, as long as they did their duty in coming.[42]

At the same time, he imputed an unusual power to the Supper. He recognized that not all the Church members who took it were filled with saving faith. The Supper, however, might fill them, might regenerate them. Here Stoddard changed the meaning of Holy Communion. For the fathers of New England and their orthodox sons, the Supper was an ordinance intended to nourish the faith of those already converted. It sealed their covenant and gave them the strength to grow in grace. Stoddard did not deny this function to the Supper but he made it something more, an instrument by which saving faith might be induced in a sinner. Hence in his sacramental theory, Church members—not the profane outside the Church—should come to the Supper even though they know that internally they lack grace. God commands them to come just as he commands them to perform any act of worship, "as no Man may neglect Prayer, or hearing the word, because he cannot do it in Faith, so he may not neglect the Lord's Supper." [43] Such a practice would benefit those men who were uncertain about their conditions too; some saints after all could not discern their own graciousness even though they examined themselves. If they stayed away in their uncertainty, "Days of comfort," which was what Communion Sabbaths were to be, would instead become "Days of Torment." [44]

Stoddard proposed this sacramental practice and instituted it in his own church knowing that Increase Mather and many eastern colleagues despised it. Like every Puritan divine who suggested changes in doctrine or worship, he knew that he urged the wishes of the Lord. Stoddard read Increase Mather's work, and he agreed that the Church of his day had "better ordinances" and "a more glorious dispensation" than the Church of the Old Testament. He declared periodically that the typical laws of Israel no longer governed, but in this case of the Supper, he could not refrain from pointing to the old model. The Lord had required that all of Israel take the Passover, the type of the Supper, even though Israel contained ungodly as well as godly men.[45]

If Stoddard inconsistently cited Israel's experience after he denied that experience any contemporary meaning, he proved himself perfectly consistent in the next step of his reasoning: though unregenerate members of the Church could lawfully take the Supper, their participation could never be acceptable to the Lord. The distinction between "lawful" and "acceptable" worship had appeared in Puritan divinity for generations.[46] Every Puritan intellectual recognized its validity, but Stoddard's application of these categories to sacramental practice marked a daring extension of the traditional theory. All Puritan divines agreed that the Lord required all men to pray whatever their internal condition; He required that they listen to the Word in His temples; He required that they fast when His representatives on earth demanded. But the sacraments were something apart; they had been reserved according to all tenets of Puritan thinking to those graciously qualified. Here was Solomon Stoddard proclaiming that it was lawful for carnal men to take the Supper, even when they knew themselves lacking in grace. And the Church should acquiesce, indeed it should welcome such men. It must because, as Stoddard never tired of pointing out, it could not get inside men's minds and hearts. It should take men's professions at face value except when scandalous behavior gave these professions the lie. God would reject unregenerate men when they appeared at the Communion Table but the Church on earth would never know it. The Church should concern itself with the visible; the invisible belongs to God.[47]

These propositions prompted Increase Mather to express his disgust and horror at their character so often that he has been accused of defining his own position on the Church and the sacraments as a reponse to them. In fact, while Increase felt compelled to answer Stoddard, he maintained those essentials of his own position which he first discovered at the time of the Half-Way Covenant. At that time he had praised the seamless continuity of the Church which extended from the models of the Old Testament. He had argued too that types provided a guide for the ordinances of the evangelical churches; they would not go out of date until the Church militant became the Church triumphant—in other words, until the Lord gathered to Himself in Heaven all the chosen from the earth. Mather persisted in these assertions throughout the dispute with Stoddard.[48]

However, Mather was not one of those grave Puritans who serenely pursued the Lord's way oblivious to what anyone else did or said. The strait gate to his mind and heart did not admit serenity until the last years of his life. He remained extraordinarily sensitive to any challenge to his views, and he reacted with extraordinary quickness and energy. In his sensitivity, in his eagerness to set things right, in his frantic desire to see his own formulations accepted by others, he forced his own ideas to the outermost limit of their application.

Typological interpretation demonstrated to Increase Mather the persistence of the Church as an institution reserved for the saints. That, he believed, was the great use of typology as a device for understanding Scripture. Ranging over that story Increase asserted repeatedly that the ceremonial holiness required of the Israelites was "typical" of the real holiness expected of New Testament churches. In David's time, the Israelites regulated admissions to the temple lest any enter not out of love of God, but out of fear; and in Solomon's time, they enforced the same strictness lest unworthy men enter in order to enjoy the great prosperity then obtaining in Israel. Later in the post-exilic temple they appointed porters to exclude the unclean. The Israelites' Passover, a type of the Supper, made a similar case for purity; as Mather noted, the paschal lamb was reserved for the clean. In Mather's account of ancient practice, the Israelites are shown searching their houses for any leaven, a symbol of the malice and hatred that believers must purge themselves of before enjoying Passover. Only saints could perform such a scrutiny. If the premise that Israel forecast New Testament experience were accepted, there was nothing startling in Increase's argument. His method was old; and others besides Stoddard insisted that it could not be made to yield truth about evangelical Church practices.[49]

The central issue between Increase Mather and Solomon Stoddard, the purity of the Church on earth, took its origins in their different understandings of religious psychology and the meaning of the sacraments. Assuming that the saints could not be separated from sinners by devices available to mere men, Stoddard proposed that membership in a church should be founded on a profession of faith in Christ by men who were "morally sincere." To a generation frustrated by years of trying to separate the gracious from the carnal, this seemed a plausible suggestion. As Stoddard pointed out, the Church cannot get inside a man's skin and examine his conversion experience. What can it really tell of his internal condition? All it can do is require that a man give a sincere statement of his belief in Christianity, and hope that some of the men making such statements have grace as well as historical faith.[50]

Increase exposed the flaw in Stoddard's reasoning with a few deft thrusts. Stoddard's argument, he said, implies that "there must be a certain Rule whereby it may be discerned what mens inward Sentiments, and the belief of their Hearts is, Whether they do not speak falsely, when they say, That they believe such Articles of the Christian Faith, as They pretend to believe." What Increase meant was that testing sincerity of belief presents the same problems as testing the graciousness of inner experience. Both cases involve assessing the truth of statements made by men. And if there is evidence that men have mistaken the movements of their carnal hearts for the operations of the Holy Spirit, or that some men have lied about their conversion, there is also evidence that men have said they believed in Christ when they did not. To prove this point Increase cited the Emperor Julian, who professed his belief in the articles of Christianity and then, in his apostasy, admitted that he had never believed any of them. And Arius had professed belief in the divinity of Christ in order to enjoy communion with Christian churches though in reality he did not believe—as he later admitted. According to Increase, Stoddard's position might be summed up in these terms: ". . . If men are knowing, and Profess they believe the Principles of true Religion, and do not Profess any Error that is inconsistent therewith; the Rule requires that Churches who cannot know the hearts and inward Persuasions of men, should accept of their outward Profession." But Increase asked: "And why then should we not believe, That men that give us an account of Their Conversion, and whose Conversations are outwardly blameless and holy, are really according to what they seem to be?" Mather's point was that a church has to judge an inward state whether it demanded historical or saving faith. In the first case it relied on testimony about beliefs; in the second, testimony about conversion. From its vantage, the difficulty was the same in each case. Why, then, should Stoddard assume he had solved any genuine problem when he required only historical faith? Stoddard never answered this question, and probably never grasped the psychological subtlety that informed it. Increase did answer it, insisting that the Lord comprised His Church from those with saving faith and no others. Typological interpretation suggested that the evangelical churches faced the obligation of sifting the good from the bad, if the Church of Christ was to be as pure as men could make it.[51]

The obvious method of keeping the Church pure was to examine all candidates for Communion with very high standards required for admission. If this were done, only those believers with full assurance of their faith could enter the Church as full members and take the Lord's Supper. The flaw in requiring complete assurance lay in the fact that grace gripped sinners with varying degrees of strength. As Increase often noted, there were degrees of faith: there were weak believers and strong believers; and there were some with more grace than others. All a man required to be saved was a shred; faith as a grain of mustard seed, Christ had said, would move a mountain. But if so little faith would save a man, discerning it taxed a church which, as both Stoddard and Mather agreed, could not peer inside hearts. A church should expect a seed to grow, Mather noted, and it might look for the same development of faith. Men might strengthen themselves by exercising what little grace they possessed, and they needed the nourishment the Church and the sacraments provided. Therefore, Increase concluded, "rigid severity" in examining candidates for admission ought to be avoided so that the weakest Christian received encouragement.[52]

A church should test the experience of those who offered themselves, but it should do so with "rational charity." In practice, Increase explained, rational charity meant weighing any evidence of the inner state and, upon detecting a bare sign of grace, admitting the person if his behavior was good and if he possessed knowledge of Christianity. In making decisions about communicants, a church was well advised to act with such charity that it receive "diverse hypocrites" rather than exclude "one Sincere Child of God." [53]

The traditional test of one's inner state was a relation of conversion experience. At the time that this requirement was instituted, churches recognized that not every growing person would be able to pass it. Women, for example, frequently could not bring themselves to testify in public; their fathers and husbands did not care to encourage them to talk more than was necessary anyway. Others, men and women alike, proved incapable of identifying the precise moment of their conversion; grace after all sometimes worked itself into the soul gradually and insensibly.[54]

Increase accepted this analysis of the varieties of religious experience and held that only "capable persons" should give a relation of their conversions. Like divines of his father's generation, he recognized the manifold ways that grace operated. And he noted the existence of men and women of "bashful tempers," who hesitated to speak publicly of their inner lives. He also admitted that conversion took strange courses, which sometimes resisted classification and description. Some conversions should not even be described; those provoked by a sense of a dreadful and secret sin should not find public expression because the sin itself, better left secret, would be exposed.[55]

If the Church should exercise restraint and charity, so as not to condemn men too easily, men should hesitate before condemning themselves. Increase was convinced that Stoddard had gone too far in urging carnal men, who knew they were still in a natural condition, to come; but a man who has "hopes" about his soul, though he may also have doubts, should come to the Supper. He need not have assurance, Increase insisted; all a man should require of himself is the "hope" that there is a "good work begun in his Soul." Typology offered instruction on this point, as on so many others: just as the Jews were to eat the Passover after they had searched their houses for leaven and found none, so were Christians to take the Supper after they had examined themselves and "cannot find that they are in a State of Hypocrisy, which is Leaven. . . ." Rational charity exercised upon the self, Mather contended, should prove encouraging to anyone who had hopes for his own salvation.[56]

Behind this view lay a rich conception of the Supper as a source of profound emotional satisfaction. Increase felt an ecstasy at the Lord's Table that he believed all gracious men should experience when they receive the sacrament. For, though Increase always denied to the Supper the power to convert sinners, he attributed more emotional power to it than most Puritan intellectuals did. To be sure, he employed the conventional terms in describing it: the Supper was a "seal" of the covenant of grace, a sign of our salvation through Christ, a commemoration of His sacrifice. But he invested these terms with an intense piety. A man who hoped to take the Supper should realize, he once wrote, that the Supper was more than a mere form, a commemorative device. One who took it had the obligation to come to the Table in a loving frame of mind, and prepared to experience a greater emotion than he knew. Indeed, soul-ravishing joys should seize him. The heart of these joys was Christian love, love of Christ for His gift of Himself to men, love of Christ's ordinances, and the love of one's brethren in the particular church. Bread and wine, the "outward elements" of the sacrament, helped induce these notions in the soul. Increase Mather always emphasized that men needed the tangible to help them comprehend the intangible.[57]

Mather, however, was not content to point to the connections of inner and outer in the sacrament; he insisted that the full beauty and power of the Supper would affect men only if its every aspect were grasped. Thus he made explicit the spiritual significance of each sacramental action. The smallest physical movement spoke of a divine loveliness. The "taking" of the bread and wine signified the incarnation of Christ in human nature; the "blessing" of the bread and the cup signified the sacred use of Christ for men; the "breaking" of the bread, the "bruising" to death of Christ on the cross; the "giving" of the elements to men, the "giving" by God of Christ for man; the "receiving," the reception of Christ as our Savior; the eating and drinking of the elements, our feeding in faith upon a crucified Christ.[58]

Other Christian groups have given themselves fully to the beauty of the Eucharist. Still there is in Increase Mather's theory more than the usual plan for participation in a right frame of mind. Since observing him as he gives the Supper to his church is no longer possible, we should not suggest that the experience carried great physical gratifications for him; nor can we say with absolute certainty that he expected communicants to feel sensual pleasures at the Table. He wrote after all only of the ravishment of the soul, not the body. Certainly he experienced—and desperately wanted others to experience—emotional satisfactions. But he may have felt more than satisfaction as he gave and received Communion. He concentrated not just on the thing symbolized, not just on the elements of the sacraments, but on the symbol itself, and the visible events which happened to it—receiving, breaking, eating—to a degree that hints that he experienced sensual pleasures at the Table of the Lord.[59]

The Supper could nourish; it could enable men to grow in grace. Thus, to Mather, it followed that only the qualified should come. A man could be transformed through a series of religious experiences, and then he could come to the Table with grace. A natural man lacked grace and he could not grow in something he did not have.[60]

Although Stoddard seems to have shared a delight as great as Mather's when he took the Supper and though his advocacy of open Communion rested in part on the belief that the sacrament should give comfort, he did not claim that it would produce bliss in communicants because he recognized that the participation of many would be unacceptable to the Lord. He encouraged all members to take it, hoping thereby to induce conversion, an experience that might be pure ecstasy. Thus Stoddard's sacramental theory reduced the importance of the sacrament in worship as it increased it in conversion.[61]

In reducing sacramental practice to the level of ordinary worship, Stoddard argued that though the participation of an unregenerate man in Communion was not "acceptable" to God, it was clearly "lawful." [62] A natural man might after all be regenerated by the Supper. Increase had replied that if the Supper were a converting ordinance it ought to be given to the profane. Why confine it to Church members? Stoddard never really answered this question except to repeat that the sacraments were designed for administration to those in the Church. Some division between the Church and the world had to be maintained. But as far as Increase could see, Stoddard threatened to close the gap almost completely.[63]

The controversy between the two ended as such disputes did

between Puritans, with each man more than ever convinced of the strength of his own position and the weakness of his antagonist's. But at the close, through the struggle in the pulpit and the presses, the arguments of each had been strangely transformed. What began in disagreement over sacramental practices finished as conflict over the meaning of New England.

Throughout, Stoddard had rested his case on a very simple proposition: good men could not be separated from bad men by the Church. That fact helped define the character of the Church in the world. The Church would contain saints and hypocrites, but far from considering such a mixture a liability, it ought to seize its opportunity to use all the ordinances, sacraments as well as sermons, to convert its members to the faith. In New England the Church occupied a particularly favored place: the entire nation comprised the Church, because the entire nation, saints and sinners alike, enjoyed a special covenant with God. This far had Stoddard's understanding and appreciation of externality brought him. In fact, Stoddard extended the theory of the national covenant—the covenant God made with a people regardless of the certainty that any people would contain men damned eternally—far beyond its conventional limits. The national covenant promised temporal prosperity to a people who lived up to its conditions, though it could not convey salvation to anyone. But as originally conceived, the nation was not presumed to coincide with the Church, a more restricted agency because of its purity.[64]

Stoddard, however, argued in the course of his dispute with Increase Mather that the "Public Covenant" between God and a people constituted the Church. As Stoddard read history, God made the first national covenant with the Jews in Israel and thereby created a national Church. In this polity the Israelites organized themselves into separate synagogues for convenience, but they relegated these smaller institutions into a subordinate position under the Church that was the nation. In fashioning this ecclesiastical polity the Israelites apparently simply followed the light of nature. At any rate, Stoddard found justification for this arrangement in nature which taught that man was "fitted for Society" so that he might worship with his fellows. According to nature's laws men ought to worship not only in "lesser societies"—particular churches—but in "Kingdoms and Countrys" as well. Nature also instructed men in the line of authority: "the whole hath Power over the parts" provided a principle that must be applied to Church organization. And therefore Stoddard proposed a system whereby the nation as a Church supervised the worship and discipline of subordinate churches. He admitted that no such national Church was mentioned in the New Testament. The reason was not that "National Churches are not according to the mind of God," Stoddard explained, but that no Christian nations existed in the days of the gospels. Now Christian nations abounded, and national churches represented the wishes of the Lord speaking in nature and through the history of Israel.[65]

Although Stoddard conceived of the nation as the Church, he never suggested in the seventeenth century that everyone in the nation should receive the sacraments. The Church, he advised, should continue to exclude the vicious and profane from its sacraments. But as he pondered the uses of externality and the impossibility of detecting saints in a world of sinners, he gradually altered his conception of the benefits of the Supper. The Lord's Supper, he maintained in the 1680's, could help regenerate men—it was a converting ordinance as well as one which nourished the gracious. Hence it should be given to carnal men, who professed faith in Christ and lived acceptable lives. Yes, he replied to Increase Mather, Communion was the seal of the covenant. No, he said, when Communion was given to carnal men it did not seal a "blank" because these men were in covenant with God despite the absence of grace, an external covenant whose condition was a morally sincere profession of belief and obedience to the law. The Supper given to such communicants might carry them to the faith that saved.[66]

By the early years of the eighteenth century, Stoddard had come to place a new value on the sacrament. Not only might the Supper produce faith, it might also ensure outward prosperity to the Church. God had made a "publick covenant" with the nation because it was a Christian nation; this external covenant deserved to be sealed in the same manner as the internal—through the Lord's Supper. Therefore, unregenerate men should claim the sacrament not just in hope of salvation, but as a "right" they possessed as part of the "body corporate," and as a guarantee of the blessings of "outward prosperity." By this astonishing extension of theory, Stoddard lifted the sacrament from the realm of private experience and placed it among the terms of public obedience to the national covenant. And in doing so, he unwittingly co-opted religion to secular purposes, an action Increase Mather both feared and despised.[67]

Stoddard's pronouncements contained nothing about the final meaning of New England. Presumably he believed that its character was important, but he was disturbingly content to think of New England in the terms of the national covenant alone. That covenant included sinners as well as saints and, as Increase Mather came to see, sinners could do little for the Lord.[68]

The more that Stoddard asserted that the Church in New England included the entire nation, sinners as well as saints, the more Increase felt disposed to insist that the Church must remain the haven of the pure. The struggle with Stoddard persuaded him that New England's only hope of avoiding rejection by God lay in the Church. The Church held hope only so long as it held fast to its purity. If it were pure, it could stand for the entire land. Though it contained only a fragment of New England's people, it nourished the people most precious to God. In a sense Stoddard was right, Mather conceded, the Church was New England, but not the national Church, not the Church of the impure, but the Church composed of visible saints.[69]

This New England, the New England of the Church and not of the public covenant, was a type, Mather believed, in the sense that Israel had been a type. If New England was a type, what was the antitype? The answer was one his father would have shrunk from announcing though he may have considered it: New England was "a Type and emblem of new-Jerusalem," the Kingdom of God that would flourish in the millennium.[70] The Church of the pure, the visible saints, could stand for the entire land. Though they were only a fragment of the people, they could redeem the whole. And the truly godly among them, the New England of the type, could serve saints everywhere. When these saints received the Lord's Supper, they anticipated the saints in Heaven sitting at the side of Christ, judging the world on its final day. Hence the desperate need to preserve the beauty and the purity of the sacrament; anything less would rob New England of its glory at the end of history.

8

The Invisible World

While the controversy with Stoddard was brewing, but before it reached a boil, Increase Mather was thinking about another matter that affected his ideas about the Church in New England: nature and an arena beyond nature, the invisible world. In fact Mather always pursued his scientific studies in the frame of mind that inspired not only his ecclesiology but all his scholarship. His preoccupations, which were those of his generation of New English divines, remained centered on God's designs—especially as they involved New England. It is true that in Mather's lifetime such concerns lost much of their urgency for him as he turned his attention to the problems of converting the elect, but even then his sense of wonder at the mystery in the world and his love of the power behind it, which had been reinforced by his scientific studies, continued as strong as ever.

Increase approached scientific study with the traditional Puritan assumptions about nature as an extension of God's wisdom and power. His friend Samuel Willard once said that "When God wrought the works of Creation, he had a Design in every Creature." [1] The detection of that design was recommended to all sorts of men, who were told that it was their duty just as poring over the Scriptures was. The divines who urged scientific study were aware of the dangers in what they encouraged. Scholarship and natural philosophy might completely absorb a man; they possessed the attractiveness of any of the things of this world. Some men developed an inordinate taste for meat and drink and became gluttons and drunkards; some rich men valued their vanities more than their souls; some scholars failed to see beyond second causes. This last failure was understandable because God chose to work through the laws of His created universe; but to see nothing beyond second causes was atheism nonetheless, for Providence lay behind every natural event. God's power filled the order of the cosmos. So long as men remembered that nature contrived to reconcile order and arbitrary power, they would make natural philosophy a godly enterprise. So long as they regarded nature as John Cotton had, as "a mappe and shaddow of the spirituall estate of the soules of men," they might examine it confident that they did so in the faith.[2]

Accepting these premises, Increase probed into the natural world with the eagerness, if not with the rigor, of the great figures of seventeenth-century science. The range of his interests grew throughout his life and included astronomy, geology and, under the tutelage of his son, Cotton, medicine. His most impressive study was of comets, which he discussed in several sermons and tracts, and in one major book, *Kometographia*, published in 1683. Much in these studies, and especially in the long work, suggests that a powerful curiosity pulled Increase into his investigation of the heavens. He explains in *Heavens Alarm to the World* that he was intrigued by the comet of 1680, the largest one he had ever seen.[3] He took the trouble to measure its "radiant Locks," presumably the blaze of the comet, and found them to be approximately sixty-six degrees long. As was his custom when he became interested in any subject, he read everything he could lay his hands on, but of course the great seventeenth-century works on comets were still to be written. Fortunately for his need of direction, Robert Hooke, the Secretary of the Royal Society, had published his work on the Comet of 1677; and Increase used it as a guide in his investigation of Halley's Comet, which had made one of its periodic visits in 1682.[4]

Hooke dealt with a number of problems long of interest to

astronomers. He speculated on the density of comets: the nucleus of a comet was solid, he said, with a density as great as the earth's, while the tail or blaze partook of the nature of flame. He studied the source of a comet's light and finally decided that it was its own source. Hooke also considered the traditional questions about the nature of a cometary movement and distance of comets from the earth. Before Tycho Brahe's work became known, many scientists had argued that comets were sublunary bodies which had been drawn into the air, where they were set on fire. Skeptical of the view, Brahe measured their parallax and, discovering that it was less than the moon's, properly concluded that comets were at a greater distance from the earth. But Brahe made his own mistakes, the most notable one being his assumption that comets followed an orbit around the sun.[5]

The exact course of cometary movements intrigued Hooke, perhaps more than any other issue concerning their character, and much of his study was given to a calculation of their orbits. The proposition he offered on this subject which Increase Mather found intriguing was that if exact observations of a comet's parallax could be obtained, the return of a comet might be accurately predicted.

Mather's reaction to Hooke's formulation reveals more sharply than any other single feature of his work the character of his scientific interests. He agreed with Hooke, Brahe, and Kepler, all of whom he read with care, that comets did not move within the earth's atmosphere. The argument on the basis of parallax convinced him, and he pointed to the need of precise astronomical observations from several parts of the earth. But he did not accept the views of Hooke, Brahe, and Kepler uncritically. The evidence from other astronomers, inexact as their observations were, was taken into his reckonings. He also gave weight to observations which showed the relative movements of the earth, other planets, and comets. At certain times, he noted, planets interpose themselves between comets and the earth. This suggested to Increase that comets moved "in an higher Sphere" than planets.[6]

The evidence of the senses did not carry Increase as far as it did Hooke, however. Hooke described the movement of a comet as corresponding to a natural law; Increase agreed but stopped short of the inference that Hooke found compelling: the path of

a comet was predictable and the return of comets could be precisely calculated. This last contention appalled Increase Mather.
If it were accepted, how could the doctrine of *concursus*—the
faith in a God who sustained every instant of all existence—
stand; a created being operating according to its own laws, presumably independent of the Divine, compromised the sovereignty
of God. Increase was prepared to believe that comets were generated somewhere beyond the earth's atmosphere, but not that
they possessed everlasting (sempiternal) existence. And surely
they followed the laws of nature, so far as men could understand
these laws, only as long as God decreed. God used comets, as
He did all nature for His own purposes; most commonly He
chose to employ them as signs of impending events, "Ensigns"
held up in Heaven for men to see.[7]

What comets portended depended upon Man's course along the
line of time leading to the Day of Judgment. In certain periods
their appearance forecast happy events; for example, the birth
of Christ had been announced by a blazing star. Eventually,
Mather suggested, one might anticipate a shower of comets as
the Second Coming approached. But for the most part, comets
did not bring happy tidings; rather they served to warn men of
disasters which awaited them should they fail to heed divine
commands. New England in particular had reason to recognize
the dreadful portents of comets. God had often spoken to it
through these preachers of divine wrath before sending His
afflictions on the land.[8]

If God spoke in comets, He also acted through them, using
their mysterious power as a "natural influence upon the Earth."
Increase did not presume to explain the naturalness of this
"influence"; rather, he contended himself with the assertion that
comets "caused" droughts, infestations by caterpillars, tempests,
floods, sickness, and perhaps even earthquakes. Besides signifying the coming of afflictions, which might be forestalled by
repentance and then causing them when repentance was not
forthcoming, they seemed also to predict apocalyptical events.
Thus the second woe, the crushing blow upon the Turks, was
announced by a comet; and assaults by the sixteenth-century
reformers on the Antichrist in Europe were forecast. At times
God chose to make their awful messages even clearer by giving
comets extraordinary shapes; one in 1627, for example, assumed

the form of a man's arm holding a sword about ready to descend in a crushing swipe.[9]

The belief in the grotesque stories of the shape of comets, the insistence that their orbits were unpredictable, the emphasis on their emblematic quality, the belief in their capacity to produce natural disasters, seems to comport uncomfortably with the careful observations, the sane comments about the importance of parallax, the preference for Kepler and Hooke over early superstitious savants. And in fact, Increase Mather's "science" contained jarring inconsistencies. Like the best natural philosophy of the seventeenth century, Mather's *Kometographia* was intended to brighten the glory of God in men's eyes by illuminating His secrets in nature. But Increase sensed the danger that this enterprise of opening God's mind in nature would diminish the awareness of His mysterious power. Hence the crude assertion that explanations from second causes alone constituted atheism. And hence the fact that much of *Kometographia* departed from scientific concern to explain nature on the level of the mysterious. Natural explanations sufficed for limited purposes, but for genuine understanding, the final resort had to be to piety.[10]

Increase offered *Kometographia* as an exercise in natural philosophy as well as in piety, though he inevitably blurred the conventional distinctions between the two. A year later he published *An Essay for the Recording of Illustrious Providences*, which provided additional evidence of his curiosity about nature. Yet this book, too, like his studies of comets, was designed to reinforce a sense of the mystery in life, in this case by emphasizing the power of the demonic as well as the power of the Divine.[11]

The exact beginnings of the book cannot be reconstructed. Such books of God's wonders, of remarkable providences, had appeared for centuries. The possibility of writing a book of this sort apparently first occurred to Increase when, in examining the papers of John Davenport, he discovered a manuscript that had been inspired by Matthew Pool's *Synopsis Criticorum*, an account of God's providences in such matters as storms, apparitions, floods, and possessions. (Whether Davenport had written the stories, or collected the accounts, is not clear.) Sometime in the year 1681, Increase evidently showed the collection to other Boston ministers, who, following his lead, decided to complete and publish the manuscript. Increase took the project over and finished it with the aid of his colleagues, who either contributed accounts of wonders or suggested books he might examine.[12]

The publication of the *Essay* brought to attainment a hope Increase had declared years before in the *Discourse Concerning the Danger of Apostasy*.[13] At that time he had conceived of the collection of special providences to New England, with the intention of using them to demonstrate the special character of the Lord's chosen people in America. The collection would testify to the extraordinary blessings the Puritans had received and would contribute to the rejuvenation of the faith of the fathers.

Increase's purpose survived the passage of the years; the *Essay*'s subtitle—*Wherein, An Account is given of many Remarkable and very Memorable Events, which have happened in this last Age; Especially in New England*—reflects it and the text occasionally refers to the special concern God felt for New England. But for the most part these expressions remain as afterthoughts to the main commentary, which concentrates on God's glory—not the glory of men in New England. Many of the wondrous examples of divine Providence occur outside New England, and do not involve New Englanders in any way. As in *Kometographia* these wonders are types of the Lord's wisdom and power; they are emblems of His goodness.[14]

The book carried the same purposes as Increase's studies of comets did—to undermine the authority of scientific explanation of natural phenomena and to substitute the ancient sense of divine mystery in life. To be sure, the range of subjects taken up in the *Essay* suggests a scientific curiosity which operates impartially over the varieties of nature. Sea deliverances, preservations, thunder and lightning, magnetic variations, witchcraft, demonology, storms, earthquakes are some of the subjects Increase reports on. Within this variety his intention is unvarying: to offer one level of explanation in terms of second causes, but also to insist that the Providence of God whether working through nature or outside its confines is ultimately inexplicable in this world. It is true that every case includes concrete details, suggesting the reliance upon the observation of the senses, calculated to satisfy any natural philosopher. In the accounts of preservations, boards are shattered by lightning, bricks are thrown about, positions of people tossed by wind and sea are minutely described and their injuries tabulated down to the last cut and bruise. Such details give the stories of the *Essay* their remarkable vividness; they intensify their horror and mystery. Increase wrote in the conviction that his readers would be more inclined to believe the implicit propositions about the strength and mystery of the unseen if their observed effects were fully described.[15]

Though the book is offered as observation, it is not genuinely empirical. Most of the illustrious providences were reported by witnesses whose testimony Increase accepts unquestioningly; and "evidence" of all kinds is lumped together indiscriminately. Increase repeats old folk belief—elephants fear mice, the horse abominates the camel, lions tremble at the crowing of a cock; he reports instances of strange antipathies in nature—men who swoon at the sight of eels and frogs or when they smell vinegar —with the same seriousness that he discusses current scientific speculation about magnetic variation. But given his purposes, this lack of sophistication is as it should be. What Increase most hoped for the *Essay* was that it would convince men that "There are Wonders in the Works of Creation as well as Providence, the reason whereof the most knowing amongst Mortals, are not able to comprehend." Hence a story of fish that jumped into the boat of starving sailors drifting on the sea was as important as the properties of magnets—both ultimately were "very mysterious and beyond humane capacity" to understand.[16]

The *Essay on Illustrious Providences* presumed to deal with the problems of nature in its extraordinary guises; and therefore in the four chapters on witches, possessions, and apparitions Increase made no claim that these subjects, surrounded by the occult and embedded in folklore though they were, deserved special treatment. Their study should be pursued in the way of God's illustrious providences and with the expectation that scientific explanation would carry one so far and no farther. Something of witchcraft and apparitions could be explained in terms of secondary causes just as something of magnetic variation could. But the scholar would reach the limit of such investigation soon and eventually would have to retire in the face of the demonic mystery. He could console himself with the knowledge that the Devil and his kind operated within restraints set by God who used the evil spirits for His own purposes.[17]

The method of study, Increase recognized, depended upon the

assumptions about the phenomenon studied. Some men insisted upon the total validity of natural investigation because they denied the existence of evil spirits and witches. Increase was concerned to banish these skeptics whose skepticism threatened religion itself. As Joseph Glanvill, one of the compilers of witch stories from whom he drew, said, *"Atheism* is begun in Sadducism: And those that dare not bluntly say, *There* is NO GOD, content themselves . . . to deny there are SPIRITS, or WITCHES."[18] Just who the skeptics were in New England is not clear; announcing themselves would have been a dangerous trespass against received opinion. A few years later during the outburst in Salem a few scoffers raised their voices. Martha Cory was one—she did not think there were any witches, she said— and her sniffing at the whole affair helped hasten her way to the gallows.[19]

Increase Mather rarely produced a major book for the local audience alone, and in the *Essay* he hoped to destroy the doubters in cosmopolitan Europe as well as in provincial New England. Not many genuine skeptics published their views in Europe, and Mather was reduced to attacking men who believed as seriously as he in the existence of witches but who had urged that only the most careful and scientific means of detecting them be used. The four Increase mentioned as deserving particular contempt were Reginald Scot, a sixteenth-century English author who inspired other critics for the next two centuries, Thomas Ady, John Wagstaffe, and John Webster, all well known in the seventeenth century. Increase either misread or misunderstood these men, or relied on secondhand information about the content of their books. None of them denied, as he charged, that witches and evil spirits abounded in this world.[20]

The technique Increase used to cashier the "skeptics" throughout the *Essay* and in later studies of the invisible world, relied on a mass of data. His purpose apparently was to present so much evidence—stories, attestations, testimonials, narratives— of the incursion of witches and apparitions in every corner of the world as to leave his reader no choice but to agree. As in the accounts of the remarkable use of thunder and lightning, to say nothing of earthquakes, floods, and storms, he attempted to convey a sense of the mysterious immediacy of the Devil and his dark spirits. The visible, the concrete, the stuff of ordinary existence, paradoxically, was made to suggest the presence of another order of invisible, immaterial and dangerous being. Thus, the stories abound with "evidence" of men being bitten by unseen teeth (the marks appear before the victim's astonished eyes); chairs are lifted into the air despite the best efforts of men to hold them against the floor; burning ashes are flung out of a fireplace by an unseen hand; children sicken and die at the command of a voice from an unseen mouth. Some afflicted men imagine that they have been turned into beasts; others speak in languages they do not know; still others receive dreadful information about the future. The people who endure these tortures all appear as normal Englishmen or Americans. The implication is that the same kinds of things might happen to Increase's readers, should Providence be disposed to lengthen the Devil's leash.[21]

This type of demonstration surely convinced many of the power of the demonic in the world of men and things. It employed the conventional and it connected the visible and the invisible. Still it did not convince everyone, as Increase well knew. And one who doubted the existence of the invisible world might accept the truth of all Increase's descriptions and still insist that they all could be explained in natural terms.

Those savants and skeptics who resorted to science for explanations did not presume to suggest that the laws of physics accounted for the strange levitations reported in many cases; nor did they plot the orbits of witches riding on sticks. Rather they fastened on the extraordinary behavior of the accused witches and their victims. The convulsions, the fits, the Lycanthropia—the delusion of some men that they had been transformed into animals—even the confessions by practicing witches, all took their origin from the same source, they said: disease of the body and brain. These skeptics denied that supernatural creatures inserted themselves into men. Illness could produce all the symptoms of witchcraft and it could lead men to admit crimes they had not committed when they were accused by strong-willed investigators.[22]

This argument baffled Increase who knew that calling it atheism did not constitute refutation. The best he could do was to point to the delusions of afflicted and accused, the terrors, the frightful ideas, their hatreds and enmities. How did these phenomena enter the mind? How could "meer natural Disease" produce them out of nothing, he asked. Consider, for example, the extraordinary capacity of some of the afflicted to speak with tongues, that is, to speak in languages, unknown to them. Surely what they spoke came from the mind; what baffled him was how anyone could explain "how should that be in the mind, which never came there through the outward senses." The conclusion seemed obvious to him: "This cannot be without some supernatural influence." Perhaps recognizing the lameness of his argument, he charged that the "patrons of witchcraft" favored the view that there was no mystery in the behavior that the vulgar attributed to the demonic—disease explained it all. And he added, in an opinion that had dangerous implications, witches themselves often put their godly pursuers off the scent by using this medical argument.[23]

Because the *Essay* proved to be popular, these views must have been widely known. But there is no evidence that they contributed to the venomous atmosphere that swirled around Salem Village when witchcraft appeared there in 1692. Even so, they do help us understand Increase Mather's responses to the incursions of the witches that year.

The witches first appeared in Salem Village, now Danvers, which was a small parish on the edge of the town of Salem, then a small seaport of traders and fishing men. Salem Village did not enjoy much contact with the larger community, or with any other town in New England. Its isolation probably contributed to the propensities of its inhabitants to backbiting and talebearing; and perhaps it encouraged them to resort to the courts for other kinds of satisfaction. At any rate, the petty squabbles there over land and crops and animals often ended with the parties involved appearing before the local justices.[24]

Salem Village also had a history of unhappy relations with its ministers. Two, the Reverend James Bayley and the Reverend George Burroughs, had departed the parish after quarrels with their parishioners over their salaries and a long list of lesser matters. Apparently sharing the local fondness for litigation, both ministers took their people to court in an attempt to collect, and both won judgments. But both had then left, happy to be free of such a tightfisted flock. A third minister, Deodat

Lawson, avoided the worst of these struggles but he did not remain long.[25]

The Reverend Samuel Parris who succeeded Lawson late in 1689, did not find his parishioners in a generous or charitable frame of mind. After hassling over his salary, they forced him to accept a meager sixty-six pounds a year, a third in provisions, and they refused to provide his firewood for the winter, a discourtesy that must have soured his coming. Parris was scarcely a sweet-tempered man under the best of conditions, not that he had the opportunity to enjoy the best of anything very often. He was thirty-eight years old in 1692, and he had come to the ministry not from Harvard College but after failure in the West Indian trade. His family in Salem Village included his wife, about whom almost nothing is known, his nine-year-old daughter Betty, his eleven-year-old niece Abigail Williams, and two slaves, John Indian and Tituba, apparently half Carib and half Negro.[26]

The trouble started with Tituba who, in the long winter of 1691–92, began entertaining the two girls and a number of others in the village with stories of the occult. She also instructed them in fortune telling, a forbidden art in any Protestant community. Although historians have assumed that Tituba was innocent of any evil motive in these practices, she doubtless took herself seriously, and so, evidently, did the girls. The problem of how her practices induced the pathological reactions that began appearing in this circle of female adolescents is beyond the scope of this book. Whatever was involved, by January 1692 symptoms of morbidity and soon of hysteria began to appear. Samuel Parris first noticed the abnormalities in his daughter Betty. Early in her illness, Betty seemed withdrawn and preoccupied with her own secret thoughts; she was also forgetful and began to neglect the chores she performed for her mother. She lost interest in almost all her customary activites, including worship, to the point of forgetting prayer and then rejecting the Bible when it was offered to her. Fits began in the same months, dreadful convulsions accompanied by shrieking, screams, tears, and sometimes unconsciousness.

About this time the other girls began displaying similar symptoms. Parris and other frightened parents at first attempted to keep their children's illnesses quiet, consulting the village physician, who was baffled, and then seeking the advice of ministers in Salem proper and nearby Beverly. As one girl after another began to act as if she were possessed, the chances of a rapid cure or of maintaining secrecy disappeared. Like many parents in the village, Parris suspected that the disease had a supernatural origin, but he does not seem to have announced his fear until the village doctor suggested that the girls were suffering from demonic possession. This learned opinion may have emboldened the girls, for soon in answer to the question, "Who torments you?" they named Tituba, and two village women, Sarah Good and Sarah Osborne.[27]

The accusations made during these convulsions by the demented girls were that the spectres, or the shapes of these women, appeared to them demanding that they enter a compact with the Devil by signing his black book. The girls refused with the results visible to everyone. The spectres of the witches kicked and bit them, flung them around like rag dolls, and twisted them into rigid postures. All this suffering, the girls insisted, was their reward for resisting the blandishment of the Devil and his agents, the witches.[28]

When the witches showed up in Salem, Increase was in England at the Court of William and Mary completing a successful appeal for a charter for Massachusetts Bay to replace the old one which had been withdrawn eight years earlier. He finished the last of his business in March 1692, and with the new Governor, Sir William Phips, sailed for home on the twenty-ninth. He had not seen New England since 1688. His ship anchored in Boston on Saturday night, May 14, 1692.[29]

The return brought him joy until he recognized the danger of the distress at Salem. The jails bulged with the accused, whose numbers would certainly grow as the afflicted girls cast their nets more widely each day. The girls drew the sympathy of those who watched their torments, but the accused too had their supporters. Devout families could not comprehend the justice of having pious members snatched out of their houses on nothing more than the charges of the suffering girls. Of course, the Devil roamed this world; of course hypocrites sat in churches along with the saints. But these families also believed that when the charge of witchcraft was lodged at one's door, some caution and judiciousness had to be exercised. The whole matter belonged before the courts for trial, once and for all. And those who supported the girls agreed, at least they agreed that the courts must proceed against witchcraft and drive the Devil and his cohorts from New England. The supporters, who in the Spring included Lt. Governor Stoughton and most of the Council and a number of ministers outside Salem, did not clamor for the exoneration of the innocent, however. In May when the Governor arrived, they were more interested in discovering the guilty than in freeing the guiltless.[30]

The Governor delayed any action until May 29, when he commissioned a special court to try the cases. The judges, who sat without a jury, included nine distinguished members of the Council. Lt. Governor William Stoughton presided.

Increase certainly approved referring the witch cases to the court; established procedures in England called for judicial decision, as he had noted years before in his studies of witchcraft. But the creation of the court did not assure equitable proceedings, and he watched the first two weeks of the court's actions with a growing sense that long established practices were not being followed. The first trial lasted one day, and the conviction was clearly based on "spectral evidence," testimony by the afflicted girls that the spectre of an accused person was doing the tormenting. Bridget Bishop, the defendant, was not an attractive character; common gossip had it that she was an immoral woman, fond of gambling, prone to keep unusual hours and receive company of doubtful reputation on doubtful business. Her neighbors dredged up stories of unpleasant encounters with her, several going back as far as fifteen years. The most telling evidence was the accounts of the horror her spectre wrought: it had beaten Deliverance Hobbs, mother of one of the girls, with iron rods. Bridget Bishop was also supposed to have murdered several children, and given suck to her familiar, which turned out to be a snake. The judges found this testimony convincing and at the end of the long day of the trial, Stoughton sentenced her to hang. Phips was preparing to leave about this time to lead the fight against the Indians and may not have followed the trial closely; on June 8, six days after the trial, Stoughton ordered the execution for June 10. Bridget Bishop hanged that day.[31]

The trial troubled Nathaniel Saltonstall, one of the magistrates, so much that he resigned from the court as soon as it was over. Perhaps this resignation shocked Phips, for soon after he appealed to the leading ministers in Boston and nearby towns for advice as how best to proceed. The "Return of several ministers" to the Governor, issued from Cotton Mather's pen almost immediately, and was approved by Increase and twelve other ministers.[32] This report reeks of the awful tension the ministers felt between the dangers of convicting the guiltless, and of the opportunities of ridding the land of the witches. The ministers were clearly offended at the bedlam of the pre-trial hearings; such investigations—they urged—should be conducted as quietly and discreetly as possible so that "Noise, Company, and Openness" might be avoided. They were also perplexed by the indiscriminate accusations, commenting especially upon the girls' insensitivity to social status, which is what led to their fear that "persons formerly of an unblemished Reputation" might be lightly accused. Nor, they declared, should the accused be convicted on the basis of spectral evidence, a clear rebuke to the court.[33]

The opportunities presented by the affair were no less on the ministers' minds. And therefore while the disorder of the hearings and the quality of several of the accused dismayed them, they did not hesitate to exhort the Justices to a "*vigorous* Prosecution" of the witches. And if spectral evidence was inadmissible in court, it clearly had its uses in the pre-trial investigation of accused persons, and the ministers were careful to urge only that it not be admitted as convicting evidence.[34]

Increase felt both dispositions which informed the ministers' "Return" and he continued to feel them as the trials resumed, convictions mounted, and executions took a toll. Five witches died on the gallows on July 19; another five on August 19; and eight on September 19, the last day of the hangings. Three days before, Giles Cory, an old man of steadfast courage, was pressed to death in a field by heavy stone in return for his refusal to answer the charges against him. His standing mute before the court protected his property for his heirs, but he experienced the terrible torture prescribed by English common law procedure.[35]

Cory's brave death shook the watchers in the field. Increase did not witness it, nor any of the executions as far as we know. His alarm arose from the knowledge that the court continued to rely on spectral testimony. Governor Phips returned from the Indian Wars about this time to learn that the court and the executions had served neither to purge the land of the witches nor to persuade an increasingly large body of critics that justice was being rendered. No one could deny that the court continued to receive the most doubtful sort of evidence, nor could anyone doubt that a number of those cried out upon by the girls remained at large, untouched by the law, because they came from the best families. Among them were Saltonstalls, Thatchers, and even, it was rumored, Lady Phips, the wife of the Governor.[36]

Bewildered, the Governor did the only thing left for him to do —he went to Increase Mather and several other leading ministers for a way out of this tangle. Increase delivered his answer almost immediately and in the following year published it as *Cases of Conscience*.[37] While Increase refrained from criticizing Stoughton and the other judges directly, indeed he disavowed "any Reflection on those worthy Persons who have been concerned in the late proceedings at Salem: They are wise and good Men, and have acted with all Fidelity according to their Light," his essay constituted a repudiation of their methods. For Increase insisted once more that the Devil could impersonate persons innocent of witchcraft and denied that evidence based on the claims of the afflicted that they could identify their tormentors' shapes should be admissible in court. He also branded the trial by sight and touch, which the magistrates had resorted to in the preliminary hearings, an inadmissible technique; its efficacy rested on the demonic power, Increase pointed out, and one using it compacted with the Devil. But the problem of what evidence was good remained. The free confessions of witches constituted solid grounds for conviction, Increase argued; there were still confessing witches in jail; and at the time he wrote the *Cases* he believed in their sincerity. But the evidence he found most reliable was the testimony of two credible witnesses, the sort of evidence required for conviction in any capital crime.[38]

This argument persuaded Phips, who trusted Increase and who also was impressed by the array of ministers who subscribed to the views expounded in the *Cases of Conscience*. The Governor dismissed the court on October 29, freed on bail many of the imprisoned, and urged the judges to find other ways of relieving the remaining prisoners. Early in January, a Court of Assize and General Jail Delivery met in Salem and, proceeding along the lines suggested by Mather, exonerated almost fifty accused, and condemned three of witchcraft. Lt. Governor Stoughton regarded these proceedings with disfavor and ordered the "speedy" execution of these three along with five others, who had been convicted through special judicial action. Phips, now seeing the need to act with dispatch, stayed all these judgments, and thereby "inraged" Stoughton who, filled with "passionate anger," left the bench of the court then sitting in Charleston. The special court charged with hearing the witch cases took up again the following year in April but there were no more convictions; and in May 1693 Phips granted a general pardon.[39]

At several times while the hysteria over the witches convulsed New England, Increase Mather had acted to restore sanity. He declared privately that it was better for the witches to escape detection than that one innocent person be punished. He urged the court not to admit spectral testimony as evidence; and he pointed out that the ordeal by sight and touch was no more reliable. On one occasion he was able to discourge a prominent citizen of Boston who was seeking a warrant from the magistrates against a local woman named by the Salem girls. The Boston gentleman had taken his daughter, suffering from an undiagnosed illness, to Salem for treatment by the girls. They obliged him by proclaiming that far from having an ordinary disease, his daughter was bewitched. Increase disagreed with this mode of treatment and berated the gentleman for forsaking the Lord in Boston in favor of the Devil in Salem. The magistrates in Boston may have received some advice from Increase too. The most admirable act, of course, was the advice given to the Governor in *Cases of Conscience*. Increase, more than anyone else, had stopped the whole grisly business.[40]

He did not do so out of scientific skepticism, or because he was a "liberal" in any sense, or because he doubted that witches were tormenting the people of Salem. Indeed, it was precisely because he entertained not a shred of scientific rationalism that he was able to argue that the methods of the court were unreliable. What he, and only a few others realized, was that the rationalists were the ones who had made the dreadful mistakes and perhaps had even shed the blood of the innocent. The court had proceeded on the assumptions that things in this world were what they appeared to be, that the world was orderly and reasonable and susceptible to understandings rooted in common sense. The court had denied that the Devil could take the shapes of men innocent of any compact with him and harm others, precisely because they believed such a situation could not be reconciled with God's government of the world. The judges saw chaos lurking in this doctrine of demonic power, the subversion of government, the "ruine" of society. There "would be no living in the World," if it were true, the court said. Reliance on spectral testimony was the fruit of the belief that the world conformed to men's reason, that things must be what they seemed, that appearances must be trusted. Increase, of course, could not accept it—he knew that appearance must not be confused with reality. Hence in his critique of the court's practices he returned to what he had found so fascinating in his studies of comets—the unpredictability and mystery in life.[41]

He could not rest his case on the simple assertion that the court's view of the demonic badly underestimated the Devil's power. Renewed demonstration was needed and in the *Cases* he provided it, along with a mass of data calculated once more to remind New England of the remarkable providences of the Lord. Therefore he filled the pages of the *Cases* with stories of men gifted with supernatural sight on Tuesdays and Fridays, but not on other days of the week, of fruit on plum and pear trees that shriveled up when the owners became mortally ill, of men who were offended by the stink of the corpses of men not yet dead but who died while apparently in good health a few days later, of an "inchanted pin" which could be run two inches into a man and not draw blood. This world did not begin to yield all of its secrets, these stories implied—not to natural philosophers, not to judges, not to ministers, nor to the shallow rationalists who denied the Lord because they could not see Him.[42]

The same set of emphases appeared in Increase's selections from the array of scientific and Christian examinations of witchcraft. His preferences in this vast literature, which he studied with his usual dedication, were for the Protestant commentators who, while repudiating Popish superstition, also recommended means for the detection of witches that conceded the full mystery of Providential and demonic power. The "Return" of the ministers of June 15, prescribing methods for the eradication of witchcraft, endorsed the techniques outlined by the great William Perkins and the Reverend Richard Bernard of Batcombe in

Somerset. Both Increase and Cotton Mather praised these authorities on several occasions, and explicitly drew from their works.[43]

What Increase found valuable in these writers were the precise
prescriptions for the identification and conviction of witches.
Both Perkins and Bernard despised the ancient folk practices;
no test by water nor by scalding for them (a suspect tossed into
water who floated was guilty, as was one who was burned by a
hot iron). And neither advised accepting spectral testimony for
conviction. Yet each approved devices for detecting demons that
seriously compromised seventeenth-century scientific views. Perkins and Bernard both agreed that charges of witchcraft by
neighbors should be grounds for investigation; and a single witch
in a family brought other members under suspicion, Perkins said,
because the practice of demonology could be taught. A curse by
one man of another, followed by some calamity, was also grounds
for suspicion that ought to be officially probed. And unusual
body marks such as those sucked by Satan and his demons should
bring a formal probe. A magistrate whose suspicions were aroused
by any of these "tests" ought to question the accused vigorously
and even to use torture if confessions were not forthcoming,
Perkins argued. Medical authorities, such as Dr. John Cotta, a
Northampton physician who had taken an A.B. and an M.A. at
Cambridge University and who was widely respected in the
seventeenth century, were also willing to accept "Common def-
amation" and family association as grounds for pursuing an
investigation of witches. But Cotta urged caution against credulous acceptance of rumor and the findings of unqualified examiners. And he left little doubt that what gave one expertise in
such examinations was not a knowledge of theology but medical
training. Grand juries, magistrates, town officials, ministers, all,
he wrote, should have resort to medical opinion before bringing
any charges. The problem in detection—he implied—lay as
much with the afflicted as with the accused. The problem was
first to identify the bewitched. Since the identification came
down to discriminating between natural disease and supernatural
possession, a physician ought to be the only one to attempt it. A
physician knew that disease sometimes produced horrible fits
and delirium that closely resembled the attacks experienced by
the bewitched. There were cases in medical records of dreadful
symptoms, which seemed to indicate witchcraft; and indeed some

suffers rolled, shrieked, and complained that they were being tortured by demons and witches. The credulous considered the symptoms and the claims of the afflicted and agreed that they were witnessing witchcraft. Then, according to Cotta, physicians took over and discovered the natural causes—in one case, a boy who endured such torments and complained of witches was found to be suffering with nothing more than a bad case of worms! And in another case, the true disorder was so mild as to be cured in the most prosaic fashion by a stay at the baths. Increase read Cotta, praised him, and ignored all such deflationary prescriptions. He felt no doubt that the witches were abroad in Salem and that the girls were what they claimed to be, bewitched. To be sure, the girls were deceived by the spectres which did not usually represent the persons they seemed to resemble; but the girls' testimony about their own sufferings was to be trusted. Increase knew, of course, that scientific rationalism suggested skepticism of the girls' statements about both themselves and others. Only the evidence of the senses, rationally construed, could help in the identification of those tortured by demons and spirits, Cotta said. Though the girls' "evidence" was simply not accessible to anyone else's senses and the girls' rational faculties had obviously been disordered by the horror of their experiences, Increase persisted in taking their claims seriously—on the grounds that the inaccessible "evidence" could indicate only one thing in this case, the operations of demonic forces. His opposition to the admission of spectral evidence in court arose not from scientific reasonableness, but from the traditional Christian belief in the Devil's capacity for trickery and deceit.[44]

Still, following the prescriptions of Perkins and Bernard, he was willing to approve of convictions based on the confessions of guilt by witches. Here again he departed from medical opinion as given by Cotta and Merci Casaubon, another seventeenth-century Cambridge scholar, whom he praised and ignored. Casaubon emphasized the connections between disease and such disorders as enthusiasm. Perkins had urged that convictions of witchcraft should be obtained on only two bases: one, the confessions of guilt of suspected witches, and the other, the testimony of at least two witnesses that the accused had made a league with the Devil, or had performed some recognized demonic practice.

Calling on the Devil for help constituted evidence, in Perkins' eyes, of a league; and divination, or a supposed conference with the Devil, who most likely appeared as a creature, say a cat or a mouse, provided evidence of the entertaining of a familiar spirit. These grounds satisfied Increase, though the scientific writers he professed to admire agreed that confessions under any condition should not be accepted, and implied that brains deluded by illness might seem to call on the Devil, or hold a conference with his agents.[45]

The doubts about the authenticity of the experience of the afflicted girls that medical opinion introduced shook Increase, but did not persuade him that the meaning of Salem could be explained by scientific rationalism. In the thirty years following, he often returned to the problems of understanding the invisible world, especially the difficulty of separating fancies produced by sickness from genuine apparitions. Though in these years he remained faithful to his first insights, he reread the medical commentators—Cotta and Casaubon—and studied fresh accounts of the appearance of demons and evil spirits. From these authorities he learned that melancholy, epilepsy, an imbalance of the humors, and disease, all might contribute to the delusions of men. But Increase refused to believe that such afflicted persons were suffering from physical disorders alone. Physicians might satisfy themselves that the afflicted were simply deluded, but he would not be so easily convinced; by reducing such cases to physical terms such explanations reduced the power of God. The facts were, he said, that in virtually every report he had received, the Devil had taken advantage of physical weakness to insert himself or his agents into the mind of the sick. The sufferers at Salem had even sometimes been deceived by devils impersonating good angels; the sick—Increase argued—were especially prone to the delusion that they were attended by angelical apparitions, while in fact only their imaginations were affected and then only by diabolical illusions. Increase did not raise the possibility that the Salem girls had only imagined that they were afflicted by the agents of the Devil. That experience had not been illusory.[46]

Increase put most of these truths into print in a book about angels published only five years after Salem.[47] He was not altogether comfortable with them because he knew that they did not remove suspicions that a terrible crime had been committed in the Salem episode. If delusions had physical origins, who was to say that some bodily disorder had not been at the root of the whole business? No one could deny that the judges had made use of spectral testimony at least in their pre-trial examinations; and Increase admitted that they had used it in the trials themselves. Minds disordered by disease—he conceded—sometimes "imagine that they see and hear wonderful things." Increase wrote this line in 1706, when he was clearly still troubled by what had happened almost fifteen years earlier. But by this time he had worked out a view of the actions of spirits that must have eased his mind. Sometime after 1694 he had come across *An Essay upon Reason, and the Nature of Spirits* by Richard Burthogge, an obscure English physician, who was deeply influenced by the Cambridge Platonists.[48] Increase recognized in Burthogge a "master in reasoning" and especially admired his argument that the apparitions of spirits, of which a witch's spectre was one type, did not affect the senses of men however much they seemed to, but struck directly into their imaginations. Burthogge did not "prove" this assertion, nor did Increase, though he pointed out that it agreed with the ancients who called apparitions "Phantasms" and "Images." But he hastened to add they are not "meer Phansies or Imaginations," they are "real." [49]

This was the line that Increase held to for the rest of his life. It was, of course, entirely compatible with all his instincts and his contention announced in *An Essay for the Recording of Illustrious Providences* that some subjects were not susceptible to scientific study. Science, after all, dealt with the evidence of the senses. But Increase, with the assistance of Burthogge, lifted witchcraft out of this realm. For if apparitions and spectres of of witches do not affect the senses but jump across them directly into the imagination, what could science tell men of Salem? In this world the invisible controlled the visible. Men in New England now had been reminded of this fact—that was one meaning of Salem.

There were other meanings. But it was not Increase who made them clear to the land. Cotton Mather took up that task in the *Wonders of the Invisible World*, written as the whole dreadful affair ended in the Fall of 1692.[50] Increase endorsed the book's version of what happened at Salem, and thereby joined his son in the gallery of villains who attempted to excuse the bloody trials. There is no need to defend either Mather for his part in the trials or in the public discussions that followed. Neither of course took part in the judicial proceedings, though Increase observed for himself the trial of George Burroughs who, he reported, was justly convicted on the evidence of two witnesses. And Increase, more than any other man, was responsible for stopping the prosecutions. But he defended the judges for acting according to their lights and he denied that the guilt of innocent blood hung over the land.

It is clear that in 1692 both Mathers *felt,* whatever they *believed* or said they believed, that the judges had made a horrible mistake in permitting the evidence of the spectres to be used against the accused. Both admitted that this testimony was received in court, but argued that it alone was never allowed to convict. They knew better and five years later Cotton Mather said so publicly: "Nevertheless, divers were condemned, against whom the chief evidence was founded in the spectral exhibitions." Increase made no such public confession.[51]

If the Mathers are guilty of not being honest with themselves and the court in time to save the lives of the innocent, they were sincere in proclaiming that the incursion of the witches was a judgment of God sent to punish the land for its violation of the covenant. Neither ever repudiated this interpretation of the outbreak; each continued to believe it as long as he lived. Cotton, who first announced it as he called for reform and repentance in the *Wonders,* has been charged with having "prostituted a magnificent conception of New England's destiny" to save "the face of a bigoted court."[52] Certainly New England's destiny did not shine more brightly as a result of the killing of the witches in Salem. Yet the fault was not the Mathers' who understood the whole miserable affair no more clearly than anyone else. Nor was Cotton Mather the first to conceive of the witches as a judgment of God on the land for its sins. The people in Salem Village reacted almost instinctively in a way that revealed their own convictions on the matter. They held fast days, and days of humiliation, all calculated to move the Lord to forgive them their sins and to lift His judgments. Shortly after these attempts the General Court proclaimed a general day of fasting throughout the colony with the same purposes in mind. Cotton Mather followed this lead in the *Wonders,* and a few years later others, even more profoundly convinced than he that the court had erred, did the same. Eighty-two-year-old John Higginson of nearby Salem Town in 1698 said simply that the witches had been sent by God as an affliction "for the Punishment of a declining People." [53]

Higginson wrote this in a preface to a book by the Reverend John Hale of Beverly. Long a student of witchcraft, Hale had questioned the accused at Salem and studied their judges and the evidence they accepted. He agreed with almost everyone else that the court had tried to do the right thing, but he, more clearly than anyone else, understood the extent of its failure. He did not shrink from saying that the innocent had been destroyed. Nor did he hesitate to say that not only had his generation proceeded on mistaken grounds against witches, but so had the founders. In summing up one meaning of Salem, Hale likened New England to Israel in the Wilderness punished by famine for a breach of the covenant made four hundred years before by the patriarchs. And he asked: "Why may not the Lord visit upon us the misguided zeal of our Predecessors about Witchcraft above forty years ago, even when that Generation is gathered to their fathers?" The children had also sinned according to Hale, and the larger meaning of the witchcraft at Salem lay in this long-standing judgment of God on the land for its sins.[54]

Although Increase Mather could not bring himself to speak so forthrightly, he remained as troubled as Hale was about what the crisis at Salem portended for New England. His generation had created the noble myth of the Puritans' errand into the wilderness. His generation had uncovered the meaning of New England, a magnificent enterprise typifying the purity of the millennium. That meaning had now apparently been seriously challenged by the incursion of the witches. Increase knew better: the corruption of New England had brought on the judgment of the witches and threatened its typological significance. In this knowledge of the evil abroad in the land, Increase dreaded the immediate future and yearned for the conversion of the elect and the coming Kingdom of God.

9

The Word in Boston

From his pulpit in the North Church, Increase Mather looked out upon a congregation of solid citizens. Some of Boston's best sat before him every Sabbath, merchants who regularly sent ships to London and the Levant, rich men with their handsome wives, officials of the town and the colony who professed that they wished only to serve God and their people. There were others too, less exalted men, not so well endowed with money and position, who worked with their hands in markets and workshops. A sprinkling of the poor also attended, and here and there a black face appeared.[1]

As their minister, Increase owed them much—not because they paid his salary but because he occupied an office created by God. His understanding of his responsibilities as one of the Lord's ambassadors did not differ from his colleagues' or from what his father before him had taken to be the minister's calling. Though Increase commented throughout his life upon the heavy burdens the clergy carried, what he emphasized most were the great opportunities the vocation offered and how the minister should strive to train himself to seize them. Any ordinary Church member could recite the duties of his calling—to convert the sinners and to nourish the faithful. And the qualifications necessary were well-accepted too. A minister must be a man of piety—he ought to be converted at least in the judgment of the Church—and he must have learning. Increase's insistence upon these standards was unvarying throughout his ministry, and by the most rigorous application of them, he was superbly qualified to lead his church. To lead them meant more than anything else to preach to them. The Word as preached was the most important component in his, or any other teacher's, ministry.[2]

The Word was clear to Increase and his friends in New England's pulpits; they were the heirs of a complex theology that embraced every aspect of man's relation to God. But how the Word appeared in their sermons was insensibly affected by the reality they experienced. Among New England's leaders, none surpassed Increase in the ability to sense the direction of social change. Increase did not usually comprehend the forces altering New England but he sensed the slightest slippage in the foundations laid by the fathers. Throughout his life Mather was prone to take any departure from ancient practice as evidence of declension; and objectively he knew that considerable political power had shifted from the devout to less pious men—in England as well as in America.

If these alterations dismayed him they also encouraged him, for the sin in customs and manners and the upheavals in Church and State indicated to the hopeful student of the prophecies that the end of the world was imminent. Hence the peculiar tensions in his preaching, tensions born of despair and hope. To the unconverted in his flock he must convey his sense of the passing of time; the day of grace for them was growing short. Once passed it would never return, and a man who went to his grave without the Spirit would never look upon Christ. To the saints he must point out the necessity of growing in grace and in making their callings sure. For a man might deceive himself as well as others as to his internal state, or he might be deceived by the Devil and his agents. The joy available to the converted in this world ought not to be despised either; a saint could enrich his own life and that of others if he worked and strived and labored.

In the first half of his ministry, Increase often spoke to his people of their souls in the context of New England's mission in the New World and of their responsibilities to the land. Their conversions aided the land, made it lovely in God's eyes. New England's fate was tied to their own, he reminded his church as he led them in the renewal of their covenant. He never exhausted this theme, nor did he repudiate the conjunction of regenerate souls and a prosperous land. But he came to make the connection infrequently in the final twenty-five years of his service to the North Church, as his belief in the redemptive powers of the whole nation weakened. During these last years, he fastened his hopes to the elect, their powers to please the Lord and to redeem the Church in the final days of history. Therefore he gave all his heart to the effort of saving souls. He had learned, he said, that God wanted him to convert the chosen, and to that noble task, he would give the remainder of his unclean and sinful life. Many of Increase's lamentations about his own sin were conventional Puritan expressions—but not lightly felt for all their conventionality. By his own gauge he had failed often, and now, in his last years, the final great opportunity to serve God had narrowed to the traditional objective of Protestant teaching, the saving of sinners. The objective was simple and straightforward and so was his preaching in its service. The language he chose, the texts he selected (largely from the New Testament rather than the Old Testament) all reveal the altering emphasis in his homiletics.[3]

In approaching sinners, Increase like Richard before him employed the conception of the covenant of grace in carefully limited ways. Like virtually all Puritan divines, he accepted the covenant theology as a description of one way in which God dealt with man. But his method of saving souls was not to outline the terms of the covenant in the hope of enticing a sinner to take them up. He did not lay out a contract to sinners with instructions that suggested that if man did his part, by believing with heart and mind in Christ, the Lord would do His with the gift of grace. Nor did he bedazzle his listeners with the insidious language of commerce—promises, seals, bargains—that suggested the equality of God and man in an Arminian universe.[4]

As Increase explained the covenant of grace, it offered not the terms of an agreement between equal parties, but provisions of total capitulation. It was not a contract in any sense familiar to his auditory. The relationship it described would hardly embolden sinners to claim God's favors by right; rather, the arrangement it suggested would be available only to those who accepted the cruel facts of predestination and the omnipotence of God.

The Lord of the covenant granted it, and entered it, as a master; man received it, took it up, as a "servant." [5] The man who received grace put on the "livery" of Christ.[6] The Lord Jesus is the "Captain of our Salvation," Increase told his listeners; we are His soldiers, and only because He has conscripted us, not because we have enlisted.[7] Increase chose these figures to exemplify man's dependence upon a power infinitely greater than himself. Men preferred their own righteousness to Christ's, he knew, and if they were to be saved they must learn that only the righteousness of Christ was sufficient. Hence the language of dependence which left no one doubting who was superior and who was inferior in the covenant.

If the covenant of grace in this preaching appears less as a business agreement than a treaty of unconditional surrender, the covenant of redemption between God the Father and Christ the Son appears in a conventional way in Increase's sermons. But the emphasis is not conventional. In fact, Increase's Christology supplied the central techniques in all his attempts to secure the salvation of souls. The Lord does not need you, Increase told his church. He saves some of you because it suits His pleasure. Of course, by your sin you have chosen to make your own salvation difficult for Him. In His wisdom He has decreed that the law must be satisfied; but since in your corruption you are helpless to satisfy its terms, He has chosen to accept the sacrifice of His Son as full payment. And if you—a sinner—can believe graciously in Christ, your salvation is assured.[8]

Phrased in this manner the covenant of redemption does not seem on first sight to reduce greatly a man's power to help himself, to enter the covenant of grace as an equal to a Lord who voluntarily binds Himself to fulfill its terms. But Increase not only never suggested that men enter the covenant of grace as equals, he "preached Christ" with such intensity as to suggest the total helplessness and dependence of man. Drawing on the warrior-Christ of Revelation was one way of emphasizing man's dependence and the Lord's command. Christ as a ruler over men, His subjects, is also a familiar figure in Increase's sermons. By "preaching Christ" Increase intended not only to nourish the faithful (this purpose was a favorite one in his sacramental meditations) but to bring sinners into the fold.[9]

Though in these sermons Increase described the unregenerate standing helpless before the conquering Christ, he did not attempt to frighten his listeners into conversion. He wished to reduce their pride and to destroy their confidence that they could find salvation in their own righteousness without the benefit of Christ's, but he realized that by itself fear could not permanently induce submissiveness in the soul. And therefore, though he sometimes pointed to the precariousness of the unregenerate state—for example, in this sentence that Jonathan Edwards must have pondered, "Thy soul is hanging over the mouth of hell by the rotten threat of a frail life: if that breaks, the devouring Gulf will swallow thee up for ever"—he did not often rely on sermons of sustained terror. What he had to establish for his sinful hearers was the fact that although Christ's human nature added to the efficacy of His sacrifice for the redemption of the elect, it in no way implied that a man could achieve as much for himself. Not surprisingly, Increase, in praising the magnificence of Christ's sacrifice, professed wonder that God as Christ should take on the nature of man with all the "sinless infirmities" of man. For in His human nature, Christ—like ordinary men—suffered fatigue, and He experienced hunger and thirst. He suffered abuse at the hands of men, finally enduring the torture of crucifixion. He did not sin Himself; in His human character He possessed a holiness above all created beings including, Increase Mather took pains to point out, angels. Yet He suffered and felt much as any man did. He lowered Himself, Increase Mather explained, to give His sacrifice power, and to demonstrate His enormous capacity to assume the guilt of men. Throughout His first appearance on earth, He remained essentially "one" with God the father, and yet in His human form, "personally distinct." [10]

The demonstration of Christ's divine authority and His power should have been easy to Increase, and yet by his emphasis he indicated that he anticipated most resistance from his listeners to this proposition. The trouble in persuading men lay in their pride, their self-regarding insistence that they could lift themselves by their own bootstraps. Lest they seize the fact of Christ's human nature to demand salvation from Him on their own deserts, Increase in sermon after sermon reminded them of how things were. Christ was not a mere man: He was not to be forced into a contract. He existed above men; His sacrifice stood *"above Reason"* and could not ever be fully comprehended in human terms.[11] The warrior-Christ may not have chosen to spill much blood, preferring to redeem men by sacrificing Himself, but He possessed the full powers of God, sitting with God as an equal. He was not a servant who stood before the throne, as men would on the Day of Judgment.[12]

Typology provided one technique of persuading men of the majesty and greatness of Christ. And Increase employed it to full advantage. In particular he drew on the types to illustrate the dimensions of Christ's sovereignty. God gave evidence of His intention to save men only through the mediation of Christ, Increase said, in His use of Moses. For only Moses ascended the mountain to receive the law; and Moses was a type of Christ. Later, the High Priest went into the Temple alone, again to forecast the sole mediation of Jesus. As for Christ's wisdom and power in the salvation of men—they appear in the great figures of the Old Testament who also were types of Christ. The names were familiar to every listener in the North Church—Solomon, Joshua, and David.[13]

Thus, Increase concluded, men should enter the covenant of grace as servants standing before their Lord—in full obedience and humility. Their rights in the covenant existed solely because of the rights conferred by Christ's testament for them. Every figure chosen by Increase to indicate the act establishing the covenanted relationship described Christ's supremacy and man's subordination. Men may claim the "right and title" to an inheritance, he said in a sermon on the Beatitudes, through a number of devices—gift, birth, adoption, and purchase. And in each case the "right and title" are founded in Christ's sacrifice. Believers receive the gift from the Lord; they are born of Christ and are His heirs; they are adopted by Christ, hence receive His inheritance; and finally, Christ's "purchase" by His sacrifice entitles them to Heaven. In a similar figure—though from commerce and not law—men are "debtors," Christ their "surety" who pays up for them.[14]

Increase Mather never conceived of grace entering the believer except as a free gift, as he said, a "favour of God." Nothing a man could do would earn it, for grace was not a "debt" to be paid over as "wages." Nor should a sinner ever believe he would come by it because of his misery, for grace was not a "mercy" to be bestowed only on the deserving. It might go to the unworthy should giving it suit God's pleasure. Increase also distinguished between grace and love, saying that though love was the "original grace," love might flourish between a variety of men. Love—he insisted—may exist between "equals," "inferiors," and "superiors," subjects and rulers, but "Grace imply's Superiority." In the understandings of men, God resembles a "king," and kings "single out whom they please to be their favourites. . . ." [15]

The way Increase presented the covenant of grace to his people reflected not only his understanding of Providential design but also his assumptions about the psychology of conversion. In preaching the covenant he told his listeners that they were "rebels" to be subdued by the conquering Christ. The intention of the "Plain, Practical Sermons" he preached to promote Conversion was to induce those in rebellion to surrender—to enter the covenant on the only terms possible, as abject captives of Christ. [16]

Increase wanted to affect his listeners—to convince them of their vile and weak characters—but he was not content simply to move them. Throughout his ministry he spoke slightingly of the "sermon-sick," those temporarily contrite because of something they heard in church, who soon fell back into the old, evil grooves of their lives. A minister who wished to bring saving faith to others had so to reduce their will to live that their only possibility of survival lay in the acceptance of the Holy Spirit. [17]

In these sermons calculated to convert, he explained the process of conversion in most men. He described this process as starkly and simply as he could without bending down to patronize his listeners. He did not presume to tell them how God and the Spirit operated; there was mystery in life, he said, and most of the Lord's ways were hidden to all but Himself. What a minister could do was to take men inside themselves. Here is the way you are, he said, what you think and feel, and why. Here are your hidden thoughts, your deceptions, your secret preferences. When you see what you really are—what dreadful, sinful shape you are in—you have a chance. Then you can seize the opportunity to strive after Christ, and to accept grace should He offer it.[18]

Sitting in the North Church, a listener learned that a man really has only one problem in this life, the problem of the self. Most men preferred their own righteousness to Christ's, Increase insisted; they hated to admit that they needed anyone else, so puffed up with pride were they. Looking at the prosperous, the complacent, and the rising entrepreneurs in front of him, Increase pointed out that pride led men to place serving themselves above glorifying God. Most men were "practical Atheists"; despite their professions of love for Christ, "the Farm or Merchandise has their hearts." To be converted they must renounce their idols, the creatures of the world, and most importantly they must deny the self, the chief idol of every sinner.[19]

Like other ministers in New England, Increase knew that his congregation contained men who professed an inability to believe. God had not given them faith, they said, and though they longed to believe, they could not. Toward these men Increase adopted a stern and unforgiving attitude. Your "cannot," he told them, is a "wilful cannot." You love yourselves and your lust. If you could be converted you would not accept it, you hate conversion because you enjoy your unbelief. Do not blame the Lord for your carnal will; you have chosen your own destruction.[20]

Still another sort of sinner listened too. The civil moral man who lacked capacity to examine himself rigorously and who therefore failed to detect his own corrupt spirit. This man thought that he loved Christ; he lived a life outwardly pure but inwardly he remained unclean. Far from loving Christ, he hated Him; his love was himself, and his sins.

Other kinds of listeners sat before Increase as he delivered the Word. Some felt an anxiety about their inner states, though they had long since experienced conversion and described it to the satisfaction of the Church. Some, also converted, felt little besides calm, though they had often heard the minister warn against security, as Puritans denoted the feeling of absolute certainty that one was saved. And still others approached despair, for they now recognized themselves as hypocrites in their teacher's description. Increase recognized them all and hoped that, however they appeared to the Church and to themselves, all possessed at least a seed of grace. A seed could grow into a mighty faith and so he watered it lovingly.

Growing in grace was never a formal doctrine in Puritan theology, but ministers had long preached as if it were. And none preached it more strenuously than Increase, who elaborated it throughout his sermons on conversion and the Christian life. A man with a particle of grace could do much for himself, and he must. He must pray for more, pray for help in leading a life in God's service. He must live with his attention fastened upon Christ: in every action however small—eating, drinking, sleeping, working—he must strive to serve Christ first, and himself second. Increase did not imagine that in thriving, bustling New England, men would go around with prayers constantly on their lips or even in their minds. Nor did he believe that a merchant selling a barrel of rum, or a cobbler driving a nail into a shoe, would act with the image of Christ dancing in his head. But there were godly ways of performing ordinary activities at work or at home, and there were ungodly ways too. A godly performance rested finally on the value men placed on the things they did. A merchant might make a sale, a cobbler might finish a shoe without ever a thought of the Lord, and do so in a holy frame of mind, if in his heart he genuinely felt that service to Christ was more important than anything else. It was this perspective that Increase strove to establish as he urged his church to live with their hearts fixed on Christ.[21]

Men should do much more if they were to grow in grace. They must examine themselves honestly. To attain the truth about oneself, examination of the heart should be conducted secretly, Increase said. Self-scrutiny often turned up sins even in the converted—conversion was always imperfect—and to remove them, Mather prescribed a "second conversion." The technique implied by this concept involved recapitulating much of the original process of conversion. But the second conversion did not affect the entire soul, at least not directly, but rather only the sinful part. A second conversion turned the believer away from a specific sin that had somehow survived in the new birth of the creature.[22]

All this concerned the inner life, assuredly the most important, vital part of any person's being. But the external often affected the internal, and a man must therefore watch his behavior in society. Indeed Mather felt the danger of the world so keenly that he preached a kind of moral separatism. The faithful—he urged —must isolate themselves from sinners; bad company corrupted good. Bad company fancied the creatures rather than Christ; bad company liked nothing better than to drag good men into the pit.[23]

But if a man succeeded in avoiding unregenerate men, if he prayed in the closet as well as in the meetinghouse, if he observed the law in all his dealings, if he worshipped, and if he wanted to believe, how could he know for certain that he was saved? Could he ever obtain assurance? Increase repeated the same answer throughout his ministry: a man could gain assurance, for grace was a discernible thing. Yet obtaining it was difficult, for grace was also a mysterious power not easily comprehended in human terms. And men might attain much in religion which would render them hopeful about their internal conditions and still remain in an unregenerate condition. They should recognize the melancholy truth that "There may be great Gifts where there is no grace."[24]

Knowledge of holy things ranked high among the gifts valued by most men, but as Increase repeatedly reported to his flock, the very Devil knew much about God and the sacrifice of Christ and yet hated the knowledge. Had not the Pharisees achieved a command of the Scriptures? By itself morality was a no more reliable guide to the inward condition of men. After all, a person might reform externally and conduct himself in the scrupulous observance of the law and remain internally a heathen. He might also perform the duties of religion, attending church regularly, keeping the Sabbath holy or at least visibly so; he might pray and take the sacraments. In the eyes of the Church he was a saint, always assuming that his description of his religious experience was taken to be genuine. But God saw into a man and recognized that the natural man had gone far, but not far enough. Hypocrites abounded in many lands, and at least a few survived in every church in New England. All these external signs— knowledge, morality, and worship—could be counterfeited; they could not provide the assurance that men craved.[25]

Nor could good feelings, or as Puritans said, good affections, give comfort. The "Sermon-Sick"—Mather's phrase—often developed strong feelings; even Herod was deeply affected by

John the Baptist for a short time. But a man might "desire" grace and still not be saved. As Increase read the parable, the Foolish Virgins wished for grace when they cried "Give us your Oil, our Lamps are gone out," but they did not receive grace. Such desires, passionate and affective as they were, often arose from unworthy motives, for carnal ends, for service of lusts, for the self, not for the Lord. To be sure, "Sincere desire is Grace," Increase admitted, but in saying so he was conceding nothing to good affections. This admission simply said that a man with grace would entertain holy affections.[26]

If behavior did not provide guidance, if good affections could not be trusted, how could a man discover the truth about himself? The answer Increase gave his church provided some comfort but only enough to reduce the tension a regenerate man ought to feel throughout his life. A man had no choice, Increase implied, but to look into himself in order to test his faith for grace at every step. Only his own inner experience could help him. The Church had to judge him by appearances; only he and the Lord could know if the Church judged rightly. A man in doubt about himself was a man who should hope, and more, a man who should strive to enrich his experience, to grow in grace. He should use every means at his disposal, including the instituted worship provided by the Church. A man who knows that he is in the unregenerate state should not come to the Lord's Supper, of course. But, Increase pointed out, there is a difference between a man's knowing that he is unconverted and having some doubts about it. Doubts and all, he should receive the sacrament, an ordinance designed by God to nourish the faith of communicants. And in a peculiar way doubts, Increase believed, and even fears of being a sinner, should give a man some ease. For a natural man did not fear his unholy state, he secretly reveled in it. He loved his indulgences; he loved himself and his sins.[27]

These themes did not distinguish Increase Mather's ordinary preaching from his father's or from that of most of his late seventeenth-century contemporaries. Richard Mather had never urged the need for a "second conversion," but he had demanded the same growth in grace that the phrase implied. Richard had recommended that "brotherly kindness" be extended to unregenerate men but he, no more than his son after him, intended that the godly should embrace the wicked with the love they gave to the brethren. And throughout their careers in the pulpit both men sought to help the saints separate themselves ecclesiastically as well as morally from sinners.[28]

Yet Increase Mather did not simply echo his father. Despite the shared values and spirit, he was different from his father and he expressed the difference—wittingly as well as unwittingly— in his approach to his church. Perhaps the most significant difference lay in his psychology of conversion. Unlike Richard Mather, Increase explained what his people must do and what they often did largely in terms of the will. If they succeeded in attaining faith it was because their wills had been broken, and if they remained unconverted it was because their wills had been permanently corrupted by sin. If they claimed they wanted to believe but could not, it was because they willed to remain unregenerate. The will was the center of corruption and had to be purified, and a man who thought he had been saved and wanted assurance would do well to examine it—and not to trust mere affections, however strong they seemed. Nor should he ever let his good works lead him into thinking he was saved. He must do them and constantly if he were to grow in grace, but by themselves they could only provide false assurance.[29]

If all this was explicit in Increase Mather's sermons, his difference from his father was even more a matter of mood, of stylistic and temperamental shading, than of doctrine. These differences arose from his altered perceptions of the world. He began as an American provincial—a son of the founders—who defined New England largely in terms of its errand, its redemptive power as a type of the New Jerusalem that would replace the carnal world in the millennium. But over the course of his ministry Increase had to face problems that did not exist for his father—scientific rationalism and an English State which after the Glorious Revolution required religious toleration in all its dominions. Even more pressing, and frightening, was the decay in piety that Increase, along with most of his generation of divines, perceived. All his impulses called for resistance to decay—for purity, for reform—and what did he face but the accommodations of Solomon Stoddard and the innovations of Brattle Street? [30]

These challenges and his defeats in meeting them stripped him of his confidence in New England as a redemptive force in history. To be sure, he admitted his disenchantment only occasionally, but the gradual evaporation of his corporate spirit is clear in the shift in his appeals from New England to the elect, to the mystical Israel of the types. Thus the types that fascinated him in the last twenty years of his ministry were those that anticipated mystical Israel, the chosen of the Lord. He recognized at least partially the change in his own mental framework. In a reflective preface to a collection of sermons issued in 1703, he said that he had learned that attempts to convert the elect were the best way of serving the Lord.[31] And from that time on he pledged himself to teaching his people about Christ, the power of His sacrifice, and the need for the faithful to gather in His Church.[32]

Suffusing all this preaching was an altered mood—openly antirational, obsessed by death, and profoundly alienated from the preoccupations of ordinary life. In these last twenty years of his life, Increase did sometimes make the ancient obeisances before the laws of nature in which he conceded that reason could fathom much about the ordinary workings of the world. He made such statements with conviction, but he also made it clear that he believed that ordinary workings were not very important—except, perhaps, for their capacity to lead men to value this world too highly. He continued to argue the willfullness of sinners, but he also began to note the unreliable character of reason as well. Some sinners may think that they love Christ, he said, but in fact they hate Him. The point of this assertion was to question the value of rational consciousness. Increase had never described entering the covenant of grace as a rational transaction but some of his earlier sermons on conversion had dealt with taking up the promises. Knowledge of Christ, he had stated in these early sermons, enable one to wish to believe, even if grace was to be given by God rather than earned by intellection. Such a proposition was not intended to imply that faith was simply an intellectual process; but it did imply that reason was in the process. But in his mood of the new century, he seemed to be most impressed with the unpredictable character of grace. He emphasized that God sometimes gave it to His enemies. The prime example was Paul, who had opposed the Lord with all his might. Still the Lord plucked him out of his corruption by a single gracious act.[33]

If Increase's preaching dwelt more on the mystery than on

the reasonableness of the covenant, it also concerned itself with death rather than life. Much that he reported about death had been familiar fare for years in Puritan homiletics—the putrefaction of the flesh in the grave and the resurrection of the body on the Day of Judgment, for example. Nor was there anything new in the attitudes he recommended to men approaching the ends of their lives. In one of the hackneyed—yet still powerful—figures of Puritan preaching, Increase reminded these men that they were sojourners in this life, pilgrims passing through the world to a glorious kingdom.[34]

By this metaphor he meant to suggest a habit of mind Protestant ministers had attempted to inculcate since the sixteenth century—one fixed on the state of the soul rather than the things of this world. Depending upon one's convictions about one's self, the figure could provide consolation or stimulate anxiety. To the believer who felt assured of his conversion, the notion of life as a pilgrimage brought the comfort that no matter what happened here on earth, his final destination would yield glorious bliss. To the sinner who felt guilt at his unregenerate state, the pilgrimage figure undoubtedly evoked different sentiments, among them the fear that his journey might end before he received grace. Increase Mather hoped these sermons would affect saints and sinners; certainly his sermons of his last years evince a desire to convert as well as to edify. Indeed the second purpose often gave way to the first, or even more commonly, edification was phrased in terms as capable of disturbing as of consoling.

The poor and the mean, for example, heard the happy news that they had as much chance of getting to Heaven as the rich and the well-born. They were also urged to cultivate contentment in their poverty, for had the Lord intended better things for them in this world they surely would have received them. Hard work in an honest calling, they were informed, was all the Lord expected from any man so far as getting a living was concerned. Of course the wicked frequently prospered; Increase Mather, like scores of divines before, was as quick to concede that unhappy situation as he was to sooth the poor with the prediction that justice would finally be done on the Day of Judgment.[35]

If this "consolation" sounds suspiciously like what the haves always say to the have-nots, it was no more removed from the conditions of ordinary life than his reassurance that the angels

were looking out for the Lord's chosen in this world. "Angelology" still claimed a place in natural philosophy early in the eighteenth century, but its hold was becoming precarious. Scientists
could find few uses for angels in the explanations they offered
of natural events, and Puritans retained Calvin's suspicion that
Catholic reliance on angelical offices was nothing more than ancient "superstition." This superstition, as Calvin argued, pos-
essed dangers of its own because its emphasis tended to obscure
the "glory of Christ." Increase Mather, who read Calvin and the
standard Protestant works on the subject, had no desire to shift
anyone's gaze from Christ, but in his preaching after the incursion of the witches at Salem, he stressed the manifold ways in
which spirits inserted themselves into men's lives. The Salem
episode was largley responsible for this emphasis as his references to it testify in his sermons on angels and demons. After
Salem, Increase could no more deny the importance of angels
than he could of witches.[36]

At the same time Increase carefully aligned himself with those
Puritan writers who denied any independent activity to angels
and who always presented them as mere instruments of an omnipotent God. Angels ought to be loved and honored, Increase told
his church; they were pure spirits who did much for the saints.
But whatever their service they must not be worshipped; such
reverence must be saved for God. It was well also to remember
that God no more needed angels than He did men; His reason
for using them was simply that it pleased Him to do so: "God's
will is the Reason of all Reasons." [37]

With these premises forcefully stated, Increase did not hesitate to tell his flock that angels did much for believers. Calvin
had professed uncertainty about the proposition that at birth
every saint had been assigned a guardian angel; Increase expressed no doubt that the Lord directed such superintendency
over His elect "from the Cradle to the Grave." This angelic
watch also included warnings and deliverances from evil. It was
true, Increase admitted, that angelic apparitions had virtually
ceased, although as Puritans in New England had learned
through the Salem experience, the Devil sometimes transformed
himself into an angel of light. But if angels were no longer to
be seen, they had ways of making themselves felt. Increase cited
angelic actions as a species of edification: angels—he told his

church—influenced men's thoughts and spirits. In the combat against Satan they served as "tutors" to the saints, inspiring them and presumably, though Increase was understandably vague on this point, instructing them as to what constituted good behavior.[38]

Because Mather knew that the way to enthusiasm lay close in claims of angelic intercession, he did not sound these themes as strongly as he did those pertaining to the service angels would give dead saints. Here, too, he betrayed his propensity to play down disappointments in this world in favor of the glories of the next. When you die, he told the saints in his church, your souls will not fall into the clutches of Satan. For the angels afford protection to the souls of dead saints, conveying them through the demonic hosts who lurk in the earth's atmosphere to the abode of Christ where eternal bliss awaits.[39]

Angelology furnished still another standard in the advice Mather gave on the conduct of life in this world. The tacit premise of all this preaching was that only the regenerate could attain a sanctified existence, although, of course, the unregenerate were commanded to try. Mather urged both sorts of men to model themselves on the angels, which was another way of saying that perfection was not to be found in this world. Lest this counsel escape inattentive ears, he spelled it out in terms used in ordinary life: to rich men he said, your wealth is all vanity, and your desire to leave your estates to your children is scandalous—so long as you regard their unconverted condition indifferently. You must work for your children's souls, not their substance. To men on the make, those rising retailers and craftsmen who filled Boston's shops, he delivered another uncompromising message: work in a calling can be overdone, especially if it carries you to violate the Sabbath, and if the voice of the creatures renders you deaf to the call of God. Such men, Increase pointed out, fell far short of the purity of the angels, whose example—though not to be equalled in Boston's counting-houses and shops or anywhere—might at least be imitated insofar as it led men to bend whatever they did and thought to the glory of God.[40]

Whether any of this genuinely edified or consoled anyone in the Second Church may be doubted; more likely, it left some uneasy and depressed. Increase Mather probably sensed a variety of responses in his church—he was at times an extraordinarily perceptive man. In any case he leavened these sermons of his last years with hope for sinners, by reminding them that God might save the most depraved of men. In giving grace to the Jews with the blood of Christ still "reeking on them," He demonstrated His mercy. To men who, though aware of God's power and mercy, remained fearful of their own unbelief, Mather spoke the reassuring words that perhaps their fears indicated that they did, in fact, believe.[41]

Mather did not often say in these sermons what he did elsewhere: men who lose this fear can degenerate into the complacent, the secure, and finally become so dead spiritually that they do not care one way or the other about their inner conditions. Mather had no wish to give assurance that paralyzed growth in grace. The tension that some in his flock felt was far better for them than complete assurance. There was still another reason that his preaching, which seemed to offer comfort, actually stimulated unease. These sermons reflected his own intensity, his growing inclination to reject this world and all its works. So as he offered the "comfort" that fear of unbelief was a good thing, he said almost simultaneously that only a few would be saved whatever they felt, and in spite of, not because of, their efforts. Relatively speaking, Heaven would be lightly populated—and justly so.[42]

He passed along these truths out of dissatisfaction with much of the preaching of his own day. In the last ten years of his life he remarked several times on the failure of many ministers even to mention Christ in their sermons. These preachers gave their listeners morality—not the doctrine of free grace—and the implication of their message was clearly that a man's own efforts were efficacious in his salvation. Increase deplored this old delusion and the language these Arminian ministers used to present it. So much of the new preaching affected a "Dramatic Style," he reported, and it brought "Playhouse Phrases into the Language of the Pulpit." Increase recognized the poison beneath the enameled language of the new homiletic mode, and he determined to oppose it with his own plain style. He had no "racy Notions" to provide, no sermons *gingling with Latin.*" What men needed was the righteousness of Christ, and they should learn too that they must obtain it soon.[43]

IO

Chiliasm

━━━━━━━━

Increase Mather attained the greatest intensity in his evangelical mood in his chiliasm, a belief that predictions of Christ's Second Coming described a literal return in time and space. Late in his life he reminded his church that he had long been a chiliast and that the first generation had contained men of similar views. This statement was accurate but it ignored the changes in his interest in the chiliad, in particular the developing fervor of his belief. His early speculations have an air of detachment; they seem deliberately to avoid raising hopes that the Kingdom of Christ would rise on the morrow with the sun. In 1666 when news of the great London fire reached Boston there were rumors in the city, as in England, that the end of the world was imminent, and that believers might hopefully scan the heavens for Christ descending with His angels. Increase took considerable pains to deflate these expectations. He did not sneer or scoff as he often did when he was uncertain of his ground, but simply observed that the time was not right and men must not expect too much just then.[1]

He also proved capable in these early years of his ministry of separating his chiliasm from his Christology. The purpose of

Increase's studies of Christ was the exaltation of Christ's power
and glory and sacrifice. Increase offered nothing original in his
views of Christ's offices, the divinity of His person, and His
equality with God, all topics which had been taken up hundreds
of times before in Protestant theology. What he argued supported his understanding of conversion, that is, that God did all
and that man deserved nothing. It was Christ's sacrifice—Increase emphasized—that fulfilled the terms of the covenant of
grace for man.[2]

By the early years of the eighteenth century, Increase was no
longer content to leave these propositions in their conventional
context. His celebration of Christ was no less fervent, his admiration and gratitude for Christ's sacrifice no less adoring, but
now besides these old categories, he began to invoke the figure
of Christ as judge at the end of history. This Christ who sepa-
rates the sheep from the goats on the Day of Judgment is the
great warrior-conqueror who in the final judgment slays His
enemies by sword and fire. Increase connected this interpretation
to the older Christology by returning to the circumstances of
Christ's own death—an event which he presented as a victory,
for the major part of Christ's conquering was accomplished, of
course, through His sacrifice of Himself. In this sense, Increase
pointed out, Samson is a type of Christ, for he killed more of
his enemies by dying than by living.[3]

The fact that Christ took a human form and suffered and died
had long raised the question of His relationship to God the
Father. Although Increase was not preaching to Unitarians skeptical of the Trinity, many of his later sermons on Christ assert
at length Christ's equality with God. The case he attempted to
make in these efforts was not that Christ's righteousness was
great enough to save men—that seemed indisputable—but that
Christ would participate in the final judgment. Thus he emphasized that the Book of Revelation described Christ sitting on the
throne with the Father. Sitting denoted "Honour and Power,"
and Christ would demonstrate His sovereignty when He with the
Father consigned some men to Heaven and others to Hell.[4]

Such sermons, preached with growing heat as the eighteenth
century advanced, fused his Christology and his chiliasm. They
also expressed his final acceptance of the failure of the New England of the national covenant. Occasionally in his last fifteen or

twenty years Increase did recall the land to its great mission and threatened it with destruction should it not repent and reform. These cries were little more than an old reflex asserting itself mechanically and hopelessly. His major concern had narrowed to the individual, to the saint awaiting the return of Christ.[5]

That return Increase believed to be "imminent." But unlike his son Cotton, he never tied his hopes to a particular date. Imminent, he explained on several occasions, meant sometime in the next few years; and one should not presume to calculate precisely the movement of the Lord.[6]

But the signs appeared so promising that in these last years of his life Increase attempted to do what he had been reluctant to undertake in 1666: the identification of events of his own day with the forecasts of Scripture. In his first treatise on eschatology, *The Mystery of Israel's Salvation*, Increase had denied that the world had entered into the final series of events inaugurating the millennium.[7] In that work, and for years afterwards, he had been preoccupied by Israel, largely because he saw in Israel a type of New England. As late as 1695 he had taken pains to explain that the conversion of Israel had not yet taken place. He was convinced it would—Paul had forecast this salvation in his declaration to the Romans that "all Israel shall be saved." This salvation would be national, embracing most Jews scattered all over the world. When it was accomplished Israel would occupy Canaan and the desert would bloom again.[8]

By 1710 Increase was saying publicly that perhaps this national conversion was under way. All the signs pointed toward the end of the reign of the Antichrist. Revolutions, wars, famine, and pestilence were breaking out all over Europe, and the Turkish Empire had fallen; in Danzig the plague had killed 40,000 people in the previous summer; and in Hamburg hundreds of Jews had recently been converted. Increase did not attempt to weave these events into a neat pattern but he could not help but ask, "May this be the *first Fruits* of a greater harvest shortly to follow?" Nine years later, shortly after his eightieth birthday, he published *Five Sermons* celebrating the power of supernatural grace and predicting that some of his listeners might hear the seventh trumpet sound which would signal the beginning of the millennium. These sermons repeated convictions of some sixty years standing: God chose whom He would regardless of merit, and their salvation is to be "wholly ascribed to the Grace of God." Men have "no Mind to believe, their *Wills* are set against believing on the Name of the Lord Jesus Christ." And Christ would have His Kingdom as God had Israel, which served as a "Type of the *Elect* of God." [9]

Working out a prophetical scheme that utilized the signs of his own day to "prove" the imminence of the end was beyond the powers of the eighty-year-old Increase. His son Cotton, who seems to have given him instruction in eschatological matters in these last years, would do that anyway. But the old man, though feeble, could still observe the European and the American events that anticipated the end. The sins of New England, the decay of the Protestant interest in the Palatinate, Saxony, Poland, and Hungary, all suggested the shakings of nations promised in Scripture as a preface to the entrance of Christ's Kingdom. [10]

These same years heard him gradually concede that his belief in corporate New England was misplaced. If the Lord had not exactly rejected the land, He no longer really depended upon it to serve Him. The Lord, of course, would preserve His Church, and individual churches in New England still retained their old purity. It was to these few remaining churches that Increase spoke, and to the elect in and out of them. Hence, whatever his speculations about the salvation of carnal Israel, it was mystical Israel that drew his major attention, the Israel that stood for God's chosen in all times and places. It was this interest in the elect that prompted him to give the simple sermons of his last years, quivering with piety and the expectation that Christ's return was near. [11]

Increase expressed this same set of concerns in still another way: in his laments that ministers more frequently than ever preached "morality" without ever mentioning Christ. These complaints which he made when he was an old man revealed his bewilderment at the growth of deism, and its associated heresies, Pelagianism, Arminianism, and Socinianism, in England. Because he never quite grasped the subtleties of these rational persuasions, he responded to them with the traditional claims that the true religion held truths reasonable enough and yet "above reason." Such assertions no longer satisfied even Boston's wits. Fortunately for Increase's peace of mind this fact largely escaped him. His son Cotton, was not spared so easily. [12]

There were still other difficulties for a minister who held to the simple message of Christ. The covenant theology in all of its ramifications had opened the way to enforce good behavior on a people. They could always be reminded of their compact with the Lord and the duties it imposed in attitude and behavior. A people who failed to honor their agreement could expect afflictions—the land would be scourged with famine, flood, droughts, wars, and sins. The way to recover from these judgments lay through repentance and reformation.[13]

This formula had served so well for so long that Increase could not quite ever give it up. Yet in his final years, he resorted to it infrequently, and then usually concentrated more closely on the fate of sinners than on the land. Thus in the sermon he preached shortly after the great fire of October 1711, which left a large section of Boston in ashes, he argued in the familiar style that the affliction had been sent as punishment for the people's sins. He said this with passion—"The People of *New England* have cause to be *Humbled and Humbled;* and Wo to *New-England,* if after all these things it shall be said of us, as 'twas of the Obstinate *Jews . . . They are not Humbled even to this Day; neither have they Feared.*" But he added a chiliastic prediction with equal intensity, "The Lord has threatned to punish Sinners with Fire: Thus has He threatned the world, and will e're long do it after such a tremendous manner, as like never was since the world began." The threat he detected was for the instruction of sinners—not the people in the national covenant.[14]

Increase did not offer this prophecy with a genial qualification that his listeners might believe it or not as they wished. He was not giving them opinion; indeed in these same years he began insisting that belief in the chiliad was a test of faith. If a man discovered that he believed in Christ's imminent return, he could take hope that he was one of the elect. Chiliasm was thereby added to one of the signs of conversion, and seemingly incorporated into the theory of assurance.[15]

No full-scale treatise developed these suggestions. They were not ideas which were intended to change doctrine so much as they were hints (perhaps not completely recognized in Increase's consciousness) which would lead the saints into primitive purity. To them Increase added one further exhortation: growth in grace would not only provide assurance of one's faith, it would secure a higher place in Heaven. There of course the saints would enjoy the ultimate glory of holy communion with Christ. There they would finally understand that true happiness lay in perfect holiness.[16]

In these hopes of which he spoke to his church in a series of sacramental meditations, Increase reached the emotional culmination of his chiliasm. He had always despised carnal chiliasts, those who prayed for Christ's coming for what it would add to their sensual lives in the New Jerusalem. Increase agreed with them that the saints of the millennium would have no worries about where their next meal was coming from. Nor would they suffer from disease or anxiety. The thousand years of Christ's reign would see a utopia brought down to earth. But the joys of these times would be nothing compared to those that would follow afterwards—when this earth was finally totally consumed and the faithful were carried up to the Third Heaven by the angels. In Heaven they would discover that "to be holy is to be happy."[17]

This vision of Increase's last years also subtly altered his Christology. In the seventeenth century Increase concentrated on Christ as the redeemer, the noble figure who sacrificed His life to save man. The sermons on this subject emphasized Christ's priestly, prophetical, and kingly offices in the traditional Puritan way. They paid particular attention to the relation of Christ's human to His divine nature, a matter Increase considered important because it provided an opportunity to make Christ's sacrifice comprehensible and moving to ordinary men. With this purpose in mind Increase carefully explained that Christ assumed a human nature in order that He might sympathize more deeply with men and so that His death would be "infinitely meritorious." Although this theme never disappeared from Increase's preaching, by the second decade of the eighteenth century he was saying less about Christ's redemption of man than of Christ's transformation of man's soul beyond the grave. To the figure of Christ as glorious savior, Increase now added the portrait of Christ the awesome judge, separating sheep from goats, who after dispensing His justice, prepared His sheep for the holiness that was the eternal happiness.[18]

While this formulation, repeated often in these final years, expressed Mather's *understanding* clearly, it conveyed only in part his *meaning*. His yearning for holiness implied a renunciation of this world. By this time his cravings for purity far exceeded the traditional exhortation to love the world with weaned affections. He wanted not to love the world at all; he wanted to separate himself not only from evil but from all that seemed ostensibly good by this world's standards. Release from the flesh, the creatures, and the world, he was telling his flock in the sermons of his last years, would be obtained sometime after all the vanities had been consumed in flames.

Like his father before him, Increase had often called for growth in grace—for the exercise of the virtues instilled by the Holy Spirit at conversion. He would never stop urging such growth. But the state of the soul that he saw in his visions of heaven far transcended anything described in these prosaic terms. No matter how rapid, growing in grace in this world could never carry one to the ultimate holiness, that is the happiness of communion with Christ. The joy of this Heavenly eternity could not be approached even in the ravishing movements of conversion, however many times conversion was repeated by men striving to improve the supernatural gift of grace. In any case, as Increase had long taught, good men who had been reared in religious families might not experience much feeling in their conversions. The truth was that no institution enjoyed on earth could forecast the bliss awaiting the redeemed in heaven—not conversion, or its repetition, or even the delights of the Lord's Supper.[19]

If Mather's renunciation of this world is clear in his celebration of Heavenly happiness, so also is it in his insistence that in the world of the resurrection, the soul would be reunited with the body. At first sight, Increase's belief in the resurrection of the body and his rejection of this world may seem paradoxical. One might assume that more than a remnant of sensuality lurks in the belief in the final unity of body and soul. Yet everything he preached on the subject in these last years contributed toward his rejection of nature in favor of the spirit. In these sermons his sensuality was transformed and in the process, he reaffirmed his profound faith in the absolute sovereignty of God.[20]

Puritan ministers facing congregations filled with men at once literal-minded and yet tough and commonsensical had long had to answer questions about the resurrection of bodies dead for thousands of years. How was it possible, ministers were asked, that bodies long since turned to dust could be put back into their original shapes? Like most ministers, Increase responded by reminding these questioners that nothing was beyond the omnipotence of God—and few things revealed it better than the joining of the old body to the soul. In a rough sense, the Lord acted in the way of a goldsmith making an old plate into a new one, Increase once said. He takes the old metal—the moldering corrupt body—and gives it new form. Although God imparts new qualities to the body, it remains "Materially and Substantially what it was before Death." It has eyes and ears, and flesh and bones—"wonderfully changed" to be sure—but still essentially the same as before death. Yet it feels no pain nor hunger; it is incorruptible and cannot die; it possesses perfect beauty; and most wonderful of all, though in glory it cannot equal Christ's, it attains a "Glory of the same Nature" and conforms to Christ.[21]

In this condition of glory the raised saint would resemble the angels, yet he would not be a spirit, but rather have a "spiritual body." Unlike several of the great theologians he respected so highly, Increase was never willing to concede that the glorified saint would ever enjoy perfect knowledge of God Himself—that claim, he implied, compromised the sovereignty of God. But the raised saint would understand completely what he saw of the Divine, and he would know perfect happiness.[22]

Increase never gave himself over completely to this vision. He became neither a mystic nor an Antinomian. And because he was talking to men of flesh and blood, men prone to follow the ways of sin, he did not urge them to renounce this world here and now. Although there is evidence that his own worship sometimes approached ecstasy, he continued even in his joy to recognize the need for controls on himself—and especially on others. Hence, even as he dreamed of glory, he used the vision to extort conformity to the law from his flock. Heaven, he told them, recognized differences in sanctification though, of course, it imputed Christ's righteousness equally to all. But men who strove after perfection on earth participated in the glory of Heaven in proportion to the grace they received on earth. Sanctification on earth was not the same for all, and those who grew in grace could expect that achievement here would eventually pay off there.[23]

Suffused with the sense that the opportunity for conversion

might soon pass with the end of the world, such statements carried a tacit recognition that New England had probably lost its opportunity to serve as a redemptive force in history. But Increase Mather did not openly renounce New England, the people of the land who were joined in the national covenant. He was too much the provincial, and if not quite mellow even at the close of his life, he was emotionally divided between his attachments to the people he had served and his enormous hunger for God. Increase may have died as Richard had before him, with his heart fixed on the godly all over the earth, but he and his generation had invented New England. That creation was their greatest gift to the world. But Increase Mather had wanted to leave behind much more, more indeed than New England could achieve; he had wanted to leave behind a people so pure that they might serve as a type of the glory at the end of the world. Had New England satisfied Mather's hopes, it would have escaped history. What he had learned was that not even a people on a divine errand could do that.

BOOK THREE

COTTON MATHER
(1663–1728)

PROPHECY

II

The Virtuous Epicure

Cotton Mather once asserted that "There is a vertuous Epicurism in Usefulness. No Epicure can swim in such Delights, as the Man that is *Useful* wherever he comes." To be useful, he explained, meant to labor, to strive and if necessary to struggle, but always to act. Even in repose a man should do something, at least he should pray strenuously in thanks for the opportunity to rest under the Lord's supervision. For those who enjoyed the assurance that they were among the chosen of God and for those who lacked it, Mather had the same advice: "*Be up* and be *doing.* Activity, Activity, in the Service of GOD, and His People; This will be most likely to be followed and rewarded with Triumphant Satisfactions." [1]

The nature of the satisfactions that Mather expected is not as clear as the nature of the utility which arose in action. His suspicion of the ordinary means of gratifying the senses found in food, drink, and sex is clear in the warning, "We must kill our lusts before they kill us," which he repeated throughout his life. Asceticism provided its own gratification for him as it has for Christians from the first century to the twentieth. He experienced the pleasures of denial from a very early age—he began fasting at fourteen—and he continued to pursue them until he died. But Mather had something more in mind than the joy in mortifying the flesh when he praised "vertuous epicurism." He was thinking of the indulgence of the emotions and the flesh that accompanied service and worship. Indulgence was not the word he would have chosen to describe the way he felt, but he clearly was physically rejuvenated, as well as emotionally delighted, in his work for the Lord. The groaning, fasting, panting, swooning, and the joy and raptures that enlivened his private conduct all testify to the gratification of the senses that marked his life of virtuous epicurism.[2]

That life was singularly free of the great outward activity that distinguished the careers of the first two generations of Mathers in America. Unlike his grandfather Richard, who crossed the Atlantic once, and his father Increase, who crossed it four times, Cotton never left New England. His longest journeys took him to nearby towns, Cambridge, Reading, Salem; and he rarely made even these short journeys. Richard Mather composed the magisterial *Cambridge Platform* for the Synod of 1647; Increase wrote the preface to the *Result* of the Synod of 1679, and presided over its second session; Cotton's major effort to establish a Cambridge synod, for which purpose he issued his *Proposals*, ended in a squabbling failure. Nor did he exercise the political power that his father held for a time, though he did write the statement of the rebels of 1689 in Massachusetts justifying the upheaval against Sir Edmund Andros. And if his attempt to introduce smallpox vaccination in Boston did not end in failure, neither was it a universally acclaimed success. Yet despite the fairly restricted limit of Cotton Mather's public activities, he honored his injunction to be up and doing.[3]

Indeed he rarely rested. His days were long and full of hard labor in his study and in his church and community. The average working day for him seems to have been about sixteen hours. The nights sometimes must have seen the exhausted man in rest, but at least several times a month he spent the night in a sleepless vigil, praying, beseeching his God for aid and comfort. He fasted even more frequently; his son, Samuel, estimated that he went without food for at least 450 days during his life; and these days too were given to strenuous prayer. The work of the ministry consumed most of his time; like his father, he preached several times a week and gave much of his scholarship to his sermons. Unlike Increase, Cotton Mather pursued the pastoral work of the ministry with dedication. This task carried him into the houses of families where he comforted the sick, catechized children, and preached to private meetings of neighborhood societies. Mather reveled in this side of the ministry as he did in all his work and in fact increased his responsibilities by encouraging the organization of neighborhood societies. He was in demand at their gatherings—young men in particular looked to him, asking his counsel, and seeking his preaching. For the most part, such responsibilities had to be met in daylight hours; in his spare time and in the long evenings Cotton Mather retreated to his study where he wrote the solid edification that filled his books and sermons. His output was staggering—it included over four hundred published works—and was all accomplished without the benefit of grants and leaves so indispensable to modern scholars. Much of his published work first took shape in the sermons he preached regularly on the Sabbath. But he also composed catechisms, translated Scriptures and creeds for Indians, and the Spanish in the West Indies (they were equally savage in his eyes); he wrote guides for the treatment of measles, a tract for midwives and mothers; he put together biographies and histories; he collected accounts of scientific curiosities and turned out several long philosophical treatises of his own. He also gave advice to ministers—one of his distinguished works, *Manuductio Ad Ministerium,* is a manual for candidates for the pulpit—but he also put his learning at the disposal of magistrates, schoolmasters, housewives, physicians, and children, though there is not much evidence that all these groups solicited his advice. Formal theology fascinated him, and he wrote dissertations on it too; one of the monuments to his knowledge of Biblical scholarship, the "Biblia Americana," still rests in six huge volumes of manuscript at the Massachusetts Historical Society. If his scholarship testifies to his interest in this world, his prophetical writings indicate his concern for the next one. On this subject too his productions ran into hundreds of pages.[4]

This impressive yield and this ceaseless activity astounded his contemporaries, as they have astounded students of Puritan history ever since. But neither Cotton Mather's contemporaries, nor ours, were to extend unreserved praise to him for his good works. Certainly he was respected, but the respect has always been grudgingly given except by his close friends and admirers; and for every expression of admiration there has been one of derogation. Thomas Prince, a friend, remarked on Mather's powers as a conversationalist, singling out for especial commendation his wit. Benjamin Franklin, no friend, playing on the same quality, transfixed Mather as "Silence Dogood" in the essays of that name published in the *New England Courant*. His family and friends found his early piety impressive—he wrote short prayers for his schoolmates—but a number of his peers, who anticipated the views of several twentieth-century historians, found this zeal cloying. His schoolmates thrashed him with their fists; S. E. Morison, repeating the beating in the pages of his history, rejoiced that the "young prig" got what he so richly deserved. Mather's learning, which sometimes decended to pedantry, was immense and was recognized by other intellectuals, but to the Quakers he was always, as they said, the New England school boy. And to a modern scholar who understood much of his thought, he was at best the source of a profound revulsion, or at worst of an upset stomach.[5]

If the variety of responses to Cotton Mather is bewildering, there is good cause—he was a bewildering man, capable of selfishness and selflessness, given both to excesses and to asceticism, noble and self-effacing at times, and petty and self-righteous at others. He could be the pleasant and witty gentleman to his friends, yet he distrusted wit and laughter. He despised and feared sexual gratification, but he married three times, fathered fifteen children, and enjoyed the marriage bed at least as late as his fifty-fifth year when his wife's illness forced celibacy upon him. He was an opponent of Quakers and Antinomianism, but his private worship approached enthusiasm.[6]

The outward circumstances of Cotton Mather's life help clarify some of the mystery that envelops his character and his behavior. He was born on February 12, 1663, the first of the nine children of Increase and Maria Cotton Mather. His mother was twenty-two years of age and his father almost twenty-four. Like his father, Cotton was a very bright boy, and he could read and write before he went to school. His early piety matched his intelligence apparently, for, as he later remembered, he prayed as soon as he could talk. In school he enjoyed the tutelage of one of the distinguished masters in New England, Ezekiel Cheever, who put him through the customary rigorous training in the learned languages. Cotton thrived on the diet of the classics and emerged when he was twelve to enter Harvard College. At this time his proficiency in Latin was so good that while listening to the Sabbath sermon, which was delivered in English, he could take notes on it in Latin. He wrote the customary Latin themes and letters, and he read Greek capably. He had only begun Hebrew grammar, however, but before he was fourteen he redeemed himself by acquiring the skill to write in it. Mather's progress at Harvard was depressingly rapid, and he was graduated in 1678, in his sixteenth year, after having consumed enormous numbers of books in most of the arts and sciences known to seventeenth-century scholars.[7]

Not even his father had expected this brilliant performance, but Cotton believed that as a Mather he could do no less. In fact in these years he had already acquired the habit of reproaching himself for his sloth, among other failures which threatened to prevent him from serving God in the tradition of his great ancestors who were never long out of his mind. His family pride shaped his character far more than his early studies or even Harvard, providing him with a standard to measure himself by and the spur to get as much out of himself as possible.[8]

He shared his father's estimation of Richard Mather and John Cotton. Although Increase had initially rejected his father's view of the Half-Way Covenant, he had changed his mind before Richard's death. And he had maintained a loving relation with his father even through the period of their disagreement. Cotton Mather was only six years old when Richard died and could not have known him well. His life of Richard Mather in the *Magnalia* leans heavily upon Increase's account of 1670 and adds nothing to it. What seems to have most impressed Cotton about his grandfather was not his contribution to ecclesiastical theory or to the practice of the New England churches, but the purity he displayed in leaving degenerate England in 1635. Richard stands as the noble exile, banished to the wilderness of America for his devotion to the true Church order. But his part in defining that order, while noted, receives only perfunctory praise.[9]

This restraint disappears in Cotton Mather's life of his maternal grandfather, John Cotton. Here again he follows a lead provided by Increase Mather, who said that John Cotton, more than any other man, gave New England its name and being. His son repeated this judgment, explaining that John Cotton had provided the most exact statement of the New England way left by the founders in his *The Keys of the Kingdom of Heaven*.[10] Yet Cotton Mather fully acknowledged that his grandfather had disagreed with the other ministers of New England in the Antinomian crisis. The paroxysms induced by these encounters with ministers, he wrote, assumed such proportions that Grandfather Cotton thought of leaving the Bay for another colony. Cotton Mather did not venture an opinion on where the truth lay in these conflicts among the ministers, preferring to emphasize that after all the struggles, they found it possible to unite in the expulsion of Anne Hutchinson and her friends.[11]

As important as the influence of his grandfather was in his conception of himself, it did not approach the power of his father's example for him. He saw his father as the great exponent of his grandfathers' system of Church polity. Increase had properly worked within the system largely devised before his birth. The only time that Increase challenged this system—in the controversy over the Half-Way Covenant—"He was in the wrong." Cotton Mather did not condemn his father for this deviation; his father had recovered his sense of proportion after all and had become a stout defender of the Synod of 1662 and all its works.[12]

On only a few other matters did the son pronounce the father in error. Increase had erred in defending persecution, but here too he had changed his mind. Increase had also published a book on the coming Kingdom of God without sufficiently studying all the evidence, Cotton believed. Yet on this issue as on all others, he eventually repaired his earlier mistakes. There were, however, differences between Increase and Cotton in ideas and attitudes, several of which remained unresolved at Increase's death. The father gave up on New England; the son did not. The father refused to concede supervisory powers over churches to ministerial associations; the son did not. The father sometimes hurt the son, for example, in 1690, when he proposed to remain in England.[13]

Cotton never publicly disagreed with his father on important issues. When the old man threatened to oppose a secessionist group in the North Church with what seemed too blunt a severity, Cotton found ways of softening his father's actions without directly resisting them. He did not manipulate the aged Increase; he diverted him, but in a spirit of love and with a desire to ease his father's final years. The last ten years of his father's life must have occasionally taxed Cotton's spirit. It is too simple a view to hold that one man ever dominated the other; each man possessed great moral and intellectual strength and respected the other's powers. Yet there is evidence that on several crucial issues the son deferred to the father. For example, although Cotton respected Increase's scholarship on the coming conversion of Israel and publicly defended it, he confessed after his father's death that he had always had serious doubts about its conclusions. Shortly after Increase died, Cotton wrote of a central argument in Increase's interpretation of the fate of Israel, "I find it will never do. Tis unscriptural." But Cotton had not even as much as hinted of his reservations to the public while his father lived; rather he had "Laboured all I could for my Life to acquiesce in the opinion." He had, however, argued—not quarreled—with Increase about the matter. His respect and admiration for his father surely helped suppress his differences— in the last years of Increase's life, a respect that is clear in Cotton's customary references to his aged parent as "Adoni Avi," the patriarch. Most of the time these two Mathers looked at the world as if they had but one pair of eyes between them.[14]

For all Increase's direct influence on Cotton's attitudes and ideas, he affected his son most of all by his example—by what he was, a member of a great family that had attained distinction in the service of the Lord. It was in this way that Cotton felt his father's force, and the power of his grandfathers, Cotton and Mather. They more than anyone else, he thought, had made New England what it still claimed to be—a model of godliness. As he once confessed, "I were a very degenerate person, if I should not be touched with an Ambition, to be a Servant of this now famous Countrey, which my two Grand-fathers COTTON and MATHER had so considerable a stroke in the first planting of; and for the preservation whereof my Father, hath been so far Exposed." Giving less than his best in the service of God would be a

"Reproach" and a "Blemish" on the Mather name. The knowledge of what was required of him increased his anxiety, and if ever a man was anxious it was Cotton Mather.[15]

If Mather's piety was greater than most—in part because his familial heritage was unusual—its sources were similar to that of other Puritans. Mather lived in a world of ideas where God reigned, and man, diseased with sin, craved His dispensation. Only the Lord could save man, and the Lord made His decisions about man's fate without consulting anyone. Man, helpless and sinful, did not deserve to be consulted. Evoking a world of uncertainty, these ideas engendered an anxiety in him that could be eased only by a conviction that he was somehow acceptable to God.

Cotton Mather never questioned the view of himself and of the world that these conceptions imposed. His description of himself would have satisfied any Puritan, for any Puritan would have recognized himself in it. All his life Cotton Mather accused himself of sin that rendered him indescribably filthy. He was a "vile" sinner, "feeble and worthless," suffering, he once told the Lord, from spiritual "diseases . . . so complicated, that I am not able so much as distinctly to mention them unto thee; much less can I remedy them." He employed these terms in describing himself when he was an adolescent, apparently in the midst of an agonizing crisis of the soul. He survived this crisis and though years later he sometimes appeared complacent, he never lost his sense of sin. As an old man he confessed in a characteristic way his "Humiliation for my . . . Miscarriages" and called himself "as tempted a Man, as any in the World." [16]

Mather's anxiety arose when he found himself unable always to bring his behavior and his state of mind into harmony with his ideas. A true Christian, he knew, was humble—not swelled with pride. A true Christian did not prize this world: he was to live in it and he was to give his best, but at the same time the attention of his heart should be fastened upon God. Mather was pained by his failure to live up to this ideal. In his pride and in his sensuality, he disappointed both the Lord and himself. Falling short of the divine imperative rendered him ugly in the sight of God; truly Cotton Mather was a filthy creature.[17]

This conception of himself must have helped induce the massive anxiety he endured for so long. From an early age Cotton

Mather had learned of his sin; and by the time he reached maturity he did not have to be reminded of it, though he reminded himself often. After a few years of life he seems not to have required the specific accusation of sin to experience the unease; it probably was always there—a part of his consciousness or not far from it. The most trivial incident could set his fears in motion. When he had a toothache he asked: "Have I not sinned with my *Teeth?* How? By sinful, graceless excessive *Eating*. And by evil Speeches, for there are *Literae dentales* used in them." [18]

This anxiety, perhaps more than anything else, made his psyche what it was. His anxiety was a psychological component of virtuous epicurism: to satisfy it, which meant simply to keep it under sufficient control to prevent a breakdown, he could take no rest. Whatever he did in his outward life, from preaching to rearing his children and performing essential bodily functions, had to be done with his entire being fixed on God. He did not create this frame of mind, of course; it had been described in Puritan divinity for a century. But as much as any Puritan divine of his generation, he felt compelled to honor it in the conduct of his life. The result was that his inner life was marked by tension that few men find tolerable for long. [19]

One side of this tension gave Cotton Mather an extraordinary sensitivity to the moods and opinions of others. Indeed he, better than anyone of his generation, sensed the cultural shifts of his time, though he never approached a full comprehension of their roots. A minister of his eminence did not often hear criticism of himself and his religion with his own ears. To gain information about popular attitudes, he had to rely on a few close friends and on his own ability to detect the hidden meanings in the casual comments of his parishioners. His task appeared much less difficult after the *Boston News Letter* began publishing in 1704; but much of importance to a minister interested in the life of religion escaped the public press. Mather's sensibilities quivered constantly, receiving the impulses of religious vitality and decay as they were expressed by people of all ages and ranks. He was especially attuned to adolescents; he recognized their concern over fine clothes; he sensed that making public declarations of their faith was especially painful for them. Youth was a time of "bashfulness," and the jibes by the Ishmaels

of Boston stung the pious.[20] He discovered too that the very
bearing of the godly—their sober faces, their grave carriage—
depressed young people, who tended to equate piety with unhappiness. Mather's characterization of saintly deportment as
"Comely gravity," and his assertion that "The *Heart* may be
Pleasant when, the *Face* is not *Airy*," may have been clumsy and
unsatisfying, but it at least contained a recognition denied to
most ministers of the distress felt by many of the young.[21]

The young, we know today, register, and sometimes create,
many of the impulses for change in society. In Puritan New
England if youth did not enjoy so full a creative part, they
expressed and felt change. Their desire for fashionable clothes,
their scoffing at religion and their sensitivity to scorn, their
perception of the variety of attitudes towards Christianity in
New England, were expressions of a larger cultural change. Cotton Mather's social senses served him well, and he recognized in
these apparently unrelated phenomena the growth of a culture
increasingly prone to take its values and direction from sources
other than the churches.

The other side of Mather's inner tension gave his introspection
its relentless analytical character. The question for the student
of his psyche is how much self-knowledge did he attain? The
answer seems shrouded in the incessant examinations, usually
followed by accusations of himself, in his *Diary*. Much of the
Diary seems spontaneous, a faithful reflection of the moods and
ideas it relays. Yet we know that Mather rewrote large portions
of it with the avowed intention of providing instruction for his
son Samuel, and for any other of his children who might survive
to study it. In his revisions he sometimes may have heightened
his private experiences, and yet on the whole these revised passages bear a striking resemblance to the unrevised.[22]

There is much of the conventional Puritan in the *Diary* and in
his autobiographical comments scattered throughout his other
works. The classic Puritan failures, idleness and waste, appear
occasionally; but they did not contribute greatly to his unease.
He knew that he was rarely idle, that the little money he
earned was not squandered; and he indulged in no false contrition on those scores. But he did recognize in himself many of
the habits of mind that Christians had always considered evil.

Although Mather's recitation of his sins sometimes takes on a ritualistic cast, the substance of his comments indicates that he saw deeply into himself and even perceived many of his true motives and his capacity for self-deception. He often thanked God for his achievements in the world, for the size of his library, for the large number of his publications; and he recognized the pride he took in these gifts. The sin of pride was almost always on his list of failures: his dissatisfaction with himself is clear in his contemptuous references to his "affectations in Grandeur, and Inclinations to be thought Somebody. . . ." To be thought somebody! He was somebody and knew it and wanted to be even more than he was. He knew this too and condemned himself for his desire. His despair for himself was expressed in his recognition of his envy of the success of others. It was his "Disposition," he said, "to envy the Favours of God unto other Men." There is honesty in his reproaches—he was jealous of the possessions and achievements of others; he felt that he had so little, they so much. He even envied the triumphs of his friends in the pulpit. These feelings were unworthy and he despised himself for them. Even as he did, he did not quite transcend them in the recognition of his own pride and pettiness, for while he castigated himself he still branded the pulpit performances he resented as "jejune." [23]

There was honesty, and considerable sophistication, in Cotton's awareness of the complexity of his regard for his children. He placed great hopes in his eldest son, Increase, named for his own father. But this unhappily named boy gave no sign of following in the great tradition of the family. He shirked his studies, failed as an apprentice in a countinghouse and as a seaman, and, worst of all, showed little evidence of piety. The distress Cotton Mather felt at these deficiencies became despair when "an Harlot big with a Bastard" laid "her Belly" to his "poor Son Cresy." Prayer and exhortation left the boy cold, and Cotton finally steeled himself to renounce him after the boy had taken to running with a gang that rioted and fought over the streets of Boston. Cotton could not hold to this resolve long and took his son back—unrepentant and apparently confirmed in his evil ways. In moments of clarity and painful introspection, Cotton confessed that a part of his grief and anger at his son arose from his disappointment of a desire for "Reputation and Satisfaction" that "a Child of more honourable Behaviour might bring unto me." Honesty compelled him to see that not even love for a son was disinterested; regard for the self polluted one of the best of the emotions. Cotton attained the same knowledge in the midst of his torment over his son, Samuel, sick with smallpox in 1721. Why—he asked—did he love his son so deeply? Wasn't there selfishness in this love too? The answer was clear: "I see *my Image* on my Children." [24]

Mather recognized his sensuality as well as his pride, but his awareness of his sexual impulses did not relieve the guilt he felt at their indulgence. Indeed the knowledge of the sensual self must have been secured only at the cost of considerable pain. To be sure, long before Cotton Mather's birth Puritan theologians had in their accommodation of nature and grace attained a remarkable frankness in dealing with the claims of the flesh. But their candid discussions of sex did not imply detachment or neutrality toward the subject. They acknowledged the necessity of the physical side of life and its legality but they did not extol the joys of the flesh even when legality was not an issue. They simply said that sexual intercourse was essential to man and lawful in marriage. Their openness in treating sexual issues was most apparent when they detailed the danger of the physical side of life and when they condemned fornication and deviance.[25]

Despite Puritans' frank discussions they felt uneasiness, even guilt, over lawful sexual intercourse, in part because they distrusted the body and in part because they recognized the capacity of sex to undermine spirituality. Puritan divines did not quite concede that the body was a part of nature in the way that the other creatures were. They did not ordinarily distrust nature as a source of truth and beauty when it was considered as a part of God's design (which included a higher and better source of truth, beauty, and enjoyment in the Scriptures). Though the body was a part of nature, it took its place in a special category, a category apart, because the body was so often a source of sin. More than the other creatures it was prone to degeneration and extraordinarily susceptible to corruption. The adjectives most commonly applied to it in Puritan discourse were "vile," "filthy," and "unclean." Jonathan Mitchell summed up the attitude implicit in these terms with his denunciation of "the old Crazy Rotten house of the body." [26]

Despite these attacks and despite the belief that the life of the senses could never match the life of the spirit, Puritans did not reject the flesh. Accept the creatures, they urged, including yourself and your need for food, drink, and sex—and enjoy the satisfaction of the need. But the satisfaction must be tempered, not just by a moderation, but by the knowledge that it is inferior to the experience of the spirit. Indeed, satisfaction of physical requirements, though good and necessary in itself, is intimately linked to human weakness and to sin.

Cotton Mather shared these complex attitudes. His response to physical urges was divided, as he was divided on so much else —he wanted gratification and he craved denial. Every part of his own physical apparatus fascinated him, and every part had—in his mind—to be related to the spirit. The pain in his teeth and the headaches that he endured throughout his life reminded him of his sin; the act of excretion humiliated him and put him to ruminating on the abased condition of man in his vile body. He accepted the contention of Puritan eschatologists that the body would be reunited with the soul on the Day of Judgment but hedged his agreement in a way that reflected his revulsion from the physical side of life. All of his writings on this matter reveal that for him (and for others) the resurrected body was not really a body at all. In the millennial state, it required neither food nor sleep; it felt no pain nor experienced disease; it had no senses; it was incorruptible; and it was completely under the control of the spirit.[27]

Yet he agreed that marriage and the marriage bed were among the good things of life, and as a young man he prayed that God would give him a spouse. His prayers were not free of reservations, however; among them the fears that marriage might carry him out of the service of the Lord and that his appeals might be animated by "misguided appetites." A few days after he entered these thoughts in his *Diary*, he had managed to suppress his unease so far as to plead with God to give His approval with the reminder "that Marriage was His Ordinance; and that He had promised, no *good* Thing should be withheld from mee." [28]

Pleading on the grounds of legality—"Marriage was His Ordinance"—could not permanently remove the sexual anxiety that he experienced throughout his life. At the age of fifty-five, when he had been widowed twice and married for the third time, two years before, he put the dilemma he felt in two classic sentences.

The first expressed his distaste for the physical: "The Diseases of my soul are not cured until I arrive to the most unspotted Chastitie and Puritie." The second, his uneasy delight in it: "I do not apprehend, that Heaven requires me uterlie to lay aside my fondness for my lovelie Consort." There are hints in these and other comments that the sexual strain he experienced did not always focus on his partner in his marriage bed, for in this entry he alludes to his "former pollutions" and he warns himself to "abhor" the thought of any person save his wife. And finally, in one last admonition, he resolved that he must be temperate in his "conversation" with her.[29]

Mather understood himself better than he did others. With the exception of his self-knowledge, the range of his psychological awareness did not extend beyond conventional Puritan limits. In fact the strength of his perception into himself may have suppressed a more generous understanding of others. In those long hours of introspection, the brooding over pride, the lonely struggles with the demonic which he felt striving to capture his soul, he came to know terror, evil, and guilt better than he knew serenity, good, and innocence. He came to suspect the worst in himself—the tainted character of his love for his children is only one example—and the worst in others. He could not see that the men who left his church in 1714 to found the New North acted for the sake of convenience, even though he had to admit that the old North's meetinghouse was overcrowded. They were a "Proud Crue" and it was their pride, their desire for pews, that carried them away.[30] When a group of his relatives attempted to collect debts from him, they did so not simply to secure their money, but to "ruine" him.[31] The Society for the Propagation of the Gospel in Foreign Parts did not send missionaries to the Indians out of a policy of spreading the faith, but because it wished to subvert the Church order of New England. He saw enemies everywhere: there were those who were bent to bring him down when he was a young man, and by the time he reached old age they swarmed around him like jackals around a wounded lion. They hated him and they had always hated him.[32]

All the tension of introspection converged on the problem of his faith and his life in the sinful world. His chief concern about himself had to be what it was for every Puritan, the state of his soul. In the language of theology, the problem concerned assurance. How could he know that he, led by the Devil, had not deluded himself in his conversion, wracking though it was? How could he know that he was dear to the Lord? Mather accepted intellectually the doctrine of the perseverance of the saints—once chosen, a man could be certain that he would not be cast aside by the Lord. But though Mather gained comfort from this doctrine, he sometimes doubted that it applied in his own case, just as he sometimes doubted the fact of his own conversion. Throughout his life he suffered from "deadness," an inability to feel anything about religion, love or hatred of God. We may suspect that these periods arrived as a result of emotional exhaustion induced by strenuous worship, but for Mather they were evidence of his sin. His periods of doubt, which he called atheism, were even more frightening. They did not occur often, but when he was free of them he sometimes found himself questioning the Trinity and even the very meaning of life itself. He once compared man to "a *Bubble* rising on the Top of the Water, and there taking a Dance or two, perhaps with some lesser ones about it. In a *moment,* it bursts asunder, and immediately the Bubble shrinks into its first Principles." [33] These were desperate thoughts, born of a precarious, yet intense, faith. Mather sometimes fell into self-righteousness, but even in that state of mind he was rarely complacent. Faith was too fragile a thing for slackness; zealous as he often was, he knew in his marrow that as a sinful creature he could not sustain it alone. He needed the grace of God: without it, he would burst and shrink to first principles like the bubble rising to the top of the water.[34]

Mather rarely found assurance quietly. Like so many of the emotions in his life, its comfort appeared only through vigorous exercise. Whatever the forms his devotions took, and there were many ranging through secret prayers, sacramental meditations, ejaculations, vigils, psalm singing, and daily spiritualizing, they all were marked by a physical strain, emotional pressure, and zealousness. Cotton Mather was incapable of contemplative worship. He sought this intensity in his worship, probably because he sensed that greater satisfactions would emerge from it. For most of his life he set aside six periods in his day in which to worship; four years before his death he increased this number to seven. Most of these devotions found him in an attitude of beseeching, begging, and pleading with all the intensity he could muster. Sometimes he stretched himself prone on the floor of his study; and many times he went without food and sleep. This regime did not satisfy him as he grew older and in his fortieth year he began his midnight vigils, all night assaults on the Lord, filled with prayer and hymns. These planned devotions were only one side of his worship: he also relied on spontaneous prayers, ejaculations in Puritan terminology, which saw him dart brief appeals to God for His blessings and His aid. The sight of almost any person or of any event could evoke an ejaculatory prayer. A tall man brought, "Lord, give that Man, *High Attainments* in Christianity: lett him fear God, *above many;*" a lame Man, "Lord, help that Man to *walk uprightly.*" Short men, ministers, merchants, the young, the old, a man carrying a package, a man on horseback, and thousands of others (by Mather's count) received the benefits of his prayers. Awareness of the condition of his own mind also produced ejaculations. When he detected a proud thought in himself, he pleaded for abasement; when he experienced an impure one, he asked for a holy one. To the reader of his *Diary* the list appears endless. Mather also seems never to have entered a room without praying that he might not leave it until the people there had received some benefit from exposure to him. One other technique was the spiritualization of ordinary objects, extracting the holy significance from the creatures.[35]

The result of this nearly constant application was an intense, and uneven, religious life. He obtained frequent "particular faiths," promises by God that a particular desire would be granted in the future. A particular faith was not given to everyone, rather "but *here* and *there*, but *now* and *then*, unto those whom a *Sovereign* GOD shall Please to Favour with it." Mather received many; as he described the experience after strenuous prayer, "The Impression is born in upon his mind, with as clear a Light, and as full a Force, as if it were from Heaven *Anglically*, and even *Articulately* declared unto him." He also experienced the crucifixion of Christ; he had interviews with angels. In such experiences his joy was "unuterable," he knew raptures and afflatus. The most gratifying climax of all occurred when he re-experienced his conversion, an event that was repeated many times in his secret devotions. After humbling himself, he passed through the familiar stages of the conversion process which ended with the assurance that he was one of the Lord's chosen.[36]

To sustain his assurance, he had to act—inwardly and outwardly. Anxiety, he discovered from experience, could be endured only if it gained release. Hence the relentless activity of his inner and outer life and his attempts to extract meaning from the most trifling events. For years he suffered from a cough when he rose in the morning. The phlegm that he raised in his throat reminded him that he should seek to cast out his lusts. The "Evacuations of Nature" reminded him of man's resemblance to the brutes and he resolved to think "abasing" thoughts whenever he relieved himself. When he suffered from a headache the barrenness of his head and of his pious activity troubled him. The usual resolve to improve himself followed. Snuffing out a candle put him to thinking of how much brighter men might shine in the service of the Lord. The theft of his papers filled him with thoughts of his approaching death. These same occurrences, or ones similar to them, stimulated him to shouting ejaculatory prayers to Heaven.[37]

Just as the ordinary acts of his life had to be examined for their Providential significance, and spiritualized, so also did the events around him. Most, of course, were beyond his control, a death, a fire, a theft, a drought, a storm, a depression in trade. Yet he felt compelled to draw out their religious significance. The longer he did this the greater the conviction was that he could little affect the circumstances of life in New England.[38]

Cotton Mather's personality was complete in its essentials by the time he reached his twentieth year. It deepened, and developed slowly after that. It remained one that required mental and emotional exercise; it thrived on activity.

The most important line of psychological development in Mather's life followed the road of Christian ascetics. There was a kind of voluptuousness in Cotton Mather's immersion in denial, sacrifice, and finally as an old man, in martyrdom. As he grew in fame as a Puritan divine, he increasingly found fulfillment in humility, especially in the imitation of Christ. In his moments of ecstasy he demanded abasement and dreamed of being swallowed by Christ. As he grew older, his dreams of this union in the Kingdom of God permeated his entire psyche and provided the framework for his greatest satisfactions.[39]

This personality leaned on, as it reinforced, Cotton Mather's intellectual development. His propensity to deny himself, to sacrifice what was dearest to him filled the theory of worship that he elaborated for all the chosen of God. His own feverish piety, and all the techniques he devised to nourish it, animated his revivalistic designs and his plans for the active life of doing good. His abasement of himself and his craving for union with Christ inspired his dream of the New Jerusalem and gave his study of the prophecies its awful urgency. Mather's inclination was always to translate his private experience into his ideas, especially when that experience bore on worship and religious psychology. But little of his thought on any question escaped the impress of his life. This relationship helps explain the emotion that his ideas carried. Cotton Mather experienced the world passionately; he could not have divorced his ideas from that experience had he tried. The history of his life indicates that he did not try.

Christian Union and the Meaning of New England

By the time Cotton Mather came to maturity the jeremiad was a well established convention. As a youth he was nourished by its sadness, its feverish appeals to the people of the Bay to honor the objectives of the founders, its claims that New England had been undertaken in the service of God. He accepted as fact that the land and the people had a special character; and if he never tired of castigating the people for their failures, he never flagged in his defense of them as the soberest and the best in an imperfect world. This divided attitude toward his country reflected ambivalence within the jeremiad which, if it were to remain true to itself, was bound to maintain that God had sifted an entire people for the choice seed with which to plant the New England colonies. From this seed a lovely plant sprouted whose delectable fruits were the Congregationalist churches. A good people watered this plant, and the State, a gentle careful gardener, drove off pests and blight in the form of Antinomians and Anglicans. But now this noble vine threatened to turn itself into a poisonous weed with the rank foliage of a backsliding people and indifferent magistrates. The second generation, including Increase Mather, used all these figures in their appeals for reform. As they preached of New England's apostasy, they also insisted that its fate was full of portent for the rest of the world. Increase, of course, elevated this insistence into the hope that his people would serve as a type for the New Jerusalem.[1]

Cotton Mather repeated much of what his father said about New England, for the jeremiad bit deeply into his mind. He shared the desire of his father's generation that the Congregational polity that developed in New England would truly serve the rest of the world. In the *Magnalia,* his greatest exposition of this idea, Mather suggested that Christ planted the churches in New England in order that "He might there, *to* them first, and then *by* them, give a *specimen* of many good things, which He would have his Churches elsewhere aspire and arise unto. . . ." Still, if Cotton made his father's hopes his own, he did so in his own way, imparting his own flavor to the conventional versions of the Puritan mission to America.[2]

The fear and sadness of the jeremiad impressed him more deeply than the claims for New England as a model. He came of age, after all, just when the Bay lost its charter; he listened to the frantic wailing in the old Puritan faction as one disaster followed another in the persons of Edward Randolph, Joseph Dudley, and finally Sir Edmund Andros. To be sure, he participated in the Glorious Revolution in April 1689 which saw these satanic agents first consigned to jail and then dispatched to England. But the next few years offered their own bag of horrors, infestation by witches, and a new charter that provided that the King should select Massachusetts' governor. These events strengthened a disposition to despair for the future of New England.

They also put Cotton Mather to examining the past for a fuller understanding of the purposes of New England. His great historical works, especially the studies of the Reformation and of Church history, coincide with the Dominion of New England and the first period of the new charter While these studies all indicate that his feeling about New England's mission persisted, they reveal chastened hopes. Cotton Mather never gave up the belief that his America had much to teach Europe, but he did not envisage the new society serving as a blueprint for the old. Its corruption, which drew relentless afflictions from the Lord, rendered any such suggestion simple arrogance. As for New England standing as a type for the New Jerusalem, for anyone who took seriously the catalogue of sins presented in the jeremiads, that notion was better left unexamined. In fact Cotton Mather never commented on this dream of his father. Typology remained for him a rhetorical device, not an instrument to be used in the analysis of history.[3]

His ideas about New England went through a long evolution. They began with a comprehension of the founding that drew more on Richard Mather's thought than on Increase's. Richard, and the divines of his generation, had felt that they were in exile. They had been banished. Though they intended always to give their best for the Lord in America, and though they believed they could do much for Him in the wilderness, their removal from England did not fill them with a sense of triumph. They despised the corruption in their homeland, and for a time expected the Lord to smite it just as He had Israel, but still they hated being driven away. And driven and persecuted they felt, even as they grasped at their opportunities in America to fashion the true Church polity in the expectation that history was rapidly nearing its close.[4]

The sons of the founders, the generation that created the legend of their fathers' grand errand into the wilderness, experienced little persecution and felt nothing approaching banishment. Nor did Cotton Mather, who reached maturity at a time when his father's hopes were in decline, when the argument about New England's decay seemed irrefutable. In this saddened mood he returned to the founders' explanations of their coming and found them true.

His pronouncements of the 1690's and of the early part of the eighteenth century emphasize the "PERSECUTION" of the first Puritans who came to the Bay Colony; they were driven from England by " 'Fire! *and* Sword!' " as the noble Blackmore's poem said. "It was indeed a *Banishment*, rather than a *Removal*, which was undergone by the glorious Generation" that settled New England. This understanding of America's beginning enabled him to make a case that he clung to for the rest of his life: the banishment of the founders included the banishment of the best part of Christ's Church from England. The founders were driven out under the benevolent eye of a Providence that watched over the true Church in the world. It had always been so, and always would be to the end of history. God always had an Israel. For a time the Jews had served, but they lost their place as the chosen of the Lord when they sank themselves in their lusts. The Savior revived the failing Church, and for a time it thrived in the days of the primitive Christians. With the appearance of Rome and the Antichrist, it was almost lost once more. Now in the last days of the Antichristian apostasy, its purest elements had been carried to New England, driven from their homes by persecuting bishops and their agents. In New England the task of the people in covenant with God was to preserve the Church until justice and mercy arrived with the Second Coming of Christ.[5]

Cotton Mather retained his faith in this broad view of New England history until late in his life. It was a view that included many of his father's cherished beliefs, but it never attempted to reconcile within itself the typological ecstasies of Increase. It did of course make use of covenant theory. New England had pledged itself to the Lord's service in the national covenant, Cotton Mather insisted. This covenant, he used the terms "outward" and "external" covenant, embraced all the people, though —in agreement with his father—he believed that only the elect would survive the final cataclysm. New England, as a people in the outward covenant, could do much for the Church. If godliness, sanctity, and good behavior prevailed, the Church could be preserved in a form pleasing to God. But if they declined— if the Church were polluted by the ungodly, the Lord would remove all His blessings from the land. Hence the need to hold the people together in a condition that honored their covenant with the Lord.[6]

There were imprecisions and vagueness in this theory. The relationship of the saints and the sinners was never clear; indeed Cotton Mather swung his emphasis on this question erratically. The one sure proposition was that the Church would always survive. But a godly land might not. At times, like his father, Cotton Mather suggested that a faithful few could protect the land. This view contained dangers of its own: if a saving remnant was all that the Church required, what grounds could be established for calling for obedience from all the people? In most sermons addressed to these questions, Mather simply assumed that the fates of the Church and the land were inseparable. If the people failed, Christ would remove His Church; and if the Church were poisoned by unregenerate members, or a flawed structure (which he believed Stoddard proposed), the Lord would blast the land.[7]

This position was not in fact as ambiguous as it seems to us. Cotton Mather, even more than his father, was an American Puritan. As devoted as he was to the Church of Christ, to the Congregational polity, he could not think of New England in terms defined solely by a single institution—however precious it was to the Lord. He loved the Church, and he ached to see its triumph at the Day of Judgment. But the knowledge that the Church would survive—God would have His Israel, however evil the behavior of a dissolute people like New England's—did not offer complete consolation. A third generation American, whose family had participated in the founding and had worked in the public arena, Cotton Mather could not take lightly the fate of his people and his land.

In thinking about New England's purposes, Cotton Mather did not prove to be a conservative, yearning only for the good old days of unchallenged Congregationalism. He recognized that the political circumstances created by the Revolutionary settlement voided the policy of intolerance which his father, following the lead of the founders, espoused. In time, as he came to believe that the unity in the essentials of religion did not lie in the forms of Church organization, he exploited the toleration that the Crown had forced on his country in 1691 to work out a fresh understanding of the meaning of New England.

All this is not to say that Cotton Mather welcomed the loss of the original charter. He regarded the Crown's removal of it with a hatred envenomed by the knowledge that the era of Congregational dominance had passed. In effect the charter of 1691 and the Toleration Act transformed the magistrate into a secular creature. Cotton Mather recognized what the new situation meant for religion: unformity was dead, and he said so openly, while he mourned its passing in private.[8]

He was not so oppressed by the new dispensation as to be unable to point out that the Act of Toleration provided protection for Congregationalists as well as for Anglicans. Indeed immediately after the return of his father in 1692, he began preaching about the immunity New England now enjoyed from persecution from abroad. In these sermons he folded "the Rights of ENGLISH-MEN" around his people, and he claimed additional privileges because "we are NEW-ENGLANDERS" who dwell in a Puritan soil where the power to persecute is "by a Royal Charter, for ever kept from coming into the Hands of any that might hereafter incline to use it on us." [9]

Mather's invocation of the rights of Englishmen and his espousal of toleration have been interpreted as signifying a momentous shift in the New England mind. This view holds that he and others now recognized the centrality of the State and that he almost, in spite of himself, testified to its prominence not only by invoking English rights but by issuing tracts on currency and by writing *The Political Fables*.[10] He also recommended the expedition against Louisbourg on the grounds of its necessity to New England's prosperity; and in other statements in the first confused years of the 1690's he carefully linked the charter to property. In these actions he has been pictured marching down the road toward secularization in lockstep with the merchants and the "moderates." [11]

Cotton Mather may have touched that road at several times in his life, but only to cross it while pursuing his own purposes. His comments on coin, business and war are not in themselves revealing of a secular tendency; he remarked on the events of his time at every opportunity in order to improve them for the Lord. He bade the old Congregational order in Church and State farewell in his sermons of the 1690's because its departure could not be prevented. But while he watched it go, he never dismissed the vision of Christian unity that animated it. By the early years of the next century he regained that vision, when it appeared before his zealous eyes in the hues and shapes of evangelical "PIETY." [12]

This development of his mind in the twenty-five years following the new charter began in the confusion and hope of the Glorious Revolution. His father had slipped out of Boston bound for the court of James II just months before. Three thousand miles away, Cotton could not realize with the certainty that soon came to his father that the old charter was irretrievable. Cotton could only wait and pray, and after Andros was jailed he could not do much more. In December of 1691, he attempted to prepare Boston for the worst by giving a sermon decrying discontent and murmuring. His first reactions to the news of the charter and the policy of toleration betray his confusion—the charter was both more than he expected and less than he wanted.[13]

During the next few years he attempted to work out the full significance of the new arrangements for New England. His first endorsements of the policy of toleration were undoubtedly insincere; he had not in the years immediately following the receipt of the charter imagined a new basis for Christian unity. Hence in these statements of the 1690's, though he repudiated the persecution of the founders, he confined the guarantees of toleration as tightly as possible. Public policy, he declared, must distinguish between the political capacities of the State and the religious capacities of the churches, The State must not persecute for belief lest it afford "a Root for Cains Club to grow upon." [14] But there are other grounds for freedom of conscience, and Mather clarified them for his listeners: "a Christian by Non-Conformity to this or that Imposed *Way of Worship*, does not break the Terms on which he is to enjoy the Benefits of *Humane Society*. A man has a Right unto his Life, his Estate, his Liberty, and his Family, altho' he should not come up to these and those Blessed *Institutions* of our Lord." [15] These rights, he explained, belong to all Christians—those in New England prized them as citizens of Britain: Mather did not mean to separate the Church and the world completely, however strong this statement may appear. For, in his view, the magistrate had responsibilities that carried into the arena of the Church. Both Church and State had to concern themselves with morality: the magistrate, for example should punish drunkenness, an offense that a Puritan church could not overlook in one of its members. Nor should the State countenance atheism or blasphemy; nor should it ignore those who reviled religion. Roman Catholics fell into one or more of these categories in Cotton Mather's judgment, and should they ever be incautious enough to appear in Puritan colonies, they must be driven out. More than that fell to the State in Mather's judgment. The true religion continued to be known whatever statutes the British Parliament approved concerning toleration and the magistrate should give protection to those who attempt to advance it. Cotton Mather prescribed "Singular Kindness,

Defense and Support" as the duties of the magistrate toward the churches of Christ.[16] In practice this meant the collection of rates for the local Congregational meetings, a practice Mather never repudiated.

The changes in this position did not all occur within the area of theory. In 1718 Mather participated in the ordination of a Baptist minister, Elisha Callender, in a Boston church. This was a remarkable action, and a praiseworthy one, accompanied by a subdued plea for the exemption of the Baptists from payment of rates for Congregational churches. His repudiation of the founders' persecution of the Quakers also required courage, though he never suggested that Quakers be exempt from rates for the established churches.[17]

Mather stated his final position on these issues in *Parentator,* his biography of Increase.[18] He did not spare his father in discussing the intolerance of the first generations in New England; Increase, he admitted, had accepted the founders' views eagerly, even going so far as to write an essay justifying them. Increase never published it, Cotton said, because he changed his mind (Cotton might have noted that Increase made his views public in a number of works which did get into print). Cotton Mather ascribed the change to Increase's understanding of the parable of the tares, and his father's comprehension of the irrelevance of this part of Israel's experience for New England; as Cotton said, the persecuting example of Israel could not "Legitimate the like Proceedings among Christian Gentiles." [19]

When Cotton Mather first repudiated the founders' position on Church and State, he probably did not realize that he was then on the way to making further revisions in ancient theory. Cutting away the old assumptions in one area left others exposed, including those on the character of the Church in history. What he did in the twenty-five years following the Glorious Revolution, or what he was in some measure unwittingly compelled to do, was to find some basis other than Church polity for that union of Christians which he expected to welcome the chiliad. By the time he had accomplished this reconstruction of prophecy, he had also worked out a new version of the meaning of New England.

The Act of Toleration forced Mather to begin to think anew about the Church itself. He realized that the Congregational churches of New England would soon need all the support they could get from other nonconforming bodies in England. He would not concede at first that in receiving it, they would compromise their claims to a pure, scriptural organization. Hence he welcomed the union of Congregationalists and Presbyterian ministers in London that his father helped form in 1691. This league, the United Brethren, joined ministers in consulting organizations and did not include the laity. Both Mathers looked upon it as not only an expression of the Christian spirit but as a device to oppose the Church of England.[20]

In the first years of the 1690's, the Church of England looked more threatening even than the innovations in sacramental practice coming out of the Connecticut Valley where Solomon Stoddard held forth. A distant, unknown enemy invariably looks more formidable than the familiar one next door—and so this one did to the Mathers. Always troubled more by the unseen than the visible, Cotton Mather almost blundered into the enemy's Northampton camp in his eagerness to sign an alliance with the Presbyterians in England. By 1690 Stoddard had begun to sneer that the Church covenant had no basis in Scripture. His distaste for the old requirements for Communion had been expressed many times. Cotton Mather ignored these western prejudices as he appealed to the East. There is, he argued, no reason to permit differences between Presbyterians and Congregationalists on principles to forestall an alliance between them. They can agree on most elements of practice and where they cannot, considerable variety is tolerable. The enumeration of the tolerable must have astonished Stoddard, for Mather admitted that some Presbyterian churches might not require the relation of conversion experience, some might not agree that ruling elders, who were qualified laymen, should assist ministers, and some might not choose to follow New England's practice of bringing the children of non-communicants under Church discipline. No matter, said Cotton, implying that these things were fundamentals only in New England. And as for the most crucial of all, the issue of regenerate membership, the New England requirement that grace must be demonstrated by a description of an experience has been considered by some, an "Humane invention!" Cooperation on a practical level ought to be encouraged, too, by the fact that Church societies are founded on natural reason.[21]

Stoddard never seized the opportunity that these incautious statements gave him, probably because Increase—always his major antagonist—did not go so far as Cotton and because Cotton did not repeat all these mistakes in later publications. In any case, the United Brethren split almost as soon as they joined, and not over practice but over an issue of principle, the justification of sinners. When this fissure became a gulf in 1696, the Mathers had begun to relax slightly in their fear of the Church of England and to eye once more their local enemies.[22]

Their problems at home in New England could not be solved by signing agreements. Stoddard continued to go his own way in the Valley; and his practice began to appear in the East. The place was neighboring Charlestown where, in 1697, the church searched for a minister to assist the aged Charles Morton. The church asked Cotton Mather for his advice in February 1697; he may have suggested Ebenezer Pemberton, who declined. The town then took matters into its hands and voted to invite Simon Bradstreet, a graduate of Harvard, class of 1693. According to established procedures, the town's action was improper, as the Mathers were quick to point out, for only a church had the power to call a minister. Angered by the presumption of the inhabitants of Charlestown, and the abdication of responsibility by the church, Increase and Cotton prepared an admonition to the Charlestown Church which their own flock endorsed and sent along. Bradsteet probably liked none of this, though he approved of the town's act which the Mathers saw as usurpation. The fact was that Bradstreet had little use for traditional ecclesiastical theory, especially that part which held that a church could be formed only by a covenant; and he made no secret of his views. Bradstreet's dismissal of the Church covenant smacked of Stoddardeanism, though there is no reason to believe that he had not worked out his own ideas independently. In any case the Mathers were horrified and protested strongly to the Charlestown Church which had endorsed him as the choice of the town. The protest changed nothing; the Mathers were beaten; they knew it and when they were invited to participate in Bradstreet's ordination in October 1698, they accepted. Cotton Mather gave the right hand of fellowship, and preached a sermon which, he reported to his *Diary*, produced weeping among his listeners.[23]

The Charlestown affair sorely tried Cotton Mather's hopes for a union of all Christians; in extending the right hand of fellowship to Bradstreet, he showed how reluctant he was to give them up. The following year all his ecumenical aspirations received a further testing and in the process he was forced to stake out boundaries which separated Congregationalism and the union of all Christians.

The new challenge had actually begun about the time that Charlestown's case took form. Early in 1698 President Leverett of Harvard, Thomas Brattle, a Boston merchant, his brother William, and several others decided to form a new church in Boston. They agreed that Benjamin Colman, a recent graduate of Harvard, then in England, should serve as its minister and that, since his and their plans did not conform to ancient procedures, he should receive ordination before coming home. Colman was ordained by nonconformists in London in August and arrived in Boston in November. Soon after he and the founders or, as the Mathers called them, the innovators, published a *Manifesto* that offered a rationale for what was known as the Brattle Street Church.[24]

A part of the *Manifesto* may have been designed to tweak the Mathers—for example, the innovators' announcement that worship in Brattle Street would be that sanctioned by the United Brethren. In fact, the *Manifesto* reeked of the "catholic spirit" that underlay all the yearnings for Christian Union. Leverett had long sniffed at fidelity to traditional rigidities and Colman was known to admire faith that cut across sectarian lines. It was in such a spirit that the *Manifesto* proclaimed its indifference to the polity of the first generation. The old standards, it implied, were a little absurd, when measured against the love that united all Christians. Therefore, though the Brattle Street Church would be gathered volunarily, its covenant should not be understood as a divinely ordered instrument but rather as one contrived under the law of nature. Moreover, its candidates for admission would not be required to make public relations of their experience; simple examination by the minister alone would suffice. The brethren's silence implied their consent. Nor would the sacraments be rigidly confined: "any" child might be baptized (and here the *Manifesto* bade the Half-Way Covenant farewell), and "visible sanctity" would satisfy requirements for taking the Lord's Supper.[25]

Cotton Mather declared that the articles of the *Manifesto* "utterly subvert our Churches, and invite an ill Party thro' all the Countrey to throw all into Confusion on the first Opportunities." [26] In the month that followed the appearance of the *Manifesto* he fumed about the apostasy he detected in Brattle Street and began composing an attack on the innovators. He did not publish it because—if his *Diary* may be trusted—some accommodation was worked out that made possible his and his father's participation in the installation of Colman. By his own account, the Brattle Street Church declared its willingness to "publickly recognize their Covenant with God, and one another" and to treat with other churches on the basis of the Heads of Agreement that had joined Congregationalists and Presbyterians in London.[27] This truce with Brattle Street, which Mather tried to convince himself was a concession to orthodoxy, largely reaffirmed the original terms of the *Manifesto*. But it did allow him to believe that he had gained much and the break was smoothed over.[28]

By such self-deceptions Cotton Mather managed to persuade himself that ecclesiastical unity continued in New England. Like the original non-separating Congregationalists, he had always maintained that the New England churches were a part of the Church of England. In these years immediately following the Revolutionary settlement this contention proved difficult to maintain and the difficulty placed further strain on his ecumenical hopes. His *Diary* reveals his growing disquiet at the vigor of "High Fliers," the Tory churchmen whom he saw attempting to crush nonconformity in England and America. But still if Christian Union were ever to be attained he knew that the Puritan churches must declare their unity with the Church of England.[29]

Mather found it possible to reaffirm this unity by redefining the ecclesiastical polity of the English Church—in effect by branding the Tory Churchmen as Antichristian usurpers. He began this task in 1698 with his *Eleutheria* [30]—the Happy Union lay in ruins and the limits of the Toleration Act had become obvious to dissenters everywhere—and completed it two years later with the publication of his *Letter of Advice to the Churches of the Non-Conformists in the English Nation*.[31] In these works he offered the theory that since the Reformation there had been two groups struggling for control of the Church of England.

The evil crowd, whom he called the Idumaeans after Lot's wife, had never accepted the reforms of the sixteenth century and despised the Puritans who carried them further in the seventeenth. The Idumaeans were the usurpers, responsible for divine right Episcopacy and Pelagian doctrine. Their usurpation had carried so far, he argued, that they now constituted a "new Church of England." [32] As a prevailing faction this new Church used the canons to justify its unscriptural rule, a rule that prescribed episcopal ordination and deprived parish ministers of their authority to teach and to administer the sacraments. This Canonical Church maintained only a slack discipline and a virtually open Communion; indeed its religion really only "lyes in Sainting their Martyr Charles I." [33]

The other party—the "True Church of England" consists, he explained, of the nonconformists, now by the Revolutionary Settlement "legal parts" of the Church of England. In fact Mather argued that the nonconformists were the only Church of England though he modestly contented himself by saying to his dissenting English brethren—"*You* are indeed among the TRUEST SONS of the *True Church of England*." [34]

What Mather derided as the New Church of England revealed plans that dampened further his ecumenical aspirations. In the Society for the Propagation of the Gospel in Foreign Parts, founded in 1701, it acquired an agency that soon produced heartburn in dissenting ministers all over the colonies. The first SPG missionary arrived in 1702 in the person of George Keith, once a Quaker but now an Anglican, and still an enemy to the churches of New England. He announced his continuing disgust with the New England way almost immediately. In the next few years Mather and other Boston ministers began complaining of SPG activities in and out of New England—Jamaica on Long Island, for example, and in Newbury and Braintree, Massachusetts. What irked them about the Society's efforts—they said—was its concentration on areas already served by nonconforming ministers and its neglect of plantations lacking any sort of Christian churches.[35]

The worst case of all as far as Cotton Mather was concerned involved Newbury where, in 1712, twenty-two citizens, spurred on by John Bridger, the Royal Surveyor of Portsmouth, New Hampshire, petitioned Governor Dudley for his protection for themselves while they set up a church conforming to Common Prayer worship. They had already sent to the Bishop of London for a minister, and they wished the Governor to cast his friendly eye on them and, incidentally, to relieve them of the obligation of paying for a Congregational minister. The Governor immediately declared himself willing to afford protection and exemption from church-rates. Cotton Mather fumed and resolved to send books to eliminate the ignorance that must have prompted such a request; Benjamin Colman, noting the plea for relief from taxes, questioned the petitioners' motives; and Judge Samuel Sewall appealed to a Deacon in the Congregational Church in Newbury to help recall the petitioners to their senses. All to no avail, of course, as General Nicholson sent money; a missionary arrived; and Queen Anne's Chapel, as the Newbury foundation was called, continued to lead a reduced but evidently effective existence.[36]

These episcopal extensions across the sea were frightening and dampened Mather's thought of a grand union of all Protestants. Still, well into the eighteenth century both he and Colman found it possible to speak of the United Brethren as a transatlantic dissenting interest. In part his motives may have been defensive, for the High Church faction was enjoying the Queen's favor in these years and making life even more trying for nonconformists in England than in America. Mather followed the attacks on nonconformity with fascination. He was temporarily elated by the trial of Henry Sacheverell, the Tory priest, who in 1709 virtually repudiated the Act of Toleration. But Sacheverell's light sentence and the activity of the mob that supported him depressed Mather. To a friend he reported the news that a Tory mob had pulled down six Presbyterian meetinghouses; civil war was likely, he said, once peace with France was concluded. Two years later he had increasingly bad news: Marlborough had been dismissed from office, and the Tories were using the Act of Occasional Conformity to drive dissenters from all places of public trust. His Glasgow correspondents told of events that further darkened his spirits: the "Episcopal men in Scotland (who are generally Jacobites)" were being protected by Parliament to such an extent that a rupture of the Union seemed likely. He continued to predict peace with France to be followed by an alliance. All the news suggested that "Men of Revolution-Principles" were on the way out "while those of the French Mode are like to carry the

Day." His worst fears were that this would bring the Church of England—or as he usually said, the new Church of England—into a "coalition with the Gallican Church." [37]

The experience of such measures as the Occasional Conformity Act did not bode well for a Christian Union that embraced all Protestants, especially those of the Anglican variety. Mather recognized this fact and dealt with it in the manner he had worked out in the 1690's: with the claim that nonconformity represented the doctrine of the true Church of England. And of all nonconformity the purest was found in New England where "The *Doctrinal Articles* of the *Church of England,* through the *Matchless Favour* of God, are more universally Held, and Preached . . . than in any Nation." The new Church of England, Pelagian in doctrine and persecuting in temper, had cut itself off from the catholic Church of Christ. [38]

Mather assumed in all his comments on the Church of England that its doctrine was now, and had always been, Calvinist. He also assumed that nonconformists in England shared the same faith that had long obtained in New England. To stake out his claim he published, and republished, those doctrinal parts of the Thirty-Nine Articles and of the Book of Common Prayer that espoused the traditional Calvinism. And with his father and other worthies in Boston pulpits, he attacked Common Prayer worship for its Antichristian taint. Increase and the others described the situation of nonconformity in England as if public policy had not changed since the Restoration, except in cases where they argued it had become more barbarous than ever. These tracts drew replies from the Anglicans living in Boston who, following the lead of the Mathers, also reprinted works which had produced controversy twenty years before. But no Anglican proved as assiduous as Cotton Mather in sending tracts and sermons throughout English America. Those he dispatched testified to the orthodoxy of the churches in New England and to the apostasy of the High-Fliers in England. This sort of evangelical enterprise was also one more way of pointing to the neglect by the SPG of the "ungospellized" plantations in America. [39]

With the death of Queen Anne and the accession of George I, Mather looked for some respite from the SPG. The Whigs and the Latitudinarians who came back into power would not try to force a bishop on the colonies, an event he had dreaded for years.

And unfriendly legislation, such as the Occasional Conformity Act and the Schism Bill, might be nullified. For these reasons, Mather greeted the Hanoverian succession with joy, preaching *The Glorious Throne* in its praise only three weeks after George I received the crown. Most ministers in New England agreed that George promised more than Anne and joined in a friendly address to the King in 1715. For a while they considered Mather's suggestion that two agents carry their memorial to the King but finally contented themselves by commissioning several nonconformist ministers in England to act for them. Cotton Mather managed the ministerial convention that met in Boston to discuss the churches' response to the new monarch; and he drafted their address. The New England ministers did not have to be pushed; most disliked the SPG and almost all wanted guarantees that the High-Fliers would not push legislation across the Atlantic. Benjamin Colman, for example, preached on the accession of the new king and the next year declared New England's happiness that the Jacobites had been put down.[40]

Both Colman and Mather used these occasions to talk about the United Brethren as a transatlantic association. In fact no such organization existed though correspondence passed back and forth between like-minded ministers on both sides of the Atlantic. And the plan for a grand ministerial association and a standing council that might advance the catholic spirit of Christian Union foundered on Congregational independence. All earlier attempts at imposing some hierarchy had failed for the same reason. Informal meetings of ministers had draw the opposition of Roger Williams in 1633 on the grounds that such gatherings might lead to the introduction of the Presbyterian polity. On at least two occasions in the next thirty years, the Reverend Thomas Parker of the Newbury Church had tried to persuade his colleagues in the Bay to strengthen the powers of synods. He was accused of Presbyterianism and his suggestions were dismissed. Perhaps Parker was encouraged by English Presbyterians; in any case, Richard Mather, John Cotton, and Thomas Hooker, among others, had spent an inordinate amount of time answering Presbyterians in England.[41]

With the Restoration, fears of Presbyterianism had faded in New England, especially as Congregationalists discovered how much the persecuted everywhere had in common. Meetings of ministers undoubtedly took place even during the worst of the transatlantic squabbles; and shortly before the end of the century there were a handful of ministerial associations throughout Massachusetts. They had no existence in law, however, and they were not empowered to discipline churches or members or indeed to do anything more than discuss common problems.[42]

But in August 1705, these associations met in Boston and agreed upon the *Proposals,* a plan for ministerial associations empowered to license ministers and for standing councils which would meet annually. The standing councils would have lay members, sent by the churches, but in all actions the major part of the ministers would retain a veto. The councils then would remain snugly in ministerial hands. The actions a council might take all bore on disciplinary matters which traditionally had belonged to the individual churches—disputes within a church between ministers and brethren for example. Under the *Proposals* a standing council might in extreme cases order the churches of the Bay to discontinue their relations with a disorderly church and to receive its godly members to their own communion.[43]

What prompted this plan is not altogether clear. Undoubtedly the motives of its projectors varied from a desire to strengthen ministerial authority in a society increasingly prone to ignore it to a sense that some fresh way of introducing godliness into a decaying society had to be discovered. Its proponents included most of the distinguished ministers in the eastern associations, though Increase Mather held himself aloof until 1716 when he publicly declared his opposition.[44]

Cotton Mather played some part in organizing the meeting that drafted the *Proposals,* and he signed them, but he said very little openly in their favor. He gave his support cautiously because he, better than anyone else, knew of his father's opposition. A part of his own favorable disposition arose in the frustration he felt over the attacks on nonconformity in England and New England. The SPG alarmed him; strong ministerial associations might help keep its High-Fliers in check. This much is hinted at in his *Diary,* where he also indulged his rage at other intruders, for example, Samuel May, "a wondrous Lump of Ignorance and Arrogance," who preached to a congregation of Anabaptists, until he was unmasked as a plagiarist and woman-chaser. In 1699 when May appeared, Mather probably would have relished the chance to bring him before an association, or better to refer the case to a standing council.[45]

Still he knew that in a state pledged to religious toleration nothing effective could be done about the Mays of Boston or about High-Fliers of the SPG. He said as much the year following in a meeting of ministers in Boston, where he savagely attacked Stoddard's recent sermon, which proposed a whole hierarchy of provincial classes and a national synod. The decrees of Stoddard's organizations, he said at this time, "will signify little, except they have a *Civil Magistrate* that will make them cutt." The possibility that the State might once more enforce the true religion, he continued, did not exist, nor never would again in New England.[46]

Mather's advocacy of the *Proposals* five years after the assault on Stoddard was not an act of pure consistency. Yet both positions—the opposition to Stoddard and the support of the *Proposals*—were deeply felt. Mather hated the suggestion for synods from Stoddard because it came from Stoddard, a man who had already repudiated long-standing conventions of Church discipline and worship. Stoddard's synods would ratify the Church organized on the basis of geography, not the covenant; and they would give Communion to unregenerates in the belief that it was a converting ordinance. These practices, Mather declared in the attack on Stoddard, would "ravish" the churches of New England and far from reforming them, would lead them into the arms of the Antichrist. But synods and standing councils committed to the true polity and holy worship would not lead the New England churches into Popery. Others thought differently, among them the Reverend John Rogers of Ipswich, who announced his opposition briefly and cautiously the next year. But for the most part the *Proposals* were ignored publicly until John Wise delivered his great *Churches Quarrel Espoused* in 1710.[47]

Even as the *Proposals* of 1705 sank in a sea of apathy, Mather groped towards a more satisfying basis for union, one that would transcend factions and varieties in ecclesiastical polity. He had begun searching for such a basis by denying the divisive force of differing principles. Agreement on practice—he believed—should placate nonconforming groups whatever their principles. Now early in the eighteenth century he sought, and found, the fundamentals of Christian Union.

The basis lay in what Mather and other evangelicals in America and Europe called "PIETY." (They rarely wrote the word in the lower case.) Mather wrote and preached about the "MAXIMS OF PIETY" from early in the century to the end of his life. His inspiration may have come from Europe; certainly he corresponded with European Pietists, including August Francke of Halle, and read their works avidly. But Piety was not just another import received by an American provincial who hoped to emulate the customs of the sophisticated world. If Cotton Mather had been born too late in the seventeenth century to believe that his country would serve as the model for the reformation of Europe, he lived before Americans turned to Europe for the correct fashions in theology. The fact that European reformers now emphasized the New Piety pleased and reassured him; but he began thinking in its language out of frustration and hopes that had arisen in his American experience.[48]

Though "PIETY" never received a single definition which Mather consistently followed in his writings, he clearly meant it to describe an attitude of mind and the substance of belief. He customarily phrased both as the "MAXIMS OF PIETY," which he reduced to three, a fear of God (including a rational and affecting belief in Him), a full acceptance of the righteousness of Christ as justifying men, and the love of one's fellow man as a way of honoring God. Piety would save a man and bind him to good men everywhere; it cut through the tangle of sects and divisions among churches. It represented a saving ecumenicalism, and men who lived according to its maxims could leave the old strife behind forever.[49]

Just how fully Cotton Mather committed himself to it as a basis for unity appears clearly in his castigations of the sectarian spirit which sought to crush the New Piety. If we prefer a man not of the "Best Morals" who supports our notions of Church polity to one of eminent piety but of a different ecclesiastical persuasion, we are guilty of the sectarian spirit, Mather argued. To be sure, New England must hold to the primitive Church—to unpolluted administrations in its forms and worship. For Cotton Mather, as for his father and grandfather, purity resided most clearly in a regenerate membership. Baptism might be extended to the children of half-way members and even to adults who lacked any connection to the Church but who strove to experience grace, but full membership must be reserved to the visibly gracious. Cotton Mather developed new techniques by which men could examine themselves; he urged that assurance was not required before taking Communion; he exhorted churches to stretch rational charity to the limits in judging those who offered themselves for the Lord's Supper. But in all these extensions of old limits, he clung to the ancient proposition that grace was visible and that the identification could be made by the Church. He expected these good men, once properly identified, to gather themselves under a covenant in a church. A voluntary covenant remained indispensable in his theory to an instituted church. To this requirement he continued to give his full support, though he badly clouded the issue by periodically insisting that church forms were human inventions and that the law of nature was the surest guide available to men interested in forming churches. If such aberrant statements did not represent his deepest commitment to traditional theory, they did reveal the direction his mind was taking early in the eighteenth century. He could never admit that at some level the fathers' devotion to the traditional polity conflicted with his own sense of the importance of Christian love as the fundamental obligation of the elect. Yet he insisted in these opening years of the eighteenth century that love of God, of Christ, and of one's fellows defined a Christian's being—not loyalty to the Congregational Church and the Congregational State. Reaching this position without directly repudiating the founders—and his father—cost him psychically almost as much as an open break would have. By 1715 his own practices were absolutely clear: the old polity distinguished New England from the world—it was New England's *"crown,"* but the crown without the "Jewels" of the vital Piety, the catholic love towards all who have the same faith, carried the rust of sectarianism.[50] The union of the faithful transcended the fact that in ecclesiastical terms they followed "very different persuasions." Piety cut across these distinctions; it required that love be shown to dissenters; it supplied a basis for the joyful unity of all in Christ.[51]

Thus a line of thought that began in 1691 with an argument for ministerial cooperation between Congregationalists and Presbyterians ended with a plea for the unity of all Christians. Whatever their differences, men who shared the faith of the MAXIMS

OF PIETY—Presbyterians, Lutherans, even Episcopalians and Antipaedobaptists—should join in the Union. They should not unite with the expectation that they could eliminate all sectarian marks before the reappearance of Christ; only a Donatist could entertain such an extravagant hope. But they could share the faith. They could serve one another; in fact they should not confine their love to only those who shared the glorious MAXIMS, but extend it to those outside, to heathens, pagans, yes to enemies.[52]

Mather found a sanction for this ecumenicalism in the failures of the past. Providence had blasted earlier attempts at union because they had not rooted themselves in the everlasting gospel. In the sixteenth century, for example, some reformers had sought to build on private judgment alone, other insisted on Scripture unenlightened by interpretation. Both groups ignored the true basis in Piety. And in their error they had missed the experience of every successful religion on earth. Those religions "in Vogue" presently, or in the past, Mather said, had subscribed to the cardinal tenets of the Christianity he advocated. Had not all of them testified to the propositions that God deserved the highest love of men and that men united in this love should treat one another with kindness and affection? The three non-Christian persuasions which attracted the allegiance of most men, Judaism, Muhammadanism, and Paganism, all paid homage to the idea of a savior who would mediate between God and man. The Jews, whose religion was but the "First Essay" of Christianity, had only to return to the faith of their fathers in the Old Testament to discover anticipations of Christ. The Muhammadans conceded miraculous power to Christ and thereby acknowledge His divinity even though they are too corrupt to worship Him. As for the Pagans, Plato—their ancient spokesman—predicted the coming of a being so perfect, so just, that he could only have meant Christ.[53]

The implications for New England of Mather's vision of a Union forecast in Plato and Muhammad, correcting the imperfections of the Protestant Reformation, and transcending all ecclesiastical traditions, were revolutionary. The New England of Cotton Mather's understanding had been reduced from the runner of the errand, from the City on the Hill, to a part and only one part of a Glorious Christian Union. Chastened by the Act of Toleration, by the new charter, by the need to define rights in English, as well as in Christian, terms, Cotton Mather had found it impossible to conceive of his country as the redeemer of the English Nation. It had much including a covenant with the Lord; and it should hold fast to the purity of its churches and their worship. It should recognize how these gifts distinguished it from much of the profane world. But it should see its faith and its hope in the context of a united religion.

Cotton Mather did not arrive at these views in an abject frame of mind. Working out his ideas about the MAXIMS OF PIETY was an enthusiastical process. And his fervor increased as he perceived the potential of a faith that at last broke down old forms even as it healed long-festering wounds. The foundations of the earth would some day shatter; even the ordinances of Heaven would alter; but not the New Piety which embraced eternal truths. Hence when it prevailed it would "introduce" into the world "the Kingdom of God." [54]

13

The Psychology of Abasement

Although Cotton Mather knew that Christ would return with His Kingdom at a time of His own choosing, he also believed that men must prepare. They must hold Christ's Church in readiness, maintaining its purity and supporting its ordinances; and surely ministers must never cease their attempts to convert the elect. None of these acts, in fact nothing that men could do, Mather had to admit, would affect the timing of Christ's reappearance in history. And yet he could hope that the efforts of good men might move the Lord. Logic, Scripture, theology all testified against his hopes but did not dampen them. The Lord worked in mysterious ways, Mather told New England, and in fact had chosen since the defection of the children of Israel to deepen the mystery surrounding His dealings with men. Did He not often reward the wicked with temporal riches and plunge the good into poverty? Did He not sometimes ignore the best efforts of faithful servants? [1]

Mather regarded the spread of the Christian Union as a necessary part of the preparation for the Second Coming. Throughout the last twenty-five years of his life this conviction helped suppress most doubts he had about the importance of ecclesiastical differences. What he had come to see by the opening of the eighteenth century was that the important fact in cosmic history was not the organizational distinctions which had long held men separate from one another, but the saving faith that joined them in Christ. Hence in all his dreams about a united Christendom, he always returned to the point from which Protestantism had begun: the problem of the individual.

A minister charged by his calling to convert the unregenerate and to nourish the faithful faced difficult problems in a society pledged to Calvin's version of the universe. Just as his father and his grandfather, and hundreds of ministers before them did, Cotton Mather listened to troubled men asking the question— what could a man do for himself in a world of predestination? By Cotton Mather's time the answer that the "preparationists" formulated almost a century before was widely accepted. Unable to agree on much, even Increase Mather and Solomon Stoddard agreed that men must "prepare" themselves for conversion. By preparation they—like Ames, Preston, Perkins, Thomas Hooker, Richard Mather, and John Norton before them—meant moral actions men might take before grace was infused into their souls. All these divines broke the conversion process into discernible stages which occurred over time. All agreed that a man predestined for Hell might traverse a number of them. Hooker helpfully explained this possibility by distinguishing between "legal" and "evangelical" preparation.[2] The law, he wrote, should inform all men of correct standards of conduct, and simple examination of the self would produce contrition in those who deviated from those standards. Man might even feel terror when the law successfully informed him of his departures from morality; and humility might follow. According to Richard Mather grace sometimes assisted these natural operations of the soul; grace thus might have a hand in legal preparation. But the sinner not chosen for salvation would go no farther and would fail of union with Christ. Usually he would not even realize that he had failed to rise out of his corruption and, secure in the external morality that accompanied legal preparation, would consider himself converted. The world was full of these civil, moral men.[3]

Evangelical preparation, on the other hand, carried the sinner to union with Christ. Its early stages resembled legal preparation with the sinner suffering the pangs of contrition and humility.

The difference occurred when the Holy Spirit, which sometimes stimulated these feelings, ceased to act on the soul and joined with it in holy union.[4]

Although all the preparationists argued that no man could save himself, all placed their emphasis on the necessity of seeking salvation. Preparation involved human exertions. Though a man could go only so far by his own efforts, and though only a few would be saved (the odds were a thousand to one against the individual, Thomas Shepard estimated), every man must try. Every man must prepare himself as fully as he could, getting himself into the right frame of mind. And since the condition of the inner man affected the conduct of the outer, he ought to pay attention to his behavior too. No one could consider himself truly informed of his sins, and contrite and humble because of them, if he persisted in evil actions.[5]

In histories of the New England mind, Cotton Mather has appeared as the third generation's leading exponent of preparation. These studies hold that he pushed the doctrine farther than anyone else until his position became almost synonymous with that of the Arminians. As an imperative to action, preparation seems totally consistent with Mather's disposition to be up and doing— and with his insistence that the Lord intended for every man to be as energetic as possible in His service. There are in Mather's writings, and in the sermons he preached to his flock, numerous exhortations to seek Christ. The figures Mather used suggest that a man should be in perpetual motion until he was converted, indeed after that glorious event as well. Try to believe, Mather urged, strive, struggle, wrestle with the Lord; work, struggle with the flesh and the Devil, expend ceaseless energy until you are sure. There are also statements accompanying these exhortations that assure the individual that if he tries to believe and finds in examining his soul that he can, he has faith.[6]

Despite these intriguing propositions which apparently abandoned the determinism of Calvin, Cotton Mather cannot be convicted of Arminianism. Nor was he devoted to the doctrine of preparation—a set of ideas that he actually rejected. Although most of his friends, including his father, were preparationists, he did not conceal his distaste for the doctrine, arguing that it was a mistake for men even to talk about preparing themselves. Of course men should "look" to God and seek His mercy. But, as Mather often suggested, they could not even begin to look by themselves—the first step that man should take, indeed the only one he could take by himself, was to pray for the power to "be enabled to Look." Only God could give this power: one can "as easily make Iron swim" as to look to Christ "by any abilities of your own." [7]

Mather's distaste extended even to the terminology preparationists commonly used—"humilitation," "contrition," and the word "prepared" itself. Far better, he said repeatedly, to think of yourself as a "perishing" sinner than as a prepared one. [8] Mather announced his disenchantment with the language of preparation in order to point out the dangers he saw in the entire conception. Believing that preparation had yielded "inconceivable prejudice" to the attempts of the Lord to save the souls of men, he did not hesitate to scrap the whole scheme from its psychological assumptions to its vocabulary of stages and steps. Its danger lay in its tendency to encourage men to believe that they would be saved because of some merit of their own—or worse, to believe that they might even save themselves. The *"propensity"* of men to wish to be justified by their own efforts was "innate," he said, in his treatise on *The Everlasting Gospel . . . of Justification.* The Lord says "come without money" but those emboldened by preparation want to come with "the money of vertuous dispositions." [9]

Cotton Mather recognized proud men when he saw them. As a young man he learned to face the pride in many of his own appeals to the Lord. And so when an anguished parishioner told him that "The Lord has no reason to save the likes of me," pride and self-righteousness echoed in Mather's ears. He told such men what really prompted their cravings and how desperate their conditions were. Every man secretly harbored a desire to save himself at some time in his life, and a man who did not fear such thoughts in himself was probably under their control. The world was full of proud men who sinned, felt contrition, even terror, and then mended their ways and began to feel themselves saved. But they had not received grace; they had attained nothing more than a damning self-righteousness. [10]

Just as this argument set Cotton Mather apart from the preparationists so also did his charge that they treated "knowledge," "contrition," and "humiliation" almost as works. As far as Mather was concerned this was a natural tendency, and he never expressed surprise at it. He expected men to overreach themselves: the civil moral man who mobilized his faculties by himself and then presumed to take up the covenant promises without the aid of grace was a familiar figure. As Increase Mather had long complained, ministers themselves made this error in their sermons which neglected Christ and His redemptive sacrifice. And ministers and laymen alike confused psychological "works," accomplished by the self, with grace, given only by God. Cotton Mather saw disaster in such confusion: "In making your Addresses to your Saviour for His Favours, you must not suppose, that you must arrive to such and such Degrees of *Humiliation*, before you may *presume* to come unto Him. You must not suppose That you must be Recommended by such and such *Contritions*, unto the *Compassions* of your Saviour, if you would not be charged with a *Presumption*, in coming unto Him. This is to bring the *Covenant of Work* into the Covenant of Grace." In the proper address to God, according to Mather's acrid view, sinners approached God "Unworthy as Dogs." But they should know that God was less likely to reject them because of their detestable condition than because of their refusal to admit to it.

Mather's psychological discussions generally departed from those of his peers in yet another way: so strong was his sense of the demonic in the world that he could not resist pointing out the stake of the Devil in the doctrine of preparation. The Devil, Mather insisted, recognized that preparation implies the worth of the self and attempts to convince men that they are in fact unworthy to be chosen by God. They must feel greater penitence and greater humility; they must feel an alteration in their lives before they dare trust Christ. Thus the Devil worked to wean men from a reliance on grace to a trust in their own efforts.[11]

Every minister in seventeenth-century New England must have encountered men who flung the doctrine of God's omnipotence back into his face as a justification for remaining passive despite all calls to convert. Since Christ is *"All"* and the self is *"Nothing,"* as Cotton Mather sometimes phrased the divine equation, these men seemed to have good cause for refusing to do anything for themselves. Mather despised this "Grand Excuse" which made the nature of things an argument for inactivity and dismissed it with the classic but unhelpful rejoinder that the hearts of such men were bad, hence their inability to come to the Lord.[12]

Yet in his steadfast rejection of the doctrine of preparation, he seems to leave men with neither a reason to exert themselves nor any basis in psychology which would indicate that they could. But he demands that they try their best to come to Christ! What did he think that a man unassisted by grace could do? The answers he gave both linked his theory to, and separated it from, the traditional version of the conversion process. Like the preparationists, he described the soul that received grace as one that had been purged from much of its ego—which he called "pride." Unlike the preparationists who believed that preparation accomplished the reduction of the self, Cotton Mather feared that preparation implied the importance of the self and its works. Hence he prescribed a psychological state in which a man would become a "perishing"—not a prepared—sinner. The frame of mind which Mather recommended involved the "annihilation" of the self. But in urging men to cultivate the feeling that Christ was all and they themselves were nothing, Mather did not mean to suggest that men should feeling nothing, but rather that they should loathe themselves and love only Christ. In effect, Mather compressed the stages of preparation into the most intense sort of humiliation. And the method he proposed for the destruction of the self constituted a type of preparation, but one which discarded the usual stages of knowledge, humiliation, contrition in favor of an acute self-consciousness and a complete abasement. In conventional theory, self-awareness, feelings of abasement, and dependency were expected to accompany preparation of course. What Cotton Mather did was to shift them to the center of good attitudes. Presumably the soul that was totally aware of its own sinful, self-serving propensities would be more likely to see the need to depend wholly upon Christ. Therefore Mather urged that the soul should regard every thought and feeling with suspicion. Only in this way could pride be purged. Preparation involved stages of feeling—degrees of guilt, repentance, humility, sorrow—it described a contest within the soul between good and evil. Cotton Mather's "method" was not intended to produce feeling—if guilt, sorrow, humility, repentance, contrition are all sorts of feeling—but rather to yield abasement and dependence.

Hence he simply told men to recognize their need of Christ and to try to induce themselves to give up everything for Him. What Mather proposed involved neither an emotional nor an intellectual process, but a fusion of the two which begins with an act of intellect and ends with a rejection of all that pertains to the autonomy of the self. The self should be given over temporarily in favor of an expected infusion of grace (or power) which will permit—he expected—a renewed affective process drawing the believer to God in love.[13]

Historians have made a good deal of the social implications of preparation. They note that a conception of conversion that broke its process into identifiable stages permitted ministers to demand moral behavior from men before saving faith passed into their souls. As far as the needs of social order were concerned, no matter that not everyone who underwent preparatory pangs would continue in the Spirit until he was born again: fearful men could be depended upon to observe the law. And for a society that conceived of itself in a national covenant with God, such observance held extraordinary value. External performance after all guaranteed external prosperity.[14]

Cotton Mather admired social order as much as any man. He made the case for the just price long after there was any hope that New England's merchants could be restrained; he criticized their usurious practices; and he urged laborers to curb their demands. Social mobility alarmed him—no man should give up a calling just to make more money, he told his unheeding people. Concern for order of another sort is clear in many of his sermons, which periodically go down the list of crimes provided by the Synod of 1679, warning the people that drunkenness, fornication, and other immoderate indulgences of the flesh could only bring down the wrath of God upon New England.[15]

When Puritan divines first began to work out their theory of conversion, they undoubtedly had nothing more in mind than the problem of how God transformed the souls of His chosen. The individual occupied their attention, not society. The focus shifted as the second generation succeeded the first, and the utility of preparation in keeping a people true to covenant obligations became clear. By Cotton Mather's day, this use was openly discussed. In one of the few accounts he wrote in the conventional language of preparation, Mather conceded that "preparatory common works, . . . such as Conviction of sin and misery by the law, and *the terrours of the Lord* that make men affraid, . . . may put a stop to their lewd courses, yea, and work a reformation in many things, and make a natural Conscience to act more strongly than before."[16] As socially useful as these works were, he added in a phrase that hinted at his reservations about the whole scheme, they did not always produce the beginning of conversion. Grace, he explained elsewhere, might work on men and yet not suffuse their beings. It sometimes operated externally, pushing the faculties of the soul this way or that, instructing the understanding in virtuous behavior, filling the will and the affections with fear when they countenanced sin, and yet leaving their nature unrenewed. Sometimes the natural conscience of the reprobate, without the assistance of common grace, aroused itself. Good preaching could do the job, and a man temporarily affected by his sins could mend his ways. At death, though the soul had achieved an outward reformation and no longer sinned so far as the eyes of the world could observe, the creature was plunged into Hell by a Lord who could see that internally nothing had really changed.[17]

A society in the national covenant did not have to interest itself in the true inner being of a man. If he behaved it could rest securely. But, of course, a man could not take his condition so lightly; he faced eternal damnation if he settled for anything less than saving faith. It was precisely on this point that the concept of preparation proved of "inconceivable prejudice" to the souls of men, as far as Cotton Mather could see. His analysis of the religious situation in New England always came back to one issue. At the heart of the decline of piety lay the pride of men. Not only did they cherish their own concerns, the flesh and the world, over the Lord's, they wanted to go to Him under their own power. What else was involved—he asked—in the satisfactions felt by the secure and the anxieties experienced by the fearful? The secure, made temporarily "sick" by a sermon or uneasy by their consciences, took up the life of the moral and believed themselves saved. At that point complacency had set in. The anxious, protesting their lack of merit, denied that the Lord would reprieve the likes of them and therefore remained in a natural condition. As different as these two types of men seemed, they were essentially alike: both preferred their own righteousness to Christ. Both indeed were unavowed Arminians. Unfortunately, as preparation was preached in New England it seemed to confirm both sorts in this delusion. It encouraged the secure to confuse works and grace, and the fearful to remain paralyzed and proud.[18]

For all Cotton Mather's concern about stability and his uneasiness at the direction of social change in New England, his primary interest was not the preservation of the order of this world, but its transformation in the expectation of Christ's imminent return. The possibilities of a redefinition of the social order by a league of the faithful of all Protestant churches fascinated him. If sectarianism could be submerged, if toleration could be continued, and if the elect could be converted—and united—then the society might consider itself prepared for the Second Coming of Christ. None of this made him a utopian—he did not expect the reformed society to refine human nature, and he did not suppose that it could continue long without divine assistance.[19]

If any holy reformation were to be attained, the faithful would first have to identify themselves. The hope for Christian Union, after all, lay solely with them. Hence, "how may I know that I am saved," always an important question, took on an extraordinarily, portentous character in Mather's mind.

Cotton Mather never doubted that most men who received God's grace would discover it in themselves. Some good men would never learn of their good fortune, however. A number who had holy educations from an early age might prove unable to discern the first workings of the Spirit in themselves. Such men rarely fell into terrible sins and therefore rarely experienced the guilt that distressed evil men. To be sure, they were evil men before their conversions, but their evil was not so great as most. After they were joined to Christ they sometimes had difficulty knowing it because the peace they had always felt simply continued, though it ripened and gave them even greater joy.[20]

Still another sort might not share the joy of the assurance that they were Christ's. They experienced the pangs of the new birth, but not the comfort that a new creature should expect. The flaw in their conversions lay in themselves—their dreadfully imperfect sanctification, and their tendency to persist in their sins. Because they continued in their sinful ways despite the presence of grace, God afflicted them, sometimes by blasting their lives and fortunes outwardly, but more often by denying them the blessed peace of a soul that knew it had gracious qualities.[21]

These cases produced unhappiness in men; fortunately most men who had saving faith did not require the correctives of such afflictions. Most indeed could be "infallibly certain" of their conversions. Mather did not mean to imply by this declaration of belief in the infallibility of assurance that one's assurance would be "infallibly" clear to others. He always insisted on a distinction between what he called "subjective" assurance and "objective" assurance, the first type referring to self-knowledge (which could be certain) and the second to the demonstration of an inner state to others in the Church (which would always be open to challenge).[22]

Cotton Mather did his thinking about the doctrine of assurance in a tradition especially congenial to him: one that suggested that only the active would find peace. The crisis of Antinomianism had produced this conviction in New England's divines. You should not except to receive comfort from God in your laziness, Richard Mather had told the Dorchester Church. A man who lies around waiting for visions and raptures will get neither. Even John Cotton, whose views of human abilities had raised much suspicion in New England, agreed that only in striving after assurance was one likely to find it.[23]

Although Cotton Mather repeated the demand to look for Christ, he knew that this seemingly simple imperative had failed to keep the churches of New England filled with converted people. The churches by his day did not act to keep people out; the people kept themselves out, for the most part because they distrusted themselves. The people were unable to find the "signs" or "fruits" of faith in themselves that ministers had recommended as evidence of faith. And if the signs appeared, they were distrusted. Self-examination, traditionally encouraged as a means of producing peace of conscience, had yielded only paralysis of will.[24]

The theories, and preaching, of the founders had given the paralyzed little aid, and had, perhaps, contributed to their incapacity. At first sight the tests proposed by divines such as Thomas Hooker and John Cotton seemed so promising; presumably any man who hoped that he was saved could examine himself for the signs and fruits of faith—a peaceable conscience yet one full of grief for its sins, a love of God, and a hatred of evil. Hooker's suggestion that the application of general promises to the believer's particular condition would give assurance was repeated many times, both before he made it and long afterwards. The trouble with all these proposals of method lay in the context in which they were offered. An examination of the self that turned up the promising signs lost its promise when the person making it rememberd how deceitful his own will was. How could he trust the results, however gratifying they seemed? And those who, after the survey of the self detected no feeling at all could not have found much assistance in John Cotton's injunction to live in the "faith" and not by "sense." Cotton's command, doctrinally sound though it was, ignored the fact that inability to detect faith denied the soul the possibility of feeling anything save hopelessness or despair.[25]

When Mather came to take up these problems the need was greater than ever before to establish some means by which the individual could test himself. This need of course involved more than the fate of individuals; the perpetuation of the churches themselves depended to some degree on techniques which would allow the elect to discover their election. Should they continue in their uncertainty, they would also remain properly hesitant about offering themselves to the churches.

Mather's theory of conversion has been seen by some historians as embodying an invitation to salvation to any who strove after the Lord. One of these historians describes Mather as an avid preparationist who "at the beginning of his career . . . was so far heedless of first principles as to represent his brother Nathanael entering into a covenant which became "an influence unto his Conversion afterwards." [26] What Mather actually said was that his brother entered the covenant which became "an influence unto his Conversation afterwards," meaning of course an influence on his behavior.[27] To be sure, on occasions Mather did urge men to try to believe, assuring them that if they did they were probably saved. Such statements were not offered as descriptions of the early stages of the conversion process, say, of the first passage of man from nature to grace. Rather they prescribed a technique by which a man could obtain assurance. Historians who have been deceived into assuming that he was urging preparation neglect to note that Mather also invariably adds that one's trial is not by one's own strength. And they fail to see that the trial he urges has a psychological dimension which included several underlying premises about assurance.

When he urged men to try to believe in Christ—"Now make a TRIAL"—and then told them that if they succeeded in trying, they probably would be saved, he did not intend to imply that they could coerce God into giving them grace. Nor did he mean that they could save themselves by the force of their own wills. He meant—and stated explicitly—that their attempt to believe argued the presence of grace before they made the trial. God's grace, he explained, "enabled" them to try to believe. What their attempt involved was a process of raising into their consciousness their true internal state. Presumably they had, previous to this attempt, emptied themselves and pled their inability, their abasement, and their total dependence upon Christ.[28]

To recognize his inner condition, a man must examine himself not simply for the content of his beliefs and feelings, but for the manner in which he held them. Other Puritan intellectuals had made this point long before Cotton Mather, of course, by reminding their people that even the Devil believed in Christ yet no one supposed that he would be saved. The Devil lacked grace, as did those hypocrites who claimed to believe but inwardly remained unregenerate. How then could they discover their miserable conditions and how could men who were apparently unable to believe and unable even to feel guilt or fear in their unbelief? The first sort of such men in Puritan parlance were suffering from security; the second from deadness. The answer that Mather gave demonstrated again the importance of the psychological framework of his theory with its emphasis on the importance of genuine self-awareness.[29]

Those self-aware enough to recognize their inability to feel guilty, and who regretted their inability should take heart, Mather argued. "Do you *Mourn* because you don't Mourn?" he asked. "This is the *Truest Mourning* in the World." To those who felt fear because they felt no regret at their corruption, he said, *"A Spirit with much Fear* argues . . . *a Spirit without Guile."* The fleshy, the secure, the hardhearted experienced no doubts about themselves. But the fearful, who did, gave "no little token of *a Soft Heart."* At times the Devil inspired such fears; he was envious, Mather explained, of the chosen of God.

He knew that he would never enjoy the delights of Heaven and so he determined to torture those who would. Secure men and hypocritical men rarely received his barbs. Satan already possessed their hearts and should he buffet them he risked awakening them to their carnal conditions. A dead-hearted man who despised himself for his coldness should take comfort then: only "a *Living* Heart" lamented its "own Deadness." And: " 'Tis in some Degree an *Humble* Heart, that complains of its own *Pride*. What can it be, but an *Holy Heart*, that complains of its own *Earthliness*, and *Selfishness* and *Slothfulness?* What but a *Sincere, Honest, Upright Heart*, that complains of its own *Formality* and *Hypocrisy?*" [30]

In Mather's psychological system, the truly introspective man would examine the "fruits," or results, of faith as well as these tokens or signs of the process of conversion itself. The critical feature of self-awareness was not to leave any faculty of the soul unexamined. Hence every idea and every feeling, including deadness and security, carried meaning that a self-conscious person must extract. Attitude and behavior weighed in the psychological scales too. There was much in the Puritan tradition that justified this assumption—Richard Mather, for one, had asserted flatly that sanctification gave evidence of justification. He had not defined sanctification as mere external performance, of course, but had rehearsed the conventional arguments about the attitudes that informed action. His grandson had learned even greater caution, preferring to limit the value of works—or fruits—to the judgment of "objective" assurance. A church must rely heavily on works, along with the person's testimony as to inner experience, but the individual himself must not be content to judge himself only by his actions in the world. Still, no man should ignore his life in the world; if his attitude was right, if he desperately desired to be saved, he should know that if he had grace it would affect every motion of his passage through life. He should know, Cotton Mather put it pithily, that a "workless faith was a worthless faith." [31]

Cotton Mather adopted this line of thought about assurance while still a young man. He had heard it expounded as a youth and would continue to hear it throughout his life. English divines had developed a theory of the works of faith in the sixteenth century and would honor it in treatises and sermons in the seventeenth. Mather never entirely discarded it, but by the early eighteenth century he had to face its imperfection: it failed in application to persuade men who were presumably regenerate, of their regeneracy.[32]

This traditional version of the doctrine of the signs had held that the causes, or "antecedents," of faith should be scrutinized as closely as the fruits which revealed themselves in a sanctified life. How one came to get faith could be as revealing as what one did after attaining it. On this point Mather agreed with the preparationists, though he believed that they had erred in attribuing merit to acts performed before justification. In his own preaching about the signs of faith, Mather gave the conventional encouragement that the weakest sign could be taken as mark of faith. But like most who made this point he had to admit that it was better to have all the signs dimly present than a few strongly and others not at all. And he shrank from saying, as John Rogers once did, that where the signs could not be found, "there is no Faith," though that conclusion was unmistakable.[33]

The complexity of the theory made its application difficult for most men, Mather gradually recognized. The marks of faith themselves, whether they were antecedents or fruits, baffled ordinary men. Some were "graces" or "virtues"—knowledge, patience, temperance, godliness, brotherly kindness, charity, as Richard Mather often had listed them—and could be trusted if they appeared in a self that denied its own righteousness. Judging the moral makeup in which they showed themselves was no easy task, and men who had been bludgeoned with the fact of their depravity shook with fear and despair rather than pronounce themselves faithful. Ministers who could not even agree on the origin of these signs, as Richard Mather (who said they were innate) and Increase Mather (who said they were inserted by God) could not, offered little aid. Other marks were feelings—"affections" or "passions" in Christian terminology, love, desire, humility, sorrow—and offered treacherous grounds on which to make a decision about oneself because pride crept into the process of evaluation, and the right emotions obviously served the self.[34]

As Cotton Mather became aware of the difficulties that his people experienced in applying the traditional tests, he began to simplify the doctrine, to insist that one of the tokens of faith took precedence over the others. He did not scrap the entire theory and occasionally repeated it in all its ramifications. But to persuade men that they had become overly scrupulous, that in practice they could trust their own good intentions, he began to suggest that they should require no more of themselves than the Lord did. All the Lord required, of course, was gracious faith in Christ. If men desired grace, if they desperately desired to believe, they were doubtless saved, for as Cotton Mather triumphantly explained, *The Desire for Grace argues the Presence of Grace.*" He repeated this contention frequently, emphasizing all the while that if a man desired to love Christ, if he desired saving faith, he had doubtless come by it through the enabling action of God.[35]

In revising the theory of the signs, Mather did not choose to depart from orthodoxy, though he just managed to skirt theological disaster. The difficulty in his revision was that in it he placed his reliance almost entirely on the affections, long considered the most unreliable of the faculties. And for good reasons, desire—to cite one—was thought by some to have its physical location in the bowels. The question every commentator who trusted desire faced was of testing its earnestness, its saving character, a problem of course that inhered too in the traditional conception of the signs.[36]

The problem had intrigued Puritans for years. The first generation in New England had approached it cautiously and had decided that the character of desire could not be accurately assessed. Thus Thomas Shepard intoned that "the desires of sons in Christ by faith, are accepted ever; but the desires of servants, men that work only for the wayes out of Christ, are not." Increase Mather, the father of Cotton, pronounced the same verdict for the second generation: "A Man may Desire and Wish for Grace in his Soul to Save him, and yet not be Saved." But just as Shepard left the door ajar for earnest desire to enter as reputable evidence, so also did Increase concede that "sincere" desire might be admitted as trustworthy. Cotton Mather knew the risks as well as anyone but, pushing the door until its hinges squeaked, he insisted that the "Desires of Grace are Grace." [37]

By claiming that a believer could discover so much about himself through his "desire" for grace, Cotton Mather used the faculty psychology in an unconventional way but certainly did not violate its basic tenets. As one of the affections, desire was among the last of the faculties to be renewed by grace when conversion occurred. The process of conversion, most Puritan divines agreed, began with the understanding, which then enlightened the will, and finally ended with the transformation of the affections. Thus, Mather postulated, if a person in examining himself found that he desired to be saved, he could be certain that his affections had been reconstructed, and if the affections, then the entire set of rational and sensible faculties must have been reborn beforehand—for desire was always changed after these major faculties.[38]

Desire had yet another meaning with its own peculiar resonance in Mather's mind. As a quality, desire approached love; and a true longing for salvation did not transpire in a selfish spirit. It involved a profound yearning for union with God. Pious desires were a sign of life, of grace, Mather explained, because the Holy Spirit of God worked in them; they were a response to the Spirit, an aching need to be *"swallowed up in Him."* [39]

Mather expressed all this most clearly late in his life, when he was obsessed with the ecumenical spirit. The congruence of the set of ideas about Christian Union and his psychological assumptions was not accidental. The same spirit informed each and in fact his psychology of conversion served as an analogue to his theory of the union of the faithful, joined among themselves and to God. The psychological theory obliterated the self; the ecumenical, the sects. The psychological re-emphasized the centrality of faith in Christian life; the ecumenical made faith the only enduring principle of holy organization. Mather, one suspects, saw the analogy, but even if he did not, he knew at least that he was influenced by a powerful strain in Protestantism, a hope to see things whole in the reduction of man's pride and the glorification of God. This hope inspired all his preaching to his people.

14

Christis and the Covenant

Through the psychology of abasement, Cotton Mather reaffirmed
two of the regnant doctrines of Puritanism—the omnipotence of
God and the helplessness of man. Translated into psychology,
the theology described an arrangement in which a man's only
hope of salvation lay in his ability to divest himself of his sinful
will. Only then, when he could say that he had given himself up
for lost and was willing to receive Christ, was there any hope
for him. He could do nothing efficaciously without the assistance
of God of course—not wish, not desire, not hope, not even pray.
All he could do was to beg for the strength to loathe himself and
to seek the Lord. When he found he could act, he might entertain the hope that he was saved.

This doctrine of God's sovereignty in conversion virtually
filled Mather's preaching to his people. In the eighteenth century when he was inspired by the new evangelicalism, he made
adherence to it the first of the "MAXIMS OF PIETY." The fear
of the sovereign God, which gives glory to Him, the first Maxim
held, is the essence of piety. The conclusion from this proposition seemed obvious to him—"PIETY" begins with man's recognition of his corruption and his need of the grace of God.[1]

Cotton Mather did not choose to preach to his church only in the terms supplied by the faculty psychology. Had he done so his fame as a teacher would have turned into notoriety, and his church would have abandoned him. The psychology was not dry, abstract stuff—not in the sermons he delivered—but it was not supple enough either in conception or language to furnish the fare a church required every Sabbath. For, a minister in the ordinary course of his preaching had to accomplish three tasks: converting the unregenerate, giving believers the assurance that they were saved and thereby nourishing their faith, and establishing the basis of moral obligation or of right conduct in life.

Like his father and grandfather, and virtually every other Congregational minister in seventeenth-century New England, Cotton Mather dealt with these problems by preaching the covenant theology. In its classic form, as developed by Preston, Perkins, Ames, and Sibbes, this theology, with its juridical bias, its suggestion that God offered man an escape from the determinism of predestination, proved as unsuitable to Cotton Mather's understanding of religious life as it had to his father's. The inventors of the Federal Theology, as the covenant theory is sometimes called, had suggested bluntly that God had so confined Himself by agreeing to live up to the terms of the covenant that man might bargain for his salvation. To be sure, the covenant did not alter God's election, but in dealing with men through contractual terms He has agreed to explain the qualifications for eternal glory and to live up to the promise He makes. The covenant theologians took great comfort from the conviction that one who demonstrated the qualifications could be assumed to be in contract with the Lord. Believers could attain absolute assurance; the covenant's terms could not be broken for, as John Cotton said, "If we be hemm'd in within this Covenant, we cannot break out." Nor would God violate its terms. Peter Bulkely asserted that God "cannot be a covenant breaker." The terms of the offer indeed might be pushed by a faithful man to force the Lord, under legal means, of course, to offer the covenant. John Preston urged men armed by faith to "sue him of his own bond written and sealed, and he cannot deny it." Preston's reasoning extended the idea as far as any of the Federalists dared: "When faith hath once gotten a promise, be sure that thou keepe thy hold, pleade hard with the *Lord,* and tell him it is a part of his Covenant, and it is impossible that he should deny thee. . . . When thou art on a sure ground, take no denyall, though the *Lord* may defer long, yet he will doe it, he cannot chuse; for it is a part of his Covenant." [2]

As interpreted by the Federalists, the covenant theory reassured men who were distressed by the iron inflexibility of predestination and election. These men of the early seventeenth century yearned for some comfort, and they received with sighs of thankfulness the news proclaimed by the divines of the first generation that God had agreed to operate in the world of men according to the logic and reason of a contract, similar to any they might sign in the world of commerce. But, as Cotton Mather reconstructed history in New England, thankfulness soon gave way to complacency, and by the appearance of the third generation, security and pride had replaced both. Mather looked with regret on the lack in New England of the mystery and the terror and the omnipotence of God. He considered the proud men of his day deluded in their confidence that their belief was meritorious, even, as Puritan theologians said, the procuring cause of God's grace.[3]

In his own preaching he readily conceded that advocates of more than one *"Form* of coming into the Covenant" existed in New England, but he announced his preference for the "consenting and Receptive and Relying way of Procedure; this Method of making *Self* to be *Nothing,* and Jesus to be all." [4] Unlike Increase, Cotton Mather did not hesitate to use the commercial metaphors of the founders in describing the covenant relationship. But with a difference—the founders' sermons portrayed the believer binding God with terms, promises, and legally enforceable bargains; the implication of such efforts was that man in covenant dealt with the Lord as a virtual equal. Mather's sense of the gulf between nature and grace; and the helplessness he felt as a man before the authority of the Divine curbed whatever impulse he might have had to approach God in anything but the most abject frame of mind. It is not man who "redeems" his soul unaided, he explained in a typical sermon, but Christ who "redeems an estate from forfeiture" and a man from destruction. As for bargaining and equality, the covenant permitted neither to man. A believer aspired to wear the livery of Christ. "Yea, He is One, whose Ear is *bored,* unto the *Service* of the

LORD, he will never go away from *Serving* of his Beloved LORD." Lest the gap between service and equality be underestimated, Mather declared that "Our SAVIOUR is then the *Owner* of the Christian. The Christian is His Possession." How was this arrangement made, or in Mather's phrase, How did Christ come to get "title" to the Christian? Again the language of business proved convenient, as Mather explained that Christ bought the believer by His sacrifice and thereby redeemed him. Business terminology evidently could be used by a divine to demonstrate subordination as well as equality.[5]

Of course, it may appear that Mather's discussion here pertains most directly to the Covenant of Redemption, the transaction between God the Father and God the Son in which Christ pays off the debt of sin by His own sacrifice. Mather may have attributed greater significance to this covenant between God and Christ than to the covenant of grace, but he did not choose to elevate the role of the believer in the second covenant. The Christian's part in the covenant of grace was hardly one which should fill him with a sense of his own importance. He must give his "consent" to the contract. Like hundreds of other New England parsons, Mather used the word, and repeated it in sermons covering more than half a century. But he always explained that consenting meant "surrender." And believers should not inflate the importance of their consent in the covenant, for as a return to the glorious mercy of the Lord it was a "very poor one." In giving it, "servants" must recognize what they do: "Coming into the *Covenant* of God, they then sign Indentures for the Service of the Saviour." [6]

Nor should they deceive themselves about the source of the power that enabled them to consent, which came from God. The original Federalists had sometimes neglected to state that God supplied the divine energy. Their oversight was understandable; their eagerness to rescue desperate men from Calvinism's rigidity made them forget to make explicit every premise of their theory. The men of their generation, they knew, possessed an abiding sense of their own depravity and weakness anyway.[7]

Cotton Mather faced a different sort. As far as he could see, a minister must remind men that though their strength was more than enough to settle the land and make it thrive, to build towns and give them life, and to push ships and goods all over the Atlantic and beyond, it availed them nothing in the world of the spirit. The old exhortation to love the world with weaned affections—to live in it but not be of it—apparently left men cold. So in preaching about conversion and the peace that accompanied it, he never allowed his listeners to forget that they could not enter the covenant under their own power. At the beginning of his ministry he insisted that "No man can come except the Father draw him," and at the end that the sinner was, of course, *"Unworthy* that He should *Enable* you." His advice remained unvarying, as he urged the sinner to beg Christ to "make me willing" to enter the covenant.[8]

Once made willing, according to the theory of the Federal Theologians, the believer could obtain assurance through his honoring the promises of the covenant. When he did so by living according to the law, he demonstrated the holiness of his faith and he could demand that God give him the comfort his actions deserved. After all, the Lord had granted men His covenant, and He had pledged Himself to keep its promises. In this mood, Mather occasionally urged that men plead the promises of the covenant to alleviate the sadness they felt in their earthly condition. But he did not ordinarily use the language of law because he did not conceive of the covenant so much as a legal instrument as one that ratified man's total dependence upon the Divine. In it men could test themselves, and others who wished, for example to enter the churches of New England; yet while they did so, they must recognize the opportunities of outwardly counterfeiting good behavior.[9]

Nor did Mather ever suggest that the believer in the covenant could require assurance from God. The obligation of attaining it, he suggested, rested with the believer, who might beg for divine assistance, but who should never expect to obtain comfort by merely reminding the Lord of the promises of the covenant. The believer's obligation arose in the covenant—he must plead his lack of merit and his inability to achieve good by his own efforts, but he must never stop trying. In the covenant he pledged his faith, depending always of course upon the gift of God, not the efficacy of his own prayers. His most reliable resource was subjective and hence not to be clearly seen by his friends or his church. He must examine his soul, test his affections, his disposition to come to God. The covenant required this internal action from him, not from the Lord.[10]

By reminding men that in entering into the covenant they pledged themselves to prove their faith by leading holy lives, the Federal Theologians established the basis of moral obligation. These theologues also saw the possibilities the theory presented for ecclesiastical and social organization. Here, of course, they may have followed the lead of medieval political thinkers; in any case, the Federal Theologians wrote dissertations expounding the covenant as the basis of all societies, including the Church order.[11]

In appropriating the theory to their own purposes and in developing the sermon form called the jeremiad, the New Englanders in the Federal tradition devised a means to whip their society into line. Yet over the course of a generation they discovered the practical limits of the entire conception. Men could be threatened; they could be enticed into renewing the covenant in their churches; they could even be persuaded to reform temporarily. Then they would return to their old ways, like a dog to his vomit, Puritan pastors sadly noted. No one saw this more clearly than Cotton Mather, who nonetheless preached jeremiads by the score. But even he could tire of ramming his head against a brick wall, and by the late 1690's he was working a new emphasis into his homiletics.[12]

Increase Mather may have given Cotton the new direction. Although always more of a traditional covenant theologue than his son, Increase had begun to protest early in his career against the neglect of Christ in favor of "meer morality," which, he said, filled much of the preaching of his day.[13] A Christian minister should concentrate on the sacrifice of Christ, emphasizing that the righteousness of the Saviour justified believers, not their own righteousness. This simple proposition had in fact disappeared from much Puritan preaching, replaced in the first generation by exhortations to assume legal obligations, to pay the price, to press the "promises," to fulfill the terms of the contract, and in the second by reasuring claims that men could take comfort from leading moral lives, that the external gave evidence of the internal condition.[14]

Neither technique comported easily with Cotton Mather's psychology of conversion, a point he made in various ways throughout his ministry. A sinner whose first duty was to beg for the strength to surrender himself to God should not be told that a life of righteousness could be attained by demanding anything from God or that he could complacently regard external behavior as adequate to satisfy the law. Men were too prone to settle for these easy subterfuges and to evade their responsibilities. They should not be encouraged to look upon the covenant as a contrivance they might enter at will, nor should they be permitted to assume that their "consent" to its terms came from themselves. That was the assumption of graceless men who pledged themselves to God and then relaxed secure in their own virtue.[15]

In many sermons, Cotton Mather used an old mode of analysis, presenting Christ in His various guises as the Priest, the Prophet, and the King; in others he examined the Trinity.[16] None of these efforts was orginal, nor was any of them an exercise in disinterested scholarship. What Mather intended was to illuminate and glorify Christ as a sacrificial figure who provided a means of redeeming sinners and a model for the righteous life. The covenant of redemption which existed between God the Father and God the Son far transcended the covenant of grace between God and the believer. The covenant of grace, he once explained, was an "Echo" of the covenant of redemption.[17] Every Puritan divine of the seventeenth century would have agreed, but most preferred to work directly on men's souls through the explication of the terms of the covenant of grace. At the same time these ministers must have sensed the inconsistency of urging men to abase themselves before Christ and telling them to regard conversion as a legal transaction. Cotton Mather did and said so. Although he was never a model of harmonies, he managed to make his psychological assumptions rest easily with his doctrine of conversion. And he found a vocabulary which expressed both.[18]

To his auditories in churches all over New England, he spoke of the need of men to repent and convert. He often delivered his message without once mentioning the covenant of grace and somtimes did not even pronounce the word "conversion." Instead he saturated his message with metaphors which suggest the sinner's dependency and which diminish the importance of his power while continually urging him to try incessantly to join with Christ. The sinner should "fly" to Christ, to unite with Him, and "nestle" under His "wings." Taking his text from Ezekiel 17.23 on one occasion, Mather told a society of young people that Christ is a "Cedar" offering "shelter" to all kinds of men; the branches are His Churches; sinners who come to Christ are "birds" enjoying a divine protection. The hackneyed figures of the shepherd and his lambs entered Mather's discourse too; their use serving for all their familiarity in the seventeenth century to emphasize the sinner's need for greater righteousness than his own.[19]

Christ provided the center in all these pulpit efforts. Mather was dazzled by the splendor of Christ's sacrifice and humble before it. If Mather's listeners heard anything he said they must have received the impression that they too should worship the miracle of Christ's incarnation. Mather lavished attention on this part of his Christology: at some point before the creation of the universe, Christ had covenanted with God the Father to take on the flesh of man, to suffer all the degradation of human kind, hunger, thirst, fatigue. And in the flesh He accepted the scorn of the Pharisees, and the afflictions of His Roman captors. Finally, He gave His life for His Church, the elect of God. In this act, Christ, the guiltless, took on the burden of men's enormities, their sins; and men, the guilty, enjoyed the immense benefit of His righteousness, which the Lord imputed to them.[20]

Theologically Mather's reasoning was impeccable: the God of predestination chose men according to His pleasure and nothing they could do affected His choice. And Christ's sacrifice supplied the righteousness to satisfy the guilt of the fallen. The knowledge that concentrating on these old verities put him on secure theological footing reassured Mather, but he chose this bent in preaching for other reasons as well, reasons which he may not have fully recognized. His tendency of thought ran to the personalizing of issues: he rarely spoke of evil without invoking demons or the Devil; and good reminded him of the best man who ever lived, the Son of God, Christ the Savior. This habit of mind and character accorded well with an ancient tradition in Christian worship and homiletics, the imitation of Christ. In the works of Thomas à Kempis and others like him Mather found inspiration and information for his own attempts to break down the security residing in the covenant of works and to provide a model of behavior for gracious men.[21]

Men required a knowledge of Christ's sacrifice if they were to be converted. Anyone could get a "speculative" or "notional" knowledge of it—we would say that anyone could understand it intellectually. Such knowledge could not save; and Mather in all his Christology argued that men must obtain a saving knowledge, or as he once said, "be very Really sensible of the Beauty and Sweetness that is in Him, and like that woman once, we should feel *Vertue going forth* from Him unto our Souls; or like Paul, find upon our selves the *power* of what is in our Lord." Should we succeed, or as Cotton Mather cautiously phrased it, should we be enabled to come to God, we might then imitate His life as closely as possible.[22]

For all those sinners schooled in the attitudes of self-scrutiny and steeled to face the worst in themselves, the imitation of Christ offered a further means of gaining assurance that they belonged to the Lord. What Mather attempted in these sermons was to supply a method by which a right frame of mind could be attained by Christians, a frame of mind which would govern every thought and action of their beings.

Cotton Mather recognized the danger implicit in his prescription. A man who imitated Christ might in time become convinced that he himself was divine. Hence Mather took pains in a number of sermons to remind his church that of course they could not conform to Christ in every respect. They could not recapture Christ's mediatory function nor could they achieve His holiness. Yet they must give their best to efforts in conforming to Him, for "Without the *Imitation of Christ,* all thy *Christianity* is a meer Nonentity." [23]

Although the methods proposed by Mather were varied, their essence was simple—the regulation of the self in all its thoughts, actions, and appetites so "that the *Sweetness* of everything shall be more or less, according to the *Service* of a glorious CHRIST, promoted in them." [24] When a believer applied this standard, he attempted to duplicate Christ's reactions when he confronted both good and evil. Human excellence should set him to thinking of Christ's; abasements must make him reconstruct the Savior's circumstances when He took on human flesh. When the believer was afflicted, he must take joy from the fact that his suffering established a tie between himself and Christ, who also suffered. In doing good to one's fellows, Christ's methods must be emulated—"convey something of Christ to those who receive your alms"; in dealing with the contentious the same rule applied—be a peacemaker.[25] The possibilities for imitation appeared endless; and the technique could be recommended with feeling by Mather because he himself used it in his own life.[26]

Like the other elements in Mather's preaching of the covenant, the technique established on different grounds Mather's psycholoy of conversion. Its aim was to enable the Christian to achieve a regulation of his life according to divine commands. Its method imposed a subordination of the entire soul—reason, will, passions—to the will of God. Implicitly the technique recognized man's terrible depravity and his helplessness, and provided gentle persuasion, as well as the means, for a surrender of the self to Christ.

Because Mather's version of Puritan Christology prescribed an emotional religion and stressed the importance of a "vital" experience of Christ, it fused smoothly early in the eighteenth century with his preaching of the New Piety. The heart of Piety was experimental religion which provided a "transforming energy" that altered human character.[27] None of Mather's new emphasis altered old doctrines; much of what he offered in the life of Piety amounted to no more than the old evangelicalism of Richard Mather, decked out in a fresh terminology. It did, however, demand more of the believer than simply taking up the covenant of grace. In signing the indentures of the covenant the believer took on more than a legal obligation; he entered more than a contract; he made more than a bargain; he agreed to testify to the renewal of his soul in a vital religious experience. But if the New Piety did not alter doctrine, nor challenge the tenets of the covenant theology, it did recommend the old theory on fresh grounds. It relegated the intellectualism of the covenant to the trash heap—replacing it with the passionate contention that only gracious experience weighed on the divine scales. The standards that men should take for their own could all be found in the experience of the believer in Christ. If men could truly make Christ their model, they would experience a glorious transformation. But to save themselves, and to do anything good, they must be born again in Christ. The figure of the new birth, important before in the primitive Church and destined for two centuries to inspire revivalism throughout the Western world, revealed the evangelical fervor of Mather's American Pietism.[28]

His fervor did not cool before the unalterable fact of human impotence. All his preaching recognized the helplessness of man unassisted by grace. But the New Piety transformed man, liberated him from sin, and gave him the power to glorify God. In its anatomy this sort of evangelicalism did not differ from the old message of the covenant theology. The skeleton and the flesh were the same—man tainted with original sin and a corrupt heart awaiting purification by divine grace. But in the New Piety, the old members have been rearranged, and draped in a brighter, more inviting, and simpler clothing.[29]

The advantage of Pietism to the minister who had to deal with an indifferent people lay in its simplicity and its emotionalism. No need now to balance free will against the necessities of an iron predestination; no need to make responsibilities commensurate with promises. No need to plod through the thickets of terms and conditions which one agreed to, but which one could not meet. The truth was simpler, Mather reported from the pulpit of evangelicalism: if a man could believe in the "MAXIMS OF PIETY"—and live by them—he would enjoy the divine glory.[30]

A believer's conformity to Christ provided, according to Cotton Mather, the only way to attain the New Piety. A typical exhortation in this mode found him calling on his church to resolve to take up the New Piety. But, Mather continued, the resolution should not be made in your own strength, for "If it be, there will be *no Strength* in it." [31] There are some, Mather preached in the winter of 1714, who resolve on a life of Piety when they feel a *"Devout Pang."* In their arrogance they resolve to carry out their intentions unassisted. Of course nothing comes of such resolutions. Cotton Mather did not hide his contempt for these failures. "They *trust in their own Hearts,* and they are *Fools."* These men, despite all their good resolutions, need a power greater than themselves. They need Christ; as Mather explained the way success was achieved, an "ingredient of every good resolution of Piety is ALL THINGS THRO' CHRIST WHO STRENGTHENS ME." [32]

The covenant of grace scarcely appeared in this scheme. The burden will be carried by Christ who has given His promise to God—not to man. In fact, during the last ten years of his ministry, Cotton Mather deliberately reduced the importance of the covenant of grace. Its function, he explained, is to "assign the Language of every good RESOLUTION with you." But redemptive power will come from the contract of Christ who promises God that He will "*Quicken,* and *Incline,* and *Strengthen* the people whom He will bring under the shadow of His Wings, to Glorify GOD in a *Walk before Him.*" The believer's role is, in the new language, to resolve on Piety; his role is to consent to the covenant.

> "The Style of the *Resolution* must be This; *O Great GOD,* Be Thou my God, I am not able to walk before thee, O my God, as I own my self under infinite Bonds to do: but I desire to do it; I desire to do it! And my dear Jesus has Engaged, that His people shall do it. And I consent, Oh! I consent, that He should cause me to do it. I put my self under His conduct, that He may do so; and Relying upon Him, I resolve to do what He will have me to do. Yes, and even in doing this also, 'tis *His Help that has bro't me to it.*" [33]

Mather did not regard the covenant of redemption as one more contrivance which could be used to bind the Lord to the terms of the covenant of grace. The Federal Theologians had so considered it, arguing that this bond between God the Father and God the Son might be adduced as further evidence of God's good intentions toward men. These theologians had further created the impression that the covenant with Christ was a less glorious device than the one with the believer by presenting it as the procuring cause of the covenant of grace. In the course of things the arrangement between Father and Son had to be prior to the one between God and man, but the Federal Theologues inferred from this order that the first step, the treaty God made with Himself, carried slightly less nobility than the second, which He concluded with man. The first was taken, was it not, only to permit the second? [34]

When Cotton Mather chose to follow the example of the Federal Theologues and used legal language in describing the two covenants, he invariably referred to Christ as the "surety" for the indebtedness of man. The covenant of redemption paid the bill for the covenant of grace; man's task was to strive to come under the covenant with Christ. This agreement that God made with Himself became for man the covenant of reconciliation. It gave the covenant of grace its power, and more, its very being.[35]

If Mather's Christology was one more expression of his belief in God's power and man's helplessness, it became by the early years of the eighteenth century a vehicle for criticizing much of the preaching of his day. As early as 1712, he hinted at what he considered were the causes of the failure to convert the people of New England. The reason men did not convert, he implied in a manual he wrote to help them find their way to grace, was that some ministers—"some Excellent Servants of God"—led men to believe that they could enter the covenant as equals with God. That *Form* of coming into the Covenant" has not been "without Blessed Effects," Mather admitted; but too often it had failed because men trusted their own strength in using it.[36]

Mather had raised again the dilemma that had inhered in Puritan theory since its beginnings in the sixteenth century. How could men act when they were helpless to act? They could not believe by themselves; they could not enter the covenant unassisted; they could not lead good lives without divine assistance. The preaching that attempted to deal with these problems by telling men that if they believed in Christ they must demand the covenant from God had produced these civil, moral men whom Puritan ministers had complained of for a hundred years. Cotton Mather recognized them in their self-satisfaction and branded them—to their faces—"practical atheists." This same preaching, through its emphasis on preparation, had also stimulated scrupulosity so great as to be paralyzing in another sort of men. This group was made overly self-conscious by the dissection of the preparatory stages and by the incessant demand that they examine themselves for grace. Mather sympathized with such men and urged them to trust Christ; he also pointed out that their belief that they must have merit before God would give them grace still lingered in this group. The old covenant preaching had yielded still a third group, Mather believed: they were men who could not feel anything about religion, either love or hatred toward God, and who were not frightened by their inability to fear God. This group appears to have been a phenomenon of the third generation, psychologically far removed from the founders, and completely the children of an emergent capitalistic society—this-worldly, recognizing godliness but not experiencing it.[37]

To move the men in all these groups Mather began preaching the psychology of abasement and his version of covenant theory. His psychological theory and his Christology "solved" in seventeenth-century terms the dilemmas that had long troubled laymen and divines alike. His "solution" readily conceded that men were helpless to act; everything Mather believed about conversion hinged on the acceptance of God's omnipotence and human weakness. All he urged was that men should beg for the strength to despise themselves; they should ask for help in order to plead for salvation; their natures after all prevented them from doing it naturally. They could not even attain a saving "fear" without Christ's aid. When they were frightened by external compulsion they resolved to please God, and set about to do it "in their own strength." And of course because they attributed worth to their efforts "*All* presently comes to *Nothing*."[38]

Mather reached this insight after years of observation. He himself had often attempted to frighten men into converting, and never really stopped. But he did translate his hard-found knowledge into his preaching. The year before he died he declared his dissatisfaction to a large gathering in Boston that had been badly frightened by an earthquake. "I freely own to you, that I am not entirely satisfied in a *Form of Covenanting* with GOD, wherein we act our selves as *Principals* and a Glorious CHRIST is brought in only as an *Accessary*."[39] Hence the emphasis he gave to the covenant of redemption.

But Mather did more than play up one covenant and play down another. He made this emphasis on Christ the most important technique of the New Piety. Almost all his preaching in the eighteenth century urged men to accept their status as accessories to Christ, to deny the value of the self in favor of Christ. Mather, of course, was not preaching a new doctrine in these sermons; he was not really preaching a doctrine at all. The psychological premise of his homiletics in the eighteenth century was the promise of the emotional fulfillment that awaited men who accepted the MAXIMS OF PIETY. They would experience raptures and joy when Christ gathered them to Himself. What Christ required of them was apparently simple—their full acceptance of their conditions as accessories to Him. At this point Mather's covenant theory, his Christology, and his psychology of religious experience were fused in the New Piety.[40]

Mather entertained great hopes for men who covenanted in this way. With generations of ministers in New England he had long called for the reformation of society in the expectation that Christ's coming would immediately follow. And men joined together in covenant with Christ, experiencing the inspiration of the New Piety, might do much for others in their land. And that—doing good to men—offered one more way to glorify God.

15

The Failure of Reformation

Three or four years into the eighteenth century, Cotton Mather realized that his hopes for the conversion of men and their cooperation in a Christian Union were going to be delayed. The collapse of the United Brethren in England was clear, though he and others continued to use that term to describe dissenting Protestants in England and America. In New England true conversions were rare, as men seemed bent on entering the covenant on their own merits. Others pled their worthlessness as reason for remaining in an unregenerate state. None of these conditions was new, and ministers responded with the language of the jeremiad, calling for reformation and predicting destruction if men failed to come to the Lord. As old as the responses, were the results: Stoddard said, "Attempts for Reformation have been like attempts to find the Philosophers Stone." [1]

Over the years of his ministry, but especially in the years before 1691, Mather delivered many conventional assessments of his people's character. In these sermons, denunciation invariably overpowered whatever inclinations he had to give reassurance that things were not as bad as they appeared. The Synod of 1679 provided the bill of indictment, and Mather followed the list faithfully, permitting himself originality only in his expressions of horror and in the fullness with which he illustrated the sins of the land. He reminded his audience that sin invariably brought afflictions and then pointed out the recent examples and predicted fresh onslaughts. Only slightly less frequently did he remark on the possibility that God would give up on New England altogether.[2]

According to ancient belief, which Cotton Mather sometimes resurrected and sent forth in his sermons, Providence decreed that good would emerge finally from the sins of men and the disasters that befell them. Providence worked in its own mysterious ways, and men were bound to accept that the Lord would find a way to transform the evil and the ugly into the good and beautiful. Mather accepted this proposition with his head, but he had great difficulty in believing in his heart that any good could proceed from the decay of New England. Of course, God would have His Church elsewhere even if He decided to cast off the people. And what would the people have? Cotton Mather knew: a blasting on earth while they remained on its face and eternal torment once they left it.[3]

Many ministers had preceded him with the prediction "Reformation or Desolation" but none until Jonathan Edwards succeeded in imparting a greater sense of urgency to the call for action.[4] Edwards succeeded through a mastery of language; Mather, by an analysis that touched every group in the community. The general problem of his society, as he said in a number of ways, was its drift from the true religion. Religion had decayed; the Church suffered from a loss of communicants, and hypocrites lurked among those it claimed for its own. New Englanders of his day simply could not match the piety of the founders. This decline also appeared in the lives men led away from the meetinghouse. In pointing this out, Mather did not hide his displeasure from the powerful, telling merchants, for example, that he did not like the way business was conducted in New England. This stand required courage because most of his church was made up of moderately fixed businessmen who were on the make. Cotton Mather warned them to curb their appetites: "stinted estates" were best, he said. He also opposed directly the growing mobility in New England, insisting that men should not give up honest callings to enter new ones simply to earn more money. Exploitation of the poor, sharp practices, high interest on loans all drew his fire.[5]

Cotton Mather's criticism gained from his concreteness. Not content to list the familiar sins of usury, oppression, and extortion, he spoke to merchants and tradesmen with unaccustomed directness. They were, it appeared, guilty of sharp and shabby business practice. They must have eyed one another, and their customers in the audience, as he indicted them in a sermon before the General Court in 1709:

> "For men to put off *Adulterated* or *Counterfeited* Wares; or, for men to work up their Wares *Deceitfully;* when the fish is naught; the Tar has undue mixtures; there is Dirt and Stone instead of Turpentine; there are thick Layers of Salt instead of other things that should be there; the Cheese is not made as tis affirm'd to be; the Liquor is not for Quantity or Quality such as was agreed for; the Wood is not of the Dimensions that are promised unto the Purchaser; or perhaps, there was a *Trespass* in the place of Cutting it; the Hay does not hold out Weight by abundance; the Lumber has a false Number upon it; or, the *Bundles* are not as Good *Within* as they are *Without; Tis an Abomination!"* [6]

The failures of the younger generation seemed hardly less abominable. Young men aped modern fashions and kept out of sight unless they could wear the latest styles. They shrank too before the suggestion that they should make professions of their religious experiences, if they had any, and they avoided the Sabbath services as carefully as they put aside last year's clothing. They drank, they rioted, they pursued the gratifications of the senses wherever carnality carried them. But most grievously of all, they rejected the ways of their fathers.[7]

If much of Mather's concern was expressed about men in business and men in their youth, these two groups did not constitute the entire array that angered him. Political factions who made the new charter their target, dissolute old men who had neglected their opportunities for salvation, traders who debauched the Indians with rum, and many others also earned his scorn. In this long indictment, one charge took precedence over all the rest—the fragmentation of the community. The separateness of all these groups severely compromised the possibilities for a true union of Christians.[8]

How fully Mather comprehended the growing differentiation of groups in New England's society is not clear. By the end of the seventeenth century new social types were emerging that would not have pleased the founders. The development of overseas commerce hastened their appearance; in fact merchants trading with London provided the most striking examples of the new sort of men in New England. To say that these merchants constituted a "class" is surely too simple; in attitudes and values they differed from one another in important ways. But they did share a rough unity of economic interests. Among other things, they needed to find money and goods to ease an unfavorable balance of trade; to maintain their ties with English merchants and officials, both of whom had so much to say about imperial regulation; and to ensure the existence of colonial governments sympathetic to their concerns and problems.[9]

They counted pious men within their number, men like Samuel Sewall, who studied the prophecies and wrote about the end of the world. Sewall had married the daughter of John Hull, a wealthy merchant who instructed his ship captains in the ways of the Lord as faithfully as he did in the ways of business. Sewall served the Massachusetts Bay Colony for years as a Superior Court judge and councillor; and he took a loving interest in all the problems of his church. And there was his interest in New England, an interest that propelled him into beliefs that some of his sophisticated contemporaries considered absurd: opposition to wigs, for example, and to the keeping of Christmas.[10]

Samuel Shrimpton, a merchant, was one of those contemporaries. Shrimpton had inherited a fortune on the death of his father in 1666, a sum of almost 12,000 pounds, and twenty years later he was the richest man in Boston. Shrimpton traded fish to Europe, imported English manufactures, and sent logs to England. He owned sizable amounts of real estate in and around Boston. Shrimpton's wealth and his overseas connections disposed him to fancy himself an English gentleman. He did not admire Puritan government, and soon after Massachusetts lost its charter he refused to recognize the jurisdiction of the local courts and the legislature. Not surprisingly he supported Andros and the Dominion of New England. A number of great merchants of his sort actually joined the Church of England; Shrimpton may not have joined, but the first Anglican marriage ceremony was performed in his house.[11]

Sewall of course did not like Shrimpton—nor his style of life. Sewall's *Diary* contains this account of the riotous excesses of Shrimpton and his friends: "Mr Shrimpton, Capt. Lidget and others come in a Coach from Roxbury about 9. aclock or past, singing as they come, being inflamed with Drink. At Justice Morgan's they stop and drink Healths, curse, swear, talk profanely and baudily to the great disturbance of the Town and grief of good people. Such high-handed wickedness has hardly been heard of before in Boston." [12]

Shrimpton and Sewall stood at nearly opposite poles among the merchants, and taken together suggest how far social complexity had proceeded in the New England that Cotton Mather wished to reform. These merchants had economic concerns in common but not much else united them. And not even economic interest joined the youth, the sects, the craftsmen, shopkeepers, sailors, fishermen, farmers, housewives, teachers, doctors, and all the others Mather hoped to bring into Christian Union. Mather, of course, did not often think of these groups in economic, or sociological, categories. He occasionally remarked on the different "tribes" in his church, explaining that he meant the rich, the middling-sort, and the poor. He saw that a desire for social status motivated the secessionists from his church who formed first the New North and then the New Brick churches— this "proud Crue," he said in his *Diary,* "must have Pues for their dispicable Families." [13] As he watched them scrambling for position, he thought he detected the "Dissolution" of his church.[14] He was exaggerating, of course, and may have realized it—he was far too compelling a preacher to lose his church and he knew it. A few years after the New North secessionists departed, their places had been filled by others eager to listen to Mather. Yet he could not help but think of dissolution when he observed secessionists in his or other churches. The fragmentation of a particular church seemed symptomatic of a splintering of institutions and communities of all kinds in New England.[15]

Cotton Mather's comprehension of the changes he observed with such distaste was limited by his propensity to see them largely in moral terms. Sometimes he blamed the Devil as the instigator; at others he saw the melancholy sins of his parishioners in them; at still other times he viewed them as the just afflictions sent upon him by God for his own derelictions. But whatever the explanation, he saw only one way out for his people—reform and repentance and the doing of good that might help reunite all men. This concern led him into an innovation that probably contributed to the division that he sought to close: he began asking his flock to suggest topics for his sermons, and at least part of the time he agreed to preach to private groups on subjects they chose. These practices inevitably led to a subtle erosion of his own authority as a minister who declared what God's purposes were for His people. Mather of course used all these occasions to say what he wished, preaching sermons designed to convert and to persuade men to join in a Christian Union. But still he was contributing to a social process he did not understand.[16]

In his confusion and fear he also preached jeremiads. If the jeremiad expressed a familiar appeal, it had, nonetheless, undergone a subtle change in fifty years. The first jeremiads had addressed a backsliding people, a people like Israel—stiff-necked, selfish, too much attached to this world—but still a good people, the chosen of the Lord. By the early eighteenth century, this assumption that goodness resided in the people was not so easily made. Ministers still addressed the people of New England as a body and assured them and the world that as things went they were the best people in the world. Their religion was purer, their morals higher, their behavior better than others'. Their need for reformation, the ministers warned, lay in the fact that though in comparison to the world they were good, they had declined disastrously from their fathers. Their fathers of course had been told the same thing. Yet in repeating the old admonitions the ministers of the eighteenth century did more than follow a respected form. To be sure, they attempted to recall a people to holiness that constituted their difference from other peoples of the world, but—and herein lies a departure from the old convention—they also sometimes suggested that perhaps this new generation of New Englanders was never any good. It had not declined; it had never arisen above the pollution of original sin.[17]

The ministers' uncertainty about their people is put flatly at times—"we are not the men our fathers were" expresses only one fear. In a few years this disavowal of the quality of the present generation became conventional, just as comparisions to the children of Israel had in the sermons of the first generation. More importantly the preachers of the new century inserted appeals to convert in their castigations of New England. They said that grace did not exactly abound in the land and that in time it might completely disappear. The reformation that they appealed for does not involve a return to the Lord, but a coming for the first time. This is what God expects; and they warned that His patience has extended as long as it has out of fondness for the fathers, not because the people deserve it.[18]

From these premises, Cotton Mather, Stoddard, Colman, and most divines who left a record of their utterances felt justified in asking for a broad reformation of society—the conversion of men of all ranks and orders and the rejuvenation of manners and morals. These divines despised the radicals of their day, the levelers who they imagined were lurking on the fringes of society and the Antinomians who, some thought, with even less reason, still survived in New England.

By the usual standards of measuring social philosophies of this age, Cotton Mather was as "conservative" as any. He exhorted men of all sorts to give their best in their particular callings; a diligent mechanic he said was a far better person than a weathly gentleman who lived on his substance and avoided work. Once a man had a calling, he should not give it up lightly, say, just to earn more money. Of course, if he were not suited to his job, if he lacked the qualifications and the gifts to perform it well, then he might change jobs. But to give up his farm in favor of trading or the sea in order to earn a larger income violated his responsibility to God who had originally called him to his occupation.[19]

This message probably did not sit well with men toiling for little return but yearning for better things. Mather gave them the comfort that the comfortable have always dispensed: stay content in your callings, he said, and resign yourselves to the Providence that has ordained you for a low, mean status in life. If honest labor does not bring you the rewards the wealthy enjoy in this world, console yourselves with the prospect that grace will bring you joy in the next. And therefore do your jobs and strive after the Lord.[20]

In time Cotton Mather came to recognize the futility of this sort of preaching. In time he saw that it would no more restrain the mobility that accompanied the search for wealth, the lust after this world, than his attacks on merchants who diluted the turpentine they sold and who concealed inferior shingles by putting good ones on the outside of their bundles. Men would act in these ways, and reform would be stalled, because some men prospered in these sins.[21]

The sermons calling for reformation in the eighteenth century continued to use the traditional formula of appealing to various classes of individuals. They addressed rich men and poor, husbands, wives, parents, children, servants, ministers, and magistrates. Each had a part to play in the reform of society, because each stood in relation to others. Mather used the term "relation" in its Ramist sense, that is, as describing a condition of connectedness inherent in the nature of things. As members of the community, or, as Mather said, in a typical expression of this American Pietism, as neighbors, men had responsibilities to one another. It followed in a Christian order that the strong must help the weak; the healthy, the sick; the employed, the jobless. Almost anyone in any of the relations he found himself could do good—and this was the essence of Christian behavior.[22]

Do-good, the moral expression of this type of Pietism, was older than Puritanism. Its ultimate source was probably in the ancient notion of salvation through good works. But if it was as old as Christianity, it was nonetheless ineffective as a means of reform in eighteenth-century New England. But a minister could not stop preaching to individuals of their responsibilities simply because not all responded as he directed—some did and thereby demonstrated the existence of grace in their souls. Still, a minister might do more, especially if he were Cotton Mather and acutely aware of what others, similarly interested in improvement of society, had done across the sea.

In England, Mather learned in the 1690's, good men had begun to combine voluntarily in religious and reforming societies. The differences between these two kinds of agencies were probably not altogether clear to him, though he came to follow the English practice, and established both sorts. The English societies had the tacit approval of the Crown; first William and Mary and then Anne issued proclamations denouncing the vices of the age and calling for a recovery of piety. Anne issued at least three proclamations "for the Encouragement of Piety and Virtue and for the Preventing and Punishing of Vice, Prophaneness, and Immorality" and received her subjects' praise for them in New England, even after her concessions to the Tories who then passed the Occasional Conformity Act. If she was fully aware of the societies' composition, the Queen doubtless regarded the reforming societies with less favor than those given to reviving religion. The reformers' organizations were largely made up of nonconformists and were highly critical of Church and State. The religious societies in contrast were Anglican and had the sanction of solid churchmen all over England.[23]

Increase Mather may have learned of these societies while he was in England, but he did not mention them in print until almost ten years after his return in 1692. And in that brief notice —in a preface to a sermon by Samuel Willard—he revealed that his chief interest in them had been aroused by a recent book, by Josiah Woodward, and lay in their requirement that prospective members give an account of their religious purposes and mode of life.[24] Recently engaged in the combat against Stoddard, Increase found in this practice Anglican endorsement of the New England requirement of a relation of conversion experience for Church membership.[25]

Cotton Mather surely appreciated this point, and he found Woodward's study absorbing, but not primarily for Increase's reasons. He saw in the English example techniques that might be applied in America, and by 1702 he was busy organizing reforming societies, or as they were sometimes called, Societies To Suppress Disorders. In part, he built upon Puritan experience with religious societies, organizations of laymen that met for prayer and worship. These agencies were voluntary and had no official connections with churches, though they were composed of the most pious of the brethren. Massachusetts had suffered one dreadful experience with such a body led by Mistress Anne Hutchinson. For a few years that trial may have discouraged other attempts to meet in order to talk over sermons in private. Not permanently, however, for Cotton Mather preached to a neighborhood society when he was sixteen years old, and an account he gave of the sermon much later indicates that other organizations were in existence in the 1670's too.[26]

How far the religious societies spread outside of Boston and how constantly they flourished within cannot be known. Mather addressed societies of young men off and on throughout his life; he also appeared before women's groups and societies composed of men of substance. It was such an organization that he formed in 1702 with the expectation that its members would discuss the state of religion and perhaps create proposals for encouraging piety. The second organization set up under his direction at this time included important men, a number of them justices, and gave itself to the problem of reform. This group Mather designated the "Society To Suppress Disorders." Although this initial separation of the voluntary societies persisted, there is evidence that at times the functions of the agencies blurred in actuality and in Mather's mind.[27]

The religious societies probably enjoyed greater favor throughout New England than the reforming societies. So long as societies occupied themselves by listening to sermons, praying, and discussing religious subjects—and not meddling with private conduct—they remained unoffensive. They had a broader appeal in any case. Societies of women could not get into the business of suppressing bawdy houses, for such behavior would have been considered unseemly. Similarly, young men might be put to investigating other adolescents, but they could not be sent into taverns to locate tipplers.[28]

The societies that dealt with such matters were small in size, the first in Boston numbered around twelve or fourteen, Mather reported. For the most part their deliberations were kept secret, and they were guided by ministers and civil officials. Mather recommended that each have a minister and a justice of the peace to give it leadership and a link with Church and State, the major institutions in New England. The disorders that Mather hoped the societies would suppress included behavior that was popular, one suspects, in all ranks of societies. Three vices seem to have disturbed Mather more than others—drunkenness, profanity, and patronge of bawdy houses. They crop up in his *Diary* and in the sermons he delivered to the societies with a regularity that suggests that neither the magistrates nor the voluntary agencies ever coped with them. Mather recommended a number of techniques to the societies which they could use in defending pure language and conduct. Surely the most unpopular involved the use of informers. In England unsympathetic observers of the societies accused them of paying informers to tattle on offenders against the moral code. Cotton Mather never even hinted that informers should be paid—the suggestion would have horrified him—but rather that good men should tell on bad out of a sense of duty to the community and in the service of the Lord. That evil corrupted good was a melancholy truth that no one could deny. Informing on drunkards and whoremasters might keep the neighborhood healthy and perhaps persuade the Lord to withhold the punishing afflictions He commonly sent against a degenerate community. Informers should not act out of malice, however; indeed, there were times when they and grand jurymen, tithing men, and other officials charged with public responsibilities should do nothing more than admonish lawbreakers. When violators fell spontaneously into some sin for the first time, they deserved a charitable admonition, Mather believed. This was a fine line for anyone to draw of course; Mather drew it himself on a number of occasions. For example, he did not go to the public authorities when one of the societies collected the names of young men who frequented whorehouses in Boston. Instead he put the society to writing reproving letters to each of the fornicators.[29]

In such cases the societies were exercising what Mather styled "Vigilant Inspection" of the laws. Understandably the victims of the inspectors did not care for this sort of vigilance. This disfavor did not trouble Cotton Mather, who urged that the societies extend their concern to lamentable omissions in private life, such as the neglect of family prayer and of religious duties. How the societies attempted to satisfy this requirement beyond spreading books and tracts which conveyed instructions on leading good lives is not clear.[30]

Mather himself sent books and tracts all over New England—and beyond. Some dealt with the conventional subjects of worship and faith; others with the treatment of the sick, the duties the fortunate owed the poor; and still others were intended for the Indians. Here Mather's society was the New England Company, as The Society for the Propagation of the Gospel in New England was known.[31]

This body had of necessity to concern itself with public policy. It was never primarily an organized lobby, however, even though it dealt with governmental bodies. Cotton Mather did not conceive of the lesser societies as lobbies either, but he did suggest that they should make the passage of wholesome laws their business. This objective was closely related to their usual concern of keeping grand jurymen and magistrates up to the mark. The step between enforcing the laws and securing the passage of other laws did not appear a long one, and Mather encouraged the societies to take it whenever necessary.[32]

Despite frequent exhortations from Mather, the societies for the suppression of disorders did not flourish after the first ten years of their existence. Their first three or four years seemed to promise a long life: Mather reported so much enthusiasm that dividing the original society became necessary in 1705. Thereafter, the North end and the South end of Boston each felt the scrutiny of its own group of reformers. But by November 1711 the North end's band was languishing, and in January 1713 Mather noted that the "General" society had dissolved—a reference that suggests that the combined groups no longer existed in Boston. In the next five years, Mather made a series of attempts to revive them—and may have enjoyed temporary success. On the whole, however, organized reform never received popular support.[33]

In contrast, the religious societies enjoyed longer lives, and in some form survived the eighteenth century. Undoubtedly several such bodies in Boston began with their reformist impulses as strong as their desires to revive piety. Yet it seems that their worship and their charitable activity held them together; reform, Mather's elliptical references in his *Diary* suggest, may have caused a falling out, probably because Puritans easily transformed loving reproofs into malicious backbiting.[34]

The religious societies may have dispensed as much charity as any private group in Boston. Cotton Mather felt a genuine sympathy for the poor and encouraged their relief. He himself gave money, collected wood for their fires in winter, sought clothing for them, and helped organize charity schools. And under his supervision schools opened for Negroes and Indians in the evenings. He also sent a steady stream of Bibles and sermons to schools and families.[35]

Mather's most ambitious project for the religious societies began in late 1712, a time when organized activity in Boston appeared near collapse, and when the Protestant interest in Europe—he believed—faced disaster. At home the societies were languishing; in Europe, Roman Catholic power seemed on the ascent, and Mather feared the Queen's government was on the verge of making peace with France. In October 1712, Mather confided in his *Diary* that he had recently learned of groups of English dissenters, probably in London, who had begun to hold a weekly hour of prayer in which they beseeched the Lord to rescue the Protestant interest. The English dissenters published their "Brotherly Agreement" in a letter in August 1712. Mather received a copy shortly afterwards and began planning for similar activities in America. He must have been stimulated in part by the English appeal to the "Godly People" in the colonies to join. In urging a transatlantic effort, the English sounded one of Mather's deepest convictions—the ecumenical interest was world-wide, "And this the rather because *they* are all bound up with us in the same *Bundle of Life,* and their fate is likely to be involved in ours." [36]

Mather had organized joint meetings of the religious societies of Boston for prayer and discussion before this time. He looked to these meetings to yield ideas about tactics and projects. Organized activity had always pleased him, and long after these hours of common prayer he would urge that combinations of saints gather to beg the Lord to intercede for Christ's Church on earth.

The readiness that Mather showed in these years to enlist in pietistic efforts throughout the world as, for example, in these concerts of prayer, does not mean that he had given up on the traditional Congregational way. He had of course long since confessed that the founders' use of the State to crush other religious persuasions was a mistake. But if the State would no longer enforce conformity he expected it to punish blasphemers and offenders against the moral code. The MAXIMS OF PIETY stripped morality down to its essentials, according to the exponents of do-good, but PIETY implied no indifference to the old violations of the law. Here the State, acting with the churches, still might play its part. Mather's expectations that in a nation committed to do-good the old alliance would retain its value is clearly put in *Bonifacius:* "When *Moses* and Aaron join to *do good,* what can't they do?"[37] To seal the league and infuse it with pietistic purposes he urged that every reforming society should have among its members a magistrate as well as a minister. The societies themselves would act as the arms of justice, reaching out to warn the tempted and to inform on law-breakers. Mather himself reprinted an abstract of the most important laws regulating behavior. Along with each offense, the penalty was carefully listed, obviously with intention of demonstrating the force of the State behind, as he explained, "the worthy Designs of REFORMATION."[38]

The entire system of societies embracing all ranks of men which act on one another to produce conformity in thought and behavior has the odor, as Perry Miller points out, of nineteenth-century midwestern small-town Protestantism. No one is neglected in the scheme, all those incapable of doing good must resign themselves to have it done to them. And yet this appraisal does not recognize the deepest impulses of the Pietists whose primary concerns were not social, or even moral, but religious. After all, only converted men could do good. At no point in the secrecy of his *Diary,* in his letters to Francke or to the English Pietists or in his published work, did Mather hint that any action of the unconverted was acceptable to God. They must live according to the law and carry out all His commandments so far as their natural state permitted, but nothing that they did could satisfy the Lord. Only those with grace could do that and they must be up and be doing, not just to curb evil and to relieve the sufferings of the poor and the afflicted. Mather's plans for easing the distress of such unfortunates surely constituted a social gospel, but the end of such works was never just to make life more endurable for such people. The good in doing good lay in the glorification of God, and apart from God's glory, good had no meaning.[39]

Christian Union had been associated in Mather's mind with the glory of God long before his plans for do-good and the societies were fully developed. Now in the first years of organizing the societies he realized that they and the entire range of do-good activities might be made the instruments of Christian unity. The attempts to do good that he and these groups undertook might miscarry, yet in time they might succeed in uniting all Christians in benevolence—and in the Holy Spirit. As the reforming societies fell into disrepair after 1710, this hope assumed more importance for him. The societies might fail to relieve the poor, they might not succeed in dissuading young men from frequenting bawdy houses, but they could persist in propagating the faith by spreading the Maxims of the Everlasting Gospel (as he sometimes called the MAXIMS OF PIETY). Mather never faced the paradox in his hope that do-good might accomplish most at a time when its chief mechanism, the voluntary society, languished. The societies did not reform vicious habits, and they did not bring a widespread revival of religion—and Mather knew it. But still he hoped that do-good might bring a Christian Union that had escaped the United Brethren and the associations.[40]

The opportunity in do-good lay not in its power to change men, Mather tacitly admitted in the years after he published *Bonifacius*. Rather it offered the basis of unity for the saints in this world. The Christian religion is not "meer *Theory*," he declared in a letter written in 1717; it is a "Practical *Thing*" which animates a vital piety and calls the saints into righteous lives.[41] They must continue to act—to do good—whatever the consequences, or the lack of results in a polluted world. Mather did not regard this injunction as an admission of defeat, nor did he ever suggest that the pious should give up their attempts to reform the world. They must never stop. The concealed implication in what Mather was propounding was that the doing was as important as the good achieved. Be up and be doing, he urged, and let the results come if God approved. The good resided finally in the action.[42]

This feeling, as much as the frustration he endured in attempting to revive languishing societies, drove him into his ultimate plan for reformation. Men, he had to concede, would resist those human agencies which were determined to make them over. But should they resist the Divine at the end of the world, they would be destroyed by the shakings and overturnings of the final revolution. Societies of men who recognized this cosmic fact, and in effect eschewed any effort to do more than prepare for the end, might be formed to bring on the Kingdom of God. These organizations would take as their purpose the advancing of history to the end of the world. Surely an objective so pure and so far removed from the disappointments encountered in trying to keep drunkards from the bottle and youth from whorehouses was one on which men could unite. Mather first expressed this simple plan in 1713 when he mused in his *Diary* on the possibility of such societies formed on the MAXIMS of the Kingdom and "uniting in them, and promoting of them, and studying of Methods to draw Mankind into their Association." [43] He had preached the MAXIMS frequently in these do-good years after having announced their essentials almost twenty years before. [44]

By 1722 his exhortations brought the kind of request he always yearned for: a group in his church asked him to form such a society. [45] In the meantime he had extended the conception to evangelism and then to all of do-good. Shortly after publishing *Bonifacius* he began to receive reports from Germany of missionary activity in the East Indies. Francke wrote him, and so did others. Delighted by the news of the spread of piety throughout the world, Mather wrote the missionaries in Malabar, and received comforting replies of the success of the gospel there. What did it mean? he asked in 1717. Did he dare hope that it forecast the outpouring of the Holy Spirit that would establish the Kingdom of God? Could he hope that it was in itself the first marks of that Spirit? The answers eluded him, but his hopes continued that the MAXIMS OF PIETY, the Maxims of do-good —truly uniting maxims—would bring divine intercession. [46]

Cotton Mather could imagine no higher end of doing good than the unity obtained in the Holy Spirit. This was the happy end of man's pilgrimage on earth. If the societies could work out the methods to bring in this glorious state, then work they must. No better way of giving expression to the grace of God existed. Given the intensity of Mather's piety, this blueprint for action seems almost inherent in his original schemes for doing good. Though the failure of less ambitious plans surely helped bring him to these yearnings to see the Spirit active in this world, he might well have arrived at the same point had do-good produced social reformation and a religious revival. A Puritan, especially one as active as Cotton Mather, had to exploit any avenue that led to the Divine. [47]

This impulse—one of the most profound in Puritanism—

pointed in other directions as well. Like countless Puritans before, Richard Mather had insisted that no activity was too trivial to be consecrated to God. Eating and drinking—indeed every
ordinary act of consciousness—must be done in a holy frame of
mind. Increase Mather repeated these commands to his generation, and Cotton Mather, the most inventive student of all, drew
on the lessons for all they were worth.

Even as he counseled good men that they might seek after the
Holy Spirit and glorify God by doing good, he told them that
they must concentrate too on the things of the world. Concentration on the creatures in the right spirit led one to God. And
no link to the Divine should ever be ignored.

Danger lurked in this prescription. The creatures often lured
men away from God and into the carnality that doomed. The
world, the flesh, and the Devil all carried attractive snares. The
history of the Church should instruct men of the dangers of
carnality. The Church after all had been blessed with the gifts
of the Holy Spirit when Christ ascended into Heaven. And it
had been enlarged and governed by the Spirit for hundreds of
years afterwards. "But when the *Carnal Spirit of this World,*
fermented with the Venom of the *Epicurean Philosophy,* entred
into the Church, and she would no more acknowledge her SAV-
IOUR as her Governour," the Holy Spirit withdrew and the
Kingdom of Antichrist succeeded.[48] Do-good attempted to deal
with carnality and vile Epicures in one way, but still they survived. The experimental philosophy offered another way—and
held, as Mather discovered, dangers of carnality of its own.

16

The Experimental Philosophy

ono

By confining Church membership to those believers giving evidence of their conversions, the founders of New England had strongly endorsed experimental religion. After them, their sons had striven valiantly to maintain their fathers' faith, yielding only to half-way membership when the people proved incapable of undergoing any but the most perfunctory religious experience. And the grandsons, addressing churches empty of believers but full of hypocrites, felt themselves standing on the edge of the abyss as their generation spurned gracious experience in favor of carnal experience.

No Puritan of Cotton Mather's day studied carnality more devotedly than he, and none warned more direly against overvaluing the creatures. Yet in all Mather's tracts on worship, his explanations of the psychology of abasement, his ruminations on the covenant theology, and his calls for reformation, the assumption lurks that the experience of things can confirm one's belief in the truths of the Christian religion. In his prescriptions for worship he made this point repeatedly. And the way a man conducted his ordinary business, his day-to-day routine including such mundane activities as eating and drinking, could be made to contribute to divine glory. Pursued in a holy frame of mind, any activity and any contact with the creatures could elevate the believer and glorify God.

At first sight, Mather's conception of experience may appear as elaborate sensationalism. Meditation on activity and spiritualizing the creatures both drew upon evidence conveyed through the senses. Mather recognized this dependence but, like Robert Boyle, from whom he learned so much about dealing with the external world, he did not confine experience to the senses. What transpired within the mind was also experience, Boyle wrote in *The Christian Virtuoso,* a book Mather pored over; and the inner perception of the data supplied by the senses, or by revelation, can recall divine glories to the mind.[1] In agreeing, Mather, as was his custom, bent the borrowed insight to his own purposes. The final reference in any process of ruminating on a text or on a creature, he said, should always be to God: whatever the data, inward experience of them should carry one to higher principles. Mather did not believe that the doctrine of the Trinity could be inferred through scientific study or that knowledge of the Day of Judgment was to be obtained through spiritualizing the creatures. The great truths of religion lay at hand only in the revealed word of God in the Scriptures. But experimental knowledge of them—the total conviction that they were true—might be enjoyed through loving experience of the things of this world. There was no iron law of necessity that men must be corrupted in the contemplation of the creatures. From an affective concentration on the meanest creation, one could be transported to Jesus Christ, the glorious Creator.[2]

Mather never made the distinction that later seemed so obvious—the worship of God and the study of nature are separable endeavours. The experience of the creatures in daily spiritualizing and the perception of them under a microscope fueled the same engine of piety he so hotly admired. He was convinced that affective experience in science and worship advanced the Kingdom of God toward the Second Coming of Christ. For that reason, science, just as surely as worship, took its place in his chiliastic expectations.[3]

Combining worship with an apreciation of the creatures was an old Christian practice. Puritans had always turned to nature as an exemplification of divine wisdom and power. To be sure, they had usually found the deviations from the course of nature to be more revealing of the divinity of the universe than the creation's ordinary workings. Cotton's father, Increase, found special providences fascinating and collected tales of them assiduously; and in the face of the new astronomy, he maintained that cometary motion had always been irregular and would continue to be so. Increase, like many of his generation, also tended to think of nature as an "art" which expressed the divine mind. Hence, it was comfortable for him to ascribe an emblematic character to the special providences in creation. The comets shooting across the sky were more than Heaven's handiwork; they were symbols, perhaps of God's displeasure, and a sign of a coming affliction. The earthquakes too possessed symbolic importance, and floods, and droughts; the task of a science was ultimately to recognize them for what they were—portents of the Lord's intentions.[4]

Cotton Mather had no desire to repudiate his father's scientific attitudes; and maintaining throughout his life a capacity for holding conceptions inconsistent with one another, he managed to repeat them even while he embraced a different, and contradictory, set. Even as Increase wrote on comets and published accounts of special providences, the science of the day was changing—and Cotton Mather came of age as it raced towards discoveries of universal laws of regularity and order. So, though like his father before him he sometimes heard God's voice in thunder and witnessed His signs in lightning, he had also to concede that the magnificent rhythm of the celestial system bespoke a God of order and regularity.[5]

The problem faced by admirers of the new astronomy was to avoid being carried away by their admiration into deism or, worse, some sort of mechanism that denied the existence of God altogether. Such a possibility had dawned slowly on New England. A few years before Cotton Mather's birth in 1663, the Copernican views had made their way into Harvard's curriculum. Most of the founders had learned the Ptolemaic cosmology, but they adjusted to the new thought with remarkable ease. They may not have accepted all the tenets of the heliocentric universe, but most like John Davenport, for example, did not consider them threatening to the true religion. Galileo, Boulliau, Gassendi, Kepler, and Wing were simply names to him, Davenport admitted; and if they contended that we lived on a revolving planet, there was no harm done. Scripture told a different story, and he would believe the old scheme "till more cogent arguments be produced then I have hitherto met with!" [6]

This easy tolerance had never existed in Europe, and even as Davenport spoke, the fears about the meaning of science for religion were finding their way to America. Cotton Mather may have learned of them while he was still a boy in Harvard College. Robert Boyle, who published a book asserting the compatibility of the new experimental philosophy and the Christian religion in the year of Cotton's birth, was his father's friend. Increase's own ideas on the subject must have been clear to Cotton by the time he left Harvard. Cotton, of course, did not absorb the new science in a mood of shock; it was well established when he entered college; and he learned to sneer at Ptolemy with an aplomb that would have recommended him to any society of virtuosi.[7]

Still, the immensity of the universe with its pluralities of stars and planets moved him deeply. He revealed his awe as he attempted to estimate the number of stars he and other observers had seen through telescopes. The distances between stars defied comprehension, and surely the void that surrounded each particle in the chaos that existed before God fashioned the earth and the heavens out of the original stuff must have been incalculable. Once formed, this matter made a universe of "so many *Worlds,* that swallow up all our Conjectures at the Circumstances of them, and of their Satellites." [8] One could not help thinking of the earth in this sea of stars and space. The fixed stars took on a size "vastly greater" than "this poor Lump of Clay." Their number defied the power of the mind to count—they are "like the *Sand* of the sea, innumerable." In these pluralities "this Globe is but as a Pins point, if compared with the mighty *Universe.* Never did any man yet make a tolerable guess at its Dimensions: but were we among the *Stars,* we should utterly lose the sight of our Earth, although it be above twenty six thousand *Italian* miles in the compass of it." The varieties of living creatures on the earth also astonished him; as he counted them in 1690, there were "above six Thousand *Plants,*" and one vegetable alone had often in the past proved so intriguing as to elicit a scholarly treatise. What, he asked, "might then be said upon the Hundred and fifty *Quadrupeds,* the Hundred and fifty *Volatils* [birds], the five and twenty *Reptiles,* besides the vast multitudes of *Aquatils,* added unto the rich variety of *Gems* and *Minerals,* in our World?" [9] One of the things that might be said was that this variety extended to a world hidden from ordinary eyes. As early as 1685 Mather had gazed at drops of water through a microscope where he spied "little *eels*"—"incredible hundreds playing about in one drop of water." [10] A few years later he was still confessing his "Astonishment" at this sight: even whales, those "moving Islands, are not such *Wonders* as these minute Fishes are." [11]

The meaning for men of these wonderful works of God appeared clear to the young Mather. The immensity of the universe with its marvelous pluralities of stars and satellites, "Regular to the Hundredth part of a minute" in their motions, the complex structure of the animalcula, thousands of which would not equal a grain of sand, suggested irresistibly the presence of a master hand. Indeed all the created wonders of the universe argued for the existence of God—"There is not a Fly, but what may confute an Atheist." [12]

These reactions to nature and the conclusions from them were of course genuine. But they were not original with the young Mather, who not only accepted the new science but also the natural theology that followed hard on its heels. Robert Boyle had said it all before him in a book published in 1663, *The Usefulness of Experimental Natural Philosophy.*[13] Mather read the book closely some time in the 1680's, and his early works on science and worship borrowed from it heavily, even to the use of almost identical language; Boyle, for example, marvels at the "fishes" in a drop of water, and in noting the immensity of the universe, compares the earth to a mere "point" in it. Boyle also made the argument from design.[14]

In all his early tracts that take up scientific subjects, Mather located himself in the context of the natural theology. The argument from design in these years before 1700 seemed especially powerful, as he learned more of the intricacy of the heavens and the minute fishes under a microscope. It was probably in these years that looking through a microscope he saw what so many of his peers observed: the "seeds" of plants and animals "are no other than the *Entire Bodies* themselves in *parvo.*" [15]

And yet the suspicion that the new science was not as amenable to the old religious values as the old science was must have occurred to him while he witnessed these marvels. For one thing the books he read, despite all their ostensible confidence in the harmony of science and faith, betrayed an uneasiness that all was not well. No one could quite put down the spectre of mechanism, of works in the world apart from God and independent of Him.[16]

Mather seems to have learned most of what he knew about the mechanistic philosophy from its critics. He probably never read Descartes' *Principles of Philosophy* (1644) or *Le Monde* (posthumously published in 1644), though he quoted on several occasions from the *Discourse on Method*.[17] Descartes's theory of vortices and his rejection of the possibility of a void did not attract Mather's curiosity, nor did Cartesian physics draw extended comment from the natural theologians Mather read. A number of these critics noted that Newton's mathematical analysis had collapsed not only the theory of vortices but the entire Cartesian cosmology. Though he must have been gratified, Mather's interest was not really aroused by this news.

What distressed him about the Cartesian hypothesis was its implication that the universe was self-governing. That God had done far more than create matter and set it in motion and that He intervened in the ordinary course of nature were propositions Mather clung to whatever Descartes held.[18]

Mather faced the challenge of Cartesianism most clearly in a work he never succeeded in publishing, the Biblia Americana, his enormous commentary on Scripture. Running to several thousand pages, the Biblia not only offers illustrations and explanations of the Scriptures, chapter by chapter, it also contains essays on various problems from philology to science, that Mather considered to bear on the Word. The problem of cause intrudes itself at several points in his commentary but nowhere more clearly than in his discussions of the creation, the deluge of Noah's time, and the miracles of Christ.[19]

Not so much as a hint of dissatisfaction about the Mosaic account of creation ever appeared in Mather's writings. In the Biblia he did concede that the usual commentaries on Genesis have certain "Difficulties" and that scholars had recently enjoyed only uneven success in relieving some of the "hardships" placed

on Moses' story. His own view made Moses out as an early Newtonian, a devotee of the corpuscularian philosophy; but unfortunately, until the discoveries made by the new science this
prevision of modernity in the Scriptures had gone undetected.
Cotton Mather owed this opinion to no man: it belonged
uniquely to his fertile mind. But to translate the Mosaic creation into Newtonian language he turned for aid to Richard Bentley and William Whiston.[20]

Bentley (1662–1742), who served as Master of Trinity College,
Cambridge, from 1700 until his death, had given the first set of
Boyle Lectures in 1692 on the evidences of Christianity. Published the next year as *A Confutation of Atheism*, the lectures
drew from the *Principia* a religious meaning that Newton himself shared. This was no accident, for Bentley consulted Newton
while revising the lectures for the press, bringing their argument clearly into line with Newton's beliefs about the religious
significance of the law of gravitation. Like Bentley, Whiston
(1667–1752), who succeeded Newton in the Lucasian Professor-
ship of Mathematics in Cambridge, popularized Newton's science
and defended the scriptural version of the nature of the world.
But Whiston was not the scrupulous natural philosopher, content
to suspend judgment about the physics of the Day of Judgment,
and in 1696 he issued *A New Theory of the Earth* which described the beginning and the end of all things according to his
own reading of the new science.[21]

Both Bentley and Whiston were able teachers, and sometime
late in the 1690's a fascinated Mather began to go to the school
of their writings. Whiston, who like most of the Newtonians
borrowed from Bentley, proved especially helpful in refuting
what had come to be called in England the "Vulgar Hypothesis,"
the persistent folk belief that God had created the entire universe from nothing in six days and that the earth reigned at
its center. This "Ptolemaic system of the world, must not have
at this Time of Day to bee entertained with considerate men,"
Mather wrote in the Biblia.[22] But he could not dismiss it intact
because he saw atheists using it to destroy the faith of the ignorant. The God of the vulgar system, he realized after reading
Whiston, was a foolish God who took four days to model the
earth—a pin's point in the Universe—and left Himself only two
days to fashion the sun and stars in all their multiplicity. And

this God seemed indifferent to His own laws of physics, especially the one governing gravitation. For if the Lord had created the heavens out of the same chaos that He had used in modeling the earth, there would be no way of explaining the remote distances of the sun and stars from the earth. One would have to postulate the existence of a law of "mutual Repulsion" instead of gravitation.[23] The few hours the Vulgar Hypothesis allows these bodies to separate from the earthly chaos in order to travel to their celestial orbits simply were not adequate to traverse their immense distances. And—Mather observed—besides denying the universality of gravitation, the Vulgar Hypothesis in assuming "that the Heavenly Bodies proceeded originally from the *Terrestrial chaos,* and cast themselves off from it every way supposes the Earth to be the *Center* of the world." [24]

Had the threat from the mechanists not existed, Mather probably would not have found it necessary to separate himself from the Vulgar Hypothesis. By attacking it he gained an opportunity to demonstrate his own attachment to the most fashionable English scientists who, not incidentally, preserved a large place for the Divine in the workings of the universe. The great figure among them was, of course, Isaac Newton. Mather may have read the *Optics* at some time in his life, though probably not the *Principia.* The mathematics of these works would have escaped him but not the inferences Newton drew from his system. These Mather learned of secondhand from Bentley and Whiston.[25]

The essential implication of mechanism had not changed, he knew, from its original version by Epicurus (c. 341–270 B.C.), though the argument in the seventeenth century was sent forth in the finery of Cartesianism. The universe—ancient and modern mechanists held—had its beginnings in the creation of matter by the Deity, but its shape in the heavens and the earth was the result of a series of fortuitous events. The prospect of this massive indifference to the creation and to human beings frightened all good men. Fortunately in the Newtonian system the best defense of a prudent and provident God stood waiting. The starting points of Mather's refutation of "meer blind material causes" [26] was Newton's warning delivered to Bentley against speaking of "gravity as essential & inherent to matter." [27] In the first version of his lectures given under the Boyle Trust in 1692, Bentley evidently nearly slipped into this manner of thought that Newton feared. But careful man that he was, he consulted Newton before sending his manuscript to the printer. Newton picked out the flaw at once and in a series of letters to his admirer devoutly pointed out that though gravitation accounted for much in the celestial system, the proposition that gravity was innate to matter implied that "one body may act on another at a distance through a vacuum without the mediation of anything else," a doctrine of such "absurdity" that Newton professed to believe that no man competent in scientific matters could entertain it.[28] Newton added in a sentence Bentley did not use—and which Mather never saw—that gravity must be "caused" by an agent who acted in accordance with certain laws.[29] Whether this agent was material or immaterial Newton left to his readers. Bentley rendered faithfully all but this last comment. The omission of Newton's uncertainty about the final agent in the process was deliberate because Bentley was untroubled by such doubts.

Mather recognized the force of Bentley's comments and repeated them. The agency of chance in the formation of the planetary system seemed unconvincing on still other grounds. As Bentley pointed out, by the best calculations—his own, of course —before the modeling of the heavens and the earth from the Mosaic chaos, each particle of matter was surrounded by an enormous void. The thought that in these infinite spaces particles joined to form the planetary system defied comprehension. But the argument that clinched the case against fortuitous mechanism for Mather rested on the most certain formulation of Newton's physics—the universality of gravitation. If gravitation was not the act of the divine Agent, but instead inherent in matter, what would prevent the tendency of the particles to carry them to the center of the universe where they would congeal into one huge spherical mass? Newton and Bentley discussed this problem and agreed that it provided an irresistible argument against Epicureanism. Newton, however, argued that the objection carried validity only if one assumed that the space through which matter was scattered was finite; if space were infinite, matter would not convene in one mass but in separate masses such as sun and stars. Blind materialism could not enter through this assumption of infinite space because, as Newton explained, chance could not account for the division of matter into the two sorts that composed "shining" bodies, the sun and stars, and opaque bodies, the earth and planets.[30]

Mather did not raise the troublesome question of the possibility of an infinite universe; he never suspected that the universe might be anything but finite in any case. And Bentley did not disturb his certainty by passing out the subtleties of Newton's views. The possibility that matter would form a huge spherical mass at the center of the universe did not terrify him. It "must really happen," he concluded, were it not for a "Miraculous power," responsible for gravitation and for all things. What saved the world from mechanism was this power of God, a God who exerted a "continuous influence" in the ordinary course of nature, sustaining the law of gravitation.[31]

Mather put more weight on "continuous influence" in his discussions of gravitation than he did upon "miraculous power." Almost none of the mechanists denied the first operations of God in the creation; the real danger in their schemes lay in their belief that God removed Himself from the universe once He set the machine going. Happily Newton rescued philosophy from blind chance and natural religion from the remote God. Mather always remained grateful to Newton and lost few opportunities to link his great name to the doctrine of a God who intervened constantly to sustain the universe—and, by implication, human affairs.[32]

If the experimental philosophy of Newton was to be co-opted to religion's purposes, it was all the more necessary to translate the natural phenomena presented in Scripture into experimental terms. Mather's account of the Mosaic creation in the Biblia represented one major effort, and he did not neglect other opportunities. The deluge of Noah's day offered one, baffling at first sight, but one which had to be fulfilled if the status of natural theology were to remain high.

Hypotheses about the flood had so increased by Mather's day that he noted on several occasions that their proponents threatened to fall into "Hypothesimania."[33] Throughout a long record of speculation on the subject, he managed to avoid this contagion—but not by much. He also never succeeded in making up his mind about whether the true explanation of the deluge had been given. A number of accounts failed to convince him because they depended completely upon second causes and thereby excluded the "Immediate Interposition" of God. Others relied so fully upon an immediate Providence that they ignored the facts of Moses' narrative and the disposition of God to use second causes in His own way. In simple terms, the problem of understanding the deluge for every commentator came down to asking where did all the water come from. Or, as Thomas Burnet, an English divine who knew something of the new philosophy, said: "The excessive quantity of water is the great difficulty, and the removal of it afterwards." [34]

Mather agreed with Burnet's formulation but he dismissed his answer as being nothing more than the old Abyssian philsophy, which had appeared almost two centuries earlier. Burnet's theory was actually no more far-fetched than most—it held that the crust of the earth was originally smooth and uniform and had neither sea nor mountains. Sometime after the creation this crust fell into the watery abyss inside the earth which then overflowed to produce the flood. Mather could not accept this account because it implied that the Mosaic creation left the world unfinished. There were other theorists more clearly affected by natural philosophy than Burnet and who agreed that the abyss had yielded its waters for the deluge. Over the years Mather pondered their writings: John Ray, William Sinclair, and Whiston; and Newton's comments also drew his attention. Until at least 1711, he conceded probability to Whiston's contention that the close approach of a comet had drawn the sea over the land, but he also admired Ray and Newton's theory that a shift in the earth's center of gravity decreed by God had sent the subterraneous waters pouring out, only to return when God restored the old center. Still another theory, Doctor Sinclair's held that divinely ordered earthquakes deep within the earth set up a train of physical causes which resulted in the flood. Sinclair, a professor of chemistry, had argued that the quakes released salty exhalations through cracks on the earth's surface which by interacting with the earth's atmosphere produced the heavy rains described in Scripture. At the same time, the shifts within the crust sent earth crashing upon the waters of the abyss, and the flood that sent Noah's ark on its voyage occurred. Sinclair had done more than speculate; as a solid empiricist he had performed experiments in his laboratory on which his theory was founded. It was this experimental basis that finally persuaded Mather to concede more probability to Sinclair's views than to any other.[35]

Obviously, a natural theologue could not accept both Whiston and Sinclair; and Mather, probably around 1715, rejected Whiston's cometary explanation, admitting that it was "engenious," but giving it up because it was "Arbitrary." [36] Discarding a theory because it is arbitrary, and choosing another because it is verified experimentally, seems to place Mather securely in the camp of the natural theology and, in fact, he belongs there, though only in one of its outposts. He did not mean to imply that nature must always work without caprice or that physical events must always fall out reasonably. What was arbitrary in Whiston's theory was its disregard of Scripture, which did not hint that a comet passed near the earth before the onset of the deluge. If one wished to follow Whiston's method of reasoning, he asked, why not argue that the flood was "altogether Miraculous"? [37] Some did, of course—but only by embroidering Scripture. These writers suggested that God created waters especially for flooding the earth which, once accomplished, were destroyed. This explanation, Mather observed, "cutt the Knott." And surely there was "no Absurdity" in attributing such a power to God; but His account, inscribed by Moses, did not cut the knot: "Wherefore wee will rather consider the causes of the flood, which are there more expressly mentioned." [38]

By itself Mather's respect for Scripture did not limit his enlistment in the army of natural theology; many better members professed a similar attachment to God's literal Word. But his assumptions about the trinity that natural theologians admired so highly—God, nature, and reason—did set him apart. Like the first covenant theorists, the natural theologians urged the reasonableness of the Christian religion. They professed to believe that the ancient conundrum of whether a thing commanded by God is good because He enjoins it or is commanded by God because is inherently good, if not exactly solved, was no longer puzzling. There was in the constitution of the universe, as Samuel Clarke, a writer Mather studied closely, said, an "eternal Reason of Things" in which the law of nature was founded.[39] In some ultimate sense, this reason might represent the positive will of God, but in another, some implied, it might even be antecedent to God Himself. Perhaps metaphysicians alone were qualified to deal with this question, but the natural theologians, openly impatient with the obscurities of traditional philosophy, scorned such riddles. The important *fact* was that God invariably acted according to the eternal and immutable reason of things, the guiding principle of the created universe. Reason thus provided moral obligation—Clarke said the "*original* Obligation of all"—to which "even God ties himself in governing the World."[40] Though not all agreed about the power of this bond on God, many implied with Clarke that God "always" acted in accordance with this principle. If God conducted Himself this way, men should also. They should listen to their consciences which would inform them of rational behavior. Of course, men did not always act reasonably and morally; and when they did not they violated natural as well as ethical principle.[41]

While the natural theologues espoused the case for reason, they craved the certainty that any ethical absolutism gives. But science, and the enthusiasm of the sects, had robbed them of most of their capacity to enjoy orthodox Christian assurance. First Descartes and then Newton shook their faith in miracles. As they studied the new science, they could not avoid the suggestion that the Trinity of the Father, Son, and Holy Ghost seemed to defy the laws of physics. Hence they gingerly handled the Scriptures, but despite their care they sometimes fell into heresies—most notably Whiston, whose fascination with Arianism cost him his post at Cambridge. They did not wish to reject revelation but only to remove it to a safe distance where it might not disturb the ordinary course of nature, which, since the great days of the patriarchs and of Christ, followed reason. Yet they did not want to give way to ethical relativism—to say with Swift that moral obligation depended solely on a compact among men. Behind Swift, they knew, lurked Hobbes and the case for obligation to God based only on fear of His unchained power. And therefore they tamed the Calvinist God, several going so far as to throw out the doctrine of election, but conceding to Him absolute sovereignty and foreknowledge. They accomplished their purposes by relocating the Divine in a universe of reason, which filled nature with eternal and unchangeable principles. Newtonianism, especially the law of universal gravitation, undoubtedly gave them courage and helped persuade them that

they really had solved the old problems of reconciling the existence of an irresistible force with a human kind that possessed
freedom.[42]

Cotton Mather sometimes made similar claims for reason and
the light of nature. And he, of course, always insisted that sinners were responsible for their conduct and for their damnation.
There are passages in his works that suggest that he saw miracles much the way pious Newtonians of his generation did, as
rare interruptions of a nature that ordinarily conformed to reason. As a matter of fact he continued to make distinctions between special providences—divine interference that remained
within natural law—and miracles—divine interference that occurred above natural law, distinctions which most men of his
day no longer respected. He did not conceive of God, however,
as bound by any eternal, rational principles embodied in the created universe. The God who extended His covenant to men
through Christ and accepted their compliance only when it was
given as total capitulation could hardly appear in the shackles of
natural law. Indeed, in a subtle way Mather gently repudiated
much Puritan doctrine on both miracles and nature in order to
reinvigorate ancient conceptions of God.[43]

What men had forgotten in their self-righteous tendency to
measure everything by human standards, Mather wrote in the
Biblia, was the simple proposition that all things are easy to
God. The categories of the "miraculous" and the "natural" were
human inventions. Once men realized that, they might begin to
understand that working through nature is no easier to God than
performing what humans regarded as miracles. To restore a dead
man, Mather pointed out in the Biblia, is as easy to God as to
produce a living man in his first conception. Men interested in
God and nature should recognize that "strictly speaking, if we
regard only the *power* of God, there is *nothing miraculous,*" but
if we regard our own power "almost everything" is. The distinction between the miraculous and the natural, then, was a human
one resting on the judgment of what was usual and unusual to
men's senses. Everyone would agree that there was nothing miraculous in the action of a man who, in a sense, overpowered
gravitation to catch a ball falling to the surface of the earth. But
in men's eyes when God stopped it, the action took on the aura
of the miraculous. Some powers of God, Mather explained, may

be "communicable" to men; some, denied to men may be held by angels; and some angels may do more than others. No Puritan would have disagreed with this nor with his belief that the power to create something out of nothing is entirely incommunicable to "any meer Creatures," including, of course, angels and devils, who are created spirits. But that does not mean that only God does things which are considered miraculous. Most Puritans had long believed that angels operated under divine restraints that prevented them from interfering in human affairs; Cotton Mather tended to dwell on the exceptions to these restraints, arguing that angels often performed acts considered miraculous by men. The important point that he made, however, was that whatever angels did—and he contended that in the affairs of men they ordinarily could do more than men—they did invisibly what men do visibly and therefore their acts appear miraculous: "Let the swimming of Iron on the Surface of the Water, or, the mounting of heavy Stones up into the Air, be Instances." [44]

Mather's intention in making this argument was not to divest nature of miracle but to suggest that the weakness of men's understandings, and their pride, had unwittingly led them to ascribe human limitations to God. Hence men, in the invention of these categories by which to understand His power, implied that He was in some way chained by the law accessible to their minds. They compounded their error when they—or the deists among them—removed God from the normal course of things in nature, as if anything could sustain itself for a moment without the assistance of God. And finally in their arrogance they persisted in attributing something extraordinary to God in miracles, though the only thing unusual in the miraculous derived from the character of men's perceptions. [45]

All this was said in an extended attack on mechanism, which Mather attributed to Epicureans and their modern descendants, the deists. But in this elaborate argument he separated himself, perhaps unwittingly, from those natural theologians who accepted orthodox views of revelation. They remained convinced that God acted in conformity to a reason expressed in nature that was in some sense removed from Him. They denied that anything contrary to—or above—reason survived in revelation. The universe and the ways of God were tractable to reason, and though not all of God's purposes were accessible to men's un-

derstandings, when they were finally exposed they would be discovered in conformity to reason.[46]

Cotton Mather did not agree and his disagreement would have
appeared clear to all had he ever succeeded in publishing his
Biblia. To be sure, the Newtonians, and Newton himself, would
not have quarrelled with his embellishment of Newton's First
Law in the Biblia: "*Matter* is no more capable of *Law* or power,
than of Intelligence, except of a Negative power," that every
part of it "will of itself always continue in that state whether
of Rest or Motion, wherein it is at present." Newton had betrayed a reluctance to define the external power that moved
things, but his popularizers showed no such hesitation: they
would have recognized their own case in Mather's argument that
all the power ascribed to matter and motion belongs "strictly
and properly" to God who acts upon the stuff of nature "continually and Every moment," either "immediately" in Himself
or mediately through created beings. But most, committed to
eternal principles of reason, could not have agreed that the order and rationality of the universe were more apparent than real,
that they were in fact strictly in the senses of human observers.
In this contention Mather took his stand, his piety curbing whatever impulses he may have had to shape God according to men's
rational specifications, and insisted that in ascribing reality to
human perceptions, men exposed the extent of their pride. For,
he argued what men called the "course of Nature" is really nothing else but the "Will of God" producing effects in a uniform and
regular manner. To God—and Mather obviously believed that
men must believe this or they would never be converted—this
way of acting is "perfectly Arbitrary" and as easy for God to
alter as to preserve. As far as men's perceptions were concerned
miracles existed, though in actuality they simply expressed God's
will.[47]

No primitive and untroubled faith underlay Mather's view, but
rather an uneasy and profound conviction that the new science
threatened to mask the very basis of reason. As all his reading
and writing demonstrates, Mather craved knowledge whatever its
source. He was too much of a Puritan, and too much of an intellectual, to deny the truth even if it came from an unbeliever.
A remark he made on William Whiston revealed the force of his
curiosity, and his admiration of inquiry—though Whiston, he

said, had deserted to the "tents of Arius" the most detestable heresy, we must not allow his desertion to deprive us of his valuable studies. But still the abyss opened its jaws in mechanism. The worst of it was that the lusting after order and law in nature seemed to go hand in hand with men who wished to approach God as His equals. Were not all bound by the eternal principles expressed in a rational universe? [48]

By focusing on perception, Mather fought his way clear of the snares that lay in the forest of natural theology. He needed, and felt that all men needed, not just to discover nature invested with divinity—the natural theology did this much—but also to grasp the fact of its root intractability despite its comforting appearance of order and rationality. Reason and the law of nature implied conceptions that served ordinary needs. Men had to operate in daily life as if these notions described reality. But disaster awaited men whose hearts could not carry them beyond their intellection. Mather once observed of Descartes' famous principle, "I think, therefore I am," that "it is no *New Divinity* to teach, that *As* men *Think, so they are.*" [49] But men must think beyond the evidence of their senses. They would achieve more if they went beyond the assumption that nature was only an expression of the creator's "art" and that nature in some sense was removed from Him. To be sure, the founders and their fathers before them had in the language of technologia commonly referred to nature as divine art, and art conceivably took a form separate from its creator. Yet all should remember that nature is not so much divine art as it is divine "will." And that "will" consults itself, not any human conception of order, justice, law, or regularity. It followed for Mather that if nature were "will," God existed unconfined by any eternal principle of nature or reason. He might speak with reason's voice, but He did so only out of His sympathy for men's limitations. His will was His own and unfettered by law or order. [50]

All this bore on Mather's conception of the God who inhabited the Newtonian universe. God's generosity in contriving the world in a way that could be comprehended by men seemed obvious. But men, Mather believed, frequently confused the created with the creator. Understandably they sometimes believed that in the apparent rationality of the cosmos, they detected a Deity observing the same laws that bound them. And hence they puffed themselves up and attempted to take up His covenant, sealed by the blood of the Savior, not as an accessory to Christ, but as a principal. Some would discover their errors too late for redemption; the fortunate few would learn that God possessed none of the accidents and qualities and faculties of the created spirits. All must learn eventually that whatever existed in God took form as "A Pure Act," "uncompounded" by any human conceptions of order and justice. In this way did Cotton Mather invest the Newtonian universe with the God of the whirlwind.[51]

Reason figures in much of the natural theology either as an instrument to be used to extract the truths of nature or as a set of self-evident principles to be applied as a standard for behavior and opinion. Most writers found both categories useful and switched back and forth between them without bothering to explain what they were doing. Cotton Mather entertained both conceptions easily enough, though he proved to be more self-conscious than most. In fact he came to elevate the claims of reason as a strategy in his campaign to advance piety. He had begun to give attention to science around 1690 for the same purpose. By 1700, as his understanding of the implications of the natural philosophy for religion increased, he was becoming aware of the possibilities of recommending Christianity as a reasonable, as well as an experimental, doctrine.[52]

Mather announced the new strategy in a tract, *Reasonable Religion,* published in 1700 for use on pastoral visits. Passages from this short book crop up in the sermons he preached in the years around the turn of the century, evidence of his interest in the new discovery. He admitted at the outset that New England had lightly ignored exhortations to convert that based themselves on arguments about faith and repentance. Therefore he would try something new: to make Christianity irresistible he would stop pleading *"Shew your selves Regenerate Christians"* and substitute *"Shew your selves Rational Creatures."* Within the next ten years he began to regret this tack as he came to see its dangers.[53]

The technique of making Christianity reasonable undoubtedly was imported from England and the Continent. And so perhaps was the recognition that the process held dangers of its own. Puritanism had always carefully restrained the claims of reason even while it conceded value to a rational mode in mental activity. Traditional theory about conversion described the Lord proceeding through men's understanding as well as their wills in saving them. A man ignorant of Christ could hardly expect to receive grace; and a man blind to the law surely could not depend upon his sanctification. But no man should ever delude himself by confusing mere belief in the Lord with the grace of God. The Devil himself believed in Christ but in no way accepted Him as the Savior, and despised God's grace. A man had to be assisted to the right frame of mind, and no matter how great his rational power he could never attain it from his own efforts. Restrained statements such as these limited the appreciation in Puritanism of reason in the life of the spirit. At the same time Puritans carefully defended their creed from charges of irrationalism. Nothing in it and nothing in Scripture opposed reason, they said, but parts surely transcended reason and therefore commanded belief on faith alone. The miracles performed by Christ, for example, defied rational understanding but they had to be accepted.[54]

Shortly before Cotton Mather began praising the rationality of Christianity in terms such as "Scripture is reason in its highest elevation," English deists threw caution aside with claims that all statements about Christianity must be proved.[55] Nothing, they said, was above reason including the revealed truths of Scripture. John Locke, in spite of his intentions to defend Christianity, gave this challenge much of its impetus in his *The Reasonableness of Christianity* (1695). Locke thought of the Christian religion almost entirely in rational terms, holding that the truth of its teachings could be established by appeals to reason unassisted by inspiration. All the available evidence confirmed Christian truth, especially the miracles which supported the ethical principles of Christ. Morality comprised the center of Christianity for Locke, not the stark relationships described by Calvin's predestination and election. To be sure, reason could not discover everything; there was mystery in life, but Locke did not agree that it deserved much attention or that its existence compromised the essential reasonableness of Christianity. He conceded, however, that while Scripture contained nothing contrary to reason, its truths sometimes transcended reason.[56]

Not all those who styled themselves his followers made this concession. John Toland denied in *Christianity Not Mysterious*, published the year following Locke's book, that there was anything "above reason" in the Scriptures. And religious experience itself, according to Toland, was entirely comprehensible by the intellect. Just as reason must provide the only basis of belief, faith is "entirely built upon ratiocination." Toland refrained from rejecting the Trinity—his ostensible purpose was after all to reinforce the truths of the religion of Christ by removing mystery from His worship. Other self-confessed admirers of Locke also took up this task; and still others presumed to answer along the line of orthodoxy.[57]

The problems raised in these discussions attracted attention for another hundred years. Within a short time of Locke's writing, the central issues were clear: the most pressing was the question of the authority of religious truth. If revelation was not to be accepted unless it proved tractable to reason, what could be claimed for the Scriptures? Was the universe as comprehensible as Toland and the deists suggested? If it was, Cotton Mather and the English defenders of orthodoxy saw no room for either the miracles described in Scripture or such mysteries as the Trinity.[58]

In England the questions forced themselves into religious discourse with the result that though there were evasions on both sides, the discussion in pulpit and press attained directness and honesty. After some understandable hesitation English clerics managed to find it possible to discuss, for example, whether the Bible really was God's Word—and why some men believed that it was and others had come to deny it. Such matters were of more than academic interest, and the discussions were pursued with more than mental exercise in mind. Indeed they were bitterly polemical, and positions taken had consequences for careers in the Church. The Trinitarian controversy, which in itself contained virtually all the questions about authority in religion, produced broken careers and ecclesiastical punishments.[59]

As he read the literature of these disputes, Mather's enthusiasm for reason cooled, though it never entirely disappeared. His fears, as his enthusiasms, are always fairly clear despite his efforts to conceal them. They are not always easy to sort out, for they invariably seem tangled in shifting hopes and inconsistent standards of judgment. But his deepest values invariably reasserted themselves as he came to sense the implications of a new strategy or a changing vision. Something of this sort occurred in the fifteen years after his first eager pronouncement in 1700, on behalf of reasonable religion.[60]

Mather's fears are clear even through the disguises he draped over the English controversy. Reading his productions for the pulpit and the press in the years after 1700, one can glimpse his distress as he learned that one after another the miracles of the Apostles, the Trinity, Christ's resurrection, the doctrine of the last judgment, were controverted by deists. Several of his colleagues outside Boston also kept abreast of the English scene, and in 1712 one of them wrote asking him to produce something to stay the epidemic of deism which threatened New England. Mather gladly responded with *Reason Satisfied: and Faith Established,* a tract very different from the happy endorsements of reason he had issued a dozen years earlier.[61] It is a work that makes many of the points, already conventional, about the uses of reason, but it also emphasizes the limitations. The sermons and books that followed in the next few years show the same cautious withdrawal from his earlier enthusiasm.

The problem in withdrawing lay in doing it in such a way as not to reveal just how fully Calvinist orthodoxy had been challenged. For the most part Mather managed to conceal the assaults on the sacredness of Scripture itself. Did Christianity give a true account of man and his Creator and Savior? He would prove that it did by verifying the central doctrine of Christianity, the resurrection of Christ. Of course the deists had proclaimed the resurrection an irrational story, but the description proved by the Gospels was irrefutable. He would prove Christ's resurrection from the testimony of the lying wretches who denied it. Did not the Roman guards insist that while they slept Christ's disciples slipped the body out of the tomb? But, Mather answered in triumph, it is not "credible" that Christ's disciples, who cowardly denied Him before His crucifixion, would develop the bravery to steal His body. And Peter, who denied Him thrice before the cock crowed, afterwards preached the news of His resurrection. Surely he would have continued to deny Christ had the resurrection not occurred. This "proof" Cotton Mather offered, convinced that it was incontestable.[62] At other points in this tract, as in other tracts, there appears a hint that the inspired basis of Scripture itself had been challenged, but the hint disappears under a flood of assertions that Scripture was the irrefutable word of God. Even as his doubts developed, Mather continued to assert that this argument was reasonable; he could not imagine any man equipped with a faculty which could put things together and dissect their relationships who could fail to acknowledge it. Turks, heathens, infidels all recognized the truth and beauty of Christ's sacrifice, and His ressurrection, even though they could not genuinely understand it and even though they rejected Him.[63]

When taken as a faculty, reason could not do much more than recognize the truth of Scriptures, but as a set of principles innate in the mind, it could tell men much more. Without God's Word in the Bible, men could know from the ideas innate in their minds that there was a God. Mather always resisted the contentions of Lockeans (which Locke himself did not make) that everything that men knew, they knew from sensation. There were ideas, a moral law in fact, that God had inscribed on men's souls with a pen of iron. Mather also believed that men could learn from reason that the soul was immortal and that someday it would have to stand before the bar of judgment. All these things—the existence of God who created and governs the world, the moral law, the immortality of the soul, and the certainty of judgment—were legibly written on the rational soul. The evidence of this power of inborn reason, he believed, was clear in the history of mankind. For Christianity was not the only religion that taught these things; non-Christian creeds held the same beliefs. Even the red pagans in the wilderness, Mather often said, worshipped a God, and trusted Him to give them a life after death. These religions were false and evil, but they possessed some truths because all men, however wicked and misled, were born with them. These rational truths, he said in *Reason Satisfied,* have a "native Evidence" of their own.[64]

Mather returned to these points throughout the remainder of his life in both public and private utterances. What began as a means, or a strategy, certainly affected his understanding of his God. Still the changes in his views took place within rather circumscribed limits. The moral principles he told New England it could find inscribed in the hearts of men were precisely those found in the Bible. One kept cropping up in his sermons as the crowning maxim of reasonable morality. It was the Golden Rule.[65]

The implication was plain in this emphasis: valuable as it was, reason could only tell men something better told elsewhere —in the word of God. And only revelation could provide the directions for salvation. Only revelation told of the sacrifices of Christ and of the miracles He and His disciples performed. Justification by faith was certainly a reasonable doctrine, but it was not to be understood by reason. The Holy Trinity might be considered reasonable by men who studied Scriptures, but they must not believe they truly understood it. Of course reason was an "Excellent Faculty," "a Noble Thing," Mather wrote in these years of his chastened rationalism; it distinguished men from beasts. But reason should not be idolized as it is when men depend upon it for their conduct rather than consulting God; when men, listening to it, presume to advise God, rather than depending upon Him; "when men will Receive nothing that is Revealed from GOD, Except they can fathom it by Reason; when Men must Comprehend the Mysteries of the Revealed Religion, or else they will *Reject* the *Counsel* of GOD." Of course men must listen to their reasons and to their consciences, but they must never attribute to them the power to save. That power belongs to Christ and will remain mysterious until the end of the world.[66]

As Mather knew, but hesitated to admit, the mystery that aroused extraordinary contempt among English deists was the Trinity. Cotton Mather never even outlined the dimensions of the attack on it in English circles, but his defense revealed the limitations he found in reason. While writing about the Trinity in these years, he repudiated efforts to confine reason by the rules of logic—vulgar logic he said—or by scholarship. Most study, pursued in universities, he said in his *Manuductio ad Ministerium*, deserved to be consigned to the rubbish heap, and logic which only proved itself in "logomachies and altercations" merited no higher resting place. Teaching one to think—which scholarship and logic presumed to do—Mather believed a ridiculous task; one might as well be teaching the act of eating and drinking. Reason took its origin in custom and nature, and required no tutor.[67]

And not even reason freed of the dead hand of logicians could solve the mystery of the Trinity. The deistic authorities pronounced the notion of three-persons-in-one contradictory and, worse, absurd. And, of course, as Mather pointed out by the standards of a faculty as limited as reason, it was. Neither reason nor science could properly "exhibit" this mystery, he said in the Biblia. All the descriptive terms the mind devised— "persons," "essence," "procession," failed before its magnificence and power. Yet the Trinity deserved faithful respect nonetheless as one of the articles of revealed religion.[68]

While Mather declared his respect for natural reason, in his praise of the glory of the Trinity he resorted unself-consciously, and perhaps insensibly, to the old Ramist logic. At the end of the chapter "Of Man" in *The Christian Philosopher,* a book celebrating the compatibility of the new science and the New Piety, Mather declared that the very construction of the universe was in some mysterious way analogous to the Trinity. "All *intelligent compound Beings* have their whole Entertainment in these three Principles, the DESIRE, the OBJECT, and the SENSATION arising from the *Congruity* between them . . . ," and this analogy, he inferred, permeated the entire spiritual and material world. So universal a pattern could have its source only in the archetype of the infinite God. Were men able to penetrate to its "Source," they would find the Holy Trinity of the Father, Son, and Holy Ghost. Of course, they lacked this ability, but this did not prevent Mather from telling them what they would find if they had it. In the Godhead there existed a powerful *"Desire,* an infinitely active, ardent, powerful *Thought,* proposing of *Satisfaction";* this representation was God the Father. Since only God could satisfy Himself, and fulfill the desire of happiness, He contemplated Himself, and the glorious *"Image* of His person";* the OBJECT, then, of this reflection was God the Son. The joy, the love, the *"Acquiescence* of God Himself within himself, yields the SENSATION, the Holy Spirit." The relationships which exist within the Trinity, Mather explained, appear "analogically" in nature; they do not inevitably, or necessarily, assume the "relations" that we observe. But in the Godhead they are "glorious Relatives." [69]

Mather did not admit that he was using the language and conceptions of Peter Ramus, the great logician in the founders' eyes. Every intellectual and every divine in New England knew these terms from their days at Harvard. They knew that although most things could be related in several ways, "Relatives" described the only possible relationship that some things could have. They were in a sense mutual causes of one another; if one ceased to exist so did the others. The Trinity fitted this notion perfectly, Mather believed: "it is impossible that the SON should be without the FATHER, or the FATHER without the SON, or both without the HOLY SPIRIT." This far and no farther could the mind carry man and "Thus from what occurs throughout the whole Creation, Reason forms an imperfect Idea of this incomprehensible Mystery." [70]

More than the imperfections of reason had led Mather to write these words. He knew that he had gone too far in hoping that reason and science could be used to make religious claims so compelling that enlightened and skeptical men of the new age would return to the true faith. And though he never repudiated reason, he recognized the heresies it had inspired.

Yet while Mather reduced his advocacy of reason he increased his support of the uses of experience. His disenchantment with reason was far advanced in 1715, the year he sent off the manuscript that was to be published as *The Christian Philosopher* five years later. Mather's praise of the natural theology in this book has often been noted—and his reservations about reason such as appear in his discussion of the Trinity—ignored. He would continue to seek scientific knowledge throughout the remainder of his life confident that it would redound to the glory of God.

Yet he no more expected the experimental philosophy to lead men into an understanding of the mysteries of religion than he did reason. But still his hopes grew that experience might reduce men's pride, stimulate them to reform society, and lead them into the Christian Union that would greet the return of Christ. Experience could do all this—but not the experience of the creatures, nor the experience grasped by reason, rather the direct and immediate experience of the Holy Spirit. [71]

Cotton Mather's private worship was always more "spiritual" than his public utterances revealed. The emphasis on the Holy Spirit in his preaching and writing only gradually caught up with these inner encounters. In one of his early expressions of reliance on the Spirit—a sermon preached in 1709—he told his listeners that conversion brought men "Experimentally to *feel* the *Main Truths* which the Christian Religion is composed of." But the Holy Spirit might do even more for such men if they exercised their grace. The Holy Spirit indeed would "Irradiate" and "Satisfy" them, "not so much in a way of *Reasoning*"— Mather had already recognized the limits of rational satisfactions—but "in a more *Immediate way*," the "way of the Intuition." [72] The way of intuition would persuade them of the truths of Christianity.

These promises would have left the natural theologians in England flabbergasted. They might have asked how anyone could recommend intuition as an instrument of truth, when a more reliable source lay at hand in the wonderful works of God. And did not Cotton Mather praise those works and their study? He did and would continue to do so, but his religious sensibilities were both finer and less restrained than theirs. His religion, which in these years he began to refer to as American Pietism, looked to both science and the Spirit. [73] Eventually American Pietism would learn to ignore science, and then to repudiate it. But not in Mather's lifetime. Still, Mather, without intending to, forecast this development as he turned from the experience of nature to the experience of the Holy Spirit.

17

The Experimental Religion

~

Cotton Mather's first statements about the New Piety owed little to European Pietism. The term "piety" had appeared in Christian writings for centuries with both more general and more specific meanings than he gave it. Mather arrived at his peculiar emphasis after brooding for years on the nature of religious experience. New England's Church polity, by requiring that members be tested for saving faith, forced him to think long on this subject and he had complied willingly at first and then with a growing desperation as men declined to join the churches. By the year 1710, he had learned of the European Pietists and began writing them of his efforts to revive religion. His most important correspondent was Dr. August Hermann Francke, a minister whose philanthropic impulses led him to found an orphanage that became famous in Europe, as well as schools and colleges at the Frederician University at Glaucha, near Halle, in Germany.[1]

From Francke and others on the Continent and in England, Mather learned much about the organization of society along Pietistic lines, yet his ideas remained essentially, as he once said, "American Pietism." Shortly after he began talking of "PIETY" and the "Maxims of the Everlasting Gospel," he said that he had been preaching this type of religion for over thirty years, that is, from the time he first appeared in the pulpit. Mather was both right and wrong on this score: from his beginnings he was an emotional preacher who delivered an affective message. His version of Romans 12.11 was not Paul's "be fervent in spirit," but rather "be boiling hot in it." [2] Pietism was not something he picked up to repair the sagging authority of the ministry in New England. It expressed the intensity of his own spirit, and the spirits of his followers, among them Cooper, Prince, Foxcroft, and Gee. Yet, it was also a strategy, and a well conceived one, to produce the reformation which virtually every minister in New England had cried out for over the past two generations. To its advocates piety connoted "vital" religion, the faith in the Holy Spirit and a loving appreciation of the sacrifice of Christ. Experimental religion, or as Cotton Mather sometimes called the New Piety, evangelical religion, put men to examining their own immediate experience. What the believer discovered of his feelings, it implied, was far more important than a detached application of the promises of the covenant to one's own condition. One must be affected, and must experience the energy of Christ, and must concentrate one's entire being towards the advancement of His glory. Mather did not propose that experience lead the soul to riots of mystical raptures; piety carried restraints and experience of it stopped far short of emotional anarchy.[3]

Yet Mather's conception of religious experience was different from the founders'—it implied that when the ways of apprehending the truth provided by logic, science, and reason did not satisfy men, they must consult their own experience. The application of Scripture to the believer's own condition—how he felt about it, how he experienced it—would persuade him of its truth. Similarly the believer's worship itself, besides glorifying God, would confirm for him the truth of Christianity. The first generation had, of course, recommended introspection to men, but only as a technique of discovering their inner conditions. The truths of Christianity were to be taken on faith; they could not be doubted by good men. But by Cotton Mather's day, men who were good by most standards were doubting Christianity and asking questions about the authority of Scripture. It was to answer these men and to ease their doubts that the New Piety was devised, for it provided a completely subjective test of religious truth.[4]

If the New Piety provided a different basis of religious authority, there was a further departure from ancient practice in the way it was recommended. For it was preached in terms comprehensible to the weakest intelligence—a circumstance far removed from the rigorous divinity of the first generation. Mather had begun issuing his Pietistic productions in the defense of the United Brethren and soon expanded them in the advocacy of Christian Union. Piety enjoined the "Catholic Spirit,"[5] he said in these sermons; it rendered the old sectarianism irrelevant; it dampened the differences which have divided Protestants since the first Reformation. He delivered these opinions in the years immediately following the Glorious Revolution. In these years he also began simplifying the creed, insisting that the heart of Christianity could be expressed in a few eternal maxims. Most of these Pietistic sermons were intended for men of the meanest capacity—a favorite audience was one of the Boston Societies of pious young men—and doubtless some of the blurring of theological distinctions was undertaken for their understandings. Most of the simplicity inhered in Pietitism itself, however, and in its name Mather found it possible to offer general reassurance to a culture increasingly anxious and fragmented. In the *"Midnight of Confusion,"* as Mather characterized the early eighteenth century, men should learn that piety can give their souls peace.[6] He did not often discuss the doctrine of assurance in Pietistic terms; piety implied that such theological niceties were too fine-spun for ordinary men. All such men required was the happy news that piety could rid them of their uneasiness about their fates and give them comfort much longer than "the short Blaze of *Thorns Crackling under a Pot*," as he termed the duration of much conventional assurance.[7]

In recommending experimental religion, Mather faced a cruelly familiar dilemma: how to persuade men who loved their own righteousness to seek an intense private experience which—in theory—they were incapable of attaining by their own efforts. Moreover they must be convinced that not only their own salvation depended upon vital religion but the progress of history as well. For the New Piety was one of the engines of the chiliad. Of course men could not bring Christ back by themselves; He would come at a time of His own choosing. Yet according to the divine plan men must give a sign in history that they were ready. They had to go down the line of time—as eschatologists called the duration of history—doing their best. To convince a society that had come sadly to the knowledge that much on earth was beyond its control presented discouragements for anyone. So many of the old premises had fallen—the State no longer could persecute; the charter of the government rested on the good will of an English sovereign; and the idea of a national covenant seemed increasingly difficult to defend. In the face of recent history, could anyone maintain that religion was anything more than a private affair? Mather could and did—the shock of events simply fueled his burning chiliasm, With the Second Coming, he knew, the concerns of governments and public policy would fade away, and with them the antiquated distinctions that haunted churches and states. The experimental religion, then, assumed cosmic importance, and only one isolated from history could consign it to private concerns alone.[8]

Every minister knew that men expected more from religion than a performance in an historical drama. Cotton Mather, the most sensitive of pastors, recommended piety on grounds ordinary men valued. To those who heeded piety's injunctions, it would bring marvelous benefits, which he described in sermons preached to all manner of audiences. To the young it would bring moral lives; to the old, comfort in their age. The happy could expect greater delights; the grieving, a full peace. To merchants and traders, he suggested that the experience of the vital religion would produce honesty and fair bargains in business. Families, too, would find life transformed, with husbands and wives dealing lovingly with one another, servants performing their tasks without complaint, and children showing obedience to their parents and respect to one another.[9]

These claims agreed with all the traditional expectations about the power of grace to change men. In another, technical, language Cotton Mather and his father before him had declared that sanctification followed justification. Richard Mather had preached of men growing in grace, becoming better as they exercised the new power a merciful God had given them. Increase Mather had often repeated these hopes. Out of fear, and surely out of eagerness to do good, Cotton Mather could not leave the matter there. He was dealing with men of substance and men who wished for substance. In his heart of hearts he knew that they cared less for the consolations of religion than they did for the creatures of this world. Though for the moment, they were impatient of ecclesiastical divisions, they did not fear the new groups appearing on the New England scene. Nor did they attribute a plot against Christian liberty to the High-Fliers of the Church of England, as he and Increase did. They undoubtedly hoped to be among the saints Christ would draw up to Himself when He came again, but they would leave that for the future. For the moment they looked to this world, a world transformed not by grace, but by property. As he sensed this disposition, Cotton Mather played to it and exposed his unwitting participation in the corruption of his society. For the unique advantage of piety that he singled out—"one which is not every day insisted on"—was calculated to appeal to the business mentality: piety pays, Mather proclaimed, and declared that by this argument the people of New England "would be persuaded unto almost any other Thing in the World." "Piety duely Expressed will render you sure of being *in the Worst of Times* well Provided for. Oh! The *Charms* of Piety! How is it possible to be deaf unto them!" [10]

Such statements disappeared from Mather's sermons around the year 1715. They were never easily reconciled with his understanding of religious experience as an affective process; and they placed him in the absurd position of recommending Christianity on the grounds that it returned a profit while yet espousing the traditional Puritan contempt for overvaluing the creatures. As if the conjunction of these views did not sufficiently defy logic, Mather further compounded his inconsistencies by advocating a worship that placed a high value on suffering and asceticism. [11]

Worship, of course, was intended to yield the experimental religion. Over the years as he worked out his ideas on how a man should approach his God, Mather elaborated a variety of techniques which gradually contributed to a radically different understanding of religious experience itself. Considered separately, or even together, Mather's methods of worship—the systems of a man both systematic and unsystematic, and at times irrational—did not differ from much that is familiar in Puritanism. Yet, as traditional as most of the techniques he advocated were, his understanding of worship reveals his altering conception of religious experience itself.[12]

One of his earliest devices involved spiritualizing the creatures, which saw the worshipper concentrate his energy on a thing in order to experience the Divine. The experience, Mather noted, might occur largely in the reason, but ideally one should be affected as well as informed. Of course worship had always been enjoined to move the emotions of men as well as their minds. Mather hoped that spiritualizing the creatures would induce a number of different feelings—exhilaration at the power of a God who possessed the power to create an infinite variety of things in the world, and gratitude for His gifts to sinful men. These hopes were closely tied to still another purpose that became more and more explicit as Mather's religious theory became increasingly "experimental" and "evangelical"—words he used himself.[13] Worship should produce submissiveness—a condition completely in accord with psychology of abasement. Mather urged that this objective should animate virtually all the exercises of piety, from daily spiritualizing, self-examination, prayer, meditation, vigils, to fasts. Night vigils, for example, should be "Flesh-Suppressing Exercises"—and would be, he promised, if they were conducted with labor and self-denial.[14]

Mather recommended these exercises of piety with still another favorite design in mind: they would further the cause of Christian Union. His ecumenical vision described a strife-free community suffused by a warm Christian love. The exact character of that love was not always clear—even to him, one suspects. But he clearly saw it as a force breaking down barriers, uniting men in Christ. His prescriptions for worship reveal that he also thought of love as a restraining—even repressive— instrument. The love he saw emerging from the exercise of Piety would induce the self-denial that worship explicitly required. Worship that subdued the promptings of the flesh would ensure that men would not break the peace of others. Social order resulted, he said in *Love Triumphant*,[15] when carnal outbursts were prevented. And worship in PIETY could produce the control necessary to pacific men.[16]

Christian Union was one of the ends he most desired to stimulate by a worship controlled by asceticism. As these hopes gradually faded in the eighteenth century, he continued to demand fervency from the people of New England. In fact, as he became more disillusioned, his own worship and his exhortations to others grew not only more affective but came to rely increasingly on the direct influence of the Holy Spirit. It was in this dependence on the Spirit that he exposed his own altering, and at least partially unself-conscious, conception of religious experience. For it was the celebration of the Holy Spirit that ultimately defined his version of the experimental religion.[17]

The curse of the Antinomians, and their cousins the Quakers, probably slowed Mather's Pietistic progress. But even as he reviled both groups in the seventeenth century, he was yearning for some experience that would put him and others into direct contact with the Lord. For most of its practitioners, spiritualizing the creatures, like other kinds of meditation, was an affective processs but it did not bring them into an immediate encounter with the Holy Spirit. When Mather instructed his flock in its techniques, he urged them to be "boiling hot" in its use, but as late as 1702 he only claimed that it would "affect" them.[18] Formal meditation, he said in *Christianus Per Ignem*,[19] should simply see worshippers take a scriptural text or a case of conscience and "speak unto it as well as we can." The believer should take two steps meditating on a "thing": first he should consider its nature, titles, distribution, causes, effects, subjects, adjuncts, opposites, and comparisons; and second he should examine his own life and behavior, remonstrate with himself to improve, and finally resolve on better conduct. This type of meditation might be compressed "in the little *Fragments of Time,* that intervene between our more stated Businesses" but compression no more than elaborate formal meditation brought a direct infusion of the Holy Spirit. Not even close concentration on a scriptural passage, which would undoubtedly move the believer to feel that it was composed under the influence of the Spirit, could do that. So Mather's opinions stood on practice of meditation around the opening of the eighteenth century.[20]

But in the next fifteen or twenty years Mather came to see that the exercise of Piety in devotional practices might pay higher returns. He had always urged worshippers to study the Scriptures while they spiritualized the creatures or engaged in any sort of meditation. Concentration on the Lord inevitably brought men back to His word and if it did not, Mather was quite willing to advise them on scriptural study appropriate to any meditation. And in fact many of his Pietistic tracts recommend scriptural passages suitable for worshippers at almost any conceivable time. In the seventeenth century, a cooler period for Cotton Mather, he never proposed that such meditation would ever do anything more than affect men rightly and give them proof that Scripture was indeed the word of God. But by the last decade of his life he was so excited by these old techniques as to claim that intensive meditation could lead to the recapture of "like Motions of PIETY" of those who wrote the Scriptures.[21] The same Spirit that guided the pens of the authors of the Bible would inspire the devoted worshipper. And filled with the Spirit, the fervent Christian would gain the assurance of "coming to dwell in the same *Heavenly World,* which those men of GOD are gone unto." [22]

Mather's own inner life inspirited these utterances as they did so much of what he preached about worship and behavior. Long before he began telling his church about the "New Piety," he had perfected the method of the particular faith, a technique of concentrated prayer which induced in its practitioners a conviction that what they yearned for would come to pass. He had also begun his midnight vigils, continued his fasts, and intensified his meditations every year. Occasionally he experienced the delights of interviews with angels; and his private devotions were increasingly filled with rapture and afflatus.[23]

These experiences helped form Cotton Mather's preaching about the believer's covenant with God. As he became dissatisfied with his colleagues' understanding of the covenant as a transaction between "principals," he began to urge that men who entered it properly, as minor "accessories" to the major agreement between God the Father and His Son, should strive to equal the humility of Christ. Conformity to Christ, especially the imitation of His abasement, would lead men to the joy of the knowledge that they had indeed been saved.[24]

Mather's own devotions convinced him that the Holy Spirit, acting under Christ's direction, brought such divine comforts. Prostrate on the floor of his study, pleading his vileness in the dust, he yearned for more of these direct encounters with the Spirit. He knew that others shared his desires—the Pietists in Germany, for example—but he admitted that neither they nor he could do anything without divine aid. But nonetheless, in the hot moods of this Pietistic fever, he begged God for a pouring out of the Holy Spirit.[25]

Mather recognized that he was on the slippery ground of enthusiasm here; and for years he confined most such yearnings to his *Diary*. He was not an Antinomian nor a Quaker but these secret experiences placed him dangerously close to them—and he was inclined to move closer. Late in his life, his father dead and most of the second generation in the grave, Cotton Mather began to sound some of these desires in the pulpit and in the press.[26]

The ways in which the Holy Spirit acted in human affairs had divided Protestants for years. Presbyterians and Congregationalists, the Puritans of the right, had long cashiered Anabaptists and Quakers, the Puritans of the left, for their insistence that the Spirit still spoke directly to man as it had in the days of the Apostles. In New England the radicals had first made their case in the Antinomian crisis, and for years afterwards Richard Mather and his heirs complained of Familists and Antinomians. Increase Mather had rejoiced over the actions of the State against the Quakers and had publicly urged on their persecutors. Cotton Mather delivered his only reasoned argument against Quakers in 1690, but even then he stigmatized their doctrines as "vomit" and the "plague of This Age." These gentle comments came in the *Principles of the Protestant Religion Maintained;* [27] Mather had dealt with Quakers the year before in the Appendix to his *Memorable Providences,*[28] and he was to attack them again in *Little Flocks Guarded Against Grievous Wolves.*[29] He preached against them in other sermons too, in 1712 for example, riding to Salem to excoriate them. The Quakers gave as good as they got. By calling him the New England College Boy they suggested that Mather's learning was not quite as weighty as he imagined; and George Keith, an effective Quaker polemist, compared Mather and his friends to "Nightbirds and Beasts of prey." [30]

When Mather could suppress his anger, he explained that his central difference from the Quakers concerned the operations of the Holy Spirit. What Puritans found reprehensible in Quakers, Cotton Mather said, was their pleading for "Immediate and

Extraordinary" revelations *"such as the Apostles had."* That Christ opened the Apostles' minds "without ordinary helps"— reading and hearing the word—no Protestant would deny. Puritans of Mather's persuasion did deny, however, that Christ continued to work that direct way after the end of the apostolic period. The Holy Ghost spoke in "cloven tongues" then; but since then the Spirit chose to increase men's understandings only through the regular, even rational, process of operating on their faculties. The Spirit worked this way because God respected man's reasoning power, and because He had revealed all that men needed to know in Scriptures.[31]

Over the next thirty years as Mather worked out his ideas about the psychology of religion and the covenant, he came to recognize that this safe view of the Holy Spirit, so nicely calculated to prevent enthusiastic outbursts, could not be reconciled with his understanding of how God converted men. In these years he insisted repeatedly on the affective rather than the rational side of the conversion process; he declared that the doctrine of preparation was only a convenient disguise for the pride of man; he called for men to abase themselves before Christ's covenant of redemption and to realize that they were only accessories to the transaction that gave them salvation. And he preached sermons telling his people that the Lord required His chosen ones at the moment grace entered their souls to abdicate their reason and their wills. At that moment at least, prideful and corrupt human beings must resign every pretension of power and merit in order that a greater power and a greater merit give them a new birth. Had Mather been braver, or more reckless, or more creative, or had he yielded to one set of impulses deep within himself, he might in these years have abandoned the doctrine of the means which held that God dealt with men through evidence accessible to their senses and their minds. Indeed he might have given up scholarship altogether, and surrendered himself totally to the Holy Spirit.[32]

But he did not. Instead he led an emotional life that swung unevenly between conventional piety and direct encounters with the Holy Spirit. His public comments about religious experience only gradually revealed this precarious split. Until the last decade of his life most of his preaching about conversion pictured the Spirit acting rationally on the faculties of the saints.

But in these sermons Mather's commitment to the New Piety is clear.[33]

Traditional divinity had always held that a saint might detect the "signs" of his faith by close examination of the self. All three of the Mathers and most of their colleagues over the century had urged their flocks to scrutinize their psyches for evidence of conversion. The Holy Spirit, of course, provided the testimony a believer craved—not directly, but by illuminating the faculties of the soul. Thus the sense of assurance came from one's own spirit which had been affected by divine action. And happily the New Piety offered another way for the testing of the spirit, for if the individual discovered that he believed in piety's simple maxims, he could take comfort that he belonged to God. What seems especially suggestive here to a modern student is that Mather usually phrased this argument in terms that indicate that he understood self-examination as an affective rather than an intellectual process. For what one discovered about the self was not so much its beliefs as its power of empathy. If, for example, a man discovered that he felt Christ's blood in his soul, an almost incomprehensible feeling, he could begin to trust his own sanctity.[34]

What all this amounted to was a scrapping of rational tests— despite the professions of belief in the Spirit's working through the means. Mather's hymns to men's "desires" for salvation were a comparable repudiation of formal theory. Here in his sermons on the New Piety, the traditional language of the faculty psychology is discarded and "desires" become blurred into inarticulate feeling through the operations of the Spirit. For, as Mather implies, if desire and feelings could tell men so much about themselves, they must have been moved by the Spirit.[35]

Mather first began cautiously to say as much around 1710 when he began sounding his views of Pietistic religion more strenuously than ever before. There was nothing in these statements in direct conflict with traditional Calvinist theology. Yet excess seems inherent in emotional religion—if, filled with the Holy Spirit, the emotions can be trusted with so much, the next step often seems to be to look closely for the Spirit itself. Mather hinted as much in *The Heavenly Conversation*,[36] a treatise he wrote to instruct ministers in the opportunities of "the true American Pietism." In this work he again joined his psychology of religion and his Christology, but with a difference: the imitation of Christ by the believer—he told his readers—might lead to a direct experience of the Holy Spirit. For if a Christian shared the Savior's humility, if in response to afflictions he became more like Christ, he might find that his conformity will "strangely fetch in a *Light* from Heaven . . . ; a Light which will *Revive* you, *Comfort* you, *Direct* you; and not with meer Influences of Reason, but [Give me Leave to say it!] in the way of a *Vital Touch*, fill you with Pleasures that cannot be uttered; with Joys *unspeakable* and *full of Glory*." [37]

Mather did not repeat this suggestion in print for almost fifteen years and he does not seem to have developed it in the sermons he gave every week in Boston, and which remain unpublished. There was no reason for his colleagues to notice the comment; the bulk of his preaching in these years on the Spirit dealt with its operations which enabled believers to accept the MAXIMS OF PIETY. And in these manifestations, the light it gave presumably revealed nothing new to men, but rather confirmed one's fear of God, acceptance of Christ's mediation, and love of neighbors, tenets which were all part of the traditional gospel. Nothing Cotton Mather said in these sermons would have aroused his grandfather Richard—there was no hint that the Holy Spirit operated immediately and directly in the believer. Rather, all of Cotton Mather's comments, though emotional and concentrated on the passions, were quite tame; they portrayed the Spirit under Christ's tutelage affecting the faculties of man in a rational and logical manner.[38]

But while Mather was publicly describing the Holy Spirit working in these orthodox ways, he was privately learning a great deal more from it. His *Diary* in the years around 1715 is filled with claims that God had given him extraordinary knowledge of the coming Kingdom.[39] This information—conveyed in rapturous interviews in the dead of night—did apparently go beyond Scripture, at least in the knowledge Mather claimed of the return of Christ. But as enthusiastic as these encounters left him, he never quite fell into Antinomian frenzy. And yet he must have come close in the last five years of his life. At this time he publicly repented of his old views of the Quakers, saying to them in *Vital Christianity* [40] that "God has raised you up *to chastize us for the vile Contempt and Affront which People generally cast on the Light* of God within *them;* and *for our usual and criminal Rebelling* against the LIGHT." [41] Mather more than made amends in these years. He continued to say in the conventional way that the Spirit worked through means, but he put his main emphasis on its "supernatural" and immediate effects on men's souls.[42]

Still, Mather did not so far take up the religion of the Spirit as to abandon the religion of Christ (as he implied the Quakers did). In the year 1726, he carefully remarked that the Holy Ghost moved under the special dispensation of Christ, and that it left Christ's image on the soul of the believer and not its own. The believer for his part should attempt to resemble and conform to Christ as fully as possible. When the Spirit assisted the soul in a rational way, the believer obtained a testimony of his conformity to Christ. But this assurance, which Cotton Mather called "discursive," usually proved feeble and contained "much of *Darkness*" in it if the Spirit chose not to show it self in "a more *Absolute manner.*" When the Spirit, acting to give an "Intuitive" assurance, broke "*Directly*" into the soul, its "*Mighty Light* bears in upon the Mind of the Believer a powerful persuasion of it, that he is a Child of GOD, and his GOD and *Father* will one day bring him to *Inherit* all *Things.*" [43]

The comfort the Spirit brought in this intuitive way clearly affected the entire soul and all its faculties. Mather described the rational faculties as "overpowered" with the "Thoughts" of the believers' inheritance in Heaven.[44] Understandably, a man so affected felt peace and joy, but the Spirit moved his will and passions so that he experienced raptures. Presumably even this affective process might be forced into the traditional understanding of conversion, for the Spirit is not said to be bringing new revelations to the believer, but only the assurance of saving faith. But some of Mather's colleagues must have twitched uneasily as they heard him proclaim that the Spirit spoke directly to the Christian, saying "I *have taken hold on thee, and set thee apart for Eternal Blessedness.*" [45] For Mather had in fact given up most of the restraints of reason and of the "means" in favor of the direct experience of the Spirit. Publicly he declared, "I am no pretender to Extasy," [46] but privately he knew ecstasies in his worship. And what he urged on his flock publicly was calculated to give the most affective kind of experience a Puritan could conceive—a direct immersion in the Holy Spirit.[47]

It was not Cotton Mather's practice to disavow beliefs he no longer held. He did, to be sure, reject an old method of covenanting when his Christology grew extraordinarily powerful. But at the end of his life he saw no need to suggest that his grandfather Richard's view of religious experience was inadequate. He recognized that men would worship through a variety of techniques. His grandfather's ghost may have haunted him, though, as his proposals for a more spiritual worship came to be obsessive. Almost as if he were answering an unspoken reproach from Richard, he repeated the contention of the founding generation that evil conduct was utterly inconsistent with the effects of the Holy Spirit. As his grandfather had rejected Antinomian excess, so would he. However, Richard Mather, one suspects, would have deplored his grandson's position as only a step short of enthusiasm.[48]

Mather continued in these years his long flirtation with still another enthusiastic concern—the appearance of apparitions and their relationship to the body and soul. He did not suggest that apparitions were ever the manifestation of the Holy Spirit. But in the stories he told of witchcrafts and possessions, he summoned up for his listeners and his readers a world inhabited by unseen powers which surely included the Holy Ghost. "Shallow Reason," he wrote in the Biblia, simply could not cope with such phenomena.[49] His own explanation of these mysteries provided further evidence of his disenchantment with rationalism and science. He had come to believe, he said, that the operation of an extraordinary spirit accounted for much that was inexplicable—from such mysteries as the apparitions of departed saints to the puzzling capacity of birds to build nests without any apparent instruction. Mather called this spirit the Nishmath-Chajim—"the breath of life"—and declared that it was composed of finer particles than light itself. It sometimes appeared to the watchers over the dying, he suggested; and he speculated that perhaps it provided the medium by which original sin was conveyed from one generation to another. There is little of inherent importance, or interest, in this theory or in the incredible stories Mather told in his last years about the world inhabited by spirits. The theory and the stories, however, in offering no criticism of superstitious folklore deprecated by careful theologians, suggest the depths of Mather's growing anti-rationalism.[50]

His obsession with the Spirit and with subjectivity has still another meaning. It implies a recognition that his culture by the early years of the eighteenth century had relegated religious experience to a private realm. His grandfather's generation had always encouraged worship within the community of the church. There the faithful might hear the Word and enjoy exposure to the means. Of course they were instructed to pray in their closets and to prepare themselves for the joy of the sacrament. But religious experience remained closely attached to the church where sermons were preached and men grew in grace together. Cotton Mather valued this ancient practice immensely; hence in part his attempts to invigorate the churches within a protective state, and that failing, his calls for a Christian Union and the reformation of society through pious organizations. Yet all this had miscarried as far as he could see. Piety had not revived; and the mission of New England as a covenanted community no longer seemed compelling to ordinary men. What remained was the old task of bringing men to salvation. Stripped down to its essentials that task entailed making them listen to the Holy Spirit as it spoke directly, immediately, and intuitively.

Men who heeded the Spirit would be ready for the Second Coming of Christ. As Mather met the Holy Spirit in his worship, he also heard its other voice in prophecy. In these last ten years of his life he became convinced that the Lord had released the Prophetical Spirit once more; and like the Holy Spirit, it spoke in the voice it had used in the days of Christ.

18

The Prophecy of Joel

―――――

∽

The most frequent dream in Cotton Mather's life was of death. Visions of his own death haunted him from an early age, and descriptions of the deaths of sinners—their corruptions at last stopped, their polluted influence ended, their filthy voices silenced—gave him satisfaction all his life. He recommended that sinners think about their own deaths as a tactic to reduce their pride. No man, he insisted, could resist the Lord if he believed that this day, this moment would be his last upon earth. Mather recognized how difficult it was to accept the fact that one's death was inevitable and he conceded that it was "Natural to desire Life." But a good man learned that it was also "Religious to Embrace a Seasonable Death." [1]

Although death brought rest, it was not to be welcomed simply because it ended the pain that filled every life. Temperamentally, Cotton Mather was no more suited to accepting ease even in death than he was to contemplating adultery in life. The death he yearned for and encouraged men to think upon would open a new activity. Free of the flesh, the saints would eventually join a glorious Christ in the New Heavens to rule over the New Earth for the millennium. Even before that glory, the souls of the departed saints enjoyed a limited communication with Christ. Mather's restlessness, his urgent need for effort and action, are nowhere clearer than in his ideas about the soul. In his scheme of things the souls of the dead did not rest: they could "see" and "hear" in a sensible way that resembled the powers of the body. Of course the souls of the dead escaped their bodies and the burdens of the flesh. Still they might reappear as apparitions in this world acting through the medium of the Nishmath-Chajim, that divine set of fine particles which linked the spiritual and the physical in man. Separated from their bodies at death, the souls of the departed entered the Second Paradise, as Mather styled the next to the highest apartment in Heaven, and immediately engaged in the worship of God. This action was divine indeed, the sweetest fruit possible before the Day of Judgment and the resurrection of the bodies of the dead.[2]

Although Cotton Mather was comforted by this vision of souls in motion, he sometimes admitted his uneasiness that they might not enjoy union with Christ until the end of the world. On this matter, the peculiar conjunction of his literalness in reading Scripture and his fantastic imagination shaped his thought. Heaven, he always believed, surely was a place having a physical location somewhere above the stars, and surely it was made up of separate stations; but just as surely, Christ passed from apartment to apartment visiting the saints until they joined him in judging the world.[3]

And so Cotton Mather dreamed of death, not just his own, but the death of the world when all this would come to pass. In his excited moments he called on the Lord to "Overturn! Overturn! Overturn!"[4] He envisioned the world in flames; he relished the torments of sinners as they finally received their payment for their crimes against God. The satisfaction of these scenes was equalled only by his pleasure in the rewards the saints could claim. They at last would come into their own and shake off their secret sorrows. The Lord would publicly bless them and praise them before the entire universe for their services in His faith. And they would sit with Him and separate the just from the damned.[5]

Mather never tired of the speculation about the final convulsions of the earth. Until the last ten years of his life he puzzled over the meaning of the "signs" of the end. For years every earthquake appeared to him as a portent of the destruction of the earth, every large fire as an anticipation of the last great burning. Sometime around the year 1720, he decided that the signs had all been given and God would give no more, although great events might occur that would provide some notion of how things would be in the millennium.[6]

The end itself would take by surprise a world morally asleep. Christ would come as a thief in the night, but the circumstances of His coming would leave no one in doubt as to the meaning of His appearance. For He would come in clouds of smoke and fire, accompanied by legions of angels singing His praises. He would destroy the Antichrist and his cohorts with this fire and then chain the Devil for a thousand years. All this He would accomplish in a gigantic conflagration—so hot and huge that Mather hardly dared guess its extent and its duration. Those saints still living on earth would be caught up to Christ, raised above the fire, and along with the saints long dead would be given bodies completely transformed. Once the burning ended, the City of God in the New Heavens would rule over the saved nations of the New Earth. These nations would then live a thousand years on an earth marvelously refined by the conflagration. They would build their houses, plant vineyards, and reproduce themselves during this glorious period. The raised saints in the New Heavens would reign with Christ over them, would indeed serve them as angels now served men. The saved nations in the New Earth, however, would enjoy a sweet communication with the raised saints not often granted to men in their present state no matter how pure they were. And Christ Himself would occasionally walk among men on the New Earth, openly and visibly so they might enjoy His beauty.[7]

At the end of a millennium of this peace, Gog and Magog would rise from Hell, led by the Devil playing his final wicked part. Mather always felt uneasy about the details of this final act in the cosmic scenario, but he could not doubt its denouement. As dreadful as Gog and Magog were, they and the Devil would be speedily consumed by fire from the New Heavens. The last judgment would then ensue with a second resurrection of sinners. Their fates were clear: they would be dispatched to burn eternally while the saints would enjoy communion with Christ in the Third Heaven.[8]

Every form of Christianity has conceived of an end to this world. Yet Christianity has always been a religion of obscurities which have baffled the theologians and the unlettered alike. An end to all things and a judgment of men there will be, but how and under what conditions, has always been disputed. The Scriptures themselves have provided the common basis for Christian history—and prophecy—and have proven to be embarrassingly tractable to varieties of interpretations.

The Puritanism of the founders of New England reflected the deep concern of the seventeenth century that the end might be near in time. The English Civil War reinforced this preoccupation—as did indeed the migration to America. Both were deeply unsettling experiences and turned men to thinking of the final resolution of human affairs. In the New World, however, as settlement took root and Puritans discovered the opportunities as well as the agonies of life in the American wilderness, eschatological interests went into decline, except for a few pure spirits such as John Cotton. Richard Mather, who for twenty years after his arrival continued to believe that history was approaching its close, lost this certainty by the last decade of his life.[9]

Because most Puritan divines of the first generation felt little need to work out in detail man's progress on the line of time, eschatology rarely served as the chief ordering device of their thought. The theology of Calvin and the covenant supplied the structure of thought and feeling for this generation, while the theology of the end of things remained interestingly speculative and for most, obscure. Perhaps the same propositions can be offered about the generations of Increase and Cotton Mather; they too clung to the classic certainties of predestination, election, and the efficacy of Christ's sacrifice. At the same time, it is clear that Cotton Mather and his peers inaugurated an era of apocalyptical expectation in America that did not lose its force until after the American Revolution.

All the elements of Cotton Mather's thought were joined in his eschatology and were expressed by it. On one level Mather's eschatology provided no more than a homiletic device. He could —and did—threaten unregenerate men with the final conflagration, telling them that though they might savor the creatures in this life, eventually the book of the election would be opened and only the names of the saints read aloud. Then the book of the damned would reveal the names of sinners. The wicked might congratulate themselves on their prosperity in this world, only to discover that they had enjoyed a dream. The flames of the final burning warmed these words as well they might: Cotton Mather could do no greater service than saving souls, and if he had to pour oil on the fires of the end, he would do it.[10]

On a deeper level Mather's eschatology provided a coherence to all his thinking about man's relationship to God. The formal propositions of Calvinism remained as the fundamental structure of his theology and he never considered repudiating them. Indeed, he reaffirmed his belief in Calvinism throughout his career, often in response to the challenge of Arminians and Arians. The reformed theology was so much a part of his thought, however, that most of the time he announced his views unself-consciously and without indicating that he saw anything unusual in endorsing the five points of Calvin.[11]

Over the years, in attempting to deal with the inroads of Arminianism on Calvinism, Mather came to recognize in chiliastic theory another means of supporting the truths of revealed religion. This recognition did not occur as a blinding flash, or even consciously; rather, as his piety and his frustration grew, he gradually came to phrase the old formula in the language of his chiliasm. The final meaning of God's sovereignty—Mather said—would be revealed on the Day of Judgment: the sufferings of the elect would cease and the damned would receive their just deserts. What was new in this was the emphasis which shifted from divine arrangements of human affairs in this world to the final resolution of man's condition in the next.[12]

There was no comparable shift in Mather's psychological theory. It had always tacitly, and sometimes explicitly, looked toward the Day of Judgment. Eschatological speculations exalted the triumph of Christ; psychological thought, the abasement of man. Between these two poles Mather sought to devise the means men could use to glorify God. As early as the year 1692, in his *Preparatory Meditations Upon the Day of Judgment,* he juxtaposed the meanness of men in this world with the bliss awaiting the saints at the end. What he insisted upon in prescribing good conduct for men was that they renounce the self; until that were done they could do nothing towards the glorification of God.[13]

Mather's version of the covenant theory made the same point. Unregenerate men deluded themselves by regarding the covenant of grace as a transaction between equals. The Lord, however, took men into His covenant as subordinates whose obligations had been assumed by Christ. The full meaning of the covenant, Mather argued, would be realized only with the Second Coming. Then Christ would claim His chosen, those for whom He had paid the price. In that moment of union with the Savior, man would at last find his soul free from pride and corruption.[14]

There is more than a whiff of other-worldliness, or at least alienation from this world in these attitudes. Puritanism always wavered between full-scale immersion in the creatures—in an attempt to make ordinary life conform to the moral law—and a surrender to the ecstasies of the spirit. Mather's development, though by no means steady, was towards the spirit and away from the preoccupations of ordinary life. He never admitted to having a conscious desire to escape completely from the affairs of this world, yet his piety increasingly carried him away. His most concrete denunciations of his society which castigated interest groups and virtually named names are filled with eschatological expectations.[15]

These impulses are clear too in his theory of religious experience. In worshipping, he said, men are most effective, most pleasing to God, if in the course of abasing themselves they succeed in getting a taste of the judgment in store for them. Their spirits will close with the Lord if they keep the Day of Judgment before them in all their practice whether in meditation, prayer, or self-examination. "Think, Faithful Soul," Mather pleads, "what thy Account will be When Christ to an Account shall Summon thee."[16] This was the religious experience of the New Piety, a full celebration of the maxims of "the gospel of the Kingdom." PIETY required the "experience" of Christ and of the Spirit. Were it attained, men could expect the end of the world almost immediately.[17]

The eschatological urgency in this appeal appears in almost all of Mather's invocations of PIETY. The ultimate purpose of PIETY, whether conceived of as religious experience, or doc-

trine, or morality, was best understood within a chiliastic framework. Thus Christian Union—that contrivance that would have
men put aside petty squabbles over polity—anticipated the faith
that would animate the New Earth and the New Heavens. To be
sure, those Christians who put aside minor differences in Church
polity in favor of brotherly communion could not expect to enjoy all the bliss of a world refined by the Conflagration. Christian
Union could not transform the flesh; united men would still
require food and drink; they would suffer from disease and
pain; they would continue to use sexual intercourse to reproduce themselves. These requirements of the flesh did not disturb
Mather. The important fact of Christian Union after all was the
experimental enjoyment of Christ and more immediately, of the
Holy Spirit. Such experience forecast the way things would be
in the world of the millennium. Men—as far as Mather was concerned—could not ask for more on this side of Paradise.[18]

Do-good, too, gained moral authority when it was performed
with the millennium in mind. When Cotton Mather made the
connection between helping one's fellows and bringing on the
Kingdom of God, he often hastened to add that nothing men did
could hasten the Second Coming. But there were reasons for
men to try: among others, the fact that the Lord intended that
they should. Mather did not mean to suggest that the Lord
recommended fruitless exercises. Attempts at do-good that mattered, that achieved their purpose in other words, could only
be done by saints. Do-good extended sanctification, and testified
to the existence of grace within the souls of its doers. Most
importantly it glorified God.[19]

Although Mather's eschatology was supremely useful as a
medium for bringing his ideas into a grand order and for giving them intensity as well as form, it was even more expressive
of the various hues of his piety. (Putting the matter in these
terms can distort our understanding, for Mather's religious feeling found expression in virtually every explication of his ideas).
The darker side of Mather's piety is especially striking. His
sense of the demonic was probably as strong as that of anyone in
the seventeenth century who left a record of his inner life. His
Diary records the assaults of the Devil with depressing frequency, and he learned to expect buffetings from evil spirits,
particularly after he had performed some good act. Puritans of

course were never surprised at Satan's ingenuity and his persistence. They believed, however, that Satan could not exert power over them so long as they resisted temptation; the corruption of men stripped them of defenses against the Devil's authority. The Devil, in fact, needed their consent in order to gain power over them. Cotton Mather knew this but his obsession with demonic power was so great that he often spoke—and acted—as if the Devil's authority was uncurbed, that in fact the Devil might obtain authority over good men even without their consent. This suspicion bordered on irrationality even in the seventeenth century. It did not go unnoticed. With Mather in mind, Robert Calef charged in his indictment of Salem witchcraft that the ministers who supported the prosecutions made Satan into an "Independent Being." [20] The ministers reacted with horror to this charge and none professed more distress than Cotton Mather. Strictly speaking, Mather was innocent of the charge which suggested in a way that he was guilty of Manicheanism. Consciously, of course, Mather despised the Manichees; he was unaware that he sometimes espoused a "practical Manicheanism" by his tendency to attribute initiative and energy to the dark powers of the universe while he often pictured the good in the guise of a passive victim. He did not do so as a result of intellection but from feeling and temperament. He felt Satan pushing against himself, and within himself, and within the world around him. His eschatology provided the perfect vehicle for the expression of this feeling—and at the same time prevented him from giving way to it in paranoid despair. Mather's eschatological perspective revealed to him the long history of Satan's conspiracy against God and His people. Every major event in history took its place in the design of the Lord who permitted not only the Devil's plots but also the rise of empires, the falls of Kings, the wars against the Church of Christ, the Protestant Reformation, and the long struggle with the Antichrist, whose time was near its end.[21]

One way of dealing with conspirators, whether men or devils, is physically to smash them. Christian eschatology, especially in the Bible, foretells this end for Satan and his creature, the Antichrist. Mather studied Revelation with satisfaction and even relish, especially its accounts of the destruction of evil. There is in his Puritanism—and perhaps in most varieties of Christianity which conceive of historical process in terms of conflict between good and evil—some need of violence. The God of the Puritans was the scourge of transgressor, as well as the loving Father who gave His Son for the chosen. His afflictions were familiar to all: He brought death to His enemies and He took off children and old men. The anger of God filled learned scholars and untutored men with terror, an emotion strong in Cotton Mather. His *Diary* shows him dreading and welcoming the sword of fire as it would descend upon a wicked world. These feelings found nourishment and ultimately release in his eschatology. At no time in his vision of the end did he ever describe Christ's Second Coming as occurring in harmony and peace. The Lord might come as a thief in the night, that is, His appearance would surprise a world sunk in sinful sleep, but the shock sinners would receive when they awakened would leave no room for doubt that the world had reached its end. Mather enjoyed this picture he painted so often: Christ would descend upon the earth in smoke and fire with His angels. And the fire would rain down on degenerate men everywhere, and the heavens would be set on fire to torment the devils there. "This *Fire* will be that *Sword, the Fiery Sword.*" Unregenerate men would burn and with them, the works of man on this earth including whole cities and their best parts, libraries and the great achievements of man. The prospect of the burning of books distressed him, he admitted; and the idea of the loss of whole libraries was enough to make a Protestant scholar weep.[22]

Whatever reservations Mather had about the destruction of such vanities arose less from sympathy for the human beings involved than from the difficulties in explaining how the saints would survive the Conflagration. Increase Mather held out for a partial burning of the earth which would allow the saints to retire to unscorched parts to await the end. Cotton never felt easy with this solution but offered it as late as 1712. Near the end of his life, with Increase in the grave, he announced his change of mind—the theory of a partial conflagration was "unscriptural" and would never do. The fire would burn everything in "an all-devouring Rage"; there would be much more than an incomplete and leisurely destruction, there would be "universal Desolation." [23]

It is the obvious gratification Mather takes in the grand smash of all things that reveals his impulses towards violence so clearly. These impulses grew stronger late in his life when they affected his treatment of the prophetical books of the Bible. They appear in their starkest form in his new understanding of Psalms. As late as 1718, in *Psalterium Americanum,* Mather asserted that the sufferings of the Jews depicted in Psalms referred to the children of Israel. But within a few years, in "Triparadisus," he had shifted to a typological interpretation and now held that the accounts in Psalms were forecasts of what awaited the Lord's "Holy People" at the end of the world. Similarly, he began to read Isaiah not as history but as typology, discovering in the fiery destruction of Judea by the Assyrians and of Jerusalem by the Babylonians "Emblems and shadows" of the burning of the whole world.[24]

Although Mather recognized that most men would find such destruction almost inconceivable, he did not shrink before the task of justifying it. The sins of men made it understandable, he explained, and in the human scale, just. In the 1720's when he had fully absorbed the theory of total desolation, he offered his ultimate explanation of divine wrath. The sins of men had grown to insupportable proportions, he said. When real and vital piety had been banished from the face of the earth and "exploded as nothing but Enthusiasm," men should not expect anything but the Conflagration.[25] The history of Europe reinforced this harsh judgment, Mather believed: the Protestant interest there had shrunk to half its sixteenth-century size; and in Great Britain a succession of ministries controlled by Tory High-Fliers persecuted dissenters. Corruption thrived with placemen and grafters taking large cuts at the expense of the public interest. In America moral practice was not much higher; and men showed themselves to be brutes to one another. In the Caribbean, for example, the slave trade was especially shocking. But evil infected nations professing Christianity everywhere. One of the saddest reports of a benighted world that Mather received, he said, came from the East Indies, where missionaries wrote that even the heathen there expressed shock at the behavior of men professing the religion of Christ.[26]

God would punish these men some day; of that Mather had no doubt. They would burn and suffer torment; Cotton Mather welcomed that prospect. But the burning would end sometime, and afterwards good men would feel joy and divine happiness. If Mather believed the end of the world brought sinners their just deserts, he felt the horror of the scenes of the conflagration even as he relished them. His greatest satisfactions, however, were not received from the grisly harvest of the unregenerate, but in the rapture he experienced in his dreams of the union with Christ. His piety assumed beautiful as well as ugly forms in his visions of the end, and it was finally in the experience of this divine beauty that he found rest.[27]

Cotton Mather always professed a Christian modesty in describing the glories of the world to come. Seeing far into another order was beyond any man, he admitted, but fortunately God had given us strong hints in Scriptures, and anticipations in the experience of pious men might be used. Surely everyone would agree that describing the New Heavens which would come down after the Conflagration would tax the powers of the most inventive eschatologist. The New Heavens will have a Holy City in them, a New Jerusalem, made of gold and studded with jewels, Mather said in "Triparadisus," his most ambitious attempt at reconstructing the divine vision. God would place this New Jerusalem over the old carnal Israel, stretching it 1,500 miles in every direction. The resurrected saints, their bodies transformed and spiritualized and reunited with their souls would live with Christ in this glorious city. To describe the "Heavenly Things" there defied the powers of "our low, dark, scanty Language" but "the *First Thing* that offers itself unto our contemplation in the *Holy City,* is that UNION with God, into which it is the eternal purpose of His Love, to bring His chosen people." [28]

To say that the elect of God will become the "same" with Him would be blasphemy, and Mather hastened to disavow any such suggestion: "they will continue Distinct Beings; they will not putt off their Individuation." Still Mather expected much from a union with Christ and poured his own spirit into the description of its delights in the New Heavens where the raised saints were to be brought so "near to God that He will become '*All in* All' to them." Mather, in these accounts, attempted to feel the fullness of God and to capture the feeling in phrases having God "permeate" and "Replenish" and "swallow them up." The perfectionism denied to men by their sin in this world is at last attained through this union. All Mather's psychological theory had directed men to strip themselves of their obsession with the self. Now, in the City of God, the purposes of abasement would attain fulfillment: "*Self* will be entirely dethroned, the *Love* of God will govern Every Motion." With the self and all its sinful dispositions "extirpated," a perfection in thought and action would follow. The raised saints would not take a wrong step, nor speak a vain word, nor think anything but right thoughts.[29]

Puritans had always recognized the body as offering an impediment to perfection as great as the self. And most eschatology paid at least some attention to the transformation of the flesh in the Heavenly world. Few men have ever been more preoccupied with bodily functions than Cotton Mather, a preoccupation that led him to ponder the connection of physical and mental states. In the New Heavens, he concluded, all the sources of viciousness that lay buried in men's flesh would be destroyed. To be sure, the raised saints would receive bodies which would possess some conformity to the old human figure. But they would get a "wonderful accession of *New Qualities*" too, bodies of "material" but "highly *Spiritualized*" and able to fly with the ease of angels. Best of all, they would possess immortality, with neither a shred of corruptibility nor deformity. They would be luminous, shining like the stars in the firmament, with power and beauty.[30]

In Mather's theory the happiness the saints would enjoy in the New Heavens and the New Earth lay very much in the perfection of soul and flesh. It is true that many of his accounts of the bliss the saints would reach in the millennium suggest an experience similar to the best in this world. He took delight, for example, in reporting that the saints, though swallowed in Christ, would know one another. He liked to conjure up scenes of Luther and Zwingli embracing, and of white-bearded patriarchs enjoying discussions with the martyrs and the prophets. One of his dreams that did not find its way into his published work involved rapturous exchanges between Moses, Abraham, David, and himself. This was the stuff of happiness. Yet in his deepest feeling he saw happiness in still other terms—as the achievement of absolute purity. The "very Essence" of the happiness of raised saints, he said in "Problema Theologicum," "will very much consist in this Righteousness." This feeling grew with the years.[31]

Supporting these impulses of piety, these feelings of fear and trembling and love and hope was Mather's formal prophetical theory. Like the piety it sustained, this eschatological doctrine drew on many sources—an understanding of history, the new natural science, Biblical scholarship, Calvinist theology, and an anxious study of European politics. A profound religious devotion underlay all these elements in Mather's consciousness and made their study urgent. His thought of every sort was always in a state of tension with his piety. He was never the detached scholar.

Late in the seventeenth century when Mather came of age, Protestant studies of the prophecies had taken a direction they were to follow for at least another century. This direction had not appeared immediately with the Reformation, for the sixteenth-century reformers had only slowly emancipated themselves from the gloom that suffused Catholic attitudes towards the millennium. Medieval Catholicism had of course accepted the Augustinian synthesis of the prophecies, which held that the predictions of Daniel, Isaiah, and the great patriarchs did not refer to the future at all. In this ancient view the prophets had testified to events that befell the historical Israel and not events that the Church of Christ could anticipate. As for the book of Revelation, to which Augustine had denied any literal meaning, contending that it must be understood as an allegory of the passage of the soul from death to eternal life, the medieval Church had scanted its value as either history of prophecy. Aquinas received most of Augustine's views on Revelation with approval and stripped out any notion of a future millennium.[32]

As the sixteenth-century reformers and their successors in the Protestant Church gained perspective on the split from Rome, as they gradually comprehended that it was a momentous event in history, they came to regard the older interpretations with dissatisfaction. It was not just that these views were Catholic and smacked of the Antichrist. Their acceptance deprived the Reformation of its significance and of the possibilities it opened for the Church of Christ. If the break with Rome were to be seen in its proper context, some different version of the Christian past and future would have to be conceived.

For Puritans in England and America, the writings of Joseph Mede filled this need better than any others. Mede, fellow of Christ's College, Cambridge, and later Professor of Greek, was acknowledged as the most learned scholar of the prophecies in the English Church. Mede revived the theory of the millennium and cast it into the future, arguing that the present revealed progress towards that glorious period.[33]

Cotton Mather pored over the commentaries of every millennialist he could lay his hands on. He copied out long passages from many on Biblical texts, and eventually incorporated them into his own great commentary, the Biblia Americana. Mather absorbed the general view of Mede and his followers: the Book of Revelation described the history of the Roman Empire and the Church within it; the millennium lay not in the past but in future; the course of history led—despite by-passes and setbacks—to the Second Coming and the destruction of the Antichrist. From Mede, and especially from Pierre Jurieu, he learned, too, that Revelation must be regarded as a "paraphrase" of the seventh chapter of Daniel, where the creation of the fourth beast—literally Rome—is described.[34]

The influence of Mede at one end of this scholarship and of William Whiston at the other in the formation of Mather's disposition to believe that the end of all things was approaching is less clear. Each in his own way espoused the power of science to enlighten the mind and to reduce mystery including the mystery of the prophecies. Both professed to open obscure Scriptures with the new light. Like his grandfathers, Richard Mather and John Cotton, and his father, Increase, Cotton Mather connected the development of knowledge to the end of the world. John Cotton had believed, at least for a time, that Revelation had revealed its secrets in his own day. Richard Mather had told his flock that the daylight of the Gospel approached and with it the end of all things familiar to flesh and blood. And Increase Mather also saw a progressive unfolding of Scripture and the final acts of history on this earth.[35]

Cotton Mather's mentality was formed in this atmosphere of millennial expectation and scientific faith. For him and for the natural theologians he admired from a distance, piety and science joined in a reliance upon experience. Of course the New Piety had advanced once again the claims of grace by holding that men must convert before they could do anything else of merit. As mysterious as the process of conversion was, it was a discernible event and it left its marks—lives of devotion and morality. The encounters with the Spirit in the new birth was an experience that almost any man who had it might recognize— as surely as the experience of the pangs of childbirth would leave a woman aware of herself. For conversion engaged the affections and the senses and ultimately the soul. The experimental philosophy offered a similar kind of authority to men, a study of the creatures that laid bare the divine, and devising, hand. Few men—Mather believed—could observe multitudes of tiny fishes in a drop of water and escape the experience with their atheism intact.[36]

Yet despite their common indebtedness to experience, the experimental philosophy and piety could not claim an equality as authorities—in Cotton Mather's mind at least. Piety rested on revelation much more than it did on reason and its truths were confirmed by the experience of revelation and its progressive fulfillment over the centuries in the history of Christ's Church. Mather elaborated this proposition for the benefit of individual Christians in his preaching on the experimental religion. He was not alone, of course, in believing that Scripture might affect men with its truthfulness when they related it to their own experience. Among others, his friend Thomas Bridge had worked out techniques of worship whose purpose was to give the believer an immediate sense of the power of Scripture. It was left to Cotton Mather, however, more than to any Puritan in New England, to extend the experimental method to prophecy. But in doing so he imparted to the method so much of his own unquestioning faith that the truths obtained through experience inevitably gave way to the truths of revelation.[37]

Hence, when Cotton Mather went to the prophecies expecting to learn more than his fathers before him, he did so not primarily because he trusted the scientific method, but because he believed that the end of the world was near; and God had promised men greater light in the last age of history. There were Puritans in the seventeenth century whose piety was as passionate as Cotton Mather's but whose expectations about the end were far different. Intense piety did not necessarily end in heated chiliasm, but Mather's piety did—for reasons which ultimately defy explanation, I suspect. But this much can be said: if his belief that the end was imminent was not a judgment based on reason or science, neither was it the comforting escape of a clerical leader who believed that his society had gone bad. Nor was it the delusion of an alienated intellectual who saw political power in New England passing from ministers and intellectuals to hard men of business.[38]

Rather, Mather's eschatology provided the supreme expression of a temperament that craved the classic reconciliation that Christianity provided—union with Christ. In all Mather's writings on the end, he manages—perhaps unconsciously—to say that the world has come apart. Men are divided from one another; interests define social relationships. The society of New England has divided into sides, groups, tribes—just as his church has. Men hate one another and act contrary to the injunction to do unto others as they would have others do unto them. They backbite, gossip, extort, oppress and glorify the self over God. Repairing this state of affairs is the task of the Second Coming and the glory of the millennium that will follow.

If Mather's studies of the prophetic Scriptures and of events which he believed represented their fulfillment were more the acts of piety than of scholarship, they rested on highly self-conscious study. If reason—as Mather believed—could give only limited aid in understanding the prophecies, what was left to a man who loved his Lord? The answer—which took years to work out—carried him deeper into a Pietistic appreciation of experience. Reason must fail, but the working out of the prophecies over time would continue, hence one must study the history of the faithful. Eventually the study of their experience would seem a little remote to a provincial American, distant from the centers of European power, and Cotton Mather dreamed of more immediate ways of coming to a knowledge of the future. These were dangerous dreams, for they depended upon direct communication with the Holy Spirit.[39]

While Mather nourished such dreams, he continued throughout his life to put to scholarship the questions of when and under what conditions Christ would come. Only Scripture could tell the time of the Second Coming, and only Scripture could reduce the events of history to order. Like almost every Protestant eschatologist of his age, Mather accepted the general lines drawn by Mede (the "great Mede," Mather's usual form of address, indicates the respect he felt).[40] If Mede had done nothing more than connect the Revelation of St. John and the Book of Daniel, he would have gone a long way toward satisfying Protestant scholars. His contention that Revelation simply offered an elaboration of Daniel's seventh chapter, which describes the appearance of the fourth beast of ten horns "diverse from all the rest," linked a series of baffling prophecies.[41] This fourth beast, Mede wrote, referred to the Roman Empire, the last and fourth, of the great empires which followed the Babylonian, Persian, and Ancient Greek. This beast appears in Revelation where, Mede argued, its fate was projected into the future. Grotius, Hammon, Thorndike, all respected commentators, had held that these passages referred to the destruction of carnal Jerusalem and therefore should be understood as history rather than prophecy. Mede not only discarded their assumptions but also suggested that Revelation contained two prophetic systems: the first, announced in Chapter 5 in the "sealed book," dealt with the Roman Empire; the second, in Chapter 10, in the "little book open," revealed the future of the Church of Christ in the wilderness. These two systems of prophecies intersected in the second half of Revelation, Mede believed, but as far as rational understanding was concerned the visions of the prophet had to be considered separately until it was clear that he referred to a mingling of secular and ecclesiastical affairs.[42]

Until Mather read William Whiston's *Essay on Revelation*, shortly after it was published in 1706, he seems not to have questioned Mede's general view.[43] He continued to accept its main outlines throughout his life, though Whiston convinced him that the two sets of prophecies in the sealed book and the open little book referred to the Church within the empire, and that the distinction Mede made between *Res Imperii*—secular affairs— and *Res Ecclesiae*—ecclesiastical affairs—was unnecessary. What Revelation revealed, Whiston argued, was the condition of the Church within the Roman Empire from its beginning to its latter-day forms. To a twentieth-century mind, the entire matter reeks of antiquarianism, but as Whiston pointed out, the separation of the two sets of visions led Mede to make other errors of interpretation. The one that interested Cotton Mather revolved around the pouring of the vials (described in Chapter 16 of Revelation) which was widely taken as an allegorical account of the wrath of God against Rome and its Church. Mede believed that all but the seventh vial, the last, had already been poured and Cotton Mather agreed with him—until Whiston's book came into his hands. Whiston argued that the vials would not be poured on Rome until the sounding of Seventh Trumpet, which would not occur until the Antichrist was destroyed.[44]

The complicated details of Whiston's argument which changed Mather's mind need not concern us, but the sense they convey of the cast of his thought—and feeling—about prophecy is worth study. In the Biblia, where his most ambitious discussion of Revelation appears, Mather confesses his admiration for the "precision" Whiston introduces into the interpretation of these issues. This comment suggests his indebtedness to the experimental philosophy and its offspring, natural theology, which Whiston espoused with his Arian slant; but Mather had something else in mind. The precision he esteemed had fewer connections to the experimental philosophy than to the ancient science of numerology. If the vials were yet to be poured, as Whiston believed, they might be understood as being a part of the prophecy of the sealed book which has seven seals, and by consequence under the seven trumpets and by extension the seven thunders of Revelation. What delighted Mather was Whiston's precision" in bringing together, and giving coherence to "all the prophetic visions, that go successively by Sevens." [45]

There was still another reason for Mather's satisfaction in Whiston's account of the vials: Whiston's interpretation was a part of a larger one that forecast the imminent end of the world. Mede's discussion of Revelation implied that the end was far off (the pouring of each vial, as his account had it, had taken hundreds of years; the seventh vial—if it were to equal the others in its power to afflict the Beast—must take at least as long as the first six, a period of many hundreds of years). Cotton Mather desired nothing as much as he did reasons to believe that the end would occur in his lifetime. Whiston gave him hope that he would see this glorious day as early as 1716.[46]

Predicting the date of the end, of course, depended upon one's general interpretation of the prophecies and the conditions this interpretation required for their fulfillment. Mather's studies persuaded him that all the prophecies were linked to three great

events—the birth and sacrifice of Christ, the substitution of the
Gentiles for Israel as God's chosen people, and finally, the
Second Coming of Christ. Seeing the propecies in this light, he
said, provided the "key" that would unlock their mysteries. And
since only the Second Coming of Christ remained in the future,
the Scriptures, the signs that would anticipate His coming, and
the events through which history would unfold had to be
studied.[47]

Mather sometimes professed to be astonished that anyone
could believe that the millennium had already passed; as far as
he was concerned one did not need scholarship to realize that the
Church had not enjoyed a thousand years of purity and holiness
during any period of its long existence. He conceded that great
men, among them ripe scholars and theologians, had long entertained this belief. His own variety of premillennialism rested on
the premise that the millennium not only still remained in the
future but that Christ's Second Coming would give it a glorious
beginning. And so he studied the signs that might hint the dawn-
ing of this final period of history.[48]

The first sermon Mather published on the end of the world—
Things To Be Look'd For (1691)—revealed a technique of study
that he would use for the rest of his life, a careful juxtaposition
of prophecies and public events. Indeed, events in New England
and abroad had a good deal to do with the production of the sermon. Given to the Artillery Company of Massachusetts at their
annual meeting, June 1, 1691, the sermon offered "Good News in
Bad Times." [49] The colony badly needed some good news, for it
was suffering from Indian raids; its ambitious and expensive
expedition against the French in Canada had recently failed;
and it was feeling the effects of a currency crisis while its
foreign trade was drying up. As if all this were not bad enough,
it still did not have a charter of government (the old one had
been annulled in 1684) and it had just passed through a revolution against its governor, Sir Edmund Andros. This last event
was of course a happy one, though Massachusetts' leaders were
understandably nervous about the next governor.[50]

These occurrences by themselves did not persuade Mather that
the end which he yearned for was about to come. He was much
too cosmopolitan—or to self-conscious a provincial—ever to suggest that America occupied more of the Lord's concern than

Europe. And it was in Europe that blows had just been struck which signalled to him that the time of the millennium approached. What impressed him most in the European scene was what impressed European students of the prophecies: the renewal of persecution of Protestants in France with the revocation of the Edict of Nantes in 1685. France, most eschatologists believed, was the tenth kingdom of the Roman Empire. There the slaying of the witnesses described by Revelation might take place— indeed, perhaps, had just occurred in the slaughter of Protestant innocents by Louis XIV's dragoons. One who offered this interpretation of the French persecution was Pierre Jurieu, a Professor of Divinity in France and Holland who had been ordained in the Church of England, whom Mather read at this time (and cited in his Artillery Company sermon). Jurieu ventured to suggest that other evidence also testified to the nearness of the end. The vials of wrath had been poured upon the Antichrist, he insisted, and after them all that remained was the glorious blast of the seventh trumpet. Mather paused lovingly over Jurieu's careful reconstruction of the Biblical past, and his collation of prophecies and contemporary affairs; he wanted to believe that all the preliminary prophecies had been accomplished and that all the signs had been given but he dared not give himself completely to this theory. Yet, he told himself, the end must come soon![51]

He was encouraged in this view by other eschatologists who held that the Antichrist had entered the last half-time of his 1260 years at the beginning of the Protestant Reformation in 1517. A half-time, of course, equaled a period of 180 years; according to simple addition, the end of the Antichrist might well commence in 1697, with Christ, who would destroy the Beast, appearing simultaneously.

A skillful scholar, Mather believed, might test these calculations a few years hence by studying Turkish affairs. One of the commonplaces among the followers of Mede was that the second woe trumpet had signalled the beginning of the irruptions of the Turks upon the Empire, which began around the year 1300 with the Ottoman forces. Most commentators agreed that the Turkish woe would continue for almost four hundred years. Like many others, Mather believed that the time of the woe could be determined with precision to be 397 years. If the elaborate mathematics of the eschatologists were true, Turkish power would collapse around 1697. Cotton Mather told the Artillery Company that a truce in the war between Turks and Imperial soldiers might indicate the passing of this woe. This comment had inspiration of its own—eight years later, in 1699, the Austrians and the Turks concluded the Peace of Carlowicz.[52]

In the years after the sermon to the Artillery Company, Mather revised his computations but he never yielded the conviction that the end was near—so near in fact that he might live to experience the Second Coming. In the early 1690's he fastened his hopes for the end on the year 1697. Since many prophecies said that the millennium's opening would be marked by earthquakes, Mather recorded every quake that came to his attention. He was convinced, he remarked in *A Midnight Cry,* that the world had entered upon a period of earthquakes which would "assist" in the resurrection of the witnesses, one of the last events before the Second Coming.[53] He expected the earthquakes to increase in frequency and violence, and he was gratified by reports of the disastrous ones felt in Italy and Jamaica.[54]

Later in the same year, 1692, he discovered evidence in New England of the imminence of the end. To Mather, whatever else the Salem witchcraft episode indicated, it surely testified to the pervasiveness of evil in the world. The Devil, he said in *The Wonders of the Invisible World,*[55] was desolating mankind. And the evil that was abroad, he believed, was the last gasp the Lord would permit the Devil until the assaults of Gog and Magog at the end of the thousand years. Mather listed less oppressive signs too in this time of trouble: the slaughter of the witnesses had clearly passed and with it the end of persecution of the true religion in England. He would lose this certainty in the next ten years, but in 1692 he was still delighted by the Glorious Revolution and hopeful of Mary's intentions to lift proscriptions against nonconformity. In this mood he detected the completion of the second woe, which he said was clear in the military reverses the Turks had recently experienced. Mather would soon repent of that certainty, too.[56]

When Christ failed to descend from Heaven in 1697, Mather did not despair. It was widely believed in the seventeenth century that eschatological computations always carried an inherent inexactness because of the shadowy state of knowledge of the past and the prophecies. The calendar introduced still further difficulties to those who presumed to calculate the precise date of the Second Coming, or the birth of the Antichrist, or his destruction, or any of the schedule of events in the grand cosmic drama. Even Whiston, who claimed that astronomical science gave his chronology a new exactness, prefaced his treatise on Revelation with a little disquisition on the problems of translating the prophetical year into the Chaldean and the Julian year. So, although precision was always to be sought in figuring where the world stood on the line of time, it was not to be expected.[57]

The next year there seemed cause for fresh hope. In the Spring of 1698 Mather received news of William's Proclamation Against Profaneness, one of a series periodically issued late in the seventeenth and early eighteenth centuries.[58] Nonconformists in England also wrote of other promising developments: further reformation of the Scottish Church and Protestant recovery in Orange—"in the Bowels of France," Mather exulted in his *Diary*.[59] About this time through strenuous prayer he also received a particular faith that a "wondrous Revolution" was about to begin in England, Scotland, and Ireland, which could only mean that the Kingdom of God was near to realization on earth.[60]

During the next five years his speculations continued to range over the prophecies and the news from Europe with unvarying intensity. He shared his father's interest in occasional hints that the Jews might now return to the true religion. Increase Mather, of course, had long argued that the Jews must be converted before the Second Coming and that once they had been reclaimed from apostasy the climactic moment would follow. With his father, Cotton Mather shouted hosannas every time he heard of a Jew who had been gathered into a Protestant church. To advance this good work he wrote *Faith of the Fathers* in 1699 and prefaced it with an address calling out "Return, O backsliding Israel!"[61] He could not have been more pleased a few months later when he heard from the Carolinas that his little book had been a "special Instrument" in the conversion of a Jew there.[62]

Still, this instance and others like it were isolated. Moreover, Mather soon had to admit that though the second woe, the affliction by the Ottoman Turks, was passing, it had not ended. The Peace of Carlowicz gave his hopes a boost, but he could not bring himself to say flatly that the Turks had finally been stopped. By 1703, when he completed a study, "Problema Theologicum," which argued that Christ would appear at the beginning of the millennium, he had advanced the time of the Second Coming to 1736. This date was suggested in a tentative spirit not at all characteristic of Mather's normal chiliastic mood—and he would soon revise it.[63]

One other question troubled Mather in these years as he waited expectantly for a national conversion of Israel: what part would America take in the final scenes of the cosmic drama? European scholarship returned a frightening answer to this question, for Mede had predicted that America might escape the burning of the earth, not however because it was pure, but because it was evil. So evil in fact that it had been chosen to house Gog and Magog, those horrible hosts in the Devil's army who would attack the City of God at the end of the millennium. Not even Mede could find a sound scriptural basis for this theory, and Mather, in "Problema Theologicum," rejected it without the customary references to prophecies: "I that am an American must needs be Lothe to allow all *America* still unto the Devils possession, when our Lord shall possess all the rest of the world." [64] Although he continued to oppose Mede's view throughout his life, the matter remained one of uneasy concern. He knew that his own views were prompted by loyalty to New England, which for the most part, meant America to him; and the origins of Gog and Magog went unexplained in his writings for years afterwards. Eventually he brought himself to accept the argument of another European, M. Poiret, a French divine who held that the Devil's hosts hid in Hell until their dreadful assault on the New Jerusalem. In "Problema Theologicum" Mather had dismissed Poiret's opinion as a "Fancy" that one might expect to find in a poem of Milton's rather than in a treatise of divinity.[65]

Mather's uneasy resolution of the question of where Gog and Magog would rise reflected his belief that the area of cosmic history lay in Europe rather than in America; in rejecting Mede, the best that he could permit himself to hope for his own land was that it might be a "part" of the New Jerusalem—not its center. Poiret had drawn his scorn because he discovered the nest of the Devil's armies in Hell rather than in Europe.[66]

These speculations were largely the products of the years before he read Whiston, who published his *Essay on Revelation* in 1706. Mather admired Whiston's scientific credentials, his association with Newton, his ability to provide "incontestable demonstration" of his prophetical theories, his revision of Mede's interpretation of the open and closed books of Revelation.[67] But even more, Mather admired Whiston's chronology of final events, which revived Mather's hopes, after 1697 failed to bring Christ, that only a slight miscalculation had been made and that the Redeemer would almost certainly appear in 1716. Mather did not accept every feature of Whiston's argument about the end: he reluctantly agreed that the affliction of the Roman Church in the pouring of the vials was still to be accomplished but left the way clear for a change of mind with the comment that the Lord sometimes fulfilled the prophecies in a more "Exquisite" manner than anyone anticipated.[68]

With this disclaimer he found it all the more gratifying to believe in the minute set of computations Whiston proposed. Years before, Increase Mather had recommended caution to anyone who attempted to plot the location of the Lord's hand on the line of time, a warning which had been given by others before and would be repeated later, Cotton Mather among them. Whiston had not the advantage of having Increase Mather as a father and he shrank before neither prophetical mystery nor orthodox doctrine. The climactic year in history for him would be 1716; everything he examined in the prophecies, in the past, and in the events of recent years pointed towards that year. Though not a humble man, Whiston was sometimes a careful one; and he knew the danger of attempting to predict with exactness the date of the complete destruction of the Antichrist and the Second Coming of the Savior. By the opening of the eighteenth century the list of unsuccessful predictions had grown long. Hence Whiston used the technique of commentators who wished to introduce precision but not to appear ridiculous: he made a distinction between the beginning of the destruction of the Antichrist and the final end itself when the Antichrist would lose his life. Whiston agreed with most writers who periodized prophecy in this way that the beginning of the end would see the Antichrist lose his power, and his effective reign—Whiston called it tyranny—would close. After some indefinite period, but not a lengthy one assuredly, the forces of God would totally destroy the Antichrist, stamping out every shred of life from his body. If this moment could not be precisely dated, the beginning could be, and it fell in the year 1716.[69]

Mather admired this method of periodization and adopted it. For a few years after reading Whiston, probably shortly after the *Essay*'s publication in 1706, he accepted Whiston's contention that the second woe, the Turkish hostilities against the Romans Empire, had passed. (Whiston's self-confidence is nowhere clearer than in his commentary on this matter: the second woe, he wrote, began with the Ottoman becoming Sultan on May 19, 1301, and it ended with the victory of Eugene of Savoy over the Turks on September 1, 1697.) This news delighted Mather for it meant that the seventh trumpet (which in the prophetical scheme was the third woe trumpet) would soon sound signalling the appearance of Christ. And before that, the beginning of the end of the Antichrist would occur with the destruction of his power everywhere in the world.[70]

Mather discussed Whiston's chronology most fully in the Biblia Americana, which he began well before reading the *Essay on Revelation* and continued to revise until a few years before his death. Although by 1717 the failure of Whiston's prediction was clear, Mather never got around to expunging the excited passages he wrote on the wonderful developments to be expected in 1716. Every prophecy, Whiston had written, pointed to that glorious year. For example, John's first vision under the "little book open" had forecast the future state of Christ's Church. The primitive Church, Whiston said, had been pure until 456 A.D. when it was infested by Antichrist. When one added the 1260 years prescribed for his reign to that date, the result was 1716, when Antichristian idolatries were to be cast from the temple. This was one result of his "precision," indicating that 1716 was the year—and the slaying of the witnesses provided another.[71]

The second vision, the slaying of the two witnesses, had always confused theologians, who divided over the question of whether it had already occurred or was still to come. With many other scholars, Mather had announced his belief in 1690 that with the Edict of Nantes and the slaughter that followed, particularly in France, the prophecy had been fulfilled. He acknowledged the influence of Pierre Jurieu on his thinking, and of Peter Boyer's

History of the Vaudois.[72] The eleventh chapter of Revelation, where the slaying of the witnesses is described, also predicts that they will arise and ascend to Heaven three and a half days—three and a half years in prophetical reckoning—after their deaths. In 1692, Mather published his opinion that they had been resurrected.[73] But the discouragements of the next few years persuaded him that he had been mistaken and he retracted his conjecture that the slaying of the Vaudois fulfilled the prophecy. Whiston, however, led him to retract his retraction, and to declare in the Biblia that the Vaudois were the witnesses, that they had been slaughtered in 1686 by the French army, and that late in 1689 they had revived. The evidence he offered came from Whiston's *Essay*, which cited the re-entry of armed Vaudois into their old homes from Switzerland where they had fled in 1686. Their resurrection was complete, as far as Whiston was concerned, when the Duke of Savoy recalled the rest in June 1690 with a new edict of toleration. Whiston's calculation of the testimony of the witnesses rested on the belief that Christ's testimony in his first ministry to the world "typified" the experience of the witnesses.[74] In a series of tortured computations, he showed the correspondence and forecast the ascension of the witnesses, not surprisingly, in 1716. And so his figuring went—the Antichrist, the Church, the witnesses, and remnants of the Roman Empire all would experience great things in that year.[75]

As Mather watched the events of the years preceding 1716, he clearly felt uneasy. For one thing, his friend Samuel Sewall, also an eager student of the prophecies, refused to share his hopes. The witnesses had not been slain, Sewall insisted; and until they were, much remained to be accomplished. There was also the matter of Anglo-French relations and the success of the High-Fliers in England—who, Mather believed, represented the French interest—in getting their way over the nonconformists. Mather's English correspondents kept him informed of developments there, and the news was not good. To be sure, English arms won battles in the war but these victories meant nothing if French power survived. If the clichés of prophetical scholarship that described France as the tenth and last kingdom of the Roman Empire were true, its collapse in war would certainly mark a diminution of Antichristian authority. Therefore Mather followed the course of the French war eagerly, celebrating every victory, mourning each defeat. The news of Utrecht first pleased him, though he had long worried that peace might be made without an English victory. When he heard of the nonconformists' despair over the peace and of their belief that the French interest in England had a voice in state councils, he too despaired. The tenth kingdom survived in 1713; Mather preferred war to this sort of peace.[76]

Three years later the fateful year arrived and passed while Mather waited. It was a year of hope and, as one day gave way to another, of torture. He hopefully published *The Stone Cut Out of the Mountain*,[77] a short tract that compressed the MAXIMS OF PIETY into a few pages, maxims which Mather believed might unite godly men so firmly together that the Lord would send His Kingdom to earth for the millennium. Shortly after Mather had received the first copies, he sent several to a friend in England, confessing in an accompanying letter that the work "is of greater Expectation with me, than anything that I have ever yett been concerned in." [78] Even as he wrote these lines he was worrying that perhaps he and the others who gave their hearts to the year 1716 may have miscalculated. Sewall's skepticism about the year remained strong and he did not hesitate to announce his opinions to anyone who asked.[79]

In August, with about half the year ahead, Mather began to beg the Lord to fulfill the prophecy of Joel—"And it shall come to pass afterward, that I will pour out my spirit upon all flesh . . . "—convinced that the return of the Prophetic Spirit would introduce the Kingdom of God on earth. His conception of the operations of this Spirit provides further evidence of the increasingly affective bent of his thought. As he imagined the event, the "supernatural" shower of the Spirit would be transmitted by holy angels. These angels would "enter and possess" the Lord's ministers who, inspired, would speak with a divine "Energy" and "fly through the World with the *everlasting* Gospel to preach unto the Nations. . . ." [80] Such actions, Mather asserted, would do more in a day to advance the Kingdom of Christ than an "age" had managed previously. As was almost always the case when Mather prayed strenuously for his heart's desires he became convinced that he would soon see angels descending from Heaven bearing the Holy Spirit. He expressed this conviction with his usual repetitions—*"They are coming! They are coming! They are coming! They will quickly be upon us; and the World shall be shaken wonderfully!"* [81]

When the angels did not come and 1716 finally gave way to 1717, Mather, temporarily downcast, remarked, "Doubtless, it will now be said, *The Days are prolonged and Every Vision faileth."* [82] He renewed his supplications to his Lord, however, for a shower of the Prophetic Spirit that would make its appearance in the primitive days of the church appear as drops. In the Spring of 1717 this praying seemed lonely work and Mather confessed that sometimes he felt that he was the only man engaged in it. Yet he had to persist, thoroughly convinced by this time that all other methods of introducing piety into the world had failed. As he thought about the failures of his society to reform and to convert, he did not explain its decay simply in terms of its attachment to traditional ways of entering the covenant—those ways that exalted the power of man. He was in fact depressed by the failures of all human means to do good. Among them—prominently—was reason. We have already noted that in his disenchantment with it and in his immersion in the worship of the Spirit, Mather had exposed the anti-intellectualism of his pietism. He was less suspicious of science than reason largely because science depended, like the New Piety, on experience. (He also idolized Isaac Newton, to whom he imputed an inspired perfection.) But he was learning in these years of the limitations of science, and he was increasingly prone to point them out.[83]

Now with his chiliastic hopes rising again in the Spring of 1717, he issued *Malachi*,[84] a treatise designed to present the MAXIMS OF PIETY in such a guise as to be irresistable to a world that had resisted all other appeals to prepare itself for the Second Coming. In *Malachi*, Mather proposed that all institutions be brought in conformity to piety. What this meant—he explained—was that the languages and the sciences ought to assume a "due subserviency to piety"; ethics should promptly be consigned to "Rubbish," and with it "All Academical Erudition" which "is but a spendid, and noisy Ignorance. . . ." [85] The import of all this was clear to him by 1717. Nothing devised by man worked and nothing that the pride of man valued led to the gracious union that would usher in the Kingdom of God. And hence the only resort that remained to man was to appeal for the satisfaction of Joel's prophecy, the pouring out of the Spirit upon all flesh.[86]

In this mood he pondered the meaning of the experience of German missionaries in Malabar in the East Indies who had been sent there as early as 1705. After encountering resistance to the Gospel among the natives, they had begun to convert them. Mather learned of their trials in correspondence with them and with Francke. These German Pietists preached the Maxims of the Everlasting Gospel, he assumed; and their success, he dared hope, hinted that the Holy Spirit was once more making itself felt, perhaps as Joel had forcast.[87]

For the remainder of Mather's life, a period of about ten years, this mood persisted as he strained to persuade the Lord to send the Spirit in all its glory. His methods, the familiar ones of his worship, saw him confess his sin and attempt to divest himself of pride—"I annihilate myself before the Lord"; then followed his appeals for the Holy Spirit guided in its operations by the angels who would also accompany Christ on His return. Rapturous interviews with angels sometimes followed these appeals and Mather felt delights he could not express even in the privacy of his *Diary*. But the most satisfying returns of these efforts appeared after the death of his father. Increase had not been in the grave a year when Cotton revealed that in these interviews he had learned of how things would really be in the Kingdom. And about the same time, it was now Summer 1724, he repudiated his father's belief that the conversion of national Israel was a necessary condition of the Second Coming. This break with Increase's theory may have strengthened his conviction that the end of the world was imminent. He "daily looked for" Christ's coming, he admitted in July 1724; all the signs of the end had been given—repeatedly. The frequent earthquakes of the last thirty years, the comets, the political upheavals in Europe, all signified the closeness of the end. He found reassurance in nearby New York where the Governor, William Burnet, a friend of Newton, wrote that the Antichrist's destruction had begun in 1715. It would not be finished for years, perhaps not until 1790 by Burnet's calculations, but it had begun.[88]

A single confusion ate into Mather's confidence. What of the witnesses? Did their slaughter lie in the future as Sewall and others argued? As much as he wanted to believe that the signs were "ALL FULFILLED" as he shouted in "Triparadisus," he confessed his fear at the prospect of a great slaughter. But the fear notwithstanding, he was convinced that only an angelic possession of men could bring on the Savior—and so he continued to plead with his Lord for the pouring out of the Spirit on all flesh.[89]

These exalted hopes for an angelic possession, these feverish desires for a Union of Saints saturated with the Holy Spirit, reveal how far Cotton Mather had travelled from the provincialism of his father's generation, the generation that had invented New England. His father had sustained a splendid chiliastic vision throughout his life, and he always entertained some hope that New England might play a part in bringing on Christ's return. The types that described the history of one peculiar people dazzled Increase, and he could not help but strive to make them speak of another, better people in the wilderness.

Like his father before him, a good New Englander, Cotton Mather loved, and despised, the people of the land. Both feelings —love and hate—had found expression in calls on the land to reform, to give up its evil ways. But after years of begging his people to change their sinful hearts, Cotton Mather admitted that New England should not be confused with the New Jerusalem and that perhaps the seers who said that New England had "done the most that it was intended for" were right.[90] This saddened him but his sadness was not free of satisfaction in the afflictions he saw ahead for the people of New England. For Cotton Mather hated them, even as he loved them. His hatred made it easier perhaps to lift his eyes to a vision of the end that transcended New England's history, and New England's ecclesiastical forms. But ultimately it was Mather's love of his God —not his hatred of men—that made him plead for the fulfillment of Joel's prophecy, and gave him the extraordinary dream of the glory that awaited good men wherever they were.

19

"On the Borders of Paradise"

═══════════
ᏅᎳᎯ

While he awaited the end of the world, Mather kept up the
active life. The years that followed the disappointment of 1716
until his death in 1728 saw him continue his attempts to do good.
But sometimes when one of his proposals miscarried or drew
opposition he felt discouraged. Early in 1722, still suffering from
the savage abuse he had received for his part in attempting to
stay the recent smallpox epidemic, he threatened in a speech
before a meeting of Boston ministers to withhold all his proposals. In the past, he said, he had done his best for his community only to encounter opposition from all ranks of men no
matter what he proposed. This situation baffled him; confessing
his bewilderment, he noted how odd it was that his opportunities
to do good—"the Apple of my Eye"—inevitably evoked angry
responses from almost everyone. And he had to admit that if a
proposal came to be known as his, it drew a "Blast." This public
intractability did more than confuse Mather—it angered him so
much that he announced to the Boston ministers that he had
"done treating" them to any more suggestions for good works.
He had decided to limit his proposals to far off places, where, he
might have added, he was not known. As for doing good at home,

he would support the projects of others, but quietly and anonymously.[1]

The ministers listening to his explosive "I have done, I have done, I have done," contained men who knew their man, better than he knew himself (as least so far as impulses to do good were concerned), and one of them, William Cooper, responded to this outburst with *"I hope the Devil don't hear you Syr!"* [2] The reminder that leaving the field of battle was conceding victory to Satan was enough to send Cotton Mather back into the fray, and soon projects for good works were coming from him as fast as ever.

Even in his outrage he probably had not intended to give up his quiet efforts to relieve the poor; and he continued to try to find money and in some cases food and firewood for widows and their children. Books and instruction were almost as precious as food and Mather tried to spread both as widely as possible. He somehow found the money to maintain a small school for Negroes. There these black slaves were taught the essentials of Christianity and how to read the Scriptures for themselves. The flow of tracts and sermons which would profit ministers and their flocks maintained its force from Mather's church. He asked the well-off among his church to pay for some; he himself put up the cash for others and distributed many copies on pastoral visits and at ministerial associations.[3]

And, of course, there was preaching to be done—besides the regular services and lectures on Thursday and the Sabbath, Cotton Mather attended as many private meetings as possible. During these last years of his life he occasionally complained that two groups had deserted his church, the young and the sailors. He must have known what he was talking about, but it is clear that he remained in demand at the meetings of religious adolescents. The religious societies of the young may have outlasted those of their parents—in any case Mather seems not to have passed up opportunities to preach to them. Sailors who had never formed themselves into religious societies, as far as his private writings reveal, now abandoned his church as well.[4]

Mather more than made up for this disappointment at home by sending his proposals abroad. The correspondence with German and English Pietists never flagged as Mather reported his feelings about the Prophetical Spirit and received news of its outpouring in Europe. He had long wanted to do something for France which, as the tenth kingdom under the Antichrist, faced baleful prospects. In 1721, he finished *Une Grande Voix du Ciel A La France,* which he hoped would awaken the French and persuade them to reform before they were struck by the "tremendous Judgments of GOD." He managed to get it published four years later, after a period that saw him not only consult his friends on the best way to pay for the printing, but also seek the counsel of the Governor on how it might be distributed.[5]

Important though publishing the truth in Europe was, it had to be subordinate to Mather's efforts in America. His production of his last years made the familiar connection of PIETY and the Kingdom of God, but made it more strenuously and, as Mather might have said, more "affectuously," with a concentration on the emotional apprehension of the Holy Spirit. These works included a relatively matter-of-fact proposal for an "Evangelical Treasury," a small fund collected from particular churches, managed by deacons, and carefully audited, which would be used in the propagation of religion in frontier villages, in missions to the Indians, and in support of the poor. Not so quiet was Mather's version of Psalms, an immense rendering in blank verse designed as an "engine of the most spiritual sort of piety." Mather's account of New England's Church discipline appeared in these years too—the *Ratio Disciplinae Fratrum.* He had worked on this history off and on for twenty-five years. The last revisions of the manuscript reflect the heat of his piety and contain an admission that New England had now run most of its errand into the wilderness. What was important now, he said in a familiar plea, was that good men everywhere should now put aside their denominational differences and unite in the faith in Christ in preparation for His coming. The same hope filled Mather's *Manuductio ad Ministerium,* which like the *Ratio,* was issued in 1726. This book, Mather's instructions to candidates for the pulpit, reaffirmed the traditional view that the clergy must be learned. Richard and Increase Mather would have approved Cotton's urgings that young ministers get the learned languages under control and they would have seconded his endorsement of theological and scientific study. But Cotton Mather, characteristically going one step farther than his ancestors, infused these recommendations with his own conviction that whatever the intellectual form, the power of the minister remained in his spirit. Mather had told a convention of ministers the same thing four years before when he urged them not to come to their pulpits with a sermon that they had not already profited from on their knees in their studies. "Set the Truths on Fire" was Mather's meaning then, and he repeated it in the *Manductio*.[6]

Mather did all this good while engaged in several public disputes and while suffering disappointment and even defeat. The last decade of his life had openly inauspiciously with his taking the losing side in the fight between Ebenezer Pierpont (A.B., 1715; then Master of Roxbury Latin) and Harvard College. In 1718, the Harvard Corporation denied Pierpont his M.A., usually awarded automatically three years after the Bachelor's degree. The exact reasons for this action are not completely clear, but they lie somewhere in the history of a nasty struggle that developed when Pierpont challenged the College decision denying admission to two of his students because, as Tutor Nicholas Sever declared, they were badly prepared. Shortly after their rejection, and Pierpont's complaints, the Harvard Corporation decided that the sad state of these boys' knowledge proved the incompetence of their schoolmaster—and Pierpont need not apply for the Master's degree. The Corporation's judgment of Pierpont's quality may have been affected by his calling the Harvard fellows " 'Rogues, Dogs, & Tygars.' "[7] From that point on, all parties lost their balance and Cotton Mather's entrance into the affair did not restore it. Mather's motives were undoubtedly complicated and, like other aspects of this case, elusive, but one thing is clear—he did not like President Leverett and he had not forgiven the Corporation for having forced out his father over fifteen years before. As time was to reveal, he also wanted to be President himself.[8]

Understandably, Pierpont got his support in the attempt to secure the Master of Arts. Mather rallied Governor Shute to Pierpont's side, but even though Pierpont got a hearing before the Governor, nothing came of it. Pierpont then took his case to the Middlesex County Court where it was tossed out and he went through life with only an A.B. Mather did not cease sniping at the College but he had lost and he knew it, and may also have realized that his chances for the Presidency of Harvard were slim indeed.[9]

The defeat in Pierpont's case could not have been pleasant for Mather, but it was a minor irritant compared to the "victory" he achieved three years afterwards, in 1721, in the inoculation controversy. Inoculation for smallpox was not new in the eighteenth century, having been tried in Europe, Asia, and Africa before. Published accounts of the practice appeared in Leipzig in the 1670's, and others indicate that it was tried in the eighteenth century in Turkey and Greece. In 1714, the *Transactions* of the Royal Society carried an account from Emanuel Timonius, a physician in Constantinople, of successful inoculations in Turkey. Two years later the Society issued a similar report from Jacobus Pylarinus.[10]

Cotton Mather, Fellow of the Royal Society, read its *Transactions* as eagerly as any member and contributed more to them than most. But he did not see the Society's publications regularly and had to borrow the issues describing inoculation from William Douglass, a Scottish physician who had recently arrived from Edinburgh. The news from Constantinople fascinated him especially since it seemed to confirm what he had already learned—or soon would learn—from Onesimus, his black slave. Onesimus and other blacks in Boston, telling the story of inoculations in Africa that successfully suppressed the disease, described a technique of cutting the skin, and infecting the body that closely resembled the Turkish practice.[11]

Mather might never have made anything out of his new knowledge had a smallpox epidemic not begun in Boston in the Spring of 1721. A significant number of cases were identified in May and by late June their number was so great as to persuade Governor Shute to call for a day of fasting and humiliation. Shute's proclamation repeating the language of sixty years of jeremiads, appealed for a "thorough Reformation of this whole Land." This call indicated that public authority considered the situation dangerous; Mather had already reached that conclusion and had sent a summary of the Timonius and Pylarinus' reports to all the medical practitioners in Boston.[12]

Only one of these men, William Douglass, had much formal medical training, and he was skeptical of the value of inoculation and was soon to explain that he feared that it would spread the disease. All of Boston's medical practitioners shared this fear to some degree, but Dr. Zabdiel Boylston (the Dr. was a courtesy title) indicated a willingness to try the new method. With Mather urging him on, Boylston inoculated his six-year-old son and two black slaves on June 26. They took a mild infection and soon recovered. Encouraged by this success, Boylston continued, and by July 19 had inoculated ten people.[13]

As the news of Boylston's experiment got around—Boston was a town of 11,000 people—public clamor against inoculation began. And it continued despite Boylston's attempts to ease popular fears by explaining the practice in the *Boston Gazette*. The Selectmen, the officials who carried out the wishes of the Town Meeting and who provided day-to-day government, responded to the opposition on July 21, by telling Boylston to stop. Three days later William Douglass, in the *Boston News-Letter,* questioned Boylston's qualifications, calling him "illiterate" and accusing him of lacking the ability to read the communications of Timonius and Pylarimus. This produced an answer from the Mathers and other Boston ministers, including Benjamin Colman, within a week. The following week William Douglass took to the pages of the *New England Courant,* James Franklin's paper, to lash Boylston for the inoculations, "the Practice of Greek old Women." Douglass knew that to stop Boylston for good he would have to discourage his chief supporters who were, of course, Cotton and Increase Mather. Therefore, Douglass hit them too, pointing out their medical incapacities by asserting that they recommended inoculation on the basis of their characters—not their knowledge. Cotton Mather, of course, could not ignore this attack—and the battle for public support was on. While the controversy kept the local printers busy, Boylston added to the public's anger by resuming inoculations—in violation of the Selectmen's order. In August he inoculated seventeen persons; in September, thirty-one; in October, eighteen; in November, one hundred and four. And other practitioners in the town were trying their hand at it too.[14]

When, early in June, Mather had proposed to the practitioners that they consider inoculation, he had urged caution upon them. To Douglass and evidently to much of the town, caution had been thrown to the winds when Boylston deliberate infected his son and slaves. The success of vaccination in our own day should not make us regard the opposition unsympathetically. Although no one in Boston died from inoculation, as Douglass pointed out, there was little evidence that the practice was not dangerous to the persons inoculated. The reports in the *Transactions* of the Royal Society hardly constituted an unimpeachable source. For years the *Transactions* had carried reports of folk remedies that at times resembled collections of remarkable providences—so full were they of fantastic stories. Furthermore, Boylston did little to ease public fears that his practice contributed to the spread of the disease. He failed to isolate his patients, who received visitors while they were still sick; and several of the inoculated even went out-of-doors while their sores were still running.[15]

Mather, and probably Boylston, recognized the danger of contagion. Mather's June letter which Boylston had found so instructive had repeated Timonius' warnings that the person collecting the pus should not carry it to those who were to be inoculated lest he also spread the disease in the natural way. But the chief medical defense was that inoculation worked. Boylston and Mather admitted that the fever of the inoculated sometimes rose higher than expected before the eruption of the pustules and that the number of their pustules exceeded expectations. Still the inoculated did not die and did not contract the disease afterwards in the natural way.[16]

None of this made Cotton Mather the "first significant figure in American medicine," a statement made in 1954; nor did his insistence that all inoculation really amounted to was another technique in preventive medicine, comparable to spring and fall tonics or to purges given to forestall the bloody flux. (Douglass called this comparison of "the taking of preventing physics to the Procuring a Contagious Disease" "Wild"). We do not in fact need to take the claim for Mather's medical wisdom seriously. His actions in this affair, from its onset in his prudent letter to its conclusion in shrill wrangling, were prompted by non-medical considerations—and his decisions in it were taken primarily on non-medical grounds. He was lucky in his discovery, as Perry Miller argues, and lucky, we might add, not to have blundered into a disaster.[17]

The opponents raised but did not make much of the argument that inoculation attempted to forestall one of the most dreadful judgments of God. Traditional theory held, of course, that men should attempt to prevent afflictions only by repenting their sins and reforming their lives. Inoculation clearly involved a different kind of prevention. Both the Mathers agreed with common opinion that the epidemic represented a judgment sent upon the land for its sins. Increase Mather had in fact predicted the year before that smallpox would strike New England soon unless it threw off its sins. But neither Mather ever really answered the charge that inoculation constituted a challenge to the purposes of God in afflicting the people.

For one thing both were soon busy answering other charges, and returning abuse that fell upon their heads. Neither turned the other cheek; neither was the innocent victim of a blind public—rather both struck hard and did not confine themselves to answering the Douglass camp. And as often happened in New England disputes, the issues in question were soon shrouded in vilification and personal attack.

Publicly Cotton Mather may have been more restrained than his father in the exchanges between advocates and opponents of inoculation. But he caught more barbs than Increase—more indeed than anyone who favored the practice, including Boylston. No one escaped completely; even the gentle Colman—who defended inoculation without scurrility—had to read his *Observations* styled as a "little vain Book." Increase Mather had his great age in his favor, and Douglass for one confessed a reluctance to attack him. Cotton Mather had no such defense and in any case all parties recognized him as the leader of the inoculators. During the course of the controversy he was referred to as the "Promoter," a sneer at his propensity to do good, "the young *Cub*, a Chip off *the old* Block (by Direction)," and simply as being "mad." Probably the most difficult charge he had to bear came when he referred to a passage defending inoculation in the *London Mercury*. His enemies denied that the *Mercury* carried the passage and managed to suggest in passing that Mather had no right to claim membership in the Royal Society. The *Courant* printed this charge, causing Increase to withdraw publicly his "support" from the paper and to warn its subscribers that they were "Partakers in other Mens Sins." Lest there be any doubt about Douglass' eternal fate, Increase had already informed the community that Douglass was a man who lacked "the least spark of Grace in his heart." Cotton Mather went one step further in his *Diary*, recording his belief that the Devil had taken possession of the people who attacked him and inoculation.[18]

The ultimate expression of rage against Mather occurred in November when someone tossed a bomb through his study window at three o'clock in the morning. The bomb failed to explode and Thomas Walter, Mather's nephew, who was sleeping in the room escaped injury. As if the bomb was not message enough, the thrower had attached a note which said "COTTON MATHER, You Dog, Dam you: I'l inoculate you with this, with a Pox to you." Mather, as was especially characteristic of the last dozen years of his life, reacted with powerful feelings of martyrdom. He reported in his *Diary* that "when I think on my suffering Death for saving the lives of dying People, it even ravishes me with a joy unspeakable and full of Glory." He found it impossible, he noted, to ask the Lord for the deliverance of his life. Nevertheless, he was angered at the attempt and shocked to discover that fresh trials at killing him might be in the offing.[19]

There was still another reason for dismay even though no one had died from inoculation by the end of 1721. The affair had revealed, as well as stimulated, anti-ministerial feeling in Boston— and probably in nearby communities as well. There is, of course, no way of measuring how pervasive this feeling was in the society. Its bitterness, however, appeared unmistakable; and the evidence of popular attitudes—from the anger of the *Courant* to the melancholy defenses of ministers in the Mather group— suggests that it was widespread. The feeling against the ministers accompanied clear ideas about their roles—from the layman's perspective. Douglass' jibe that the inoculating ministers were "Conscience Directors" was his way of saying that they lacked the qualifications to pronounce on public policy about the community's health. Of course Douglass, and others—not just those in the Hell-Fire Club—said the same thing in less sardonic terms. Someone even had the wit to remind Cotton Mather that in his *Bonifacius* he had written that the clergy had no business meddling in practical physic. And someone else resurrected memories of the Salem witch episode, suggesting that the ministers had long been the instruments of mischief in the community.[20]

Cotton Mather knew that the authority of the clergy had been called into question, and that his own prestige in the community was at stake. This recognition undoubtedly explains much of his own anger and bitterness. It does not, however, explain his original decision to propose inoculation or even to see things through once the opposition rallied itself. The recognition that ministerial authority had long since diminished had penetrated Mather's mind years before. He did not admire the reduced power of the ministry, but he had accepted it. Whatever his yearnings for power and status, his impulses cannot be reduced to a desire to dominate his society and to reassert the standing of the clergy. Mather proposed inoculation and clung stubbornly to its side because he saw in it a genuine opportunity to serve his God. His piety, more than his pride, made him urge Boylston on; his piety made him question the blacks in Boston about the practice and to try to make sense out of their stories; his piety made him scan the Royal Society's reports so eagerly. The third Maxim of Piety required men to do good to their neighbors and thereby glorify their God. Mather began the business of inoculation with this imperative in mind just as he had so many other projects for doing good. But in this case, though the persons deliberately infected by Boylston survived and proved immune to smallpox, Mather received the fury of his community—not its thanks. Good luck turned bad, but not without cause. He and Boylston had proceeded heedless of rudimentary standards of safety and they had shown themselves insensitive to legitimate fears about the dangers of their practice. Mather, however, never really understood his community's reaction, nor, for that matter, did he fully grasp the complexity of his own.[21]

The conflict over inoculation had passed by the summer of 1722, although resentments lingered for years. As the shock of the episode eased, New England felt another—lesser to be sure, but frightening nonetheless. In September at the annual commencement at Yale, a college founded in part as a conservative counterpoise to liberal Harvard, the head of the college, Timothy Cutler, two tutors, and four ministers of nearby churches announced that they had decided to give up Congregationalism in favor of the Church of England. This news stunned men of all persuasions all over New England. The *Courant,* for once printing an opinion that Cotton Mather could second, stated that what the renegades had done was as bad as if they had declared for Popery.[22]

Three of the ministers were persuaded to give up their heretical intentions, but not long after commencement, Cutler, the tutors, and the fourth minister sailed for England letting everyone know before they departed that they would return in Holy Orders. As if this was not bad enough, news soon arrived in New England that an Episcopal Church would soon be built in Stratford, Connecticut. Like everyone else, Mather was surprised by the defection, but he must have taken a grim satisfaction in the affair when it became known that Cutler and the others had come to Anglicanism through the reading of Arminian books. Mather after all had long predicted an Arminian incursion and he had fought the High-Fliers, as he called the false Church of England. Now the High-Fliers, through their Arminian henchmen, had corrupted good men in New England. Sober men perhaps would now put up their guard.

Cutler soon returned as Rector of Christ's Church in Boston. Mather listened to all the gossip about him, welcoming every hint that not all was well in the Anglican communion. In fact, the Church of England did not thrive in New England in these years. The rumor soon circulated that its support lay principally among men who wanted a complete exemption from paying rates for any religious establishment. Mather repeated this nasty charge privately but there is no evidence that he aired it in public. But the damage was done; Cutler did not help his cause a few years later, in 1727, when he appealed to London for an exemption for his church from paying taxes in support of the Congregational churches. He had every right to make this request, of course, which had been granted to the Quakers in 1724. But justified and just, as it was, the appeal set Congregational teeth on edge.[23]

The same year that Cutler spoke for tax reform he demanded representation on the Board of Harvard Overseers. Cutler based his demand on the College Charter which provided that "teaching elders" of the Boston churches should sit on the Board; Christ's Church was one such church and obviously should contribute representatives to the Overseers. Cotton Mather did not live long enough to see Cutler turned down but he would have been gratified by the explanation which accompanied the denial of Cutler's request. According to official reasoning, the Charter referred only to Congregational teaching elders.[24]

Mather worried about Harvard on other grounds during these last years. He worried in particular about its leadership in the person of its President, John Leverett. Mather had long envied and disliked Leverett, envied him the Presidency which Mather coveted for himself at the time of Leverett's selection in 1708, and disliked him for his early association with the Dudleys (they later fell out), his opposition to Pierpont, and probably most of all for his educational policy which emphasized a broader learning than Mather thought suitable in a college. Leverett's death in May 1724, prompted Mather to remark only on "that unhappy Man" and to begin to dream of at last succeeding to the Presidency. Mather's desire to head Harvard was transparent to his friends, and at least one of them proceeded to tell him what he wanted to hear—that what was generally wished for in New England was that he be chosen to follow Leverett. Mather immediately considered approaching the tutors, who were temporarily in charge, with a proposal for reviving learning and especially PIETY among the Harvard students.[25]

Sensitive and insecure creature that Mather was, he may soon have got a glimmer that he would not be the Corporation's choice. In June he recorded in his *Diary* his fear that the College might dissolve, and in July he stayed away from Commencement in order—he said—to pray for a president who would be a blessing to the College. The next day he addressed a meeting of ministers who had gathered for Commencement and recommended that they too beg God for a good president. The Corporation, unmoved by this lobbying, met in August and chose the Reverend Joseph Sewall, minister of the Old South Church and son of Judge Samuel Sewall. This selection, contrary, Mather noted, to the "epedemical expectation" of the country brought out the worst in him. The Corporation's act proved two things to him—that "if it were possible for them to steer clear of me, they will do so," and "if it be possible for them to act foolishly," that too "they will do." [26]

As in the crisis of smallpox inoculation, he reacted as he did in part because his profound impulse to advance piety—to do good—had been thwarted. But this motive probably was less important than his pride, a deeply personal and family pride in this case. The pride is clear in Mather's sneer that the Corporation had chosen "a Child" rather than come to him. Sewall, at thirty-six years of age, did not impress him in any way, either in learning, governing skill, or in piety. To be distressed at this baby's selection would be a "Crime," Mather wrote, but as he moved his pen over his *Diary,* he committed the crime.[27]

All this anguish was unnecessary, for Sewall declined the appointment. By this time Mather had prepared himself to be disappointed again; the Corporation did not fail his expectations, choosing Benjamin Colman in November. Mather's response was his ultimate way in dealing with rejection: he rejoiced that he now conformed more closely to Christ than before. After all, Christ too had been despised and rejected by men. But Mather attained one shred of self-knowledge at this time which saved him from the worst of his self-pity and self-righteousness. He recognized his own anger for what it was and asked God to help him govern his resentments at these affronts. Still, the anger and the sense of martyrdom broke through frequently. The anger appears in the last years of his life most often in his denunciations of his community—"this abominable Town"; the martyrdom achieved its most revealing expression in his reaction to the malicious letters he received, which he carefully saved and then when he had enough, tied into a bundle inscribed on the outside with " 'Libels: Father, forgive them!' " [28]

Mather's concern for his reputation and for his projects to help bring on the Kingdom of God could not relieve him of family obligations. Cotton Mather was at his best as a son, and very near it as a father. These last years of his life saw him straining in both roles. After his mother died in 1714, his father was often in his thoughts. He wanted to make the old man comfortable, gradually a more difficult problem, for Increase Mather's health slowly declined after his wife's death. Increase remarried in 1715; his second wife, Anne Cotton, must have helped ease his old age, but he needed the care and support of his son, too. Cotton Mather gave both unstintedly hoping always to make his father's last years happy and useful.[29]

Cotton enlisted his father's aid in the inoculation crisis but there was not much the old man could do. The abuse that his son and other ministers received obviously distressed him. This controversy began just as one involving the New North Church was winding up. The churches of New England were dear to both Mathers' hearts, of course; and Increase at least may have been more disturbed by the conflict over the New North than he was over smallpox.

The New North had been formed in a way that displeased him—and his son as well. In 1713 with the Old North, the church of the Mathers, badly overcrowded, a number of members appealed for lawful dismissal in order that they might build a meetinghouse of their own. Cotton Mather did not like the idea, seeing in it the ambitions of prideful men who wanted the status of well-located pews, but he went along. Increase, however, was "greatly wounded" by the secession and his son had considerable difficulty in restraining his father's attacks on the secessionists. Cotton managed to deal with both sides tactfully and the removal was managed without irreparable damage. The secessionists built the New North Church and things quieted down.[30]

Seven years later they blew up within the New North in a way that distressed Increase Mather even more. The issue was the call extended by the church—over the protests of a minority —to Peter Thacher, then of the Weymouth Church, to join the Reverend John Webb, as pastor. Webb approved the invitation, but the Mathers, Colman, Benjamin Wadsworth, William Cooper, and Thomas Prince did not. And apparently the Weymouth Church contained members who believed that Thacher had not been properly released. By themselves the splits within these churches would have been troubling. What made them of particular concern to Increase and therefore to Cotton was that Webb and Thacher wrapped themselves in the principles of the *Cambridge Platform* declaring for the autonomy of particular churches. They also cited Increase Mather's *A Disquisition Concerning Ecclesiastical Councils* (1716) as further justification for their conduct in not consulting the neighboring churches. Their opponents in the New North responded by saying that "men can make a nose of wax of the Platform and bend it as they please." Increase Mather, whose own long nose was twisted in the affair, expressed his indignation over Thacher's ordination by declaring that the entire procedure was "an heinous Transgression of the Third Commandment; the like of which was never before known in New England, no, nor in the Christian World. . . ."[31]

There is no doubt that Cotton Mather shared his father's sentiments but he kept remarkably quiet throughout the episode. Two things embarrassed him. First, the fact that the critics of Thacher and Webb within the New North were not for the most part men in full communion (that is, full Church members) and secondly, the evidence that part of his own church planned to secede and join the minority in the New North to establish still another church. The New Brick Church resulted from the efforts of these seceders and dissidents—again to the outrage of Increase Mather. But again Cotton soothed his father and eventually preached the sermon at the dedication of New Brick in May 1721.[32]

From September 1722, when Increase Mather suffered a stroke, until his death on August 23, 1723, in his eighty-fifth year, Cotton had to do more than console his father over secession from the church, for Increase suffered terrible pain during his last months. Samuel Sewall reported several of the old man's cries, and Cotton Mather later explained that his father had endured emotional as well as physical distress. Good man though Increase Mather was, there were days when he doubted that he had God's grace and he lamented the bitter fate ahead of him. These days saw the son attend the father with loving assurance.[33]

Two days after Increase Mather's death, Cotton preached one of the funeral sermons. And he spent much of the next two months writing *Parentator*, his biography of Increase, a restrained assessment of his father's life. Despite the book's reticence and Cotton's professed intention of sticking close to the evidence, it is a revealing document. It does not offer a full statement about Increase's psychological workings—no Puritan biography ever did that. It acknowledges that Increase possessed human frailties, but Cotton Mather does not describe them himself. Instead, he quotes extensively from his father's diary. This is an unrewarding exercise, for Increase's record of his own sins is completely conventional. In his diary he accused himself of misusing time and of unfruitfulness, weaknesses that Cotton laid to the remainder of indwelling sin.[34]

What *Parentator* reveals is the detachment the son was able to attain on his father. His love and admiration for Increase were great but they did not prevent him from seeing his father's mistakes. To be sure, the mistakes do not for the most part expose flaws of character so much as errors of judgment;

and in any case Cotton Mather did not disclose all he knew or thought about them. He gently reproached his father for defying Richard Mather over the Half-Way Covenant and he declared that his father had been mistaken in persecuting the Quakers. These admissions were easy to make because Increase himself had conceded that he had been wrong. But Increase had never changed his mind about the conversion of national Israel as a pre-condition of the Second Coming and in *Parentator,* Cotton at least hinted at the deficiencies in his father's view. He also admitted that his father's pastoral visits had not been frequent enough to suit his church, a serious charge against the conduct of his ministry. However, most of the book extols Increase's great services and his piety. Although it was written in sadness, it was not marked by shattering grief. This is the final mark of Cotton's detachment. His father had died full of years and after great achievements. Increase had served his calling well, and Cotton had no doubt that heavenly bliss awaited him.

Cotton Mather could not regard the death of his son, Increase Mather II, lost at sea, which he learned of in August 1724, with such assurance. Young Increase had already brought him humiliation and guilt; now he brought grief. Eleven of Cotton Mather's children had already died; Increase—his adoring father sometimes called him Cresy—was the twelfth; and a daughter, Elizabeth Mather Cooper, died in 1726, leaving him just Hannah and Samuel. The death of young Increase shook him as badly as any, despite his belief that his son had brought shame on the Mather name. What especially troubled Cotton was the fear that his son might have died unregenerate.[35]

While he grieved for Cresy he had reason to grieve for himself and the dreadful condition of his wife. He had remarried after the death of his second wife in 1713 (a year that saw three of their children die). His third marriage, to Lydia Lee George, was a disaster. Along with a new wife he soon took on the administration of the estate of her widowed daughter, Katherine George Howell. This estate was badly encumbered with debts, a fact that the widow Howell's creditors soon brought home to him. For several years the responsibility for these debts oppressed him so much that he considered selling his library to pay them. He counted upon friends to bail him out but they "keep at a Distance from me," and his wife's family upon whose

benefit he took on the debts behaved "like Monsters of Ingrati-
tude." His fears became so great at one point that he thought
he might end his days in debtors' prison. Finally, after seven
years of anxiety, several loyal members of his church came to
his aid and paid off the debts.[36]

While all this was going on, his wife began to display symptoms of madness. It is, of course, impossible to say with certainty today that she was insane, but Mather came to think so—
and her behavior was extraordinary. They had married in 1715;
the first signs of her unbalance seem to have appeared two years
later. By the next year, 1718, and periodically for the last ten
years of Mather's life, there was no doubt that she was deranged.
At times, Cotton Mather feared that evil spirits had taken possession of her. In these periods, she raged at him and the two
children of his second marriage who lived at home. Mather's inclination was to hush the whole business up but the grotesque
scenes that occurred in the household could not be concealed. In
one of the first, he reported that his wife had abused him because
"my Looks and Words were not so very kind as they had been."
When he could stand her "prodigious Paroxysms" no longer, he
retired to his study and his wife fled to a neighbor where, he
was convinced, she told lies about him. To make matters worse,
his wife rummaged through his papers, hiding some and spilling
ink on others. During one of these trying periods, a time when
he was also burdened with debt, and worried over Cresy, he
thought of Job and like Job referred to himself as a Brother to
Dragons. But more often he thought of Christ's martyrdom.[37]

There is little doubt that his unhappiness strengthened his
faith—and his faith made his unhappiness supportable. As he
feared affliction, he also gloried in it. Yet his love of his God
was no mere rationalization, no simple device to deal with the
disappointments of this world. He said in these years that he
felt "on the borders of paradise," and meant that the world was
near its end and that Christ would soon come. This statement
was sung, sung in piety and in love of God. Mather—despite all
his grief—continued to love his God with a remarkable intensity.
He rarely accused himself of security and "deadness" in these
years. There seemed too little time for such indulgence.[38]

Mather's sense that he was approaching the end of his life
grew strong late in 1724 and early in 1725 when he fell sick for

weeks at a time. Like his father, he had predicted his own death long before, but this time there was something different in his feeling. And because of the difference—"I seem to be upon a new Song"—he decided in order to save time to reduce the number of entries he made about do-good in his *Diary*. He did, however, introduce a new category, "Precious Thoughts," the extraordinary "Insights" into the mystery of Christ and His Kingdom given by the Lord. The most precious of his thoughts, of course, concerned the Holy Spirit and its manifestations in prophecy. Mather continued to yearn with all his soul for the Prophetic Spirit to show itself in an unmistakable way; and his appeals to the Lord for a pouring out of the Spirit remained as passionate as ever through his illness and his despair over his wife and son. And when on occasion he was so sick that these prayers took more energy than he had, and he could neither preach nor write, he at least found the strength to sing hymns celebrating the glory of the Lord.[39]

In the winter of 1727–28, he was again sick and weak, and on February 13, 1728, he died. As a young man he had seen visions, and he continued to see them as an old one. He had also had dreams of the end with the Spirit pouring out on all flesh. He died, an old man, still dreaming those dreams.

Notes

―――――

ᴄᴧᴑ

CHAPTER 1

1. Richard Mather, The Summe of Seventie Lectures Upon The First Chapter of the Second Epistle of Peter, Lecture 3, [30 June, 1646], 21. Mss. in American Antiquarian Society (henceforth abreviated A.A.S.)

2. Increase Mather, *Awakening Truth's Tending To Conversion* (Boston, 1710) 67–69.

3. Increase Mather, *A Discourse Concerning Faith and Fervency in Prayer* (Boston, 1710), 82.

4. Increase Mather, *Practical Truths Tending to Promote the Power of Godliness* (Boston, 1682), 200. See also Urian Oakes, *New England Pleaded With* (Cambridge, Mass., 1673), 11–13; Urian Oakes, *A Seasonable Discourse Wherein Sincerity and Delight in the Service of God Is Earnestly Pressed Upon Professors of Religion* (Cambridge, Mass., 1682), 4–5, 9, 17; William Stoughton, *New Englands True Interest Not to Lie* (Cambridge, Mass., 1670), 20–25.

5. "The Diary of Michael Wigglesworth, 1653–1657," edited by Edmund S. Morgan, *Publications* of the Colonial Society of Massachusetts, xxxv, 311–444 (Boston, 1951). The quotation is from 385. For a full account of Wigglesworth's life see Richard

Crowder, *No Featherbed to Heaven: A Biography of Michael Wigglesworth, 1631–1705* (East Lansing, Mich. 1962).

6. William Perkins, *A Declaration of the True Manner of Knowing Christ Crucified* (London, 1611), 27.

7. Increase Mather, *The Life and Death of That Reverend Man of God, Mr. Richard Mather* (Cambridge, Mass., 1670) contains biographical details. See also, Kenneth Ballard Murdock, *Increase Mather: The Foremost American Puritan* (Cambridge, Mass., 1926), 11–18, and the sources cited there. *Life and Death* relies heavily on an autobiographical account left by Richard, now apparently lost.

8. *Life and Death*, 2–3.

9. For an excellent discussion of Puritan educational ideas, see E. S. Morgan, *The Puritan Family* (revised ed. New York, 1966), 87–108.

10. *Life and Death*, 3.

11. *Ibid*. 4.

12. *Ibid*. 4.

13. *Ibid*. 4–5.

14. *Ibid*. 5–6.

15. The statement appears in John 3.3; its effect on Richard is discussed in *Ibid*. 6.

16. *Ibid*. 6.

17. Among the most revealing of Perkins' works are *Death Knell* (11th ed. London ?, 1629), *A Declaration of the True Manner of Knowing Christ Crucified* (London, 1611), and especially *A Graine of Mustard-Seed* (London, 1621).

18. *Life and Death*, 6.

19. Perkins, *Graine of Mustard-Seed*, 5.

20. *Ibid*. 11.

21. *Ibid*. 5–14.

22. *Ibid*. 42–43.

23. *Life and Death*, 25.

24. Richard was admitted to Brasenose on May 9, 1618. See Joseph Foster, *Alumni Oxonienses: The Members of the University of Oxford, 1500–1714* (4 vols., Oxford, 1896) III, 987. Increase Mather reports in *Life and Death* that Richard read the works of Peter Ramus at Oxford (see 5).

25. *Life and Death*, 7.

26. For Richard's uneasiness about his conformity see *Ibid*. 7–8.

27. *Ibid*. 8.

28. *Ibid.* 8-9.

29. *Ibid.* 31.

30. *Ibid.* 10-11.

31. Richard's Journal has been printed in Alexander Young ed., *Chronicles of the First Planters of the Colony of Massachusetts Bay* (Boston, 1845), 445-81. This quotation is on 477; those in the remainder of this chapter appear on 477-78, 460, and 474.

CHAPTER 2

1. Alexander Young ed., *Chronicles of the First Planters of . . . Massachusetts,* 447.

2. Quoted in Increase Mather, *Life and Death of . . . Richard Mather,* 11.

3. Quotations from *Ibid.* 12, 17. Increase seems to print the arguments from a manuscript left by Richard.

4. *Ibid.* 17 and *passim.*

5. *Ibid.* 17-18. The notion of England as the chosen nation of God has been explored in William Haller, *The Elect Nation: The Meaning and Relevance of Foxe's* Book of Martyrs (New York, 1963).

6. (7th ed., London, 1615). The work has four parts, published separately, each with its own pagination. Richard cited most frequently *The Third Part of the True Watch . . . Taken Out of the Vision of Ezekiel, Chapter 9* (London, 1622).

7. Brinsley, *The Third Part of the True Watch, passim,* and especially 216-27.

8. *Ibid.* 216.

9. *Ibid.* 219.

10. Brinsley, *The True Watch,* Pt. 2, 18.

11. Most of what I say in this, and later chapters, about Puritan eschatology is based on my reading of sixteenth and seventeenth century sources. I have also learned from Ernest Lee Tuveson's *Millennium and Utopia* (New York, 1964) and his *Redeemer Nation* (Chicago, 1968). Haller's *Elect Nation* (see note 5 above) is also helpful.

12. Quoted in Haller, *Elect Nation,* 136.

13. *Ibid.* 136-38.

14. *Ibid.* 150-57.

15. *Ibid.* 157-67.

16. Increase quotes Richard in *Life and Death,* 12. Winthrop's views on the everlasting Church are in the *Winthrop Papers* (Boston, 1929, 5 vols. published to date) III, 10.

17. John Winthrop, "A Modell of Christian Charity," *Winthrop Papers,* II, 282–95. The quotation is on 295.

18. *Life and Death,* 18–19, and *passim.*

19. The scriptural passages are Psalms 119.27; Daniel 12.4; 2 Timothy 3.7, 3.1, 3.2; Revelation 6.12; Joel 2.30, 31.

20. The text for commentators on the conversion of Israel was Romans 11.26: "And so all Israel shall be saved: . . ." Protestant theologians took comfort from the fact that the ancient fathers, including Origen and Chrysostom, had expected a conversion of Israel; they also pointed out that Aquinas and the Schoolmen had subscribed to the belief.

21. The quotations are from John Cotton's *The Powring Out of the Seven Vials: or an Exposition of the Sixteenth Chapter of the Revelation, With an Application of it to our Times* (London, 1645), 3, 4, 32, 58, 79. Cotton discussed related eschatological problems in *The Churches Resurrection* (London 1642) and *An Exposition Upon the Thirteenth Chapter of the Revelation* (London, 1655); this last work was based on sermons preached in 1639 and 1640.

22. *Life and Death,* 11–19, and *passim.*

23. Richard Mather and William Thompson, *An Heart-Melting Exhortation Together With a Cordiall Consolation* (London, 1650), 61–70. This work was written in 1645.

24. *Ibid.* 67, 79–80.

25. Richard Mather, "To The Christian Reader," in John Eliot and Thomas Mayhew, *Tears of Repentance . . . Narrative . . . . of the Gospel Amongst the Indians in New England* (London, 1653), reprinted in Massachusetts Historical Society (M.H.S.) *Collections,* 3d Series, IV, 217–25. I have used the M.H.S. edition; see especially Mather's contention (218) that the conversion of the Indians in New England was evidence that the Kingdom of God "is now beginning to be set up where it never was before, even amongst a poor people, forlorn kind of Creatures in times past, who have been without Christ. . . ." Virtually everything that Mather wrote, which still survives, is shot through with an eschatological expectation. It is not intense in such works as *Church-Government And Church-Covenant Discussed* (London, 1643), where his indebtedness to Foxe is clear (24–27), but it is present; and in such works as The Summe of Seventie Lectures, mss. A.A.S., it is burning. Mather's great

contemporary, Thomas Hooker, shared his belief that their age would be one of increasing knowledge about the Church, which was widely believed to be one of the signs of the imminence of the end; see the "Preface" to *A Survey of the Summe of Church-Discipline* (London, 1648). See, too, Thomas Parker (pastor in Newbury, Mass.), *The Visions and the Prophecies of Daniel Expounded* (London, 1646) for another expression similar to Mather's mood.

26. Perry Miller, *Errand Into the Wilderness* (Cambridge, Mass., 1956), 12.

27. Mather and Thompson, *An Heart-Melting Exhortation*, 81.

28. John Cotton joined Richard Mather in making this suggestion. See his *An Exposition Upon the Thirteenth Chapter of the Revelation*, where he says to Puritans in New England "Let us help them what we can by Prayer." (262)

CHAPTER 3

1. Richard Mather and William Thompson, *An Heart-Melting Exhortation*.

2. For the details of Increase's departure for England, see "The Autobiography of Increase Mather," ed. Michael G. Hall, *Proceedings* of the A.A.S. (1961) (Worcester, Mass., 1962).

3. The standard account of the Marian exiles is C. M. Garrett, *The Marian Exiles* (Cambridge, England, 1938).

4. Patrick Collinson, *The Elizabethan Puritan Movement* (Berkeley, 1967), 65–66, and *passim;* J. E. Neale, *Elizabeth I And Her Parliaments, 1559–1581* (New York, 1953), 132–33.

5. The documents of the Admonition controversy have been reprinted in W. H. Frere and C. E. Douglas eds., *Puritan Manifestoes: A Study of the Origin of the Puritan Revolt* (London, 1907). I have also relied on Collinson, 118–21, and Neale, 295–97. See, too, A. F. Scott Pearson, *Thomas Cartwright and English Puritanism* (London, 1925).

6. Neale, *Elizabeth I And Her Parliaments*, 193–203.

7. On the "prophesyings," see Collinson, *op. cit.,* 169–78; on Grindall, Collinson, *op. cit.,* 194–98, and Neale, *op. cit.,* 371–73. Collinson also summarizes the literature on Martin Marprelate, 391–97; see, too, his account of the classical movement, 323–55 and *passim.* J. E. Neale, *Elizabeth I And Her Parliaments, 1584–1601* (London, 1957) 145–65. 216–32 is also valuable.

8. Quoted in Perry Miller, *Orthodoxy in Massachusetts, 1630–1650* (Cambridge, Mass., 1933), 26; Miller gives an excellent account of Anglican views on 25–32.

9. Quoted in Henry Dexter, *The Congregationalism of the Last Three Hundred Years* (New York, 1880), 99, fn. 151.

10. *The Works of John Robinson* (3 vols. Boston, 1851), II, 487.

11. *Ibid.* II, 487–88.

12. *Ibid.* II, 295.

13. *Ibid.* II, 293–94.

14. Henry Ainsworth, *Counterpoyson* (Amsterdam, 1608), 35.

15. Robinson, *Works,* II, 490.

16. Ainsworth, *Counterpoyson,* 106, 127–28, 205, 226–27.

17. *Ibid.* and Robinson, *Works,* II, 487–92. See, too, Henry Barrow, *A Brief Discoverie of the False Church* (Dort, 1590), and *A Plaine Refutation of M. G. Giffarde's Reprochful Booke* (——?, 1591).

18. For the Separatists' ideas about the Church, see Edmund S. Morgan, *Visible Saints: The History of A Puritan Idea* (New York, 1963), 33–63.

19. (Cambridge, Mass., 1933).

20. Miller, *Orthodoxy,* 84.

21. *Ibid.* 84–85.

22. *Ibid. 86–98.*

23. *Ibid.,* 23–24 for the two quotations in this paragraph.

24. All the great divines among the founders emphasized the survival of the Church of Christ. The most important sources are cited below.

25. William Ames, *The Marrow of Sacred Divinity* (London, 1643), 136–37; Miller, *Orthodoxy,* 86.

26. Richard Mather, *Church-Government and Church Covenant Discussed,* 27. Although published in 1643, this work was written in 1639.

27. For a superb modern study of New England polity, see Morgan, *Visible Saints.* See also Larzer Ziff, ed., *John Cotton on the Churches of New England* (Cambridge, Mass., 1968), 1–36. Ziff's *The Career of John Cotton* (Princeton, 1962) contains an excellent discussion of Church polity.

28. Samuel Rutherford, *The Due Right of Presbyteries* (London, 1644); Chares Herle, *The Independency of Churches* (London, 1643). Hooker answered Rutherford in *A Survey of the Summe of Church Discipline.* John Cotton refers to Rutherford, Herle, and other Presbyterians in his *The Way of Congre-*

gational Churches Cleared (London, 1648), but it is directed primarily at Robert Baillie's *A Dissuasive from the Errours of our Time* (London, 1645). The definitive statement of Cotton's theory is *The Keyes of the Kingdom of Heaven* (London, 1644).

29. Richard Mather, *A Reply to Mr. Rutherfurd* (London, 1647), 11–12, 14–20, 40–44, 58–60, 102–9; Richard Mather and William Thompson, *A Modest and Brotherly Answer To Mr. Charles Herle his Book . . .* (London, 1644), 1–8, 11–15, 17–20, 28–30, 44–47, 51–58. Mather's most important published work on ecclesiastical polity is *Church-Government and Church-Covenant Discussed, see especially,* 45–59, 65–66. Mather's *An Answer to Two Questions* (Boston, 1712) was written in 1645 and published at the instigation of Increase Mather. In it Mather refers approvingly to Cotton's *Keyes,* see 9–20.

30. *A Platform of Church Discipline Gathered Out of the Word of God . . .* (Cambridge, Mass., 1649). Richard Mather drafted this document at the instruction of the synod which met 1646–48. For a convenient reprinting see Williston Walker, *The Creeds and Platforms of Congregationalism* (New York, 1893, reprinted Boston, 1960), 194–237.

31. Genesis 17.1. Morgan, *Visible Saints,* 64–112.

32. Mather first publicly answered questions about membership in *Church-Government and Church-Covenant,* 10–23, 30.

33. *A Platform of Church Discipline,* Chapter 12, 18.

34. Morgan, *Visible Saints,* 113, 128.

35. *Church-Government and Church-Covenant,* 20.

36. A Plea was never published; it may have been commissioned by the Cambridge synod. Part I of the manuscript was an answer to William Rathband's *A Narrative of Church Courses in New England* (London, 1644). The "Preface" of "A Plea" is dated 10m 2d (Dec. 2), 1645. In the "Introduction," Mather says that Rathband wrote the thirty-two questions answered in *Church-Government and Church-Covenant.* Mather expressed uncertainty about baptism in a letter to William Rathband, June 25, 1636 copied into A Plea, Pt. I, 362–70. His change of mind is clear in portions of the manuscript composed before 1645. See Pt. I, 171, Pt. II, 71–73. The manuscript is in the M.H.S.

37. A Plea, Pt. II, 71; Richard Mather, *A Disputation Concerning Church Members and their Children* (London, 1659), 20–23.

38. A Plea, Pt. I, 350–51; Pt. II, 64.

39. Richard Mather to Thomas Shepard, April, 1636, in John A. Albro, *The Life of Thomas Shepard* (Boston, 1870), 219.

Shepard's dissatisfaction is explained in his letter of April 2, 1636 in Albro, 212–18.

40. A Plea, I, 350–51.

41. *Ibid.* I, 52.

42. *Ibid.* I, 66.

43. *Ibid.* I, 66. For Mather's use of Ball, Baynes, and Cartwright see Pt. II, 27–29.

44. *Ibid.* I, 69.

45. *Ibid.* I, 69–70.

46. *Ibid.* I, 70. The Biblical passages cited are 2 *Kings* 25.24, 25; *Acts* 8.37; *Revelation* 2.2.

47. See John Cotton, *Of The Holinesse of Church Members* (London, 1650), *passim.*

48. A Plea, I, 72.

49. *Ibid.* I, 72–73.

50. *Ibid.* I, 81–83.

51. *Ibid.* II, 27–29. On the uses of hypocrisy, see Perry Miller, *The New England Mind: From Colony To Province* (Cambridge, Mass., 1953) 68–81.

52. A Plea, I, 142–47; II, 48–62.

53. *Ibid.* II, 72–73. Mather's ideas about the growth of grace are discussed in the next chapter. The sources are The Summe of Seventie Lectures, and *The Summe of Certain Sermons Upon Genes:* 15.6 (Cambridge, Mass., 1652).

54. Written with Jonathan Mitchell. (Cambridge, Mass., 1664), 51–52. Mitchell wrote the first part of this work; Mather, the second.

55. *Ibid.* 51.

56. *Ibid.* 33–35.

57. John Davenport, *Another Essay For the Investigation of the Truth* . . . (Cambridge, Mass., 1663), 9–10.

58. *Ibid.* 23.

59. The argument can be followed in *Ibid.,* especially 22–23, 33–45 and in Mather, *A Defense of the Answer,* 57–59, 75–84. Increase Mather wrote "An Apologetical Preface To The Reader," which was published with Davenport's tract.

CHAPTER 4

1. Richard Mather, The Summe of Seventie Lectures, 145. This was said in November 1647.

2. *Ibid.* 144.

3. *Ibid.* 145.

4. Mather treats the despair felt by men in *Ibid.* 88–89 and *passim;* and in *The Summe of Certain Sermons,* 23–24. Despair and deadness are also discussed in many sermons by Increase and Cotton Mather. The latter's *Diary* contains accounts of his personal encounters with such feelings. At times laymen also complained of the harshness of Calvinist doctrine. See Thomas Shepard, *The Sincere Convert: Discovering the Small Number of True Believers, And the Great Difficulty of Saving Conversion* (4th ed., London, 1646), where complaints are recorded that the ministers' insistence on predestination sometimes were enough to drive a man "out of his wits," 125; see, too, 128, 133.

5. The quotations in this paragraph are from *Summe of Certain Sermons,* 23–24.

6. There is a searching discussion of the covenant theology in Perry Miller, *The New England Mind: The Seventeenth Century* (Cambridge, Mass., 1954); Miller's *From Colony to Province* discusses the Arminian implications of the theology.

7. Summe of Seventie Lectures, 70–76, 85–88, 91, 120.

8. *Ibid.* 138.

9. *Ibid.* 393.

10. Richard Mather, *A Farewel-Exhortation to the Church and People of Dorchester* (Cambridge, Mass., 1657) 16.

11. Summe of Seventie Lectures, 105, 109, 112–13, 131–32, 237–39, 242.

12. Mather discusses preparation and "legal" preaching in *Ibid.* 62, 65–67, 131–32, 292. For scholarly studies of the doctrine of preparation see Perry Miller, " 'Preparation For Salvation' In Seventeenth-Century New England," *Journal of the History of Ideas* IV (June 1943) 253–86; Norman Pettit, *The Heart Prepared: Grace and Conversion in Puritan Spiritual Life* (New Haven, Conn., 1966).

13. These views are clear in Mather's Summe of Seventie Lectures.

14. *Ibid.* 105–8, 112–13, 265–66.

15. The sources through which the Antinomian crisis can be studied are in Charles Francis Adams, *Antinomianism in the Colony of Massachusetts Bay, 1636–1638* (Boston, 1894). Study of these documents persuades me that Mather's view was widely held. There are excellent accounts of Antinomianism in Miller's *From Colony To Province,* E. S. Morgan's *The Puritan Dilemma: The Story of John Winthrop* (Boston, 1958), and Emery Battis' *Saints and Sectaries* (Chapel Hill, 1962). For a modern edition

of important documents and a perceptive commentary see David D. Hall, ed., *The Antinomian Controversy, 1636–1638: A Documentary History* (Middletown, Conn., 1968).

16. Summe of Seventie Lectures, 124–48, 204–10, 236–38; *Summe of Certain Sermons*, 22–26.

17. Summe of Seventie Lectures, 63.

18. *Ibid.* 62–63, 65–67, 104–10, 211, and *passim*.

19. Thomas Hooker, *The Application of Redemption* (London, 1656), 345. See also 305, 307, 335.

20. *Ibid.* and *passim*.

21. Thomas Shepard, *The Sincere Convert*, 116–17, 151, 158; John Cotton, *The Way of Life* (London, 1641), 4–13, 182; John Cotton, *Christ the Fountaine of Life* (London, 1651), *passim;* John Norton, *The Orthodox Evangelist* (London, 1654), Chapter 6, especially 139.

22. Summe of Seventie Lectures, 122–48, 209–34, 262–72.

23. Hooker, *Application of Redemption*, 345; Cotton, *Way of Life,* 133.

24. Mather, Cotton, Hooker, Shepard all make comments that indicate that they were questioned by anxious men. See especially Summe of Seventie Lectures, 88–91, 256–57, 264–65.

25. *Ibid.* 104–5, and the works by Cotton, Hooker, and Shepard in note 21.

26. Summe of Seventie Lectures, 89.

27. *Ibid.* 88–91.

28. *Ibid.* 128–31, 249–52.

29. *Ibid.* 104.

30. *Ibid.* 104, 105.

31. *Ibid.* 105.

32. All major Puritan writers shared this view.

33. Summe of Seventie Lectures, 105–10.

34. *Ibid.* 255–73, and *passim*.

35. *Ibid.* 329–33.

36. In urging temperance upon Dorchester, Mather once said that God punished sexual offences with "monstrous births" and "leprous children." *Ibid.* 140.

37. *Ibid.* 241.

38. *Ibid.* 241; he makes this point often in these sermons.

39. *Ibid.* 236.

40. *Ibid.* 292 for his discussion of legal and evangelical preaching.

41. *Ibid.* 209–12 for his discussion of 2 Peter 1.8, and 235–36 for the "actings and operations" of grace.

42. *Ibid.* 265–68, 273; and see *Summe of Certain Sermons, passim.*

43. Summe of Seventie Lectures, 237.

44. *Ibid.* 237–38.

45. *Ibid.* 144–45.

46. *Ibid.* 333.

47. *Ibid.* 329–33, 348.

48. *Ibid.* 24, 297, 333.

49. Richard Mather, *A Farewel-Exhortation,* 7–8.

50. Jonathan Mitchell and Richard Mather, *A Defence of the Answer* (Cambridge, Mass., 1664), 51–52. Mather wrote the second part of this work in which the statements about grace appear.

51. Increase Mather, *Life and Death of . . . Richard Mather,* 27.

CHAPTER 5

1. Benjamin Colman, *The Prophet's Death Lamented* (Boston, 1723), 16.

2. *Ibid.* 31–37.

3. This paragraph is based on my reading of dozens of funeral sermons. Increase and Cotton Mather preached many.

4. In the "Preface" to Cotton Mather's *Hades Look'd Into* (Boston, 1717), Increase wrote "Funeral-Sermons *are sometimes in danger of* over-doing . . ." He added that those by his son did not fall into this category. For an example of his predictions of his own death see *Solemn Advice to Young Men* (Boston, 1695), "To the Young Generation." In 1715, eight years before Increase's death, he told his church that he would be "glad . . . if I might dye before I stir out of this Pulpit!" See *Several Sermons* (Boston, 1715), 60.

5. There is a fine old biography by Kenneth Ballard Murdock, *Increase Mather: The Foremost American Puritan* (Cambridge, Mass., 1926), which is full on Mather's early life. See, too, "The Autobiography of Increase Mather," ed. Michael G. Hall, *Proceedings* of the A.A.S., 71 (1961) Pt. 2, 271–360 (Worcester, Mass., 1962). There are also autobiographical comments scattered throughout Mather's other works; and Cotton Mather's *Parentator* (Boston, 1724) contains valuable information.

6. Murdock tells the story of Richard's courtship of Kath-

arine, *Increase Mather*, 15; Increase's appraisal is in the *Autobiography*, 278.

7. Increase recalls his mother's comments in the *Autobiography*, 278.

8. *Ibid.* 278.

9. *Ibid.* 278–79.

10. *Ibid.* 279–80.

11. *Ibid.* 279; Increase Mather, *Awakening Truth's Tending to Conversion* (Boston, 1710), "Preface", ix.

12. *Autobiography*, 280.

13. There was nothing unusual, of course, in Mather's doubts; his conversion experience in fact resembled those of many others.

14. The fullest account of Mather's conversion is given in his *Autobiography*. But his *Awakening Truth's* (note 11 above), tells the story of his mother's hopes for him. Mather's Diary in manuscript at the A.A.S. contains a brief entry on his inner state; the published portions in the M.H.S. *Proceedings*, 2d Series, XIII (Boston, 1900), 337–74, ought to be consulted too.

15. Cotton Mather, *Parentator*, 14–15.

16. *Autobiography*, 281; Cotton Mather, *Parentator*, 16; Murdock, *Increase Mather*, 59.

17. Murdock, *Increase Mather*, 60–62.

18. *Ibid.* 62–67.

19. *Ibid.* 68; Cotton Mather, *Parentator*, 23.

20. Murdock, *Increase Mather*, 72–73. Increase Mather commented on his wife's character in the sermon he preached shortly after her death in 1714. The printed sermon, *A Sermon Concerning Obedience and Resignation to the Will of God* (Boston, 1714) included some of his wife's writings.

21. Increase Mather, *The Times of Men Are In The Hand of God* (Boston, 1675), "To The Reader." For the full range of Increase Mather's writing see Thomas James Holmes, *Increase Mather: A Bibliography of His Works* (2 vols., Cleveland, Ohio, 1931).

22. Increase Mather, "An Apologetic Preface to the Reader," in John Davenport, *Another Essay for Investigation of the Truth* (Cambridge, Mass. 1663). For Mather's change of mind on baptism see his *A Discourse Concerning the Subject of Baptisme* (Cambridge, Mass. 1675) and his *The First Principles of New-England* (Cambridge, Mass. 1675).

23. *Autobiography*, 287; Diary, M.H.S. *Proceedings*, XIII passim.

24. *Autobiography*, 288–89.

25. *Ibid.* 288–89.

26. *Ibid.* 290–97; 313–21, 340–41, 351–52; Murdock, *Increase Mather*, Chapters 12–16.

27. Stoddard is discussed below in Chapter 7; for Mather's feelings about Harvard see the *Autobiography*, 351–52. There is an excellent account of his Harvard Presidency in Samuel Eliot Morison, *Harvard College In The Seventeenth Century* (2 vols., Cambridge, Mass., 1936), II, 472–537.

28. Mather quoting his Diary, December 30, 1672 in *Autobiography*, 299.

29. *Ibid.* 299–300; Cotton Mather, *Parentator*, 34.

30. *Autobiography*, 303–4.

31. *Ibid.*

32. Increase Mather may have fulfilled his pastoral functions more carefully before the middle 1680's than I have indicated. His Diary, MHS *Proceedings*, XIII, records many visits to church members. See 341, 345, 363, 365, for example. His preaching is discussed below and in Chapter 9.

33. Increase Mather, *Five Sermons on Several Subjects* (Boston, 1719), 3. Increase wrote "Coyned," which I have rendered "coined."

34. William Perkins, *A Graine of Mustard-Seed* (London, 1621), 48–52. See, too, Perkins' Deaths Knell (11th ed., London ?, 1629).

35. Examples of these ideas may be found in the following by Increase Mather: *The Greatest Sinners Exhorted and Encouraged to Come to Christ* (Boston, 1686), 119 (eating and sleeping with one's attention on God); *Practical Truths Tending to Promote the Power of Godliness* (Boston, 1682), *passim; Sermons Wherein Those Eight Characters* (Boston, 1718), *passim*.

36. Increase Mather, *Practical Truths Tending to Promote the Power of Godliness*, 188; *Some Important Truths Concerning Conversion* (Boston, 1684), 24–31; *Ichabod* (Boston, 1702), 31–32; *Practical Truth's Tending To Promote Holiness* (Boston, 1704), 59–97; *Soul-Saving Gospel Truths* (Boston, 1703), 57–59, 154–57; *Awakening Truth's Tending to Conversion*, 39–41; *Practical Truths Plainly Delivered* (Boston, 1718), 16–17.

37. Cotton Mather tells of his father's fears in *Parentator*, 207–8; see too Samuel Sewall, *Diary of Samuel Sewall*, 1674–1729, M.H.S. *Collections*, 5th Series, V–VII (Boston, 1878–82), VII, 325, 326.

38. For a discussion of these works see Chapter 3.

39. Increase Mather, *Several Sermons* (Boston, 1715), ii; *Practical Truths Plainly Delivered*, "Preface."

40. Increase Mather, *The Mystery of Christ Opened And Applyed* (Boston, 1686), 145.

41. Almost all of Increase Mather's sermons dealing with sin and regeneration employ some of this language. For a representative example see his *Awakening Truth's Tending to Conversion*, 66–78, 82–87, and *passim*.

42. Richard Mather, *A Farewel-Exhortation* (Cambridge, Mass., 1657), 5; Increase Mather, *The Folly of Sinning* (Boston, 1699), 56–57.

43. Increase Mather, *Practical Truths Tending to Promote the Power Godliness*, 160–72, 178–79.

44. Increase Mather, *Pray For the Rising Generation* (3d Impression, Boston, 1685), 191, 196–98. See also Mather's *A Call From Heaven* (Boston, 1679) and his *An Earnest Exhortation to the Children of New England* (Boston, 1711).

45. This rigidity is clear in his "An Apologetical Preface" to John Davenport's *Another Essay For Investigation of the Truth*.

46. These feelings are clearest after the early 1680's.

47. See the *Autobiography* and the Diary for his introspection.

48. Diary, M.H.S. *Proceedings*, XIII, 342.

49. Parts of Maria Mather's papers were reprinted in the Preface to Increase Mather, *A Sermon Concerning Obedience & Resignation To The Will of God*.

51. *Autobiography*, 361–18; Increase Mather, *Practical Truths Tending to Promote the Power of Godliness*, 119–48, passim.

CHAPTER 6

1. See Chapter 2, above, for a discussion of Puritan mission. Increase Mather, *The Life and Death of . . . Richard Mather* quotes Richard Mather's statements about the founding.

2. The sources cited below in this chapter have stimulated my interpretation. Perry Miller's *New England Mind: From Colony To Province* (Cambridge, Mass., 1953) discusses these matters brilliantly.

3. Increase Mather, *A Discourse Concerning The Danger of Apostasy* (Boston, 1679), 65. This sermon is bound with *A Call From Heaven* and its pagination follows consecutively.

4. Jonathan Mitchell, *Nehemiah On the Wall* (Cambridge, Mass., 1671), 28. Mitchell preached this sermon May 15, 1667.

5. For Winthrop's sense of mission see Edmund S. Morgan, *The Puritan Dilemma* (Boston, 1958), Chapter 6.

6. See above, Chapter 2 and 3.

7. Mitchell, *Nehemiah On the Wall*, 18.

8. Richard Mather, *A Farewel-Exhortation* expresses his mature ideas on New England.

9. The works by Increase Mather, Mitchell, Samuel Danforth, William Stoughton, Thomas Shepard, Urian Oakes, Samuel Willard, William Hubbard, and John Higginson, below all carry this implication.

10. Increase Mather, *A Call From Heaven*, "To The Reader."

11. An election day sermon, May 23, 1677, (Boston, 1679).

12. *Ibid.* 55–56.

13. *The Life and Death of . . . Richard Mather.*

14. John Higginson, *The Cause of God and His People In New-England* (Cambridge, Mass., 1663), 11.

15. Besides those already cited in this chapter see Samuel Willard, *The Duty Of A People That Have Renewed Their Covenant With God* (Boston, 1680) and his *The Child's Portion* (Boston, 1684); William Hubbard, *The Happiness Of A People* (Boston, 1676), William Stoughton, *New Englands True Interest* (Cambridge, Mass., 1670); Urian Oakes, *New England Pleaded With* (Cambridge, Mass., 1673), *The Soveraign Efficacy of Divine Providence* (Boston, 1681), *A Seasonable Discourse* (Cambridge, Mass., 1682); Samuel Danforth, *A Brief Recognition of New-Englands Errand Into the Wilderness* (Cambridge, Mass., 1671). Increase Mather's prefaces to the following are also revealing as are the sermons themselves: Thomas Thacher, *A Fast of Gods Chusing* (Boston, 1678); Samuel Torrey, *A Plea For the Life of Dying Religion* (Boston, 1683); Samuel Torrey, *An Exhortation Unto Reformation* (Cambridge, Mass., 1674).

16. Increase Mather, "An Apologetical Preface" to John Davenport, *Another Essay For Investigation Of The Truth,* (no pagination); *The First Principles of New England* (Cambridge, Mass., 1675), *passim; The Divine Right of Infant-Baptisme* (Boston, 1680), 27; *A Brief History Of The Warr With The Indians in New-England* (Boston, 1676), 49–51. See, too, *An Earnest Exhortation To The Inhabitants of New England* (Boston, 1676).

17. Thomas Shepard, *Eye-Salve* (Cambridge, Mass., 1673), "To The Christian Reader."

18. *Ibid.* 31–33.

19. William Hooke to John Davenport, October 12, 1661, in M.H.S. *Collections,* 4th Series, VIII (Boston, 1868), 177–78.

20. *Ibid.* 177; see, too, the letter of the following March 1662, 194–95.

21. *Ibid.* 222. See also the letters on 11, 15, 173, 175, 185.

22. Increase Mather's book on Israel is *The Mystery Of Israel's Salvation* (London, 1669); his other important works on the subject are *A Dissertation Concerning The Future Conversion Of The Jewish Nation* (London, 1709, probably also published in 1695 or 1696 in Boston); *A Discourse Concerning Faith and Fervency in Prayer* (Boston, 1710); *A Dissertation Wherein The Strange Doctrine* (Boston, 1708), especially 92–135.

23. There was a vast literature in these subjects in England at the time of the founding of New England.

24. The best way of studying Puritans' use of typology is to examine the sources. There are several useful guides, however. Among them see Samuel Mather, *The Figures Or Types of The Old Testament* (Dublin?, 1683 and later editions), and two articles by Jesper Rosenmeier, "VERITAS: The Sealing of the Promise," *Harvard Library Bulletin,* XVI (1968), 26–37, and "The Teacher and the Witness: John Cotton and Roger Williams," *William and Mary Quarterly* XXV (July 1968), 408–31. Sacvan Bercovitch, "Typology in Puritan New England," *American Quarterly,* XIX (Spring, 1967), 166–91, is aso helpful.

25. For Williams see Perry Miller, *Roger Williams* (New York, 1953) and Edmund S. Morgan, *Roger Williams: The Church And The State* (New York, 1967).

26. The quotations are from Increase Mather, *The Mystery Of Christ Opened and Applyed,* 83 and *The Order Of The Gospel* (Boston, 1700), 15. For other examples of Mather's typology see *Discourse Concerning The Danger of Apostasy; The Blessed Hope And The Glorious Appearing of . . . Jesus Christ* (Boston, 1701); *Dissertation Wherein The Strange Doctrine; Several Sermons; Five Sermons On Several Subjects.*

27. For the ideas in this paragraph and their implications, the key works are Mather's *Mystery Of Israel's Salvation,* his jeremiads discussed above, especially the *Discourse Concerning The Danger Of Apostasy.* See, too, Increase Mather, *Heavens Alarm To the World* (Boston, 1681).

28. The quotations are from *Discourse Concerning* the Danger Of *Apostasy,* 57; see 57–59 for this brief history of decline.

29. *Ibid.* 65.

30. *Ibid.* 61. (The pagination of the printed tract is incorrect; I have corrected it.)

31. *Ibid.* 61.

32. See, for example, *Ichabod* and works cited in note 22.

33. *Ibid.* and works in notes 16 and 22.

34. Increase Mather, *An Historical Discourse Concerning The Prevalency of Prayer* (Boston, 1677), 11. And see Mather's *Brief History of the Warr* and his *A Relation Of The Troubles* (Boston, 1677).

35. Perry Miller, *From Colony To Province*, Chapter 11 and *passim;* Increase Mather, *A Narrative of the Miseries of New England* (London, 1688), in *Andros Tracts*, II (Boston, 1869), 1–11; Increase Mather, *New England Vindicated* (London, May 1689), in *Andros Tracts*, II, 111–23; Increase Mather, *A Further Vindication* (probably London, 1689), reprinted in Thomas J. Holmes, *Increase Mather: A Bibliography* I, 273–74.

36. The later preaching, especially *Several Sermons,* and *Five Sermons* reveal some of Mather's uncertainty.

37. *Discourse Concerning The Danger of Apostasy,* 57–61, and *passim.*

38. Mather's *The Great Blessing of Primitive Counsellours* (Boston, 1693) reveals much of his attitude in the 1690's.

CHAPTER 7

1. John Higginson, *The Cause Of God And His People In New-England,* 11; William Stoughton, *New-Englands True Interest,* 9–10; Jonathan Mitchell, *Nehemiah On the Wall,* 26; Samuel Danforth, *A Brief Recognition Of New-Englands Errand Into The Wilderness,* 23 and *passim;* Increase Mather, *The Day of Trouble Is Near* (Cambridge, Mass., 1674).

2. There were, of course, appeals to groups and interests in the first jeremiads, but the burden of these early appeals was to the whole people, the people whom God has "culled out," as Increase Mather said in the *Day of Trouble,* 27. In part, the difference in the later jeremiads is one of tone and emphasis, as I have attempted to show.

3. (Boston, 1679).

4. The quotations are in Increase Mather, *Discourse Concerning The Danger of Apostasy,* 70, 81. See, too, 69–75, and *passim.*

5. *Ibid.* 74–75.

6. *Ibid.* 79.

7. Increase Mather did not make these points explicitly, and in fact as late as 1702 in an election sermon dedicated to Joseph Dudley—*The Excellency of A Publick Spirit (Boston, 1702)*—seems to indicate that he still trusted the State. But the old hope and trust were not there, and, of course, the Mathers soon broke with Dudley.

8. All the jeremiads cited above and in Chapter 6 appeal to sinners as well as saints.

9. (London, 1641).

10. *Ibid.* 71, 80.

11. *Ibid.* 71–79.

12. The jeremiads cited above and in Chapter 6 reveal this direction in Mather's thought. See especially the *Discourse Concerning The Danger Of Apostasy*.

13. For the founders' ideas on ecclesiastical polity see Chapter 3. And see, too, Edmund S. Morgan, *Visible Saints* (New York, 1963), Chapters 1–4.

14. Increase Mather, *The Order Of The Gospel*, 14–17 and *passim*. The jeremiads also frequently make these same points.

15. *Ibid.* 18.

16. (Cambridge, Mass., 1663).

17. *Ibid. passim.*

18. Morgan, *Visible Saints*, 113–38 discusses these matters with discernment.

19. The synod's statement on baptism has been reprinted in Williston Walker, *The Creeds And Platforms Of Congregationalism* (New York, 1893 and Boston, 1960), 313–37.

20. Increase Mather, "An Apologetical Preface."

21. *Ibid.*

22. *Ibid.*

23. *Ibid.*

24. Increase Mather announced his agreement with the synod of 1662 in *The First Principles of New England* and *A Discourse Concerning The Subject Of Baptisme*. In this second work he indicates that the *First Principles* was written in 1671.

25. *Discourse Concerning . . . Baptisme*, 31–32.

26. Among many sermons Increase Mather preached along these lines see *Soul-Saving Gospel Truths*, 49–56, 82–85, 103–8, and *passim*.

27. In the sermons Increase published as *The Blessed Hope* (Boston, 1701), he wrote: "What is the *Glory* of the churches?

But that they consist of *Holy Members*, of Regenerate Persons; and that great care be taken, that so far as men are able to judge, none but Godly persons be admitted into their Communion." (114)

28. See *Discourse Concerning . . . Baptisme, passim; First Principles of New England, passim.*

29. All parties to the dispute over the Half-Way Covenant agreed on these points.

30. The quotations are from *Discourse Concerning . . . Baptisme*, 19, 20, 21.

31. *Ibid.* 40.

32. Besides Stoddard's works cited below see Perry Miller, "Solomon Stoddard, 1643-1729," *Harvard Theological Review*, XXXIV (1941), 277-320.

33. *Ibid.* 277-84; see, too, Perry Miller, *From Colony to Province*, Chapter 15.

34. Solomon Stoddard, *The Doctrine of Instituted Churches* (London, 1700), 3.

35. Solomon Stoddard, *The Safety Of Appearing At The Day of Judgment In The Righteousness Of Christ* (2d. ed. Boston, 1729, first published 1687), 56.

36. Solomon Stoddard, *Doctrine of Instituted Churches*, 18, and *The Inexcusableness Of Neglecting The Worship of God* (Boston, 1708), 10-12.

37. *Ibid.* 18. And see 19-23.

38. *Ibid.* 19.

39. Solomon Stoddard, *Safety of Appearing*, 8-12, and *The Inexcusableness Of Neglecting The Worship of God*, 14-21. After the controversy with Increase Mather ended, and indeed after Mather's death, Stoddard published a sermon in which he said flatly that the argument "*that frequently men are ignorant of the Time of their Conversion . . . is not good Preaching.*" A man, he said, could know, even if he could not demonstrate to others, that he was converted, for "Conversion is a great change, from darkness to light, . . ." See Stoddard, *The Defects of Preachers Reproved* (New London, Conn., 1724), 10.

40. Stoddard, *Safety Of Appearing*, 3.

41. Stoddard, *The Way For A People To Live Long In The Land* (Boston, 1703), 4.

42. Stoddard expresses these attitudes in much of his work and especially in *The Inexcusableness Of Neglecting The Worship of God*.

43. Stoddard, *Doctrine Of Instituted Churches*, 21.

44. *Ibid.* 22.

45. Solomon Stoddard, *An Appeal To The Learned* (Boston, 1790), 13.

46. Stoddard makes the distinction in *Ibid.* 9, and in *The Inexcusableness Of Neglecting The Worship of God*, 3.

47. Stoddard, *Safety of Appearing*, 109; *The Inexcusableness Of Neglecting The Worship of God*, 4–12.

49. Increase Mather, *The Order Of The Gospel*, 15; *A Dissertation Wherein The Strange Doctrine*, 12–14, and *passim.*

50. Stoddard, *Doctrine Of Instituted Churches*, 18. Stoddard makes these arguments in his other works during the controversy too.

51. Increase Mather, *A Dissertation Wherein The Strange Doctrine*, 81, 82, for the quotations in this paragraph.

52. Increase Mather, *The Order Of The Gospel*, 19.

53. *Ibid.* 19. Mather made the same point in *Awakening Soul-Saving Truths* (Boston, 1720), 47–48.

54. Increase Mather, *The Order Of The Gospel*, 29–33.

55. *Ibid.* 29–30.

56. Increase Mather, *A Dissertation Wherein The Strange Doctrine*, 84. See, too, Increase and Cotton Mather, "A Defense of Evangelical Churches," in John Quick, *The Young Mans Claim Unto The Sacrament* (Boston, 1700), 53–54.

57. Among many discussions of the Lord's Supper see Increase Mather, *Practical Truths Tending To Promote the Power of Godliness*, 119–26; Increase Mather's *The Blessed Hope* (Boston, 1701), 109–10; and the controversial literature issued in the struggle with Stoddard, discussed in this chapter.

58. *Ibid.* See, too, the discussion above, Chapter 5, on Increase Mather's emotion on taking and administering the Lord's Supper. Mather's *Autobiography* contains much material on this subject.

59. *Ibid.*

60. In *Dissertation Wherein The Strange Doctrine*, Mather argued that since the Supper was a "seal" of the covenant of grace and therefore a seal of the grace of the faithful, to give it to the unregenerate was to seal a "Blank." (30)

61. In the *Safety of Appearing*, 121–22, Stoddard emphasizes the symbolic significance of the bread and wine in the Supper.

62. Stoddard, *Inexcusableness of Neglecting The Worship Of God*, 3.

63. Increase Mather argued in these terms in the *Order Of The Gospel*, and in the *Dissertation Wherein The Strange Doctrine.*

64. For the theory of the national convenant see Miller, *From Colony To Province*.

65. The quotations are in Stoddard, *Doctrine of Instituted Churches*, 25–26, 27. See also 28–32.

66. Stoddard, *Safety of Appearing*, 119–21; *An Appeal To The Learned*, 21, and *passim*.

67. Stoddard, *An Appeal To The Learned*, 21–22.

68. *Ibid.* For Mather's views about saints and sinners in the land, see above, Chapter 6.

69. Increase Mather, *Dissertation Wherein The Strange Doctrine*, 85, asks "But would he [Stoddard] bring the Churches in *New-England* back to the Imperfect Reformation in other Lands, and so deprieve us of our Glory for ever?"

70. The quotation is from *A Discourse Concerning The Danger of Apostasy*, 56.

CHAPTER 8

1. Quoted in Perry Miller, *The New England Mind: The Seventeenth Century* (New York, 1939, reissued Cambridge, Mass., 1954), 207.

2. Quoted in *Ibid.* 212.

3. Increase Mather, *Heavens Alarm To The World*, "To the Reader." The comet was first noticed in New England on November 14, 1680; it could not be seen after the middle of the following February. Mather gave this sermon January 20, 1681.

4. *Ibid.* "To the Reader" for the measurement of the comet's "radiant Locks." Increase Mather read the following by Hooke: *Lectures and Collections Made By Robert Hooke, Secretary of the Royal Society* (London, 1678).

5. Hooke, *Lectures and Collections*, 7–10, 15. Hooke discusses Brahe and Kepler on 17–19.

6. Increase Mather, *Kometographia, Or A Discourse Concerning Comets* (Boston, 1683), 7, for the quotation. See also 2–6, and *passim*.

7. *Ibid.* "To the Reader," and 16–17. For Hooke's views on the regularity of cometary movements see *Lectures and Collections*, 27–30.

8. Increase Mather, *Kometographia*, 129–31; *Heavens Alarm To The World*, 1–16; *The Latter Sign* (Boston, 1682), 25–27.

9. *Kometographia*, 21, 78, 96, 132. On 132, Mather says that comets may be supposed "to be not only signal but causal" of various natural afflictions.

10. *Heavens Alarm* and *A Latter Sign* are less critical, of course.

11. (Boston, 1684).

12. Mather reconstructs the origins of the book in its Preface. There is a full account in Thomas J. Holmes, *Increase Mather: A Bibliography*, I, 240–49.

13. (Boston, 1679), 70–72.

14. Increase Mather, *An Essay For The Recording Of Illustrious Providences*, 32–72, and *passim*.

15. *Ibid.* 74–75, and *passim*.

16. *Ibid.* 99–100, 109, for the quotations. The stories fill the book.

17. For the interesting comments on magnetic variation see *Ibid.* 104–5.

18. Joseph Glanvill, *Sadducismus Triumphatus* (London, 1681), "Preface."

19. For Martha Cory, see Marion L. Starkey, *The Devil in Massachusetts* (Garden City, N.Y., 1961), 66–68, 72–75, and *passim*.

20. For biographical and bibliographical information on these writers, see Holmes, *Increase Mather*, I, 248, notes. I have read their works cited there, and this paragraph is based on my reading.

21. Increase Mather, *An Essay, passim*.

22. One such writer, discussed below, was Merci Casaubon, author of *A Treatise Concerning Enthusiasme, As It is An Effect Of Nature: But Is Mistaken By Many For Either Divine Inspiration, Or Diabolical Inspiration* (London, 1655). Casaubon did admit that witches existed, however.

23. Increase Mather, *An Essay*, 199, 186, for the quotations, and the comments on disease as a source of irrational behavior.

24. Besides reading the standard collections of documents and records of the Salem episode by George L. Burr, *Narratives of the Witchcraft Cases* (New York, 1914), and William E. Woodward, *Records of Salem Witchcraft* (2 vols., Roxbury, Mass., 1864), I have read much of the secondary literature. The accounts by Miller and Morison are valuable; Marion L. Starkey, *The Devil In Massachusetts* is excellent. Frederick C. Drake, "Witchcraft In The American Colonies," *American Quarterly* (Winter 1968) XX, 694–725, is also useful.

25. Starkey, *Devil In Massachusetts*, 26–27.

26. *Ibid.* 24–29.

27. *Ibid.* 31–51.

28. *Ibid.* 40–41.

29. Murdock, *Increase Mather* 284–86, tells of his return home. There is no evidence that Mather had heard in England of the beginnings of witchcraft in Salem.

30. Early ministerial reaction followed the same lines. See Deodat Lawson, *Christ's Fidelity The Only Shield Against Satan's Malignity* (Boston, 1693), a sermon preached in Salem, March 24, 1692.

31. Starkey, *Devil in Massachusetts,* 153–56.

32. "The Return," dated June 15, 1692, was printed in Increase Mather, *Cases of Conscience Concerning Evil Spirits* (London, 1693). A part of the "Postscript;" its pages are unnumbered.

33. There is no doubt that spectral evidence was used. Virtually everyone connected to the affair admitted it. Other doubtful tests—doubtful by seventeenth-century standards—such as the ordeal by sight and touch were used in pre-trial hearings and in the trials. See Deodat Lawson, *A Brief and True Narrative Of Some Remarkable Passages Relating to . . . Witchcraft* (Boston, 1692), and *A Further Account of the Tryals of the New England Witches* (London, 1693).

34. "The Return of Several Ministers."

35. Starkey, *Devil In Massachusetts,* 204–7.

36. *Ibid.* 219.

37. (London, 1693). Fourteen ministers, including John Wise, signed it.

38. *Ibid.*

39. Phips to Earl of Nottingham, Feb. 21, 1693, in Burr, *Narratives,* 201, for the quotations. See 198–202 for Phips version of the end of the affair. See, too, his letter to William Blathwayt, Oct. 12, 1692, in *Ibid.* 196–98.

40. There is a careful and sane account of these matters in Murdock, *Increase Mather.* See Starkey, *Devil In Massachusetts* for careful assessments.

41. The quotations are from *Cases of Conscience, To the Christian Reader,* written by Samuel Willard, and from the body of the text, 8, written by Increase Mather.

42. *Ibid.* 12–15.

43. *Ibid.* 18, 34.

44. Richard Bernard, *A Guide To Grand-Jury Men* (London, 1627), Book 2, 214 (water test); Book 2, 209–10 (spectral evidence); Book 2, 111–12, 219 (sucking marks); Book 2, 240 (use of torture). Bernard used and cited Cotta, discussed below. Wil-

liam Perkins, *A Discourse Of The Damned Art of Witchcraft* (London, 1631), 643 (water and other tests), 643–45 (spectral and other evidence, witch marks, and torture). John Cotta, *The Triall of Witchcraft* (London, 1616), 70–78, 104, 115–22, and *passim*.

45. Merci Casaubon, *A Treatise Concerning Enthusiasme*, 90, and *passim;* Perkins, *A Discourse*, 644–45.

46. Increase Mather, *A Disquisition Concerning Angelical Apparitions* (Boston, 1696), 17–18. Bound with this work, but with separate pagination is another by Mather which deals with some of these matters—*Angelographia, Or, A Discourse Concerning The Nature and Power of the Holy Angels* (Boston, 1696). See 64–66.

47. There are other references to New England in these works.

48. The quotation is from Increase Mather, *A Disquisition Concerning The State of The Souls of Men* (Boston, 1707), 34; Burthogge's *Essay* was published in London in 1694.

49. Increase Mather, *Disquisition Concerning . . . Souls*, 33.

50. But not published in Boston until 1693.

51. Cotton Mather made this statement in his life of Phips, *Pietas in Patriam* (London, 1697), reprinted in his *Magnalia* (London,1702), Book II, 62.

52. Miller, *From Colony To Province*, 204.

53. John Higginson, "An Epistle To The Reader," in John Hale, *A Modest Inquiry Into The Nature Of Witchcraft* (Boston, 1698), 6.

54. *Ibid.* 166.

CHAPTER 9

1. For information about the Mathers' church, the Second, or Old North Church, see Kenneth Murdock, *Increase Mather*, Chandler Robbins, *History Of The Second Church* (Boston, 1852); and Cotton Mather's *Diary* (2 vols., New York, 1957) contains material on the church.

2. Increase Mather left no great manual for the guide of ministers, such as the *Manuductio* written by his son. But his ideas and his practice are clear from many scattered comments in tracts and sermons. Perhaps the most important is "The Work of the Ministry described" in *Practical Truths, Plainly Delivered* (Boston, 1718), 104–38.

3. In *Soul-Saving Gospel Truths*, 5, Mather reviews the

varied subjects of his own work over the years and concludes that 'I *have* observed, *That* Plain Practical Sermons, *the design whereof is to promote* Conversion and Holiness, *do the greatest Good.*"

4. For the Arminian implications of the covenant theology, see Miller, *From Colony To Province.*

5. Increase Mather, *Practical Truths Tending To Promote the Power Of Godliness,* 98 and *passim; Renewal Of The Covenant The Great Duty* (Boston, 1677), 3–4; *Sermons Wherein Those Eight Characters.*

6. *Practical Truth's Tending To Promote . . . Godliness,* 98.

7. *Ibid.* 129.

8. Mather's Christology appears in almost all his sermons after 1700 and in many before. See *The Mystery of Christ* (Boston, 1686); *Meditations On The Glory Of The Lord Jesus Christ* (Boston, 1705).

9. Increase Mather, *Several Sermons* (Boston, 1715), 1–22, 28–34.

10. The quotations are, in order, from Increase Mather, *Mystery of Christ,* 145, 83, 31.

11. *Ibid.* 46.

12. Increase Mather, *Meditations On The Glory Of . . . Christ,* 42–67.

13. Increase Mather, *Mystery of Christ,* 131–32; *Meditations On The Glory Of . . . Christ,* 45–60.

14. For the quotations, in order, see Increase Mather, *Sermons Wherein Those Eight Characters,* 24; *A Plain Discourse Shewing Who Shall, and Who Shall Not Enter Into The Kingdom Of Heaven* (Boston, 1713), 12–13, 104. See also 88–91, 105–6.

15. Increase Mather, *Five Sermons On Several Subjects,* 36–37. See also 38–45.

16. Increase Mather, *A Plain Discourse,* 90–91, 106; *Soul-Saving Gospel Truths,* 5.

17. *Five Sermons,* 38–45, 61–65; *Awakening Truth's Tending To Conversion, passim;* and see also *Sermons Wherein Those Eight Characters.* The phrase "sermon-sick" appears in *A Plain Discourse,* 55, and in many other sermons.

18. *Ibid.* and most of the sermons cited in this chapter.

19. Increase Mather, *A Discourse Concerning the Existence and Omniscience of God* (Boston, 1716), Preface.

20. *Awakening Truth's,* 69. See also 66–68, 70.

21. Increase Mather, *Practical Truth's Tending To Promote Holiness,* 61–62, for a representative statement about living with

one's attention fixed on Christ. In *The Doctrine of Divine Providence* (Boston, 1684), 147, Increase Mather tells the story of a poor husbandman who, when asked what he was doing cutting wood replied: "I am cutting wood for God." This was the perfect reply and Mather commented, "you should buy and sell and build houses and ships, and all with some respect to the glory of God." (147)

22. Increase Mather, *Some Important Truths Concerning Conversion,* 16–17; *Ichabod* 31–32.

23. *Practical Truths Tending To Promote . . . Godliness,* 160–79.

24. *A Plain Discourse,* 32. See also 41–57; and *Sermons Wherein Those Eight Characters,* 279–96.

25. *Ibid.* 32–41, and Increase Mather, *Awakening Truth's,* 84–5.

26. *A Plain Discourse,* 48–51, for Increase's argument and the quotations. These points are made in many other sermons cited in this chapter.

27. Increase Mather, *Sermons Wherein Those Eight Characters,* 294. See, too, *An Ernest Exhortation To The Children of New England,* 33; and *Awakening Truths,* 66–69.

28. See above, Chapter 4.

29. See the works cited in notes 26 and 27.

30. These matters are discussed above in Chapter 7, and below in Chapter 12. The Brattle Street Church in Boston did not require a relation of conversion experience for membership.

31. *Soul-Saving Gospel Truths.*

32. Mather's Christology is discussed more extensively in Chapter 10, below.

33. For a representative expression of the themes discussed in this paragraph, see Increase Mather, *Meditations On Death Delivered In Several Sermons* (Boston, 1707). On the irrationality of sinners, and the unreliable character of reason, see *Awakening Truth's,* 66–70; and for Paul, 54. See too *Awakening Soul-Saving Truths,* 92.

34. Increase Mather, *The Blessed Hope And The Glorious Appearing Of Christ* (Boston, 1701), 11–16; *Meditations On Death,* 4–16, 155.

35. Increase Mather, *Burnings Bewailed* (Boston, 1711), 19–36, and *passim;* and *Sermons Wherein Those Eight Characters,* 18–35.

36. *Institutes Of The Christian Religion,* trans. Henry Beveridge (2 vols., Grand Rapids, Mich., 1953), I, 149.

37. Increase Mather, *Angelographia*, 48, for the quotation. See also 40–47, 75, and *passim*. There is frequent mention along similar lines in later sermons. See *Several Sermons*, 94–126.

38. *Angelographia*, 88 (guardian angels from cradle to grave), 42–45 (influence on minds), and *passim*.

39. Increase Mather, *Several Sermons*, 94–126.

40. Increase Mather, *Meditations On The Sanctification Of The Lord's Day* (Boston, 1712), 18–62, and *passim*. See, too, *Angelographia*, 96–98; and *A Disquisition Concerning Angelical Apparitions*. On angels as models, see also *Meditations On the Glory Of The Heavenly World* (Boston, 1711), 170–75.

41. Increase Mather, *Five Sermons*, 66, and *passim*.

42. Increase Mather, *Meditations On The Glory Of The Heavenly World*, 226, and 263, where Mather says that "few of those who belong to the Visible Church will be Saved."

43. These comments on preaching are in the prefaces to *Awakening Truth's* and *Several Sermons*.

CHAPTER 10

1. For the statements about the founders, see Increase Mather, *A Discourse Concerning Faith and Fervency In Prayer*, "Preface." Mather's reactions to the London fire may be studied in *The Mystery Of Israel's Salvation*.

2. Increase Mather, *Mystery of Christ*.

3. Increase Mather, *Meditations On The Glory Of The Lord Jesus Christ*, 42–67, a sermon called "The Lord Christ Jesus is the most glorious Conqueror."

4. *Ibid.* 92, and *passim*.

5. Increase Mather, *An Earnest Exhortation To The Children Of New England* is a jeremiad; it carries a note of chiliastic expectation.

6. Increase Mather, *A Dissertation Wherein The Strange Doctrine*, 130–32.

7. Increase Mather's belief that the conversion of national Israel would inaugerate the last days was widely shared; this belief made scholars holding it reluctant to claim that the millennium had commenced.

8. Increase Mather, *A Dissertation Concerning The Future Conversion Of The Jewish Nation*, 3–12. This was written in 1695. Paul's forecast is in Romans 11.26.

9. Increase Mather, *Faith and Fervency In Prayer*, 98–104,

for the information on the Turks, Danzig, Hamburg; the quotation is from 99. *Five Sermons* (Boston, 1719), 50, 61, 54, for the quotations (in order); see, too, 120–25.

10. Increase Mather, *Five Sermons,* 123–25.

11. Mather could, however, occasionally still call for repentance and reform. See *Ibid.* 125–28.

12. *Ibid.* Preface; see also Increase Mather, *A Discourse Concerning The Existence And Omniscience Of God* (Boston, 1716), Preface; *Several Sermons,* vi–vii.

13. See above, Chapter 4.

14. Increase Mather, *Burnings Bewailed* (Boston, 1711), 8, 30–32.

15. Increase Mather, *Faith and Fervency In Prayer,* 36.

16. Increase Mather, *Practical Truth's Tending To Promote Holiness* (Boston, 1704), 98; and *Meditations On The Glory Of The Heavenly World* (Boston, 1711), 9, 269–71.

17. Increase Mather, *Meditations On The Glory Of The Heavenly World,* 9.

18. Increase Mather's *Blessed Hope* (Boston, 1701) is a series of sermons in which both themes discussed in this paragraph appear. For Christ as judge at the Second Coming, see *Faith And Fervency, passim;* and see, too, *Meditations On The Glory Of The Heavenly World.* The phrase "infinitely meritorious," and similar ones, appear throughout Mather's sermons. For one of the last appearances see *Five Sermons,* 116.

19. Increase Mather attempted to convey some of this feeling in *Meditations On The Glory Of The Heavenly World,* and in most of the sermons cited in this chapter, delivered after about 1715.

20. *Ibid.*

21. *Ibid.* 117–50; see 118 and 144 for the quotations.

22. *Ibid.* 130, 131–33.

23. *Ibid.* 9–10.

CHAPTER 11

1. Cotton Mather, *The Minister* (Boston, 1722), 14.

2. Cotton Mather, *Meat Out Of The Eater* (Boston, 1703), 16.

3. I have discussed all these matters in later chapters with the exception of the revolt of 1689. The statement against Andros is *The Declaration Of The Gentlemen, . . . April 18th 1689* (Boston, 1689).

4. For Mather's working day his *Diary, passim* is revealing,

and it gives many reports of his fasts and other methods of worship. Samuel Mather, *The Life of The Very Reverend And Learned Cotton Mather* (Boston, 1729), 110 estimates the number of fasts. For the full range and nearly complete list of Mather's writings, published and unpublished, see Thomas James Holmes, *Cotton Mather: A Bibliography of His Works* (3 vols., Cambridge, Mass., 1940). The *Manuductio* was published in Boston in 1726. Cotton Mather's published diaries are *Diary of Cotton Mather*, M.H.S. *Collections*, 7th Series, VII–VIII, (2 vols., Boston, 1911–12; reprinted New York, 1957), Worthington C. Ford ed.; and, published separately, *The Diary of Cotton Mather, D. D., F. R. S., for the Year 1712* (Charlottesville, Va., 1964), William R. Manierre II ed.

5. David Levin reviews a part of Mather's historical reputation in "The Hazing of Cotton Mather: The Creation of a Biographical Personality," *In Defense of Historical Literature* (New York, 1967). For Morison's comment see his *Harvard College In The Seventeenth Century* (2 vols., Cambridge, Mass., 1936) II, 417. Mather reports the Quakers' jibe in *Little Flocks Guarded Against Grievous Wolves* (Boston, 1691), 3.

6. Cotton Mather's gentility was noted by his friends, but judging from their comments after his death, they were more impressed by his piety and learning. See, for example, Benjamin Colman, *The Holy Walk and Glorious Translation of Blessed Enoch* (Boston, 1728).

7. Most of these external details of his life are in Samuel Mather's *Life Of . . . Cotton Mather.*

8. Mather's family pride is discussed below in this chapter, and in Chapter 19.

9. Cotton Mather, *Magnalia Christi Americana* (London, 1702), Book III, Pt. II, Chapter 20, 125–26.

10. *Ibid.* Book III, Pt. I, Chapter 1, 29.

11. *Ibid.* 21–23.

12. Cotton Mather, *Parentator* (Boston, 1724), 50.

13. *Ibid.* 58. Increase Mather's views on stated councils appear in his *A Disquisition Concerning Ecclesiastical Councils* (Boston, 1716). Cotton reproached Increase for desiring to remain in England in a letter of May 17, 1690, in *Diary*, I, 137–40.

14. Secession from the Second Church (North Church) is discussed in Chapter 19; and the issue of Israel's conversion in Chapter 18.

15. Cotton Mather, *A Companion For Communicants* (Boston, 1690), "Dedication."

16. Cotton Mather, *Diary*, I, 5, 9; II, 483.

17. *Ibid.* I, 24, 38, 62, and *passim.*

18. *Ibid.* I, 24.

19. The *Diary* reflects this tension throughout.

20. Cotton Mather, *A Servant of The Lord* (Boston, 1704), 17.

21. Cotton Mather, *Victorina* (Boston, 1717), 29.

22. It is impossible, of course, to show in detail how I have used passages of the *Diary;* I have attempted to assess them with the circumstances of their peculiar composition in mind.

23. For the quotations see *Diary . . . 1712,* 108; *Diary,* II, 117, 354. See also 123, 124.

24. *Ibid.* II, 484, 466, 642, for the quotations and the details of these relationships.

25. For an excellent discussion of Puritan attitudes toward sex see Edmund S. Morgan, "The Puritans And Sex," *New England Quarterly* (Dec. 1942) XV, 591–607. Morgan's *The Puritan Family* (rev. ed., New York, 1966) is also valuable.

26. Jonathan Mitchell, *A Discourse Of The Glory To Which God Hath Called Believers* (2d ed., Boston, 1721), 90.

27. Puritan attitudes toward the body seem especially clear through the study of eschatological writings. Cotton Mather's major works, discussed below in Chapter 18, include Triparadisus, mss. at A.A.S. Increase Mather held the same views of the resurrected body. See his *Meditations On the Glory Of The Heavenly World* (Boston, 1711), 108–50. Jonathan Mitchell, *Discourse Of The Glory,* 45–49 makes the same points.

28. Cotton Mather, *Diary,* I, 107, 110.

29. *Ibid.* II, 523.

30. *Ibid.* II, 194.

31. *Ibid.* II, 330.

32. *Ibid.* II, *passim.*

33. Cotton Mather, *A Short Life, Yet Not A Vain One* (Boston, 1714), 13.

34. I have discussed at some length several of these problems of Mather's inner life, incuding "deadness" in "Piety and Intellect in Puritanism," *William and Mary Quarterly,* 3d. Ser., XXII (July 1965), 457–70.

35. Cotton Mather, *Diary,* I, 83 for the quotation. See I, 81–84 for a list of the objects of his ejaculatory prayers. Mather tells of beginning his vigils in I, 421–22. I have discussed his "daily spiritualizing" in "Piety and Intellect." For an example see his *Agricola* (Boston, 1727).

36. For his "particular faiths", see "Piety and Intellect." The

quotations are from Mather's *Parentator*, 189–90; *Diary* I, 343, 355, 400. For a repetition of the conversion process, *Diary*, II, 696.

37. For the quotation, *Diary*, II, 69. Although Cotton Mather was an inventive man, he did not originate most of these techniques of worship. Many indeed were hundreds of years old, and he read about them in medieval and Reformed commentaries. There were also Puritan models close at hand, as his life of John Eliot, *The Triumphs Of The Reformed Religion, In America* (Boston, 1691) reveals. An English writer, whom both Increase and Cotton Mather seem to have read, also may have been suggestive. See Isaac Ambrose, *Prima: The First Things* (London, 1654) and *Media: The Middle Things* (London, 1657).

38. The events mentioned in this paragraph often occupy his attention in the *Diary* and in his preaching.

39. See "Piety and Intellect" for his imitation of Christ. See, too, Chapters 18 and 19 for this and the other topics noted in this paragraph.

CHAPTER 12

1. For the jeremiad see above, Chapters 6 and 7.

2. Cotton Mather, *Magnalia Christi Americana*, "General Introduction," Sect. 3.

3. Cotton Mather used typology more later in his life; his style was always heavily metaphorical, in part because he believed that God employed "certain Metaphors, for the use of our understandings." *Unum Necessarium* (Boston, 1693), 106.

4. See above, Chapters 2 and 3.

5. Cotton Mather, *Magnalia*, Book I, Introduction, Ch. 4, 15, 17, for the quotations.

6. Mather made these points, and used these terms, in many sermons. He also sometimes argued that a faithful remnant served the land in temporal affairs. See, for example, *Pascentius* (Boston, 1714), 32.

7. For examples of these views see the following by Cotton Mather: *Winter-Meditations* (Boston, 1693); *The Short History of New-England* (Boston, 1694); *American Tears Upon The Ruines Of The Greek Churches* (Boston, 1701); *The Good Old Way* (Boston, 1706); *Pascentius*.

8. For a typical statement of the 1690's (others are cited later in this chapter) see *Optanda* (Boston, 1692), 43–44. In *Christianus Per Ignem* (Boston, 1702), 151, Mather declared "I never

much admired, the violent pressing of *Uniformity;* but there may be *Unity* without Uniformity."

9. Cotton Mather, *Winter-Meditations* 49–50.

10. The *Political Fables,* written around 1692, circulated in manuscript in Mather's lifetime. For a modern edition see Kenneth B. Murdock ed., *Selections From Cotton Mather* (New York, 1926), 363–71.

11. Miller, *From Colony To Province,* 170–71.

12. In the eighteenth century, Mather usually capitalized all the letters in this word. Its meaning and its implications are discussed throughout much of the remainder of this book.

13. Cotton Mather, *Fair Weather* (Boston, 1692). See especially, 26–33, 37–69, 77–82.

14. Cotton Mather, *Optanda,* 44.

15. *Ibid.* 42–43.

16. *Ibid.* 45. See 45–46 for the other duties summarized in this paragraph.

17. For Mather and Callender, see Cotton Mather, *Brethren Dwelling Togther In Unity* (Boston, 1718).

18. (Boston, 1724).

19. *Ibid.* 58–60; see 59, for the quotation.

20. The *Heads Of Agreement* (London, 1691) establishing the United Brethren has been reprinted in Williston Walker, *The Creeds and Platforms of Congregationalism* (New York, 1893 and Boston, 1960), 455–62. For Cotton Mather's initial reactions see *Blessed Unions* (Boston, 1692). For later accounts see Carl Bridenbaugh, *Mitre and Sceptre* (New York, 1962), 32–34.

21. Cotton Mather, *Blessed Unions,* 57–65.

22. Bridenbaugh, *Mitre And Sceptre,* 33–4 tells the story of the Congregational Presbyterian split, briefly and well.

23. This case can be followed in Cotton Mather's *Diary,* I, 218, 226, 275–76 and in *Collections* 4, M.H.S. VII, 119–21. For Bradstreet see Clifford K. Shipton, *Sibley's Harvard Graduates: Biographical Sketches Of Those Who Attended Harvard College* (14 vols. to date, Boston, 1873–1968), IV, 154–57.

24. The *Manifesto* was published in Boston in 1699. There are good accounts of the Brattle Street Church in Walker, *Creeds,* 472–79 and in Miller, *From Colony To Province,* 240–42, and *passim.* Most of the documents may be seen in Samuel K. Lothrop, *A History of the Church in Brattle Street* (Boston, 1851).

25. *A Manifesto Or Declaration, Set forth by the Undertakers of the New Church . . . November 17th 1699* (Boston, 1699), 2.

26. Cotton Mather, *Diary*, I, 326.

27. *Ibid.* I, 332.

28. The breach was publicly patched up when Increase Mather preached to the Brattle Street Church early in 1700; on this occasion—a fast—Cotton Mather concluded the meeting with a prayer. *Diary, I,* 332-33.

29. In August, 1699, Mather reported that the "bloody Bishop of London" had written one of his Boston curates asking for information about Cotton Mather's "treasonable or seditious Passages. . . ." *Diary,* I, 312.

30. *Eleutheria: Or, An Idea of the Reformation in England* (London, 1698).

31. (London, 1700).

32. *Ibid.* 13; and *Eleutheria,* 59-60, 63-64, 70-71, and *passim.*

33. *Ibid.* 28.

34. *Ibid.* 20.

35. *Diary,* II, 60, 64, 81, 120, 145, 147-48, 151, 326-30. Mather wrote *The Old Pathes Restored* (Boston, 1711)to combat the *"Pelagian* Encroachments." *Diary,* II, 81. For the background of Anglican activity, see Bridenbaugh, *Mitre and Sceptre,* 57-67. For further evidence of these and other aspects of Mather's attitude toward the S.P.G. and the Church of England see *Diary* . . . 1712, 21, 38-39, 41, 45, 87, 91; and *Diary,* II, 88-89, 212, 221, 291, 412.

36. The Newbury case can be reconstructed from the following: *Diary* II, 147-48, 171, 194, 218, 223, 231; *Diary* . . . 1712, 15, 40, 76, 80; Sewall *Diary,* II, 838; Sewall *Letter Book,* I, 416-19. And see too, Joshua Coffin, *A Sketch of the History of Newbury, Newburyport, and West Newbury* (Boston, 1845), 175-85.

37. For the United Brethren, see Benjamin Colman, *A Brief Inquiry Into The Reasons* . . . (Boston, 1716), 31, and *A Sermon Preach'd at Boston* . . . (Boston, 1716), 28; and Cotton Mather, *Diary,* II, 310-12 ("TO THE REVEREND . . . MINISTERS . . . , IN . . . LONDON"). For Mather's reaction to the impeachment of Sacheverell, and to the news of the destruction of the Presbyterian meetinghouses, *Diary,* II, 36; for Marlborough, the Act of Occasional Conformity, *Diary,* II, 172. The quotations are from letters reprinted in the *Diary,* II, 173, 174, and in *Collections* 4 M.H.S., VIII, 414.

38. Cotton Mather, *A Pillar of Gratitude* (Boston, 1700), 22.

39. These controversies can be followed in these works by Increase Mather, *A Brief Discourse Concerning The Unlawfulness of The Common Prayer Worship* (Cambridge, Mass., 1686; London, 1689); "To The Reader," in *A Letter From Some Aged*

Nonconforming Ministers (4th ed., Boston, 1712); *Some Remarks On A Pretended Answer* (Boston?, 1713?). The important Anglican tracts are: William King, *A Discourse Concerning The Inventions of Men* (5th ed., Boston, 1712); John Williams, *A Brief Discourse Concerning the Lawfulness of Worshipping God By the Common Prayer* (2d ed.? Boston, 1712). See, too, Cotton Mather, *A Seasonable Testimony To The Glorious Doctrines of Grace* (Boston, 1702), part of which was reprinted in 1711 as *The Old Pathes Restored*. Holmes, *Increase Mather*, II, 534-38 gives many bibliographical details. For Mather's activity in distributing the tracts against the Anglicans, *Diary*, II, 175; *Diary* . . . 1712, 76, 80.

40. Cotton Mather, *The Glorious Throne* (Boston, 1714). The address is in *Diary*, II, 300-3. See, too, Benjamin Colman, *A Sermon Preach'd at Boston*, 26.

41. For early attempts at increasing synodical power, see *Collections* 4, M.H.S., VIII, 193; Walker, *Creeds*, 137-39, 267; James K. Hosmer, ed., *Winthrop's Journal* (2 vols., New York, 1908, reprinted, 1959), I, 112-13. There is a good, brief account of English experience in Geoffrey F. Nuttall, *Visible Saints* (Oxford, 1957), 122-23.

42. Cotton Mather gives information about the history of New England associations in various places, including *Thirty Important Cases* (Boston, 1702); *Magnalia* (London, 1702); and the *Ratio Disciplinae Fratrum Nov Anglorum* (Boston, 1726). See, too, the "Records of the Cambridge Association," M.H.S. *Proceedings*, XVII (Boston, 1880).

43. The *Proposals* of 1705 are in Walker, *Creeds*, 486-90.

44. Increase Mather's opposition was declared in *A Disquisition Concerning Ecclesiastical Councils*.

45. For May and the quotation, *Diary*, I, 313; and see 314, 315-16, 324, 328-29. Mather's *A Warning To The Flocks Against Wolves In Sheeps Cloathing* (Boston, 1700) was one result of the May episode.

46. *Diary*, I, 385 for the quotation. The full sermon is on 384-88.

47. John Rogers, *A Sermon Preached Before His Excellency, the Governour* (Boston, 1706), 48. Ebenezer Pemberton delivered a strong defense of the Proposals in *The Divine Original and Dignity of Government Asserted* (Boston, 1710), 102-3, where he said that they had been "misrepresented, and Prophanely descanted on." The year before, Grindall Rawson in *The Necessity of a Speedy and Thorough Reformation* (Boston, 1709) gave a

clear, though less ambitious, endorsement of the Proposals. John Wise, *The Churches Quarrel Espoused* (2d ed., Boston, 1715) is justly celebrated. Wise referred to Cotton Mather as "an *Anomulous* Author" (58) and quoted *Eleutheria* against him.

48. For further discussion of these points see below, Chapter 17.

49. For a representative collection of Mather's sermons on PIETY, see his *Malachi. Or, The Everlasting Gospel, Preached Unto The Nations. And Those MAXIMS of PIETY* (Boston, 1717).

50. Cotton Mather, *Icono-clastes* (Boston, 1717), 15, for the quotation.

51. *Ibid.* 15. See also Mather's *Brethren Dwelling Together In Unity,* for the comment about the sectarian spirit that leads men to prefer a man of their own persuasion to one of the "Best Morals." *Malachi,* and *Piety and Equity United* (Boston, 1717), also deal with these and related issues raised by the New Piety.

52. Cotton Mather, *Brethren Dwelling Together,* 6, 17–19, 24–25, 26–27, and *passim; Malachi,* 51, where Mather declares that all good men are "United in the Maxims of Piety" and "indeed a sufficient Basis for an UNION in *Religion,* is provided and afforded in them." In *Coelestinus* (Boston, 1723), Mather says that he has seen Baptists, Congregationalists, Presbyterians, Episcopalians, Lutherans, and Calvinists at the Communion Table together (v–vi).

53. Mather, *Malachi,* 40, for the quotations, and 39–42 for his argument developed in this paragraph.

54. *Ibid.* 35.

CHAPTER 13

1. Cotton Mather, *A Companion For The Afflicted* (Boston, 1701), 6–9, 18–23, 25–26.

2. Thomas Hooker, *The Application of Redemption* (London, 1656), Book III, 152.

3. See above, Chapters 4, 9, and the notes to these chapters.

4. Not every Puritan divine agreed on the character of these stages. Edmund S. Morgan, *Visible Saints* contains a fine discussion of the conversion process.

5. Thomas Shepard, *The Sincere Convert* (4th ed., London, 1646), 75, 110.

6. Miller, *From Colony To Province,* 53–67, and *passim* is

chiefly responsible for the view of Mather. See, too, Miller's "'Preparation For Salvation' In Seventeenth-Century New England," *Journal of the History of Ideas* (June 1943), IV, 253–86; this article has been reprinted in *Nature's Nation* (Cambridge, 1967).

7. Cotton Mather, *The Call Of The Gospel* (Boston, 1686), 33, 35, 36, 37.

8. Cotton Mather, *The Armour Of Christianity* (Boston, 1704), 140–41. This work was originally given as "Thursday Lectures", June–October 1703. See, too, Cotton Mather, *Balsamum Vulnerarium* (Boston, 1692), 46–47.

9. Cotton Mather, *The Everlasting Gospel. The Gospel of Justification* (Boston, 1700), 32 for the quotation "innate propensity". See, too, 29–45; and *Utilia. Real And Vital Religion Served* (Boston, 1716), 17 for quote on "money."

10. Mather cautions against becoming "listless" in the *Armour of Christianity*, 116. See, too, Mather's *A Conquest Over The Grand Excuse* (Boston, 1706) for a related set of psychological scruples.

11. For Mather's comments on the Devil and preparation, see the *Armour of Christianity*, 126–27. The quotations in the preceding paragraph are from Cotton Mather, *The Christian Cynick* (Boston, 1716), 33, 36. In *Utilia*, 7–8, Mather wrote: "The posture wherein we are to *come* unto our Savior, is *upon our Knees*. 'Tis in the quality of Petitioners, yea, and of poor ones, too, that we are to sue unto our Saviour, when we *come* unto Him. As a Beggar coming for an Alms, or as a Criminal for his *Life*. . . ."

12. For the quotations, see Cotton Mather, *A Soul Well-Anchored* (Boston, 1712), 12. See also *Conquest Over The Grand Excuse.*

13. Besides Mather's works already cited in the notes to this chapter see his *Faith At Work* (Boston, 1697), *Free-Grace, Maintained and Improved* (Boston, 1706), *The Heavenly Conversation* (Boston, 1710), *The Greatest Concern In The World* (2d ed., New London, 1718), *The Converted Sinner* (Boston, 1724).

14. Miller, *From Colony To Province*, 53–81.

15. See the following by Mather: *The Religious Marriner* (Boston, 1700), 18–20, 23–25; *A Christian At His Calling*, 38–65, and *passim; Lex Mercatoria* (Boston, 1705), 10–39; *Fair Dealing* (Boston, 1716), 13–14, 27.

16. Cotton Mather and others, *The Principles Of The Protestant Religion Maintained* (Boston, 1690), 110. Note that he says "preparatory common works."

17. These opinions on the powers of unregenerate man to rouse and reform themselves, temporarily, were widely shared.

18. See Mather, *Armour of Christianity*, 34-157, *passim;* and his *Utilia*, 16-44, *passim.*

19. All these matters are discussed at length in Chapters 15 and 18.

20. In *Menachem* (Boston, 1716), Mather reported that some conversions, notably those of men who had good religious educations, occurred in an *"Insensible* manner." (14)

21. Cotton Mather, *Meat Out Of The Eater*, 16-20, *passim.*

22. Cotton Mather, *A Companion For Communicants* (Boston, 1690), 87. This is a very important work for the understanding of Mather's psychological theory.

23. See above, Chapter 4.

24. Mather recognized this problem as early as 1690 and probably much earlier. See *Companion For Communicants*, 76-77.

25. Hooker, *Application of Redemption*, Bk. I, 44; John Cotton, *The Way of Life* (London, 1641), Pt. IV, 331. Cotton also recommended applying the general promises to one's particular condition (Pt. IV, 319-24).

26. Miller, *From Colony To Province*, 67.

27. Cotton Mather, *Early Piety, Exemplified In The Life And Death of Mr. Nathanael Mather* (London, 1689), 20.

28. Mather, *Utilia*, 47; and Mather, *Converted Sinner*, 16-17. Almost all of his sermons cited in this chapter bear on these points.

29. Cotton Mather, *Companion For Communicants*, 87-93, and *passim.* See, too, *Balsamum Vulnerarium*, and *A Soul Well-Anchored.*

30. Cotton Mather, *Balsamum Vulnerarium*, 90; *Companion For Communicants*, 76; *A Comforter Of The Mourners* (Boston, 1704), 27.

31. Cotton Mather, *Everlasting Gospel*, 66. See too *Faith At Work* where the same arguments are made.

32. Cotton Mather, of course, continued to recommend good works. He seems always to have extolled works in funeral sermons. See, for example, his *Tibitha Rediviva* (Boston, 1713).

33. John Rogers, *The Doctrine Of Faith; Wherein Are Principally Handled Twelve Principall Points, Which Explain The Nature And Use of It* (London, 1632), 370. Rogers was one of many who argued that it was better to have all the signs weakly than a few strongly. Cotton Mather discusses assurance and self-examination in many sermons and books. See, for example, *Com-*

panion For Communicants; Armour Of Christianity; Utilia; A Soul Well-Anchored; The Religion Of The Closet (Boston, 1705).

34. See above, Chapters 4 and 9; and *Menachem,* 16-22. In *The Tryed Professor* (Boston, 1719), Mather discussed signs of hypocrisy as well as of grace. See 9-16.

35. Cotton Mather, *Comforter Of Mourners,* 32. And for similar expressions, see Mather's *Winter Piety* (Boston, 1712), 29; *Utilia,* 185-90; *Christianity Demonstrated. An Essay To Consider The Sanctifying Work Of Grace* (Boston, 1710), 8.

36. G. S. Brett, *A History Of Psychology* (3 vols., London, 1921), II, 71 discusses the theory of psychological states localized in the body.

37. The quotations are from Shepard, *Sincere Convert,* 150; Increase Mather, *A Plain Discourse, Shewing Who Shall, and Who Shall Not Enter Into . . . Heaven* (Boston, 1713), 50; Cotton Mather, *Companion For Communicants,* 131.

38. The ultimate expression of Mather's emphasis on desire appears in his *Pia Desideria* (Boston, 1722) where he said "A *Desire,* a *desire,* to *Fear* the *Name of* GOD. If such a *Desire* be found in us, we shall be found among the True Servants of GOD; and His Ear *will be attentive unto our Prayer.* Verily, *As a Man Desireth in His* Heart, so is He.'" (3)

39. *Ibid.* 6.

CHAPTER 14

1. Cotton Mather, *Malachi. Or, The Everlasting Gospel,* 7-8 and *passim.*

2. See above, Chapters 4 and 10; and John Cotton, *The Covenant of Gods Free Grace* (London, 1645), 18; Peter Bulkely, *The Gospel-Covenant, Or The Covenant Of Grace Opened* (2d. ed., London, 1651), 321; John Preston, *The New Creature* (London, 1633), 23, and *The New Covenant, or The Saints Portion* (London, 1629), 477. I have been guided to these works and to several of the quotations by Perry Miller's essay, "The Marrow of Puritan Divinity," in *Errand Into The Wilderness* (Cambridge, Mass., 1956), 50-98.

3. Cotton Mather always carefully argued that faith "justified" men only in a limited sense—"*Organically* and *Relatively;* Inasmuch as it is the Instrument by which a man apprehends the *Righteousness* of the Lord. . . ." It did not justify men as "a

Work." The material and meritorious cause of the believer's justification was the righteousness of Christ. See his *Faith At Work* (Boston, 1697), 3; and *The Everlasting Gospel*, 8–15 and *passim*.

4. Cotton Mather, *A Soul Well-Anchored*, 12.

5. Cotton Mather, *Meat Out Of The Eater* 148–49; and Mather's *Genuine Christianity* (Boston, 1721), 4, 5.

6. Cotton Mather, *Coelestinus*, 7, 8, and see also, 9–10; *Christodulus* (Boston, 1725).

7. Mather, of course, did not often make clear every premise of his theory, but he left no doubt that the power in the covenant came from God.

8. Cotton Mather, *The Call Of The Gospel*, 36; *Nails Fastened* (Boston, 1726), 13, 15.

9. Cotton Mather, *The Cure of Sorrow* (Boston, 1709), 35, for an example of Mather's urging men to plead the promises of the covenant.

10. But, of course, Mather always emphasized that the power for these inner, "subjective," actions came from God. See, for example, Mather's *Faith At Work* and *The Everlasting Gospel*. This matter is also discussed in Chapter 13.

11. There is a brilliant discussion of the covenant in Perry Miller, *The New England Mind: The Seventeenth Century* (New York, 1939; Cambridge, Mass., 1954), 365–462.

12. It is impossible to date precisely the shifts in Mather's preaching, for they occurred gradually. It should also be noted that he preached jeremiads until the end of his life, though their frequency falls off, comparatively, in his last years.

13. Mather said this often; he also warned against "meer Doctrinal or Historical Faith" in contrast to genuine saving faith. See, for example, *A Plain Discourse Shewing Who Shall, and Who Shall Not Enter into the Kingdom of Heaven*, 17.

14. Perry Miller discusses these developments throughout *From Colony To Province*.

15. Mather, *Faith At Work; Utilia; The High Attainment* (Boston, 1703) are representative of many works in which these themes are treated.

16. Cotton Mather, *Several Sermons Concerning Walking With God* (London, 1689), 81–2; *The Great Physician* (Boston, 1700), 7–20, and *passim; Parental Wishes And Charges. Or, The Enjoyment of A Glorious Christ* (Boston, 1705), 55–56, and *passim; Reason Satisfied: And Faith Established* (Boston, 1712), 35; *Things To Be More Thought Upon* (Boston, 1713), 28–34; and see below, Chapter 16.

17. Cotton Mather, *The Salvation Of The Soul Considered* (Boston, 1720), 15.

18. See above, Chapter 13.

19. Cotton Mather, *The Resort of Piety* (Boston, 1716), 7, 8, 10, and *passim*.

20. Mather sometimes used these figures in other ways too, as for example in this reference to ministers: *"Death* is a *Wolf,* that will Sieze, even on the *Shepherds of* the *People,"* in *Orphanotrophium* (Boston, 1711), 15.

21. I have not been able to discover when Mather first read Thomas à Kempis. He wrote an ambitious preface to Samuel Lee, *A Summons Or Warning To The Great Day of Judgment* (Boston, 1692) in which à Kempis is mentioned. Mather was reading à Kempis in 1719. See *Diary,* II, 582–83. It is worth noting again the enormous force of Increase Mather's *Christology.*

22. Cotton Mather, *Addresses To Old Men, and Young Men, and Little Children* (Boston, 1690), 7–8.

23. Cotton Mather, *Christianity To The Life* (Boston, 1702), 17.

24. Cotton Mather, *The Heavenly Conversation* (Boston, 1710), 13; and see also 16–25.

25. *Ibid.* 23–24.

26. The *Diary* is full of his attempts at the imitation of Christ. I have discussed some of them in "Piety And Intellect In Puritanism", *William and Mary Quarterly* 3d. Ser. (July 1965), XXII, 457–70.

27. The terms "vital", "strengthen", "quicken", "overpower", in this context, all connotative of a new energy, appear repeatedly in Mather's sermons of the eighteenth century.

28. For these themes, see Cotton Mather, *A Life of Piety Resolv'd Upon* (Boston, 1714); *The Stone Cut Out Of The Mountain* (Boston, 1716); *The Resort of Piety; Utilia; Genethlia Pia* (Boston, 1719); *The Words of Understanding* (Boston, 1724).

29. Mather's fervor is clear in the works cited in note 28, and in such efforts as *Pia Disideria* (Boston, 1722), and *Divine Afflations* (New London, 1722).

30. Cotton Mather, *Resort of Piety, passim;* and the sermons cited in note 28.

31. Cotton Mather, *A Life of Piety,* 28.

32. *Ibid.* 28; and see also 29–32.

33. *Ibid.* 29, for the quotations.

34. Miller, *New England Mind: Seventeenth Century,* 405–7.

35. See, for example, Cotton Mather, *The Converted Sinner* (Boston, 1724), 26–29.

36. Cotton Mather, *A Soul Well-Anchored*, 12–13.

37. Cotton Mather, *A Companion for Communicants*, 67–80; *Utilia*, 15–17, and *passim;* see above, Chapter 13.

38. Cotton Mather, *Boanerges* (Boston, 1727), 14.

39. *Ibid.* 33.

40. For Mather's psychology of religion, see Chapter 13.

CHAPTER 15

1. Solomon Stoddard, *The Way For A People To Live Long In The Land That God Hath Given Them* (Boston, 1703), 16.

2. In 1714, for example, in a sermon before the Governor and the General Assembly, Mather describes God saying to New England: *"Thou hast Sinned against my Covenant."* *Duodecennium Luctuosum* (Boston, 1714), 10. See also, Cotton Mather's *Small Offers Towards The Service Of The Tabernacle In The Wilderness* (Boston, 1689), *The Way to Prosperity* (Boston, 1690), and *The Present State Of New-England* (Boston, 1690).

3. Mather also dealt with these themes in his prophetical writings which I have discussed in Chapter 18, below.

4. Cotton Mather, *The Day, And The Work Of The Day* (Boston, 1693), 60.

5. Cotton Mather, *Lex Mercatoria. Or, The Just Rules Of Commerce Declared* (Boston, 1705), 10–39; *A Christian At His Calling* (Boston, 1701), 60–71; *The Religious Marriner*, 20.

6. Cotton Mather, *Theopolis Americana* (Boston, 1710), 19.

7. Cotton Mather, *Addresses To Old Men, and Young Men, and Little Children,* 71–80; *Necessary Admonitions* (Boston, 1702), 29–30; *A Monitory Letter* (Boston, 1702), 16; *The Best Ornaments of Youth* (Boston, 1707), 29–30; and see also Chapter 11, above.

8. Mather, *Present State of New-England,* 20–29, 41–47, for a representative series of statements on internal divisions. See *Sober Considerations, On a Growing Flood of Iniquity* (Boston, 1708) for Mather's attack on rum.

9. The standard account of these merchants is Bernard Bailyn *The New England Merchants In The Seventeenth Century* (Cambridge, Mass., 1955). Samuel Eliot Morison's studies of several in *Builders of the Bay Colony* (rev. ed., Boston, 1964) are very helpful. For the general context, Carl Bridenbaugh, *Cities In The Wilderness* (New York, 1938, reprinted 1955) is one of many useful books.

10. For a modern account see Ola E. Winslow, *Samuel Sewall* of Boston (New York, 1964). Sewall's *Diary, Collections* M.H.S., 5th Ser., V-VII (3 vols., Boston, 1878-82) is more revealing.

11. Bailyn, *New England Merchants,* 192-93.

12. *Ibid.* 193, quoting Sewall's *Diary.*

13. Cotton Mather, *Diary,* II, 194.

14. *Ibid.* II, 195, and *passim.*

15. The great "Dissolutions" were, of course, still in the future, awaiting the Great Awakening.

16. *Diary, passim.* The large imperatives guiding Mather's actions should not be overlooked, of course. He wanted always to glorify his God, but he may have had difficulty in focusing the variety of his activities—projects, charities, preaching, visits, writing—as clearly as he desired.

17. See above, Chapters 6 and 7, for the development of the jeremiad.

18. Samuel Belcher, *An Essay Tending To Promote The Kingdom Of Our Lord Jesus Christ* (Boston, 1707), 15, for the quotation. See also, Solomon Stoddard, *The Way For A People To Live Long In The Land,* 17, where Stoddard says: "It is to be lamented that many men are grown ignorant of the doctrine of Regeneration. Some take Baptism for Regeneration, some think men may be Regenerate, without any antecedent Preparation." The following are also revealing: Joseph Estabrook, *Abraham The Passenger* (Boston, 1705); John Rogers, *A Sermon Preached Before His Excellency* (Boston, 1706); Peter Thacher, *The Alsufficient Physician* (Boston, 1711); Samuel Cheever, *Gods Sovereign Government* (Boston, 1712); Samuel Danforth, *An Exhortation To All To Use Utmost Endeavours* (Boston, 1714); Benjamin Colman, *A Brief Inquiry Into The Reasons* (Boston, 1716), 28, where Colman says: "We are sadly on the decay as to serious Piety and vital Religion."

19. See the works cited in note 5.

20. Cotton Mather, *Pascentius,* 2-4, 8-17, 25-27.

21. The old attacks on mobility, and on over-valuing the world, never entirely disappear from Mather's work, however.

22. The classic expression of these ideas appears in Cotton Mather, *Bonifacius. An Essay Upon The Good* (Boston, 1710). David Levin has provided a new—but accurate—version of this work (Cambridge, Mass., 1966) with a superb "Introduction."

23. Dudley W.R. Bahlman, *The Moral Revolution of 1688* (New Haven, Conn., 1957), 16, 67-108, and *passim.*

24. Increase Mather, "To The Reader," in Samuel Willard, *The Peril of the Times Displayed* (Boston, 1700).

25. *Ibid.* 8–11. The book Mather discussed was Josiah Woodward, *An Account of the Rise And Progress Of The Religious Societies In The City of London* (London, 1689).

26. Cotton Mather, *Religious Societies* (Boston, 1724), 1–19 (in the second part, separate pagination). See also *Diary*, II, 712. Mather next called for the creation of orderly societies in *The Wonders Of The Invisible World* (Boston, 1693), 64. There evidently was a religious society of Negroes in Boston as early as 1693. See Mather's *Rules For The Society of Negroes. 1693* (Boston, 1693?); *Diary*, I, 176.

27. *Diary*, I, 418–19; Cotton Mather, *Methods and Motives For Societies To Suppress Disorders* (Boston, 1703).

28. Cotton Mather, *Methods and Motives*, 8, and *passim* urged that the reforming societies (of mature men) suppress vice. And see, Cotton Mather, *Private Meetings Animated and Regulated* (Boston, 1706).

29. *Methods and Motives*, 7, and *passim;* Cotton Mather, *A Faithful Monitor* (Boston, 1704), 50, 54, and *passim; Diary*, II, 150, 160, 206, 229, 235, 283; *Diary For . . . 1712*, 19.

30. *Methods and Motives*, 7, 8.

31. See the excellent study by William Kellaway, *The New England Company, 1649–1776* (New York, 1962).

32. *Methods and Motives*, 1–8, *passim.*

33. *Diary*, I, 516–17, 522–23; II, 2, 27, 42, 107, 118, 131, 275, 767, and *passim.*

34. *Diary*, II, 44, 315, 369, 397, 439, 573, 712; *Diary For . . . 1712*, 13, 15, 16, and *passim.*

35. *Diary*, II, 356, 360, 370, 372, 373, 388, 391, 442, 646, and *passim.*

36. *Diary For . . . 1712*, 86, 101, 113; the four-page English letter is reproduced in facsimile between pages 114 and 119 of the *Diary For . . . 1712*. The quotation is from 4.

37. Mather, *Bonifacius* (Levin, ed.), 96.

38. *Faithful Monitor*, 3, and *passim.*

39. This is especially clear in *Bonifacius*, but also in all of Mather's pietistic writings.

40. The English writer Josiah Woodward had prescribed an ecumenical function for the societies too, but as Bahlman points out, Woodward's union was "within the Church rather than toleration and peace among different sects." *Moral Revolution*, 81.

41. Cotton Mather to Bartholomew Ziegenbalgh, Dec. 31,

1717, in Cotton Mather, *India Christiana* (Boston, 1721), 66 (for the full letter, 62–74).

42. *Ibid.* 64, and *passim*.

43. *Diary*, II, 202.

44. See above, Chapter 14.

45. *Diary*, II, 667, 673.

46. Mather, *India Christiana*, 57–60, 69–74.

47. I have tried to establish this point about Mather in Chapter 11.

48. Mather, *India Christiana*, 71.

CHAPTER 16

1. Robert Boyle, *The Christian Virtuoso* (London, 1690), 54. Mather originally referred to his *The Christian Philosopher* (London, 1721) as the *Christian Virtuoso*. See *Diary*, II, 324, 332, 511. In *Christianus Per Ignem*, he wrote of "the Incomparable *Robert* Boyl" (13).

2. Mather, *Christianus Per Ignem*, 12–14.

3. See *Thoughts For the Day of Rain* (Boston, 1712), 2, where Mather says that scientific study provides a way of doing something toward the restitution of the "Primitive and Paradisian State" and "a little to bring on the State for which the whole creation groaneth!"

4. See above, Chapter 8.

5. For one of Mather's conventional statements on thunder see his *Brontologia Sacra: The Voice Of The Glorious God In The Thunder* (London, 1695), reprinted in the *Magnalia*, Book VI, 14–20.

6. Quoted in Samuel Eliot Morison, *Harvard College In The Seventeenth Century*, I, 216.

7. See *Ibid.* I, 208–51 for an account of science at Harvard.

8. Cotton Mather, *The Wonderful Works of God Commemorated* (Boston, 1690), 26–27.

9. *Ibid.* 25, 26–27.

10. Cotton Mather, *An Elegy On The Much-to-be-deplored Death Of That Never-to-be-forgotten Person, The Reverend Mr. Nathanael Collins* (Boston, 1685), 5, and 5n.

11. Cotton Mather, *Wonderful Works*, 26.

12. Cotton Mather, *Winter-Meditations*, 20; *Wonderful Works*, 25.

13. I have read it in Boyle's *Works* (6 vols., London, 1772).

14. Boyle, *Works,* II, 20, 21, and *passim.*

15. Cotton Mather, Biblia Americana, Genesis, 1; mss. in M.H.S. There is no reliable pagination in this work (in fact few pages are numbered). I will refer to the biblical chapter where Mather's commentary is found.

16. Mather betrays this uneasiness even in his early works. Boyle may not have felt it.

17. See, for example, *Christianus Per Ignem,* 7.

18. Mather's late work, including the *Christian Philosopher,* emphasizes these propositions even more than the early.

19. Biblia, Genesis, 1, 7, 8, and *passim;* Matthew, 12 and *passim.* Portions of Mather's commentary were written in 1699; still others in 1702 and 1706.

20. Biblia, Genesis, 1, 7, and *passim.*

21. The *Dictionary of National Biography* gives the essential biographical information about Bentley and Whiston. Julius H. Tuttle, "William Whiston and Cotton Mather," *Pub. Col. Soc. Mass.,* XIII, 197–204, discusses briefly a theological dispute between Mather and Whiston.

22. Biblia, Genesis, 1.

23. *Ibid.*

24. *Ibid.*

25. Mather discussed briefly Newton's *Optics* (1704) in the "Preface" to *Thoughts For The Day Of Rain.*

26. Biblia, Genesis, 1.

27. H. W. Turnbull et al., eds., *The Correspondence Of Isaac Newton* (4 vols. to date, 1959–1967; Cambridge, England), III, 240.

28. *Ibid.* III, 254. Bentley's *A Confutation of Atheism From The Origin and Frame of the World* (London, 1693) rendered Newton's view in this way: "meer Matter cannot operate upon Matter without mutual Contact." (31)

29. Turnbull, *Correspondence of Isaac Newton,* III, 254.

30. Bentley, *Confutation,* 16, 33; Turnbull, *Correspondence of Isaac Newton,* III, 234. And see also, as Mather did, William Whiston, *A New Theory Of The Earth* (London, 1696), 37, and *passim.*

31. Biblia, Genesis, 1. Mather admits his indebtedness to Bentley and to Whiston on this and other points. Much of his language, in fact, reproduces, or closely paraphrases theirs.

32. Mather does this in many works including *The Christian Philosopher.*

33. Cotton Mather, *Thoughts For The Day Of Rain,* 9.

34. *Ibid.* 10–13; Thomas Burnet, *The Theory of the Earth* (London, 1684), 28.

35. Burnet, *Theory of the Earth*, 66–67; Mather, Biblia, Genesis, 7, 8; *Thoughts For The Day Of Rain*, 9–14. Mather read John Ray, *The Wisdom Of God Manifested In The Works Of Creation* (London, 1691). Theodore Hornberger, "The Date, the Source, and the Significance of Cotton Mather's Interest in Science," *American Literature* (Jan. 1935), VI, 413–20, discusses ably Ray's influence on Mather.

36. Biblia, Genesis, 7.

37. *Ibid.*

38. *Ibid.*

39. Mather seems to have read the digest of Clarke's *Discourse concerning the Unchangeable Obligations of Natural Religion* (London, 1706) in *The History of the Works of the Learned* (Jan.–Feb. 1706) VIII. The quotation appears on VIII, 107.

40. *Ibid.*

41. Clarke argued that the law of nature, "being founded in the Eternal Reason of Things is eternal, universal, and absolutely unchangeable. . . ." *Ibid.* 109.

42. *Ibid.* 97–105, for example, where Clarke deals with both Swift and Hobbes. There is a solid book on related issues by Roland N. Stromberg, *Religious Liberalism in Eighteenth-Century England* (London, 1954).

43. Biblia, Matthew, 12, and *passim*.

44. *Ibid.*

45. See Samuel Clarke's *Discourse concerning the Unchangeable Obligations of Natural Religion.*

46. Biblia, Matthew, 12.

47. *Ibid.* and *passim*.

48. Cotton Mather, Triparadisus, Pt. III, Sect. XII.

49. *Christianus Per Ignem*, 7.

50. Biblia, Matthew, 12.

51. *Ibid.*, Matthew, 28.

52. For an account of Puritan conceptions of reason, see Miller, *The New England Mind: Seventeenth Century*, 181–206.

53. Cotton Mather, *Reasonable Religion* (Boston, 1700), 4.

54. Miller, *New England Mind: Seventeenth Century*, 181–206, *passim*. Both Increase and Cotton Mather made virtually all of these arguments.

55. Mather, *Reasonable Religion*, 40, for the quotation.

56. Locke, *Reasonableness of Christianity, passim.* Locke accepted the biblical account of the miracles.

57. John Toland, *Christianity not Mysterious* (?, 1696), 127 for the quotation. Sir Leslie Stephen, *History of English Thought in the Eighteenth Century (2 vols.,* New York, 1962; first pub. 1876), I, 78-100, is still a distinguished guide to Locke and Toland's thought on these questions, and to many sides of English deism.

58. Stephen, *History of English Thought, passim;* Stromberg, *Religious Liberalism* should be consulted about the English controversies.

59. Earl Morse Wilbur, *A History of Unitarianism In Transylvania, England, and America* (Boston, 1945), 208-70.

60. One stage in Mather's retreat from his first eager endorsements of reason can be seen in his *The Man of God Furnished* (Boston, 1708). *See especially,* "The True Child of Light," 72-83; and "Divine *Revelation* Victorious over carnal *Reason,*" 84-92. These essays should be compared with care to the entry on reason in the *Diary,* II, 144 (Dec. 1711).

61. (Boston, 1712). Mather tells of the origins of the work on iii. Increase Mather had already attacked the deists strongly in *A Discourse Proving that the Christian Religion Is the Only True Religion (Boston,* 1702).

62. Mather, *Reason Satisfied,* 11-14.

63. *Ibid.* 34; Cotton Mather, *Malachi (Boston,* 1717), 39-43.

64. *Reason Satisfied,* 34; *Malachi,* 40-42; and especially Mather's *A Man of Reason* (Boston, 1709). This sermon was written in 1709. In it he argues for the existence of innate ideas (3-4).

65. Cotton Mather's fullest statement on the Golden Rule appears in a sermon he gave to it, "The Measures of Equity," in *Piety and Equity United* (Boston, 1717), 1-42 (separate pagination for each sermon).

66. The quotations are from Cotton Mather, *Icono-clastes,* 18. See also, *A Man of Reason,* 13-15, for a more conventional (and earlier) warning. Since most ministers in New England did not embrace reason with Mather's eagerness, most did not go through the deflationary process he experienced. For traces of the rationalism of the new century in others, see Jonathan Russell, *A Plea For The Righteousness of God* (Boston, 1704), 22; Ebenezer Pemberton, *A Christian Fixed in His Post* (Boston, 1704), 6-7; Experience Mayhew, *A Discourse Shewing That God*

Dealeth With Men As With Reasonable Creatures (Boston, 1720), 6–7, 14–15, 17–18, 33–34, and *passim;* Benjamin Colman, *God Deals With Us As Rational Creatures* (Boston, 1723), 1–8, 11–15, 16–19. Colman in his *The Government and Improvement of Mirth* (Boston, 1707) expressed his distaste for those who used their "Grovling Reason" to ridicule the doctrines of revealed religion. (69)

67. Mather, *Manuductio ad Ministerium* 35, 36.

68. Biblia, 2 Corinthians, 13: "Yea, so far is *Nature* from finding it [the Trinity] out, that now when *Scripture* hath Revealed it, she cannot by all the help of Art, comprehend it or Exhibit it, as she does other things; . . . . " And "though Reason be able from the Creatures, to infer an Essential power and Godhead, yett it cannot from them a Trinity; . . . " Mather admits his indebtedness at this point in the Biblia to an old book by John Arrowsmith, *Armilla Catechetica. A Chain of Principles* (Cambridge, England, 1659). Arrowsmith had served as Regius Professor of Divinity in Cambridge University. His book describes a reason beholden to revelation in dealing with the Trinity. Mather makes heavy use of examples and arguments from the following pages: 128, 130, 135–36, 137, 138. Mather seems also to have resorted to William Sherlock, *A Vindication of the Doctrine of the Holy and Ever Blessed Trinity* (London, 1690).

69. *Christian Philosopher,* 303–4.

70. *Ibid.* 304. See also Cotton Mather, *Things To Be More Thought Upon* (Boston, 1713), 28–41,

71. See Chapter 17 for the evidence for this view. It is worth noting here that the Biblia, "An Essay for a further Commentary on the Sacred Scriptures" contains much on the experience of the Holy Spirit.

72. Cotton Mather, *Christianity Demonstrated* (Boston, 1710), 23, 26.

73. Cotton Mather, *The Heavenly Conversation,* "Preface".

CHAPTER 17

1. Kuno Francke, "The Beginning of Cotton Mather's Correspondence with August Hermann Francke," *Philological Quarterly* V (July, 1926), 193–95.

2. Cotton Mather, *Winter-Meditations,* 74.

3. Mather developed these ideas in many places; see, for

example, his *Nepenthes Evangelicum* (Boston, 1713); *A Life of Piety Resolv'd Upon,* and *Utilia.*

4. The fact that Mather recommended many techniques of worship—fasting, meditation, self-examination—that were completely conventional should not lead us to believe that his major views were the same as those of the founders. He wanted the experience of these old ways of worship to be different.

5. See above, Chapter 12; and for typical statements of Mather's "catholic" or ecumenical spirit, *Brethren Dwelling Together* and *Malachi.*

6. Cotton Mather, *Nepenthes Evangelicum,* 8.

7. *Ibid.* 7.

8. See, for example, Mather's *The Stone Cut Out of the Mountain.*

9. Mather, *Nepenthes Evangelicum,* 25–30; *Piety and Equity United,* "Measures of Equity" (separate pagination), 20–23.

10. Cotton Mather, *Pascentius,* 5–6.

11. Cotton Mather, *Winter Piety,* 14, where he says that "The more the *Flesh* endures, the more the Soul receives!" See also, Cotton Mather, *The Religion of the Cross* (Boston, 1714) and *The Sacrificer* (Boston, 1714). Mather's *Diary* contains much on his own asceticism.

12. For examples of his techniques of worship, see the works cited in note 11, and the following by Mather: *A Present of Summer-Fruit* (Boston, 1713); *Utilia; Family-Religion Excited and Assisted* (4th Impression, Boston, 1720); *Agricola.*

13. Mather, *Utilia,* 62 and *passim;* Biblia, "An Essay for a Further Commentary on the Sacred Scriptures."

14. Cotton Mather, *The Words of Understanding* (Boston, 1724), 5.

15. (Boston, 1722).

16. *Ibid.* 16–27, and *passim.*

17. For Mather's private worship, see *Diary, passim.* His theory of the Holy Spirit is discussed below.

18. Cotton Mather, *Christianus Per Ignem.* 9.

19. Although *Christians Per Ignem* was published in 1702, it seems to have been written in 1700. See page 125 of it. It is one of the most important of Mather's works on worship.

20. *Ibid.* 9, 10, 12, for the quotations.

21. Cotton Mather, *Coelestinus. A Conversation in Heaven,* 68.

22. *Ibid.*

23. For all these, *Diary, passim.*

24. See above, Chapter 14.

25. *Diary,* II, 376, 396, and *passim.*

26. For example, Cotton Mather, *Deus Nobiscum* (Boston, 1725) and *Vital Christianity* (Philadelphia, 1725).

27. (Boston, 1690), Preface.

28. *Memorable Providences Relating To Witchcrafts And Possessions* (Boston, 1689).

29. (Boston, 1691). See, too, Mather, *Dust and Ashes (Boston,* 1710), 33; and *Diary For The Year . . . 1712, 79.*

30. George Keith, *The Presbyterian and Independent Visible Churches in New-England And else-where (Philadelphia,* 1689).

31. Mather, *Principles of the Protestant Religion,* 27, for the quotations.

32. See *Ibid.* 21–35, for a full explication of Mather's early ideas on the Spirit.

33. The *Diary, passim,* offers evidence of his inner life.

34. Cotton Mather, *Signatus* (Boston, 1727).

35. See, for example, Cotton Mather, *Divine Afflations,* 3–10, 12, 22–36; *Pia Disideria,* 3–10, and *passim.*

36. (Boston, 1710).

37. *Ibid.* 30, and see also 32–34.

38. There are occasional departures from these comments, however. In his "Introduction" to *Psalterium Americanum* (Boston, 1718), for example, he urges the Christian to "Harmonize and Symphonize" with the Holy Spirit in the Scriptures. (xxiii)

39. *Diary,* II, 387, 733 (this entry is for June 21, 1724).

40. (Philadelphia, 1725).

41. Ibid. "The Dedication."

42. See, for example, Cotton Mather, *Signatus,* 14–15, and *passim:* and *Deus Nobiscum,* 7–8.

43. Mather, *Signatus,* 14, 16, 20.

44. *Ibid.* 16.

45. *Ibid.* 20.

46. Cotton Mather, *Restitutus. The End of Life Pursued* (Boston, 1727), 24.

47. *Ibid. passim.*

48. Cotton Mather, *The Marrow of the Gospel* (Boston, 1727), 22–23, for Mather's comments on bad behavior and the Holy Spirit. See also, Mather's discussions of the Holy Spirit in the following: *Columbanus* (Boston, 1722); *Bethiah* (Boston, 1722); *Juga Jucunda* (Boston, 1727).

49. Biblia, "An Appendix Containing Some General Stores. . . . "

50. *Ibid.* for the stories. I have studied Mather's theory of the Nishmath-Chagim in Triparadisus, mss. in A.A.S.; and in The Angel of Bethesda, mss. in A.A.S. The relevant chapter has been included in Otho T. Beall and Richard H. Shryock, *Cotton Mather: First Significant Figure in American Medicine* (Baltimore, 1954). And, see also Cotton Mather, *Coheleth* (Boston, 1720).

CHAPTER 18

1. Cotton Mather, *Successive Generations* (Boston, 1715), 20. And see also, *Tela Praevisa (Boston, 1724),* 10–11.

2. Cotton Mather, Triparadisus, Pt. II, 18–27, 36–41.

3. *Ibid.* Pt. II, 40–41; and Mather's *Coelestinus,* 145–47 (second series of pagination), and *passim.*

4. Cotton Mather, *Shaking Dispensations* (Boston, 1715), 28.

5. Mather described the end of the world many times; I have relied heavily on his accounts in Problema Theologicum, mss. in A.A.S.; Triparadisus, Parts II and III; and Biblia, especially the commentary on Revelation. The important published works are cited in my notes below.

6. Mather, Triparadisus, Pt. III, Sect. VI, "Signs of the Conflagration Coming On."

7. *Ibid.* Pts. VII, VIII, IX, X. See also the following by Mather: *Things To Be Look'd For (Cambridge,* Mass., 1691); *Perswasions From The Terror of The Lord* (Boston, 1711); *The World Alarm'd* (Boston, 1721); *Terra Beata* (Boston, 1726); Biblia, 2 Peter, Revelation, *passim.*

8. Mather, Triparadisus, Pt. X ("Where to find *Gog* and *Magog*," appended, 4pp.)

9. See above Chapter 2.

10. Cotton Mather, *A Midnight Cry* (Boston, 1692), 11–25, 34–35, 50–55, and *passim; Successive Generations,* 3–4, 24–28; *Tremenda* (Boston, 1721), 11–19, and *passim.*

11. For Mather's responses to Arminians and Arians, see above, Chapter 16.

12. Mather, Triparadisus, Pt. III; Biblia, Revelation, *passim;* Coelestinus, "Heaven Convers'd withal" (2d series of pagination), 2–162, *passim.*

13. Mather's "Preparatory Meditations Upon The Day of Judgement" was prefixed to Samuel Lee, *A Summons or Warning to the Great Day of Judgment* (Boston, 1692).

14. Cotton Mather, *Perswasions From The Terror of the Lord,* 20–28; and *Terra Beata,* 18–25. See also, Chapter 14, above. Increase Mather made the same points in his chiliasm.

15. See, for example, Mather's *Theopolis Americana* (Boston, 1710).

16. Mather, *Perswasions From the Terror of the Lord,* 28.

17. *Ibid.* 28–29.

18. Cotton Mather, *The Stone Cut Out of the Mountain,* 2–8; and *passim; Malachi,* 81 and *passim.*

19. Mather, *Things To Be Look'd For,* 50–56.

20. Calef's charge came in *More Wonders of the Invisible World* (London, 1700). The ministers' response, including Cotton Mather's, in Obadiah Gill and others, *Some Few Remarks Upon A Scandalous Book* (Boston, 1701).

21. Cotton Mather's ideas about Satan may be studied in his *Batteries Upon The Kingdom of the Devil* (London, 1695); and *The Armour of Christianity.* The Devil is a prominent figure in the Biblia and in Triparadisus.

22. Mather, Triparadisus, Pt. III, Sect. VIII for the quotation. This section describes the conflagration in great detail. See also Mather's, *Things To Be Look'd For,* 67–68; *A Midnight Cry,* 22–24; *Things For a Distress'd People to Think Upon* (Boston, 1696), 34–37; *The World Alarm'd,* 3–5.

23. Mather, Triparadisus, Pt. III, Sect. VII, X; Biblia, Revelation, 22.

24. Cotton Mather, Psalterium Americanum (Boston, 1718), xxix–xxxi; and Triparadisus, Pt. III, Sect. III.

25. Mather, Triparadisus, Pt. III, Sect. VIII.

26. *Ibid.*

27. *Ibid.* Pt. III, Sect. IX.

28. *Ibid.*

29. *Ibid.*

30. *Ibid.* See also, Cotton Mather, *The Soul Upon The Wing* (Boston, 1722), 11–19; *Colestinus,* 149, and *passim.*

31. Mather, Triparadisus, Pt. III, Sect. IX; Problema Theologicum, 73.

32. For this background see Norman Cohn, *The Pursuit of the Millennium* (2d. ed., New York, 1961) and Ernest Lee Tuveson, *Millennium and Utopia* (Berkeley, 1949; New York, 1964).

33. *The Key of the Revelation* (London, 1643) was Joseph Mede's most important eschatological work, and the one that Mather studied most carefully. Mather also seems to have been

influenced by Mede's *The Apostasy of the Latter Times* (London, 1641).

34. Biblia, Revelation, 1. Mather copied long passages into the Biblia from Jurieu's *The Accomplishment of the Scripture Prophecies* (London, 1687). In Part I, 28 Jurieu argued that Revelation was nothing but a paraphrase of Daniel, 7.

35. William Whiston, *An Essay On The Revelation of Saint John* (Cambridge, 1706). For the views of Richard Mather and John Cotton, see above, Chapter 2; for Increase Mather, Chapter 10.

36. See above, Chapter 16.

37. On experience, worship, and prophecy see Mather, Biblia, "An Essay For A Further Commentary on the Sacred Scripture;" and *Benedictus* (Boston, 1715), 49–58 (statement by Bridges).

38. Miller, *From Colony To Province* tends to emphasize the passage of political power through ministerial hands.

39. The dreams mentioned here are clear in both the Biblia and Triparadisus.

40. It is probably impossible to work out a list of all of Mather's reading on the prophecies. Besides Mede, Jurieu, and Whiston, the following were especially important in the development of his eschatology: Thomas Philipott, *A New Systeme of the Apocalypse* (London, 1688); Drue Cressner, *Applications of the Apocalypse* (London, 1690); Pierre Poiret, *The Divine Economy* (London, 1713; originally pub. in French, Amsterdam, 1687); Thomas Goodwin, *The World To Come* (London, 1655); William Burnet, *An Essay on Scripture-Prophecy* (New York, 1724); and, of course, the commentaries of Increase Mather.

41. Daniel 7.19. The *Geneva Bible* says "unlike to all the others."

42. See especially Part I, *passim,* of Mede's *Key of Revelation.*

43. He did not, so far as I can tell from reading the Biblia, and the published works on these Scriptures.

44. Whiston, *Essay on Revelation,* 42–61. Mather reviews all these issues in Biblia, Revelation, *passim,* and "Coronis."

45. Biblia, "Coronis."

46. Whiston, *Essay on Revelation,* 222, and *passim;* Biblia, "Coronis."

47. Biblia, Revelation, 1, following (and often quoting) Jurieu.

48. Biblia, Revelation, "Coronis"; *Diary*, II, *passim*.

49. (Cambridge, Mass., 1691), text caption.

50. Mather had just read Jurieu's commentary on the vials, but he was not completely convinced by the argument. See *Things To Be Look'd For*, 42–43.

51. Jurieu, *Accomplishment of the Scripture Prophecies*, 78–224; Mather, *Things To Be Look'd For*, 42–43; *Midnight Cry*, 1–9, 30–32, 63.

52. Mather, *Things To Be Look'd For*, 32, 39–40.

53. *Midnight Cry*, 60.

54. Cotton Mather, *The Wonders of the Invisible World*, 26–27.

55. Composed in 1692.

56. Mather, *Wonders*, 22–25, and *passim; Things To Be Look'd For*, 32, 54–55. Mather said about this time, "I am verily perswaded, There are Some already Born, who shall see the most Glorious Revolutions that ever happened in any former ages. . . . " This age, he explained, was "in the very Dawns of our Lords Coming to Destroy the Wicked one." *Winter-Meditations*, 51.

57. Cotton Mather, himself, never insisted that his predictions were wholly exact.

58. Mather, *Diary*, I, 261–62.

59. *Ibid*. I, 262.

60. *Ibid*. I, 261–62.

61. Mather, *Faith of the Fathers* (Boston, 1699), 4.

62. Mather, *Diary*, I, 315.

63. Mather, Problema Theologicum, 52–56, 89.

64. *Ibid*. 68.

65. *Ibid*. 67–68 (the quotation is from 68). Mather had read the French version of Poiret's *L' Economie Divine* (Amsterdam, 1687).

66. In *Theopolis America* (Boston, 1710), Mather suggests that America may become a part of the city of God; see 43–51. In Triparadisus, Pt. III, Sect. X, he returned to the question, still puzzled, but determined to reject Mede's views. Although Mather did not declare himself fully satisfied with Poiret's suggestion that Gog and Magog came from Hades, he clearly preferred it to Mede's contentions about their American orgins.

67. Biblia, "Coronis."

68. *Ibid*.

69. Whiston, *Essay on Revelation*, 52–92, and *passim*.

70. Biblia, "Coronis"; Whiston, *Essay on Revelation,* 187, and *passim.*

71. Whiston, *Essay on Revelation,* 215. Whiston qualified his prediction at this point, saying that conclusion of the Antichristian state might not occur until 1736.

72. (2d. ed., London, 1692).

73. Mather, *A Midnight Cry,* 60; Biblia, "Coronis."

74. Biblia, Revelation, 11; Whiston, *Essay On Revelation,* 209 and *passim.*

75. Whiston, *Essay on Revelation,* 209–10.

76. Samuel Sewall, *Letter-Book, Collections,* M.H.S. (6th Ser., Boston, 1888), II, 53–54, 64–65, 78, 83; Mather to Samuel Penhallow, April 17, 1712, *Diary,* II, 171–74. See, too, II, 176.

77. (Boston, 1716)

78. *Diary,* II, 416.

79. See citations in note 76 above.

80. Joel 2.28; *Diary,* II, 365.

81. *Diary,* II, 366.

82. Mather, Triparadisus, Pt. III, Sect. XII.

83. *Diary,* II, 454; *Biblia,* "An Appendix Containing Some General Stores."

84. See *Diary,* II, 456–57 for Mather's hopes for this work.

85. Mather, *Malachi,* 63.

86. *Diary,* II, 376, 396, 453, 460.

87. Cotton Mather, *India Christiana,* 69–72.

88. *Diary,* II, 522, 740; Triparadisus, Pt. III, Sect. XI; Biblia, Revelation, 11, where a letter from Governor Burnet, April 5, 1725, is copied into the manuscript. In the entry in Triparadisus, Mather says that the belief in a national conversion of the Jews, before the Second Coming, produces a *"Dead* Sleep."

89. Triparadisus, Pt. III, Sect. XII.

90. Cotton Mather, *Ratio Disciplinae Fratrum Nov Anglorum: A Faithful Account of the Discipline Professed and Practised in the Churches of New-England* (Boston, 1726), 196.

CHAPTER 19

1. Mather's address to the ministers from which the quotations are taken is in his *Diary,* II, 670–71.

2. *Ibid.* II, 671.

3. *Ibid.* II, 665, 666, 669, 670, 674, 676, 697, 700, 702, 721, 733, 747, 764, 768.

4. *Ibid.* II, 705–6.

5. Holmes, *Cotton Mather*, I, 447–49; *Diary*, II, 651–52, 653, 661, 665, 768, 774, 776, 786 (for quotation).

6. Cotton Mather, *A Proposal For An Evangelical Treasury* (Boston, 1725), 2–3; *Ratio Disciplinae Fratrum*, "Introduction," 3–10 (separate pagination), 195–96; *Psalterium Americanum* (Boston, 1718), vi; *Manuductio ad Ministerium*, 1–6, 115–18, and *passim; The Minister* (Boston, 1722), 31.

7. Shipton, *Sibley's*, VI, 99.

8. See *Ibid. VI*, 98–102, for Pierpont's life.

9. *Ibid., Miller, From Colony To Province*, 455–56.

10. See Royal Society of London, *Philosophical Transactions*, no. 339, XXIX (April, May, June 1714) and no. 347, XXIX (Jan., Feb., Mar. 1716).

11. See Cotton Mather's *An Account of the Method and Success of Inoculating The Small-Pox in Boston in New-England* (London, 1722) for his description of inoculation in Africa, based upon Onesimus' information.

12. There are excellent accounts of the smallpox epidemic in John B. Blake, *Public Health In The Town of Boston, 1630–1822* (Cambridge, Mass., 1959), and in Miller, *From Colony To Province*. For Mather's letter of June 6, 1721 to the physicians of the town, see *A Vindication of the Ministers of Boston, From the Abuses and Scandals Lately Cast Upon Them* (Boston, 1722), 7–8 (where it is reprinted). See, too, Zabdiel Boylston, *Some Account of What is Said of Inoculating or Transplanting the Smallpox* (Boston, 1721). George L. Kittredge, "Some Lost Works of Cotton Mather," M.H.S. Proceedings, XLV (1911–12) 418–79, is a helpful guide to Mather's writings on the smallpox crisis.

13. Blake, *Public Health*, 56.

14. *Boston Gazette*, July 17, 1721 (Boylston); *Boston New Letter*, July 24, 1721 (Douglass); *Boston Gazette*, July 31, 1721 (the Mathers, B. Colman, T. Prince, J. Webb, W. Cooper); *New-England Courant*, August 7, 1721 (Douglass); Blake, *Public Health*, 58–59.

15. Blake, *Public Health*, 65–68; *A Vindication of the Ministers of Boston*, 8–9.

16. Boylston, *Some Account of What Is Said of Inoculating*, 11–14; Cotton Mather, "A Faithful Account of What has occured under the late Experiments of the Small-Pox," *Boston Gazette*, Oct. 30, 1721.

17. Otho T. Beall, Jr. and Richard H. Shryock, *Cotton Mather: First Significant Figure in American Medicine* (Baltimore, 1954); Cotton Mather, "Sentiments on the Small Pox In-

oculated," in Increase Mather, *Several Reasons Proving That Inoculating or Transplanting the Small Pox, is a Lawful Practice* (Boston, 1721); William Douglass, *Inoculation of the Small Pox As Practised in Boston* (Boston, 1722), 9 (for quotation); Miller, *From Colony To Province,* 348.

18. For this paragraph and the quotations see Benjamin Colman, *Some Observations on the New Method of Receiving The Small Pox* (Boston, 1721); Douglass, *Inoculation of the Small Pox,* 18, (on Colman) and *The Abuses and Scandals of Some Late Pamphlets In Favor of Inoculation* (Boston, 1722), for attacks on Cotton but not Increase Mather; Cotton Mather is called "mad" in *A Friendly Debate; or, A Dialogue Between Rusticus and Academicus* (Boston, 1722), 2; *New-England Courant,* Jan. 22, 1722; *Boston Gazette,* Jan. 29, Feb. 5, 1722 for Increase Mather's comments on the *Mercury* and the *Courant;* Increase Mather, *Some Further Account From London, of the Small Pox Inoculated* (2d. ed., Boston, 1721), 5 (on Douglass). For Cotton Mather's comments on Boston, see *Diary,* II, 631–32.

19. *Diary,* II, 657–58, 659, and *passim* for further feelings of martyrdom.

20. For a sample of anti-ministerial sentiment see *New-England Courant,* Aug. 21, Nov. 6, Dec. 4, 1721; Jan. 22, 1722. Douglass' sneer against the ministers as "Conscience Directors" is in his *Inoculation of the Small Pox,* 9. In the *Courant* of Jan. 22, 1722, the comments about the ministers as "Instruments of Mischief and Trouble, . . . , from the Witchcraft to Inoculation," is made. The same article refers to *Bonifacius,* not exactly fairly or accurately. What Cotton Mather recommended in *Bonifacius* was that the *"Country Minister* (or at least, his wife) should be much of a physician to his flock." In a city, he suggested where there was an "accomplished physician," perhaps medical studies would be only a "diversion" of the minister. See *Bonifacius: An Essay Upon the Good,* David Levin, ed., 82.

21. For Mather's private thoughts on the entire episode, see *Diary,* II, 618–62, *passim.*

22. Franklin B. Dexter, *Documentary History of Yale University . . . 1701–1745* (New Haven, Conn. 1916), 225–33; Mather, *Diary,* II, 695; *New-England Courant,* Sept. 24, Oct. 1, 8, 1722.

23. *Diary,* II, 797, 804, 806n.; Miller, *From Colony To Province,* 475.

24. Carl Bridenbaugh, *Mitre and Sceptre,* 72–73; Miller, *From Colony To Province,* 475–76.

25. *Diary,* II, 723–24.

26. *Ibid.* II, 730, 736–38, 748–49 (the quotations).

27. *Ibid.* II, 750–51.

28. *Ibid.* II, 774; for Mather's references to Boston, *Ibid.* II, 655, 656; Samuel Mather, *The Life of the Very Reverend and Learned Cotton Mather* (1729), 65.

29. *Diary*, II, 194, 196, 236, 246, 252, 474, 476, 520, 530, 539, 579, 586, 629, 652, all entries on his concern for his father; and for his interest in his children, see the following examples, 134, 136, 151, 155, 205, 207, 245, 248, 249, 251, 255–61, 266 357, 362, 379, 387, 450, 484, 525, 578.

30. *Ibid.* 181, 182, 188, 191, 194, 195 ("greatly wounded"), and *passim.*

31. *An Account of the Reasons Why a Considerable Number, . . . , Belonging to the New-North . . . , Could Not Consent to Mr. Peter Thacher's Ordination* (Boston, 1720), Preface, for the first quotation; Increase Mather, *A Further Testimony Against The Scandalous Proceedings of the New North Church* (Boston, 1720), 2. See also Increase Mather, *A Seasonable Testimony To Good Order In the Churches* (Boston, 1720); Peter Thacher and John Webb, *A Brief Declaration* (Boston, 1720); Peter Thacher *A Vindication of the New-North* (Boston, 1720).

32. Cotton Mather, *A Vision In The Temple* (Boston, 1721).

33. Samuel Sewall, *Diary,* 5th Ser. M.H.S. *Collections,* VII, 325, 326; Murdock, *Increase Mather,* 387–88.

34. Cotton Mather, *Parentator.* The book contains a great deal of information about Increase Mather's piety and worship.

35. *Diary,* II, 753–54, 755–57, 763, 764–65.

36. *Ibid.* II, 599–600, 703, 714, 739, 745, and *passim.* See, too, Holmes, *Cotton Mather,* III, 1134.

37. Mather, *Diary,* II, 583–91, *passim.*

38. Mather, Triparadisus, Pt. III, Sect. XII.

39. Mather, *Diary,* II, 778 ("new song"), 780–81, 786, 804, and *passim.*

A NOTE ON THE SOURCES

Because the notes to this book are rather full, I have decided not to repeat in an essay, or a list, the titles of the sources I have used. A full discussion of the sources would make this book much longer than it is. Examination of the notes should reveal that the major sources were the printed works and manuscripts of the Mathers. In the course of my research, I believe that I have read all the published writings of the Mathers and most of the manuscripts. The weary reader of this book may assume that I have discussed and cited them all too, but I can assure him that I have not. The character of the other Puritan tracts that I have used should be apparent from the text and the notes.

Discussing the Mathers' writings here is probably not necessary in any case, since valuable information about them has been available for a number of years in the distinguished bibliographies by Thomas James Holmes. They deserve mention here as the single most valuable bibliographical aid to my work. They are *Increase Mather: A Bibliography of His Works* (2 vols., Cleveland, Ohio, 1931); *Cotton Mather: A Bibliography Of His Works* (3 vols., Cambridge, Mass., 1940); and *The Minor Mathers: A List Of Their Works* (Cambridge, Mass., 1940).

Several other works proved so valuable to me that I want to mention them once more. Clifford K. Shipton, *Sibley's Harvard Graduates: Biographical Sketches Of Those Who Attended Harvard College* (14 vols. to date, Boston, 1873–1968) is a splendid piece of scholarship and I have drawn on it more times than I have been able to say in my notes. In a different way, I am deeply indebted to Perry Miller's *The New England Mind: From Colony To Province* (Cambridge, Mass., 1953), one of the great histories written in the twentieth century. My view of the development of Puritanism is different from Miller's, but his book has helped me to see things differently. Miller's other work on the Puritans has been only slightly less useful to me in this study.

I have discussed Miller's work at length in an essay in Marcus Cunliffe and Robin Winks, eds., *Pastmasters: Some Essays On American Historians* (New York, 1969). There I also deal with the work of a number of other able scholars of Puritanism whose studies have helped me in writing this book. Of that scholarship, the histories by Edmund S. Morgan have affected my method and thought most deeply. Morgan's *Visible Saints: The History of a Puritan Idea* (New York, 1963), in particular has helped me work out my understanding of Puritan Church polity.

Index